General introduction

Margaret Donaldson, Robert Grieve and Chris Pratt

This book is concerned with the period of life that stretches from around three to around eight years of age – a period of momentous significance for all people growing up in our culture. It is during this time that children enter the social world beyond the family and establish themselves, more or less easily and successfully, as members of a community of their peers. It is during this time too that they first encounter and deal with the challenges set to them by our system of education – challenges which, for many children, are unlike any they have ever met before. By the time this period is over, children will have formed conceptions of themselves as social beings, as thinkers, and as language-users, and they will have reached certain important decisions about their own abilities and their own worth. This places a very special responsibility on those involved in the teaching of young children during this period, either at preschool or at school. The decisions children reach about their own worth and abilities are important, not only for their self-respect and general well-being, but also for their subsequent progress.

While most children learn to adjust to school with a reasonable measure of success, some do not. If children do not fit in well at school, if they find school mostly tedious, or if they encounter great difficulty with the challenges of learning to read, write, and master number, then they may begin to regard themselves, or be regarded by others, as failures.

Before schooling was universal, those who lacked academic opportunities could blame their circumstances or station in life for lack of success. But now that schooling is universally available in our culture, all children have been officially given an equal opportunity. Thus children who do not succeed may look on themselves as stupid for failing, or else defend themselves against this judgement by blaming the school and rejecting everything they were encouraged to value there. They may of course do both of these, outwardly rejecting the merits of an education, while inwardly questioning their own worth.

The school activities which many children find difficult, and at which some children fail conspicuously and woundingly, are those involved in the traditional intellectual core of the curriculum. It is not a great disgrace in our culture not to be good at art, or at music, or not to be 'good with your hands'. However not to be literate, or not to have at least a basic competence with number, is quite another matter, for in our society a reasonable competence with words and numbers is considered an essential mark of the intelligent person.

To acknowledge the importance of literacy and numeracy is not to deny or undervalue other educational aims. Educators should have many other concerns, such as the development of a sense of society, of individual character, of morality, of creative powers, and of sensitivity to beauty and worth. We should certainly not concentrate so much on intellectual skills that we forget the importance of these other essential aspects of human life.

However, we are still left with the fact that in the society with which we currently have to deal, children who fail initially to learn the 'basic subjects' with reasonable ease may suffer both lack of self-respect, and subsequent lack of scholastic achievement. It is therefore important to ask why children may often find it difficult to acquire basic skills quickly and readily, and, in the light of the best answer we can find, to go on to ask how we can most effectively give help in the crucial early years of a child's formal education.

In addressing these questions, one possibility to be considered is that children who fail to master the basic subjects are not capable of these intellectual achievements – they are simply 'not up to it'. Here, the influence of genetic inheritance should not be ignored, for it contributes to all manner of differences between individuals. However, we are at present far from having to conclude that children who fail simply possess an impoverished genetic inheritance. This is certainly not proven. In fact, there is a highly complex interaction between genes and environment going on throughout development. Even if we allow that our genetic endowment sets some kind of upper limit to what we can achieve, there is no reason to suppose that most of us come close to that limit.

What other possible reasons are there, then, for initial failure at school? Here we can consider a particular case, of a girl called Annie. Annie, the second child of parents who married at seventeen, lived in a two-roomed house in a poor district. When Annie was one year old, her father left the household and did not return. While her mother did her best, and while there was a kind and supportive grandmother living nearby, things were hard. In addition to the disadvantages of her background, Annie had a speech defect, so that when she went to school she did not seem at all promising. At first she failed to read. The school used a reading scheme in which children did not get a book until they had first managed to learn a number of words presented in isolation. Annie failed to master this task, which made no kind of sense to her. She knew she was failing, and as time passed, and she still did not get a book, her morale sank lower and lower.

Fortunately, she then encountered a remedial teacher who took her in hand, to such effect as to change the whole course of events. Annie's experience of failure turned into an experience of success. By the end of her third year in school, her teacher's report said: 'Annie has a special aptitude for reading and writing.' The first thing Annie wanted when she got out of bed in the morning was a book to read. Now, at the age of eleven years, she reads very well and writes splendid imaginative stories.

Annie's initial failure arose from a combination of factors. Her disadvantaged background, speech defect, and inability to jump the hurdle of reading words in isolation – all no doubt contributed to her initial lack of success. While she may indeed have a special aptitude for reading and writing, it certainly did not reveal itself early, and it might well never have done so had she not received appropriate assistance.

Unfortunately, we often do not know how best to assist children who are finding school difficult. We simply do not yet understand as well as we might do how best to help them. To say this is not to criticize teachers, who, for the most part, do a difficult job with much skill and care. However, there are three important implications. The first is that we should not write off as stupid chidren who initially fail to do the strange new things which we demand of them in school. The second is that we must continually try to get a better understanding of what it is that may lead to failure: what it is that is strange and new, bewildering, and potentially defeating about the school experience. And third, we must continually strive to obtain a better understanding of young children – of the skills and capacities which they possess, of their limitations, of the problems which they encounter. The readings in this book are especially directed towards this last end. And if we have begun by placing some emphasis on the importance of achieving a good start in a child's school career and on the potentially damaging consequences of failure to do so, this does not mean that the rest of the book is principally about children who fail. On the contrary, we have made the guiding assumption that the aim must be to *avoid* failure; and that, if we are to have the best chance of achieving this aim, what we need is a good understanding of the basic principles governing the ways in which all children develop. In particular, we need to know what children are likely to be good at doing by the time they come to school and how this relates to the learning which we then expect of them. We need to understand both their strengths and their weaknesses.

Over the past few decades, the study of children's development has been strongly influenced by the theories of Piaget, and we owe him a great deal. The questions he asked were of central importance, he devised many highly ingenious situations in which children could be observed, and he formulated a theoretical account that is remarkable for its scope and power.

However, as Piaget himself repeatedly acknowledged, scientific thought is 'a process of continued construction and reorganization' (Piaget, 1970). That is, in science no one has the last word – no one arrives at final and immutable truth. We must therefore be ready from time to time to consider things afresh – to look at new evidence with an open mind, and to see if we find reason to change our opinions. To do so now is particularly appropriate, for the last ten or fifteen years have yielded many new findings which have about them a considerable coherence, and which suggest that a new picture is emerging.

The set of readings collected here has been planned to give some indication of the ways in which this picture is taking shape. To prepare the way for them, we first sketch in some general background.

This can best be done by considering three recent trends in developmental psychology. The first of these – and it is a particularly interesting one – is that we now see more clearly than before the significance of the fact that language and thought develop in interpersonal contexts. That this is true in infancy and early childhood has been shown by various investigators, notably Bruner (1974), Trevarthen (1974), and Halliday (1975). It continues to be true throughout the preschool years.

In most interpersonal contexts, there is a complex interplay of different human purposes, and early childhood thought is interfused with purpose and with the recognition of purpose. A child's thinking functions with the support of intentions which the child understands, and which are usually directed to fairly immediate goals. What we are now coming to realize is that thinking assessed in contexts which lack such features is a strange activity for young children to be expected to engage in. Thus any task, if it is 'set' to children for reasons which make no sense to them, calls for thinking of this unfamiliar, if not unnatural, kind, no matter how 'concrete' and familiar its terms may be.

The recognition of the importance of interpersonal context also has implications for the study of language development. While it is obvious that language is learned through interacting with other people, what has not always been recognized is the extent to which young children interpret language in ways influenced by the particular setting in which the language is uttered. Generally, children seem more concerned to discover what a *person* means than to determine precisely what his *words* mean. Thus in trying to extract meaning, they use a great deal of non-linguistic evidence: they take account of what the speaker does as well as what he says. There is of course nothing odd about this when it occurs in an everyday setting: we all do it most of the time. But what was not fully appreciated until recently is the extent to which young children interpret language in this interpersonally context-dependent way when they are presented with formal tasks – tasks of the sort commonly used by teachers in school. We may call these tasks 'disembedded', in the sense that they are not embedded in the context of everyday human interaction, where goals typically arise in a spontaneous way. Disembedded tasks are not spontaneous – they are 'set' by the adult, and children must in turn 'set' their minds to them with deliberate constraint and self-control (see Donaldson, 1978).

Early Childhood
Development and Education

Early Childhood Development and Education

READINGS IN PSYCHOLOGY

Edited by

Margaret Donaldson, Robert Grieve and Chris Pratt

Basil Blackwell

First published in 1983 by
Basil Blackwell Publisher
108 Cowley Road
Oxford OX4 1JF

Introduction and editorial matter copyright © Margaret Donaldson,
Robert Grieve and Chris Pratt 1983.

A Grant McIntyre Book

British Library Cataloguing in Publication Data

Early childhood development and education.
1. Cognition in children
I. Donaldson, Margaret   II. Grieve, Robert
III. Pratt, Chris
155.4'13   BF723.C5

ISBN 0-631-13361-5
ISBN 0-631-13362-3 Pbk

Typeset in 10 on 12pt Baskerville by Oxford Verbatim Limited.
Printed and bound in Great Britain at T.J. Press, Padstow

Contents

Contents

Acknowledgements

EDITORS' ACKNOWLEDGEMENTS

The editors make grateful acknowledgement as follows for permission to reprint the papers and extracts included in this book:

The author and Penguin Books Ltd. for 'Some properties of social play' by Catherine Garvey, pages 510–83 from *Play*, edited by J. S. Bruner, A. Jolly and K. D. Sylva, reprinted by permission of Penguin Books Ltd. The author and Fontana Paperbacks for 'The skills of friendship', pages 50–63 from *Childrens Friendships* by Z. Rubin. The author and Pergamon Press Ltd. for 'Social isolation from agemates among nursery school children', by W. G. Scarlett, *Journal of Child Psychology and Psychiatry*, 1980, **21**, 231–40. The authors and Routledge and Kegan Paul Ltd. for 'Nicknames', pages 98–103 and 115–16 from *Nicknames: their Origins and Social Consequences* by R. Harré, J. Morgan and C. O'Neill. The authors and the American Psychological Association for 'Act-role relations: children's concepts of social roles' by D. R. Weston and E. Turiel, *Developmental Psychology*, 1980, **16**, 417–24; copyright © 1980 by the American Psychological Association, reprinted by permission of the publisher and authors.

The author and the Society for Research in Child Development Inc. for 'The modifications of communicative behaviour in preschool-aged children as a function of the listener's perspective', by C. L. Menig-Peterson, *Child Development*, 1975, **46**, 1015–18. The author and Cambridge University Press for 'Self-initiated corrections of the speech of infant-school children', by S. Rogers, *Journal of Child Language*, 1978, 365–71.

The authors and John Wiley & Sons Ltd. for 'Ways of reacting to communication failure in relation to the development of the Child's understanding about verbal communication', by E. J. and W. P. Robinson, *European Journal of Social Psychology*, 1981, **11**, 189–208. The authors and Alpha Academic for 'On asking children bizarre questions', by M. Hughes and R. Grieve, *First Language*, 1980, **1**, 149–60.

The authors for 'Text and Context in early language comprehension, by R. N. Campbell and T. Bowe Macdonald, adapted from 'Functional asymmetry in early language understanding', in *Salzburger Beitrage für Linguistik*, Vol. 3, edited by G. Drachman (Tubingen: Gunter Narr). The author and the National Association for the Teaching of English for 'Talking with children: the complementary roles of parents and teachers', by G. Wells, *English in Education*, 1978, **12**, 15–37. The author for 'Into print: reading and language growth', by Jessie F. Reid, printed for the first time in this book.

The authors and Academic Press Inc. for 'Interpreting inclusion: a contribution to the study of the child's cognitive and linguistic development', by J. McGarrigle, R. Grieve and M. Hughes, *Journal of Experimental Child Psychology*, 1978, **25**, 1528–50. The President and Fellows of Harvard College for 'The child's understanding of number', pages 83–104 of *The Child's Understanding of Number*, by R. Gelman and C. R. Gallistel. The author for 'What is difficult about learning arithmetic?', by M. Hughes, printed for the first time in this book. The authors and Macmillan Journals Ltd. for 'Spontaneous measurement by young children', by P. E. Bryant and H. Kopytinska, reprinted by permission from *Nature*, **260**, 772; copyright © 1976 Macmillan Journals Ltd.

To the authors and Lawrence Erlbaum Associates Inc. for 'Methods for observing developmental change in memory', and 'Metacognitive skills', pages 13–15, 18–25 and 28–30 of 'Skills, plans and self regulation', by A. L. Brown and J. S. DeLoache, in *Children's Thinking: What Develops?*, edited by R. Siegler. The author and Fontana Paperbacks for 'Children's reasoning', pages 55–7 from *Children's Minds* by M. Donaldson. The President and Fellows of Harvard College for 'Intuitive and analytic thinking', pages 58–68 from *The Process of Education* by J. S. Bruner.

The authors and the Carfax Publishing Company Ltd. for 'The use of hiding games for studying the coordination of viewpoints', *Educational Review*, 1979 **31**, 133–40. The author and the American Psychological Association for 'Piaget's mountains revisited: changes in the egocentric landscape', by H. Borke, *Developmental Psychology* 1975, **11**, 240–43; copyright © 1975 by the American Psychological Association, reprinted by permission of the publisher and author.

M.I.T. Press for 'School instruction and mental development', reprinted from *Thought and Language* by L. S. Vygotsky by permission of The M.I.T. Press, Cambridge, Massachusetts; pages 97–105. The author for 'The child as psychologist', by P. L. Harris. The authors and the Education Department, University of Western Australia for 'Language awareness in children' by R. Grieve, W. Tunmer and C. Pratt, *Education Research and Perspectives*, 1980, **7**, 5–19. The author and Agathon Press for 'Play with language and metalinguistic awareness: one dimension of language experience' by C. B. Cazden, *Urban Review*, 1974, **7**, (1).

CONTRIBUTORS' ACKNOWLEDGEMENTS

Robin N. Campbell and Theresa Bowe Macdonald: The research underlying Paper 10 was carried out as part of an SSRC-funded project, 'Semantic development in young children', in collaboration with R. Grieve and R. Hoogenraad of St Andrew's University, Scotland. The text of this paper is based on Campbell and Bowe, 1977. Martin Hughes: Most of the research reported in Paper 15 was financed by an SSRC Research Fellowship in Preschool Education.

It is essential to notice that, when we deal with disembedded tasks, the language in which they are stated assumes a new kind of importance. Instead of being supplemented by the sort of non-linguistic evidence commonly used in 'everyday' interaction, the words are now supposed to carry the full meaning – as Olson (1977) puts it, 'the meaning is in the text'. When he says this, Olson is arguing that, historically, language has acquired its primacy and carries the full weight of meaning as a result of the development of writing. Olson's arguments are compelling. The influence of literacy on the development of disembedded modes of thought is surely immense, both for human societies and in the course of individual human lives.

Thus when we 'set' problems in a formal kind of way, we expect that the language will, as far as possible, carry the meaning. This is the convention, deeply ingrained in our culture. The 'right answer' is the one which has regard only, and rigorously, to the problem *as stated*. The irony, then, is that young children, not yet having grasped this convention, may actually fail to do what our words instruct them to do, precisely because they are trying so hard to understand what we, as adult speakers, intend them to do. When we set formal tasks, we mean our words to have primacy. Teachers and psychologists are so used to this in educational or experimental settings that they are apt not to notice how it differs from what is done in everyday behaviour, where we attend to what people do as well as to what they say, and where we may well attend more to the former than to the latter should these happen to be in conflict. If we recognize that we adults have both embedded and disembedded modes in which we operate, then we may better appreciate the novelty of the disembedded mode for a young child's mind.

A second recent trend in developmental psychology, particularly marked over the past few years, is for research to pay more attention than before to children's developing awareness of what they themselves do. Psychologists such as Luria (1961) and Vygotsky (1962) have long acknowledged the importance of the increase in awareness and control in children's development, and recently many studies have appeared on children's awareness of their own language, their own thinking, and their own memory. Piaget (1977) has made the point that while children are initially aware of their goals, and of their successes and failures in achieving these goals, they are relatively unaware of the *means* by which the goals are achieved. The growth of a greater consciousness of the means of achieving goals is a precondition for the development of greater deliberate control and reflectiveness, which in turn is necessary for many of the activities demanded in school. Indeed, the contrast between the spontaneous behaviour of everyday life and the kind of mental discipline called for by disembedded tasks is again relevant. While spontaneous behaviour will often focus on goals, disembedded tasks require more deliberate control and monitoring of the processes involved in attaining goals. This second trend is therefore by no means unrelated to the previous one.

The third recent trend, while somewhat different from the first two, is no less significant. It consists of a shift of interest from what children cannot do to what they can do. Much of the research carried out in the first half of this century appears to have been curiously preoccupied with young children's incapacities. Again and again results were reported which appeared to indicate that young children were surprisingly limited in what they could understand, in the ways in which they could reason. In recent years matters have noticeably changed, and a much more positive attitude tends now to prevail. Researchers are now apt to look actively for things which young children can do; and not infrequently, when they look, they find them. (It is of course important not to swing to the opposite extreme and conclude that children have no intellectual limitations. Unfortunately, there are some signs that this danger is not always being avoided.)

The reasons for this shift in emphasis, or change of heart, are complex. Something is certainly attributable to the breakthrough in the study of infancy which occurred in the 1950s and early 1960s, a breakthrough for which we are considerably indebted to developments in methodology. Ingenious new ways of studying very young babies were devised, and as soon as these techniques were employed, it became clear that infants' abilities to act on and apprehend the world had been seriously underestimated. Newborn infants, for example, can imitate tongue, eyelid and mouth movements made by an adult. They can also learn to pattern their behaviour, for example turning their head to the right to receive a few drops of sugared water at the sound of a bell but not at the sound of a buzzer. Furthermore, when matters are changed so that the buzzer now signals the reward rather than the bell, they can learn to reverse this pattern indicating the flexibility of their behaviour. By two weeks of age, infants have social perceptions, being able to distinguish the mother's face and voice from those of a stranger. These and many other findings (see Bower, 1977) were bound to influence research with older children. If babies and infants could do so much more than had been previously supposed, then why not three-year-olds, four-year-olds, and five-year-olds?

There was, too, in the 1960s, the very considerable influence of the views of the linguist Noam Chomsky (1965). His theories about language drew attention to the apparently amazing speed and skill with which children become able to produce utterances that observe the grammatical rules of their native tongue. Although these rules are highly complicated, if children use them they must in some sense know them. Young children must therefore have a considerable capacity for rule-learning.

Initially, this was not taken as evidence of any general or pervasive competence. Rather, the tendency was to explain such rule-learning by supposing that the ability was highly specific to language. That is, the children were held to be good at formulating linguistic rules, but not necessarily rules of other kinds. The proposal was that we are all innately provided with a 'language acquisition device' (LAD for short), especially designed to acquire language rules (see McNeill, 1970).

In some quarters, the idea of a language-specific acquisition device was attractive. At least part of the reason for its popularity lay in all the findings about children's cognitive limitations which psychologists had been collecting over the years. Evidence of cognitive limitations had, after all, been obtained in systematic studies, many conducted by Piaget and his colleagues in Geneva or else inspired by their work. However, the idea that children's intellectual capacities may have been under-estimated gained momentum, and researchers began to subject Piagetian evidence to an increasing number of checks. The checks did not consist in simple replications of Piaget's studies. These had been conducted earlier, and had almost always confirmed his claims. What now began to be carried out in increasing numbers were studies which extended his work, either by finding quite new ways of looking at the topics he had studied, or by using variants of the tasks which he used. These studies, some of which are reported in this book, often showed children revealing abilities at younger ages than had originally been found.

When variants of standard Piagetian tasks are used, it is sometimes argued that if the new tasks give different results from the classical Piagetian ones, this means that they are 'not the same' as the ones Piaget used, and hence somehow invalid. But the answer to this is that of course they are not the same. If they were, given that Piaget's work is basically so replicable, they would presumably yield the same results. The question that matters is whether these different tasks yield results which would be predicted by Piaget's theory. To the extent that they do not, then the theory is in need of modification.

With this background, we can now turn to this book's readings. The readings are presented in four sections. In each section, there is a brief editorial introduction, and editorial comments are provided for individual papers. Taken together, the readings attempt to illustrate the points we have been making. (It should of course be understood that no single book can do justice to the full range of the literature.) Generally, the readings attempt to convey something of the skills and capacities possessed by young children about to enter school or in early school; and at the same time, they convey something of the limitations to their competence, and of the problems that they face.

The readings of Section I, on social development, tell us something of young children's social skills – their social play, their abilities to make friends and enter peer groups, their social uses of language, their knowledge of social rules.

The social theme is continued in Section II, but here children's skills in language and communication are considered. Do children appreciate the perspective of their listeners? Do they monitor what they themselves say, and correct speech production mistakes? What do children understand about the processes of communication, particularly the function of questions? And how does children's talk differ between home and school?

The section ends with a discussion of the extensions of language skill demanded by the learning of reading and writing. Stress is laid on the child's need to understand the nature of a written code, on the ways oral and written language can initially be linked, and on the enlargement of linguistic repertoire which literacy involves.

In Section III, the readings refer to children's intellectual capacities. While it might be supposed that we have now moved from a social to an individual theme, the importance of the interpersonal context in terms of shared meaning will become apparent, whether we are involved with children's abilities in conservation, classification, number, measurement, reasoning, problem-solving, or whatever.

In the last section, Section IV, an emphasis on the child as an individual becomes more apparent, for here the readings refer to children's development of awareness and control over their own behaviour. The readings, concerned with such matters as young children's increasing knowledge and awareness of the nature and functions of language, memory, and thought, and with aspects of awareness of social behaviour and interaction, illustrate how children begin to acquire increasing independence.

Social development

INTRODUCTION

The readings of this section are concerned with aspects of children's social behaviour and development during the preschool and early school years. For many children, their first encounter with sizeable groups of same age peers occurs at preschool, or playgroup. Prior to this, their social experiences will frequently have been within their family context, and interaction with peers often confined to the children of family friends. However, attendance at preschool or playgroup will lead to a change in children's social experiences, for now the child is expected to learn to interact and play with a range of other children.

Most teachers and parents are aware of the social demands that are placed on children during this period, and a watchful eye is usually kept on their progress and activities. As children's play becomes more social, individual preferences are revealed. Some children seek the company of many playmates, while others prefer only one or two friends. Children also vary in the extent to which they are able to form friendships. As the papers in this section indicate, the skills of friendship formation are complex, and not all children are equally adept in using them. Consequently, children may fail to form the friendships they desire, and unless help is provided, such children may become isolated from their peers.

Once children enter school, further development of their social skills is expected. While intellectual pursuits are often emphasized in school, the importance of social aspects of development should not be overlooked. School is a demanding place, socially as well as intellectually. Children must learn not only to settle in the classroom, but also to cope with time spent in the playground with their peers.

For children who have been to preschool and begun to develop appropriate social skills, interacting with their peers at school will often be a natural extension of their previous experience. But other children – those who encountered problems at preschool, and those who start school without the potential benefits of preschool experience – will either have to make the necessary social adjustments very quickly, or be provided with some assistance if they are to settle adequately into the social and intellectual ways of playground and classroom.

If children are to exist happily within the school system, they must also be able to develop an understanding of the rules that prevail and the reasons behind these rules. School is an institution, and like all institutions it is governed by sets of rules which children are expected to learn and maintain. To date, little is known about the development of children's knowledge of rules in the school context, despite its importance. While several valuable studies of children's moral development have been conducted (e.g. Piaget, 1932; Kohlberg, 1968), such studies of children's understanding of rules and conventions have not been directly associated with the school context. Children's evaluation of rules with respect to school therefore needs to be considered.

The readings selected for this section are varied both with regard to their content and method of study. In some, the investigators are content to study what happens in 'natural' contexts like school playgrounds; in others, the settings in which the observations are made have been specially devised, with varying degrees of control. Most of the papers report how children behave in varying social contexts. One, however, (from Weston and Turiel) is concerned not with behaviour but with judgements of behaviour. Taken together, the readings emphasize the complex nature of children's social play, and begin to reveal the skills involved in children's social interaction, and in their making and keeping friends. While the readings illustrate how socially adept many children are on entry into school, they also indicate some of the problems that children may encounter.

1.

Some properties of social play

Catherine Garvey

To the casual observer, children's social play may often appear chaotic, with the content and structure of the play changing frequently according to the momentary whims of the participants. In this paper by Garvey, however, careful observation and analysis shows that social play is in fact ordered, and governed by certain conventions. Although it would be a mistake to suggest that children are fully aware of all the social conventions that Garvey describes, they certainly learn to play according to these conventions. At times, they are quite explicit about the nature of the proposed play. For example, Garvey discusses the importance of the distinction between pretend play and reality, and illustrates the way in which children make this distinction. Those familiar with young children at play will certainly have heard the opener: 'Hey, let's pretend that . . .' which children use frequently to delineate the boundary between play and reality. Garvey also draws attention to more general conventions of social interaction which children exhibit during play, including turn-taking skills which regulate such social interactions. Overall, the paper reveals the extent to which preschool children are adept at dealing with various social conventions.

The literature on children's play reflects a major concern with the *functions* of play in the child's individual cognitive, physical, or psycho-social development. The few empirical studies that have examined play in a social context have failed to ask how the interaction is carried out or what kinds of skills are involved in play interchanges. It is the purpose of this paper to describe the structure of spontaneous episodes of dyadic play and to suggest some of the basic competencies which underlie social play activity.

It is useful to distinguish four possible states which may obtain when two children are alone together: social non-play, e.g. both may collaborate to repair a broken toy; non-social non-play, e.g. one or both may independently explore an object; non-social play, e.g. one or both may engage in an independent imaginative activity, as when one child irons the laundry and the other builds a wall with blocks; and social play, e.g. both are mutually engaged in a housekeeping activity such as cooking and eating dinner or are driving the toy car to a family vacation.

Social play is defined here as a state of engagement in which the successive, non-literal behaviours of one partner are contingent on the non-literal behaviours of the other partner. Viewed from the standpoint of either partner, this means leaving interstices in one's behaviours for the other's acts and modifying one's successive behaviours as a result of the other's acts. Non-literal behaviour is not necessarily not serious – for play can be a serious business – but it is abstract in the sense that the primary purpose of a given behaviour is reduced to a meaning component, and its re-interpreted function in the chain of activity becomes primary. Applying these two criteria (alternating, contingent behaviours and non-literalness of those behaviours) we can contrast a very simple example of social play with a type of engagement which we would wish to exclude from this category. Two children stand close together in a playroom near a wooden car which both want to ride. One shoves the other who immediately shoves back, and simultaneous shoving occurs until one child is displaced from the area of the car. The behaviours are immediate, not spaced; neither child waits for the other to complete a behaviour. The same setting can result in social play. Both children stand near the car and one shoves the other, the second shoves back and waits, the first repeats the shove and waits for the other to shove in turn. The tempo of the activity appears to be mutually regulated. Further, neither child is displaced for the shoving is non-literal. Aggressive and defensive gestures identify the type of meaning of the play but this meaning is not primary; the re-interpreted function (marked by giggles, smiles, or exaggerated gestures) is that of moves or turns in a mock-challenge. The play episode may end with both children getting on the car or with both forgetting the car in the excitement of the interaction.

We can now examine some properties of the state of social play, analysing first the structures underlying the rhythmic, repetitive behaviours which we will call ritual play and then tracing the same structures in less stylized play episodes.

PROCEDURES

The data on which these observations are based consisted of 36 fifteen-to twenty-minute videotaped play sessions. Children came in groups of three to the laboratory accompanied by their nursery-school teacher. Each child formed a dyad with each of the two other members of the group. All members of the groups were previously acquainted from nursery school. The children in 12 dyads fell into a younger age group (three and a half to four and a third years); twelve into a middle groups (four and a half to five years); and twelve into an older age group (five to five and a half years). In all there were 21 girls and 15 boys, all from middle-class families. A dyad was left alone in a well-furnished playroom and was observed through one-way mirrors. The membership of the dyad was changed at the end of approximately 15 minutes. The third child was occupied with a series of identification tasks in another room. Episodes of focused interaction were frequent (an average of 66 per cent of each session was spent in mutual engagement) and there was a good deal of talk in each session (on the average, one utterance every four seconds).

Three procedural safeguards were adopted to reduce the possibility of misinterpreting the meaning or intent of the children's verbal and non-verbal gestures. First, if an event (verbal or non-verbal behaviour of one child) was to be accepted as evidence of competence in distinguishing among modes of behaviour or as evidence of recognition of an obligation in an interaction, that event was required to be non-unique. That is, the event must have occurred in a similar context in more than one dyad. Second, in interpreting the meaning of lexical items or expressions, both the verbal and non-verbal context of events were taken into account. For example, in the text the meaning of 'pretend' was opposed to the meaning of 'really' or 'real'; that is, the meaning was defined in terms of contrast. Further, in the instances cited, consistently different behaviours accompanied the use of these opposed terms. Third, the children's own reactions were used to interpret the significance of an event. The immediate consequence of an event was included as evidence of the meaning of that event. For example, an assertion can be interpreted as an unintended joke when the partner laughs and then is joined in laughter by the first speaker.

Using the criteria of non-literalness and alternating contingent behaviours and observing these procedural safeguards, two investigators independently identified social play episodes in the corpus. Inter-judge agreement on the identification of episodes of social play was 80 per cent. Only episodes on which the investigators agreed were used in the subsequent analysis. From these episodes the ritual play sequences were selected and classified according to the formats described below.

The ritual episodes were defined as sequences composed of repetitive and rhythmic exchanges. The investigators were able to concur on all such sequences, which are redundantly marked as social play. The alternating behaviours are closely integrated in time. Non-literalness is signalled by exaggerated intonation, by distorted tempo, and by broad or extreme gestures. Rituals which are primarily verbal are almost chanted. They are set off from their surrounding context by abrupt changes in volume, tempo, or intonation contour.

ANALYSIS OF SOCIAL PLAY FORMATS

Recurring patterns of interaction were observed in the play sessions. The clearest examples of these patterns were found in the ritual play sequences, and we will examine these first. The structure of the inter-personal behaviours will be described in terms of the rules governing alternation of participation (turns), the substantive and formal relations of the alternating behaviours, and the manner in which sequences are built up (rounds).

Interactions may be analysed as composed of *turns* at acting. A turn is the contribution (verbal and/or non-verbal) of one participant in the interchange. The content of the second participant's turn may be the same as or different from that of the first participant. If different, the difference may be paradigmatic (a member of the same class) or syntagmatic (a member of a different class, one which has some linear or sequential relation to the first class). Using the conventions of indicating first speaker or actor as X, second speaker or actor as Y and of identifying the content of a turn by capital letters with subscript p = paradigmatic difference and s = syntagmatic difference, the basic patterns of turns can be illustrated.

In the first pattern, the rule is that all features of the second turn must be identical; relevant features appear to include rhythm, intonation, and volume. In the second pattern such features also appear to be maintained in the second turn, but the latter substitutes some component – here another term of address. The third pattern employs a sequential relation. The example is an assertion followed by a counter-assertion.

Turn patterns	X's turn	Y's turn
1 $A - A$	Bye, mommy.	Bye, mommy.
2 $A - B_p$	Bye, mommy.	Bye, daddy.
3 $A - B_s$	You're a nut.	No, I'm not.
4 $A - B_s$	I have to go to work.	You're already at work.
C_s	No, I'm not.	

The first three patterns exemplify a *symmetrical* distribution of turns. A more complex pattern is constructed of *asymmetrical* turns, as in pattern 4, where X has two turns to Y's one.

Each of the patterns forms a *round*, which is a repeatable unit of interaction. A round may be repeated intact (R_i) or may be modified (R_m).* Returning to the patterns of turns, some of the ways in which sequences are constructed can be illustrated in two-round episodes.

* Round modification also may be analysed as paradigmatic or syntagmatic, but this distinction will not be made in the present discussion.

Turn pattern, Round type	X's turn	Y's turn
1 R_i	Bye, mommy.	Bye, mommy.
	Bye, mommy.	Bye, mommy.
2 R_i	Bye, mommy.	Bye, daddy.
	Bye, mommy.	Bye, daddy.
3 R_m	Hello, my name is Mr Donkey.	Hello, my name is Mr Elephant.
	Hello, my name is Mr Tiger.	Hello, my name is Mr Lion.
4 R_m	I have to go to work.	You're already at work.
	No, I'm not.	
	I have to go to school.	You're already at school.
	No, I'm not.	

In a sequence of rounds, role assignment may be symmetrical, as in the preceding example, or asymmetrical as in the following, where roles are reversed at the beginning of the second round. (Non-verbal acts are enclosed in parentheses.)

4 R_i X I'll be the dragon and you be St George that killed him.

   Y (shoots the dragon, X).

X (falls dead).

   Y Now I'll be the dragon.

X (shoots Y, the dragon).

   Y Do it again, I'm not dead.

X (shoots again).

   Y (falls dead).

The turn patterns and round types were grouped into formats which identify the structure of many of the play episodes observed. The formats, ranked in order of increasing complexity, are as follows:

		Turn pattern	Round type
Format	1:	1	R_i
	2a:	1	R_m
	2b:	2 or 3	R_i
	3:	2 or 3	R_m
	4:	4	R_i or R_m

Format 1 is, of course, symmetrical in respect to role alternation in rounds. Formats 3 and 4 may be symmetrical or asymmetrical. Format 2 occurred in the present corpus predominantly in symmetrical form.

The 36 dyads produced 158 clearly identified episodes of social play, which were distributed among the groups as follows: younger, 44; middle, 58; older, 56. Of these episodes, 74 were instances of ritual play. No child failed to participate in at least one episode of ritual play. The distribution of the ritual play episodes among the four play formats is presented in Table 1. A fifth category included in Table 1 is that of mixed formats which includes temporally cohesive sequences with a single theme which utilized successively two or more basic formats.

Table 1 indicates that ritual play episodes occurred in all age groups. It is clear that for this sample of children ritual play episodes were still a frequent type of interaction even among the older dyads. Further, the results suggest that the relative complexity of the formats as ranked corresponds to some degree to the increasing age of the three groups, although all age groups employed both simpler and more complex formats.

The final column of Table 1 indicates that younger dyads repeated the rounds of such episodes more extensively than older dyads. While the older dyads did not tend to repeat rounds more than twice the younger dyads repeated rounds on the average 3.8 times. On two occasions, younger dyads continued the sequence for ten or more rounds.

Table 1 *Ritual play episodes of two or more rounds*

Format	1	2(a + b)	3	4	Mixed	Total episodes	Average no. rounds per episode
Younger Group*	5	14	3	2	2	26	3·8
Middle Group*	2	6	12	3	2	25	2·5
Older Group*	1	7	8	4	3	23	2·2
Total episodes in each format	8	27	23	9	7	74	

*N = 12 dyads

Although this discussion has concentrated on the alternating, contingent behaviours of ritual interchanges, it is necessary to recall that such play episodes are also characterized by the quality of non-literalness. Thus, in the corpus from which these patterns have been abstracted, each episode was marked, often redundantly, as non-literal. For example, in the 'Bye, mommy' episodes the utterances were chanted. Further, the literal leave-taking meaning was subordinated to rhythmic echoing – neither child left or turned away.

In the St George episode, non-literalness was marked by explicit preparatory role assignment, 'I'll be, you be'. That episode also illustrates another feature of the sequences, which is that a turn or round can be interrupted for clarification of rules or discussion of procedures and then resumed at the point where the break occurred. This feature supports the observation that play can be conducted seriously, i.e. that the actions must be performed in a certain way and must accomplish their intended outcome – in the St George episode, that of effectively killing the dragon.

ABILITIES UNDERLYING SOCIAL PLAY

Certain abilities must be postulated to account for the structures of play described above. We will discuss these abilities which are required to conduct ritual play episodes but will extend the discussion to include the non-repetitive episodes of social play.

(1) Reality-play distinction

First, both participants must recognize that a state of social play obtains. In order to play with another, one must have a firm grasp of reality. Since the task of explicating what is meant by 'reality', either in the sense of Piagetian cognitive theory or in the sense of phenomenologists such as Peter Winch, would take us too far afield, we can restate that condition: in order to play, one must have a grasp of what is not play – and what is and is not 'for real'. Although the play mode may be primarily assimilative (Piaget, 1951), that is, rather than accommodating itself to perceived (or absolute) reality it transforms and absorbs its object to previously held perceptions, the necessity of moving into or out of the mode requires a distinction between play and other activities. The children we observed gave ample evidence of making this judgement. One type of evidence is the children's use of the terms 'really' and 'pretend'. (We do not contend that the word meanings of these lexical items are, either in reference or connotation, identical with those in adult speech. However, the terms were used in a contrasting manner in the children's speech and that contrast was systematic and non-unique.) Example 1 illustrates the use of these terms.

Example 1: X sits on three-legged stool that has a magnifying glass in its centre
X I've got to go to the potty.
                     Y (turns to him) Really?
X (grins) No, pretend.
                     Y (smiles and watches X).

Since the state of play entails a suspension of literalness, the reality-play distinction appears to be essential to interpreting the partner's gesture in terms of its primary meaning or its non-literal meaning. Both partners must recognize that the state of play obtains in order to interpret and correctly respond to the other's behaviour. In fact, the participants often checked on the state in order to determine the appropriate response. In another dyad, the statement, 'I've got to go to the potty,' was followed by the partner's comment, 'So do I,' and both children immediately headed for the door. In example (1), some cue (X's sitting on the magnifying stool, his expression, or both) led Y to check on the meaning of X's announcement, and the information that Y received led to his subsequent response. Often the state of play was explicitly bounded. The most frequent markers opening a state of play were 'pretend', e.g. 'Pretend you called me on the telephone,' or explicit role assignment, e.g. 'I'll be the mommy and you be the daddy, O.K.?' The state might end by tacit, mutual consent, or its termination might be explicitly marked, e.g. 'I'm not playing any more.'

The reality – play distinctions as made by the children themselves may be viewed as manipulations of categories and contexts, as explorations of the 'fit' of behaviours to changing definitions of situations (Bateson, 1956). Whatever the cognitive functions served by these explorations, the important point is that the distinction was often tested, even among the younger dyads. It appeared to be a relevant factor in the attitude or alignment taken, not only to objects, but to the behaviour of the partner, whose definition of the situation is critical to the continuing interchange.

(II) Abstraction of rules

Winch (1958) has pointed out that it is only possible to talk of rule-governed behaviour when one can predict what will be done next and can recognize an error in procedure. According to these criteria, the children, often explicitly, demonstrated awareness that their social play depended on mutually accepted rules of procedure. It is necessary to make a distinction here between basic general rules for interaction and specific or local strictures applicable to a limited context. The most basic general rule which holds across both verbal and non-verbal interaction is that of reciprocity. Explicit encoding of this rule often took the form of 'taking turns', but implicit conformity to the rule was clearly apparent in the alternation of turns and their integration into rounds as exemplified in the play formats. Violations of the reciprocity rule were frequently challenged by invoking the rule, e.g. 'You go next.' Since this basic rule underlies much adult conversation, it will be useful to trace the probably simpler forms of that rule in children's play, and we will attempt to describe a portion of its development below.

The point to be made here is that the explicit invocation of a rule under similar conditions across a number of different situations indicates the ability to abstract that rule from the varied and often complex activities which it structures. It further suggests an ability to perceive actions in terms of socially distributed entities such as turns or, more complex than turns, rounds, for it is these entities rather than utterances which are apportioned to speakers in play and in conversation. An example of an interaction that reflects this ability is Example 2.

Example 2: *X* and *Y* conduct a game that consists of *X* discovering a stuffed snake, *Y* sharing the discovery, *X* playing the straight man, and *Y* expressing fear

X (holds up snake).

> *Y* (draws back in alarm) What's that?

X It's a snake! (laughs at *Y*'s
exaggerated fear).

> *Y* Do it again.

X (holds up snake).

In *Y*'s request 'it' refers to the whole round. The round was then repeated exactly as before. (Example 2, which shows asymmetrical turn structure, is classified as Format 4.)

The operation of local strictures in specific situations reveals both the orderliness and the credibility that children attribute to play episodes. One type of stricture applicable to role-centred states of play is that role behaviours and role attributes must remain consistent throughout the episode. If one partner departs from the jointly created image of the 'pretend' state, the other partner has the right to correct him. The negligent partner usually accepts the correction as in Example 3.*

Example 3: *X*, preparing to speak on telephone addresses *Y*

X Pretend you're sick.

> *Y* O.K.

X (speaks into phone) Hey, Dr Wren
do you got any medicine?

> *Y* Yes, I have some medicine.

X (to *Y*) No, you aren't the doctor,
remember?

> *Y* O.K.

X (speaks into phone) I need some
medicine for the kids. Bye. (turns
to *Y*) He hasn't got any medicine.

> *Y* No? Oh, dear.

---

* Two points should be made in respect to the figures in Table 1. First, we have no basis for comparison of these frequencies with other subject samples on such parameters as age, social class, or setting. Second, although a round in any play episode is potentially repeatable, we do not know what conditions influence the children to produce a ritual sequence, to choose another course of interaction, or to end the state of play.

Y was corrected by *X* for misinterpreting his role. *Y* then accepted the correction and returned to role-acceptable behaviour.

Rules based on concepts of what behaviours and attitudes are appropriate to a particular role or activity were often stated as normative guidelines. For example, in a role-playing episode, a boy told a girl, 'Take that [holster] off. Girls don't wear things like that.' Often the children's concepts of role-appropriate behaviours were reflected in the selection of actions and objects for the co-operatively created situation. For example, in several mixed-sex dyads, the girl expressed fear of a large stuffed snake. The boy reassured her and fearlessly killed the snake while the girl watched. Both general procedural rules (e.g. turn-apportionment rules) and rules guiding behaviour in particular situations are essential to the conduct of social play.

(III) Theme and variation

Related to the ability to recognize and abstract the format of the play state is the ability to construct jointly the theme of the activity and to develop it in a manner consonant with the jointly held image of the state. Any episode of social play entails the exercise of *shared* imagination and the shared development of the theme of the episode. An example of joint development of a theme by two boys, is Example 4.

Example 4: *X* is busy cooking at the stove; *Y* watches

X O.K. dinner is ready. Now what do
     you want for dinner? (turns to *Y*).
                                            Y Well . . . (indecisively).
X Hot beef?
                                            Y O.K., hot beef.
X Coffee, too?
                                            Y No, I'm the little boy. I'll have
                                                 some milk.
X O.K., you can eat now.
                                            Y (moves closer to stove).
X Kid, we're going to get some milk
     from the store. Come on in the
     dunebuggy.
                                            Y O.K., I'm in the dunebuggy.
(dunebuggy is a small toy car, but
 X pushes it and *Y* moves beside it).

Neither child alone determined the course of this episode. Although *X* initiated it, *Y* contributed by adopting the role of little boy, rejecting the coffee and asking for milk. This move was then accepted by *X*, who had not explicitly identified himself as mother or father, but now addressed *Y* as 'Kid'. The move led to further integrated activity, i.e. going to get the milk.

While objects are freely transformed, e.g. stool to milk carton, to conform to the needs of the episode, consistency is maintained in respect to motives and appropriate actions for the roles adopted. The little boy drinks milk, not coffee, and as they started to bring the milk home, *X*, taking into account *Y*'s 'little boy' role, assured him that it was not too heavy for him to carry. Such explicit attention to motives and to role consonant behaviours suggests greater person-centred than object-centred concern in children of the ages observed. This would explain, in part, how the children were able so efficiently to express and perceive the subtle cues necessary to the flexible and rapid development of the themes of 'pretend' play.

In summary, we have proposed that young children distinguish between play and non-play modes of interaction and we have suggested some of the competencies that underlie the observed play episodes. We will now turn to a discussion of increasingly complex interaction structures.

INTERACTION STRUCTURES

Taking turns implies an ability to identify a unit of social interaction, the turn or the round. In 'doing the same thing' as in a simple imitation of another's act one must be able to abstract the critical features of the act as well as its function in the structure or format of the interaction (Guillaume, 1971). The simplest forms of ritual play involve alternating repetitions as in Format 1 where the round composed of two turns can be repeated in virtually identical form a number of times. Non-verbal parallels were frequently observed. For example, one child threw a curtain into the air, smiled and waited while the other threw his curtain up. The round was repeated, with laughter accompanying each turn. Slightly more elaborate versions occur with identical turns when each round introduces a change of content as in Format 2a or when the content of the turns differs but each person repeats the content of his own previous turn in successive rounds, as in Format 2b. A still more complex format is achieved when the content of each turn in each successive round is progressively modified as in Format 3. This last type can exhibit considerable sophistication in use of words and syntax while still retaining the feature of constant intonation over each lexically varied event as in Example 5.

Example 5: *X* and *Y*, an older dyad, are discussing their feelings about the playroom

X Don't you wish we could get out of this place?

Y Yeah, 'cause it has yucky things.

X Yeah.

Y 'Cause it's fishy too, 'cause it has fishes

X And it's snakey too 'cause it has snakes. And it's beary too 'cause it has bears.

Y And it's hatty too 'cause it has hats.

X Where's the hats? (*X* ends the game).

Although X slipped in a double play at his turn, the intonation of the four variant sentences was the same, and each production was greeted with an appreciative smile. X's last utterance was a serious request for information. Its rapid tempo contrasted sharply with the measured rhythm of the ritual. A still more complex format can be achieved when a round is composed of asymmetrically distributed turns, as in Format 4. In this type, as in previous described formats, the turns may be verbal or non-verbal. In Example 6 only Y's turn was a verbal one.

Example 6: X puts a toy car under the magnifying glass in the stool

Y (looks in the glass) That's the
biggest car I ever saw! (with
exaggerated surprise).

(X looks in glass and laughs).

X then fetched a hat placed it under glass to begin round 2, looking expectantly at Y who intoned, 'That the biggest hat I ever saw.'

The basic formats of these social play episodes form patterns of interaction from which the ritual aspects can be abstracted. An example (7) of a conversational exchange free of ritual features is taken from an older dyad.

The first turn is echoed and elaborated in the second turn. Y produced her variant of the act produced by X, and X appeared to recognize, just as Y did, that they were doing the same thing. A minimal change in content would produce a fairly typical adult conversational exchange. Sacks (1967) pointed out that 'doing the same thing' in adult conversation provides a way of tacitly acknowledging the intent of the speaker's gesture by advancing and elaborating the meaning of that gesture.

Example 7: X and Y have just been left alone in the playroom

X (looks at Y) Hey, we have to be all
by ourselves. But there's a good
thing. I know how to be.

Y (approaches X) But there's a good
thing. I won't cry when someone
leaves me alone. Well, when I
was little I always cried when
someone left me alone. Once
mommy and daddy both left and
I cried and cried, and I've been
so lonesome.

X (attends story and nods).

Of course, many conversational and interactional structures which reflect turn taking are based on doing a complementary thing, rather than the same thing. Providing an appropriate complementary, or syntagmatic, response also requires that the first gesture be correctly interpreted, since one utterance form can often serve different conversational purposes. For example, if the interrogative utterance, 'Can you open the door?' were interpreted as a request for information the response, 'Yes, I can,' would be appropriate; if it were taken as a request for action, then opening the door, with or without a verbal accompaniment, would be an appropriate response. In two examples (8 and 9), composed of another type of request and its complementary response, the request was encoded in two different ways by X before being correctly interpreted.

Example 8: X and Y are talking while X, who is 'Mom', sets the table

X Why do brother and sister always
laugh at me?
$\qquad$ Y I don't know.

X Every once a week they go out
playing and start laughing at me.
$\qquad$ Y I know, um, that's an awful thing.

Example 9: same dyad, same roles and activities, a few seconds later

X How come our house is so dirty?
Brother and sister have to make it
dirty?
$\qquad$ Y What?

X Brother and sister have to make my
whole nice room dirty.
$\qquad$ Y I know, that's a horrible thing to
do too.

Y's commiserative response to X's complaints reveal that at least X's second utterance in each episode was interpreted as a request for sympathy. Y's final responses were instances of a conventionally appropriate complementary response (rather than an instance of doing the same thing). In Example 8 it appears that X re-coded his first message because Y's first answer, 'I don't know', did not provide the requested response. In both cases, X appeared to be satisfied with the final response. The request for a sympathetic response occurred frequently in social play among the older dyads. Although free of the rhythmic features characteristic of ritual play, exchanges of this type were marked by the somewhat exaggerated intonation associated with pretend and role play. We suggest that the ritual play formats which employ syntagmatically varied turns and round modification provide a basis for the acquisition of more specialized conversational exchange types.

But what might actually sustain the practice, or repetition, of these basic social formats? Why engage so often in the work of meshing or interrelating behaviours instead of simply chanting or performing some rhythmically satisfying monologue or individual game? It is reasonable to postulate that an intrinsically satisfying feature of social play, which is present for each participant, is the feature of control. Observations of the apparent satisfaction obtained in manipulating features of the physical environment or, differently stated, of the effectiveness of successful manipulation in maintaining behaviour have been made of infant behaviour (Millar, 1968, Chapter 4). Rapidly accumulating evidence on the sensitivity of young children to features of the human environment suggests that they would be ready and willing, perhaps before they were able, to attempt control of the human environment and derive satisfaction from successful control of another's behaviour. In the performances of ritual play such control is precise and knowledge of its success is immediate; furthermore, the satisfaction derived is mutual, since each party is instrumental in eliciting and maintaining the responsive behaviour of the other. The analogy of the acquisition of basic social interaction patterns with the modularization of physical action patterns in the development of complex skills as described by Bruner (1971) is more than a suggestive metaphor.

2.

The skills of friendship

Zick Rubin

In this reading from his book on Children's Friendships, *Rubin provides from his own work and that of others an interesting overview of the skills involved in making and keeping friends. In comparing children who are adept in establishing friendships with those who are not, Rubin makes two important points. The first concerns the complex nature of the social skills that are required to make friends. These skills include a series of tactics that are used to enter into play routines; and ways in which young children, when they recognize that another child is upset, take action to alleviate the problem. The second point Rubin makes is that given the complex nature of these skills, not all children readily use them to maintain friendships. Thus when children enter school, they reveal a range of social abilities. Some will settle securely, while others need help to establish friendships. To illustrate these differences between children, Rubin starts the chapter with reference to two children, Ricky and Danny, mentioned ealier in his book. Ricky makes friends easily, and on entry to school 'quickly proceeded to establish friendly relations with at least ten of the other children in the class'. Danny, on the other hand, has few friends, and '. . . made periodic attempts to join other children in their activities but with little success'.*

I begin with reference to two boys in the same preschool class – Ricky, who made many friends, and Danny, who made none. Ricky's greater ability to make friends could not have been predicted from the two boys' physical or intellectual characteristics. But Ricky had mastered to an impressive degree the social skills needed to establish and maintain friendships. These skills include the abilities to gain entry into group activities, to be approving and supportive of one's peers, to manage conflicts appropriately, and to exercise sensitivity and tact. They are subtle skills, by no means easy to learn, and the fact that most children ultimately succeed in acquiring them is itself one of the most remarkable aspects of social development.

Consider, first, the immediate problem confronting a child who enters a new group and wants to join other children in their play. During their first few days in a new preschool setting, children frequently avoid their peers and instead hover nervously on the sidelines. (McGrew, 1972; Putallaz and Gottman, 1981). As they become more familiar with their environment, the newcomers may try to approach other children. But these attempts – like Danny's – are not likely to succeed until the child has accumulated a repertoire of tactics for entering groups, complete with implicit rules about how and when a certain ploy can be used most effectively.

William Corsaro offers the following example of the 'access strategies' of four-year-olds in nursery school:

> Two girls, Jenny and Betty, are playing around a sandbox in the outside courtyard of the school. I am sitting on the ground near the sandbox watching. The girls are putting sand in pots, cupcake pans, bottles and teapots . . . Another girl, Debbie, approaches and stands near me observing the other two girls. Neither Jenny nor Betty acknowledges her presence. Debbie does not speak to me or the other girls, and no one speaks to her. After watching for some time (five minutes or so) she circles the sandbox three times and stops again and stands near me. After a few more minutes of watching, Debbie moves to the sandbox and reaches for a teapot in the sand. Jenny takes the pot away from Debbie and mumbles, 'No.' Debbie backs away and again stands near me observing the activity of Jenny and Betty. Then she walks over next to Betty, who is filling the cupcake pan with sand. Debbie watches Betty for just a few seconds, then says:
> 'We're friends, right? We're friends, right, Betty?'
> Betty, not looking up at Debbie and while continuing to place sand in the pan, says, 'Right.'
> 'I'm making coffee,' Debbie says to Betty.
> 'I'm making cupcakes,' Betty replies.
> Betty turns to Jenny and says, 'We're mothers, right, Jenny?'
> Jenny replies, 'Right.'
> The three 'mothers' continue to play together for 20 more minutes, until the teachers announce cleanup time. (Corsaro, 1979, pp. 320–321).

Debbie's persistent efforts to join the group illustrates a variety of strategies. At first Debbie merely places herself in the area of the interaction, a strategy that Corsaro calls 'nonverbal entry'. When this tactic gets no response, Debbie proceeds to 'encircle' the area. When this strategy, too, is ignored, she enters the area directly and produces 'similar behaviour' (she picks up a teapot). And when this attempt is rebuffed, Debbie switches to a verbal strategy, making direct 'reference to affiliation' ('We're friends, right?'). After Betty responds positively to this move, Debbie once again produces behaviour similar to that of the others, this time explicitly describing it ('I'm making coffee'). At this point, Debbie's attempt to join the group finally succeeds. Betty responds in a way that includes Debbie in the activity ('We're mothers'), and the three now play together for some time.

Corsaro notes that nursery school children rarely use more direct verbal access strategies, such as saying 'Hi', 'What ya doing?' or 'Can I play?' One likely reason is that such direct approaches call for a direct response by the approached children, and this response is very likely to be negative. Once two or more children have structured and defined for themselves a particular activity, whether it is making cupcakes or blasting off in a spaceship, they often 'protect' their activity by excluding any outsiders who might dare to request entry. Sometimes this exclusive stance is established even before the activity begins. For example:

> (David, Josh, and Jonah are in the sandbox together.)
> *David* (to Josh): Will you help me make some soup?
> *Josh*: Yeah – and Jonah can't play, right?

Unless the 'outsider' is already a highly accepted group member who has special rights of entry, young children will frequently refuse him admission. A 'Hi' may be ignored, a 'What ya doing?' responded with 'We're making cupcakes and you're not', and a direct 'Can I play?' answered with an equally direct 'No'. To enter the activity therefore, the child may have to be cautious and subtle, like Debbie. By first reconnoitring the situation unobtrusively, then quietly joining in the ongoing activity and finally making direct verbal statements – including the ingratiating 'We're friends, right?' – Debbie was able to include herself in Betty and Jenny's activity without mobilizing their resistance.

On the other hand, direct approaches may be more effective when the child wants to engage a single other child who is not already involved in a group activity. And as children grow older, specific verbal formulas for initiating interaction become more important. In a study of eight- and nine-year-olds, John Gottman and his co-workers asked children to pretend that the researcher was a new child in the class with whom they wanted to make friends. (Gottman, Gonso and Rasmussen, 1975). From the children's performance in this role-play situation, the researchers were able to assess their knowledge of friendship-making tactics. Offering greetings ('Hi, Mary'), offering appropriate information ('My favourite sport is basketball'), requesting information ('Where do you live?'), and extending invitations ('Wanna come over to my house some time?') were all scored as reflecting the child's knowledge of how to make friends. The researchers then compared these social-knowledge scores with popularity ratings derived from questions asked of all class members. They found, not surprisingly, that popular children knew more about how to make friends than unpopular children did.

'Knowing how' to make friends is no guarantee of social success, however. Some children may excel on a role-play test of social skills but at the same time may be unable or unwilling to put these skills to practical use. For example, an experience with rejection may lead some children to avoid approaching others for long periods of time; other children will bounce back from rejection much more easily. As Carol Dweck and Therese Goetz (1979) suggest, the difference in reactions may depend on the child's personal explanation of a rejection. Some children tend to blame any rejection on their own inadequacies ('I'm just a shy person') and, as a result, do not feel that the problem can be overcome. Other children will attribute the same rejection to temporary moods or misunderstandings ('Maybe her mother yelled at her that morning') and will persist in their efforts to gain acceptance. In the comparison, it is the resilient child who is more likely to establish friendships.

The skills of friendship include not only the ability to gain entry into group activities, but also the ability to *be* a friend – an attentive, approving, and helpful playmate and associate. Even in the first year of life, children have distinctive styles of interaction that can make them agreeable or disagreeable to their peers. Lee C. Lee (1973) observed a daycare group of five infants in Ithaca, New York, for a period of six months, beginning when the infants were all about nine months old. She found that one of the infants, Jenny, was by far the best-liked member of the group; throughout the six-month period, each of the other four babies approached her most often. Patrick was the least-liked group member; he was approached least often by three of the other four infants. On the basis of detailed observations of each baby, Lee was able to paint a picture of their contrasting styles of interaction. Jenny was a responsive, adaptive social partner. She displayed a range of emotions in her social encounters. And she seldom terminated social contacts that had been initiated by others. Patrick, on the other hand, was a belligerent and unfriendly baby. He frequently grabbed others and was reluctant to end encounters that he had initiated. But when others initiated contacts with him, he was passive and unresponsive. Patrick did not smile, laugh, or otherwise display positive feelings in a single one of the occasions in which he was contacted by another baby. To put it bluntly, Patrick was no fun. Not surprisingly, in light of their differing styles of response, Jenny continued to be approached by other babies while Patrick was shunned.

There is no strong reason to believe that such differences in the 'likeability' of infants are likely to persist past the second year in life. As children grow older, however, they become capable of producing a wider range of behaviour that may be either rewarding or unrewarding to their peers. In extensive observations of nursery school children, Willard Hartup and his colleagues at the University of Minnesota (Hartup, Glazer and Charlesworth, 1967) found that the most popular children – those whom their classmates enjoyed playing with most – were also the ones who most often paid attention to other children, praised them, showed affection, and willingly acceded to their requests Children who frequently ignored others, refused to cooperate, ridiculed, blamed, or threatened others were most likely to be disliked by their classmates. In short, for a child to be included and accepted, he must also include and accept.

Again, Ricky epitomizes such an inclusive and accepting child. He is an engaging, supportive boy who goes out of his way to involve others in his activities. When Caleb comes out to the big rotating swing, which already has four children on board, Ricky immediately shouts to him, 'You can get on it!' 'It's crowded,' Caleb shouts back. In Ricky's view of things, however, there is always room for one more. 'Someone else wants to get on,' he informs his fellow riders. Then he takes charge of slowing down the swing and shows Caleb where he can climb on. Ricky is a skilful social facilitator, and others like him for it.

It is important to stress, however, that 'friendly' behaviour does not always win friendship. Whether an affectionate act is in fact experienced as rewarding will depend on *how* the affection is expressed and, most important, how it is interpreted by the recipient. While some children must learn to be more outgoing, others must learn to stop 'coming on too strong'. At the beginning of the year, Fiona would regularly run up to other children and hug them effusively. She discovered, to her dismay, that this display of affection usually frightened off the others. She eventually learned that she could do better by approaching others more subtly – for example, by patting them on the arm and suggesting an activity.

What may be, for one child, a show of friendship is not necessarily viewed that way by another. Even gift giving can backfire, if the recipient attributes ignoble motives to the giver. Ann, who began to interact with other children only late in the school year, gave Craig a paper envelope she had made, as a gesture of friendship. Later Craig tells me, 'I'm not going to take it home because it doesn't have a drawing.' 'Why do you think Ann gave it to you?' I ask. 'I don't know. Maybe she doesn't like it either.' Moreover, the same overt behaviour can be regarded as rewarding if it comes from a child one already likes and unrewarding if it comes from a child one already has doubts about. 'I'll tell you why I don't like David,' Rachel explains to me. 'Because he screams around all sorts of places. But I don't mind if Steven screams because he just screams a little bit.'

Studies of nursery school children have also indicated that the best-liked children are not highly dependent on teachers (Moore, 1967). Ricky often chatted amiably with teachers and generally followed their instructions, but only rarely went to a teacher for help in dealing with routine matters. Danny, in contrast, frequently called for help in a whiny tone of voice and would cry for the teacher whenever he received a minor injury or rebuff. Ricky's lesser dependence on teachers was almost certainly related to his greater ability to be supportive of his classmates. When a child must constantly turn to adults for support and assistance, he is unlikely to have the emotional resources necessary to be rewarding to his peers.

The skills of friendship also include the ability to manage conflicts successfully. Children learn that it is often valuable to talk out their hurt feelings in order to restore good will. While playing fireman, for example, Josh and Tony managed to offend each other. After a period of sullen silence, the following conversation ensued:

> *Josh*: I'm not going to be your friend, Tony. You're talking mean to me so I'm
>   not going to be your friend.
> *Tony*: You're talking mean to *me*.
> *Josh*: You're calling me names – Bloody Boy, Fire Boy.
> *Tony*: Well, you're not letting me and David play by ourselves.

Once they put these feelings on the table, Josh and Tony quickly restored harmony. 'I can be a fireboy in the fireman game,' Josh declares. 'Let him spray out fires,' Tony orders his other fireman.

In order to maintain friendships in the face of the disagreements that inevitably arise, children must learn to express their own rights and feelings clearly while remaining sensitive to the rights and feelings of others. They must be able to suggest and to accept reasonable compromises, even as they stand up against unreasonable demands. As S. Holly Stocking and Diana Arezzo (1979) note, different children may start in different places in the quest for the ability to manage conflict appropriately:

> The overly aggressive child ... may need to learn how to listen to others without interrupting or putting them down, and how to accept reasonable disagreement gracefully, without anger or attack. The overly submissive child, in turn, may have to learn to stand up for himself with a definite posture and a calm tone of voice that communicates conviction.

As children become more sensitive to the feelings of their peers, they also learn the subtle skills of tact that are needed to maintain friendships. Even four-year-olds may begin to display such tact, especially in the context of close friendships. When Tony took his pants off to go swimming, for example, his best friend David inadvertently burst into laughter. But a moment later, David turned to Tony and assured him, 'I'm not laughing at you, Tony. I'm laughing at Neil.' Although this explanation may have involved a white lie on David's part, it also illustrates his sensitivity to his friend's feelings and his ability to act in such a way as to protect them.

I observed a particularly striking example of tact among four-year-olds in the following conversation between David and Josh, who were walking together and pretending to be robots:

> *David*: I'm a missile robot who can shoot missiles out of my fingers. I can shoot
>   them out of everywhere – even out of my legs. I'm a missile robot.
> *Josh* (tauntingly): No, you're a fart robot.
> *David* (protestingly): No, I'm a missile robot.
> *Josh*: No, you're a fart robot.

David (hurt, almost in tears): No, Josh!
Josh (recognizing that David is upset): And I'm a poo-poo robot.
David (in good spirits again): I'm a pee-pee robot.

As in the case of the interaction between David and Tony, Josh realized that he had said something ('you're a fart robot') that greatly distressed his friend. He handled the situation resourcefully by putting himself down as well ('I'm a poo-poo robot'), thus demonstrating that his insult was not to be taken seriously. David's response to Josh's move ('I'm a pee-pee robot') indicates that Josh had appraised the situation accurately and had successfully saved his friend's feelings.

Acquiring the skills of friendship can be a difficult struggle for the preschool child, especially if he has not had much previous experience in interacting with other children of his own age without direct adult supervision. Nursery schools often serve as valuable proving grounds for the development of such skills. Although the learning may sometimes be painful or frustrating, children gradually develop both more sophisticated concepts of friendship and more sophisticated techniques for establishing and maintaining such friendships for themselves. The development of communication skills through interaction with one's peers may itself be an important pre-requisite for the acquisition of skills specifically related to friendship. In this connection, Danny, who had doting parents but little experience with children of his own age before entering nursery school, probably suffered in his attempts at making friends because of his relatively undeveloped powers of communication. Ricky, in contrast, lived in the same household as several cousins of varying ages and had developed communication skills of an unusually high order. With additional experience, as it turned out, Danny, too, became more successful at making friends. When I revisited him a year after I had concluded my observations of the class, I found that he was interacting much more successfully and was sought out by several of his classmates.

Children, then, acquire social skills not so much from adults as from their interaction with one another. They are likely to discover through trial and error which strategies work and which do not, and later to reflect consciously on what they have learned. While playing with blocks one day, four-year-old Alec remarked to his teacher 'Remember that day when I gave Colin a truck he needed? That was a very nice thing to do, don't you think, Miss Beyer?' (Beyer, 1956, p. 347). Children also learn social skills from the direct tutelage or examples provided by their peers. When David whines, 'Gary pushed me,' for example, Josh firmly advises him, 'Just say stop.' In other instances, children introduce their friends to one another, help others to launch joint activities, or show others how to resolve their conflicts. Rachel is one child who is successful, in her own soft-spoken way, in promoting good feeling among other children. For example, she serves as timekeeper while several other children take turns standing in a special hiding place. When Claudia occupies the space before it is her turn, Rachel calls her back to the table where the timekeeper's hourglass is kept and gently explains, 'Here, Claudia – when it goes all the way through there it's your turn, all right?' When all the sand has trickled through, Rachel happily informs Claudia that her turn has come, and lets Alison know that her time has run out. One suspects that such advice and assistance from respected peers may often be more effective than similar interventions by teachers or parents.

There are also cases, however, when children need help from adults in mastering particular skills of friendship. When children wish to make friends but lack the skills to do so, vicious circles can be set in motion. The friendless child must interact with his peers in order to develop the self-confidence and skills needed for social success. But the lack of social skills – for example, the inability to approach other children or the tendency to scare them off – may cut him off from just such opportunities. In such cases, intervention by parents or teachers may be necessary. One approach is to steer a friendless child to a particular other child – sometimes one who also lacks friends – with whom the adult thinks the child might hit it off. In at least some cases, such matchmaking can help to give two withdrawn children an initial and valuable experience of social acceptance. Another tactic is to pair an older child who is too competitive or aggressive with a younger child to whom he can relate as a 'big brother' – and, in the process, learn that he can win the approval of others without being a bully (Furman, Rahe and Hartup, 1979).

Psychologists have also developed a variety of training programmes for both preschool and school-age children. In such programmes, children who have been identified as isolates or outcasts are given a series of sessions which may include demonstrations of specific social skills, opportunities to practise them, and feedback on their performance. In at least some cases, these programmes have been notably successful in increasing the social acceptance of initially isolated children. (For a review of such programmes see Combs and Slaby, 1977, and Oden and Asher, 1977).

Because training programmes tend to be focused on increasing 'social acceptance' or 'popularity', they bring up some troublesome questions of values. Do the programmes really help children develop the capacity for friendship, or are they geared to some 'American' ideal of glib sociability and congeniality that has little to do with real friendship at all? The answer to this question depends both on the details of the programme and on the values of the adults who administer it. In the view of at least some leading practitioners, however, 'The objective of social skills instruction is not to create "popular" or "outgoing" children, but to help youngsters, whatever their personality styles, to develop positive relationships . . . with at least one or two other children.' (Stocking and Arezzo, 1979). One can also ask whether it is ethically acceptable to impose social skills training on children who have little choice in the matter and who in some instances may not really want to be changed into 'friendlier' people. In the last analysis, though, the most compelling defence for such programmes is that they may be able to increase the child's degree of control over her own life. As Melinda Combs and Diana Arezzo Slaby note, 'A child who has the skills to initiate play and communicate with peers may still choose to spend a good deal of time alone. But that child will be able to interact effectively when she (he) wants to or when the situation requires it. On the other hand, a socially unskilled child may be alone or 'isolated' out of necessity rather than by choice (Combs and Slaby, 1977, p. 165).

Even without instituting formal training, parents and teachers can make use of similar demonstrations, explanations, and feedback in order to teach the skills of friendship in school or home settings. In making use of such procedures, however, adults must be sensitive to the fine line that exists between help and interference. Although adults have a role to play in teaching social skills to children, it is often best that they play it unobtrusively. In particular, adults must guard against embarrassing unskilled children by correcting them too publicly and against labelling children as shy in ways that may lead the children to see themselves in just that way (Zimbardo, 1977).

Rather than 'pushing' social skills indiscriminately, adults should respect the real differences between children that motivate some to establish friendly relations with many others, some to concentrate on one or two close friendships, and some to spend a good deal of time by themselves. Children's friendships take many forms and involve different styles of interaction. In our efforts to help children make friends, we should be more concerned with the quality of these friendships than with their quantity.

Adults must also recognize that there are many personal attributes, some of them relatively immutable, which are likely to affect the way a child is viewed by his peers in a particular setting, including physical appearance, athletic prowess, intellectual abilities, and family background (see for example Dion and Berscheid, 1974; McCraw and Tolbert, 1953; and Asher, Oden and Gottman, 1977). As a result, different children may be best equipped with somewhat different skills of friendship. Finally, adults must be sensitive to events in children's lives that may underlie problems with making and keeping friends. Moving to a new school or neighbourhood may create special difficulties, and so may stressful family events such as divorce (Hetherington, Cox and Cox, 1979). For the most part, as we have seen, children learn the skills of friendship not from adults but from each other. But parents and teachers who are sensitive to individual children's distinctive needs and circumstances can play a crucial role in facilitating this learning.

3.
Social isolation from agemates among nursery school children

W. George Scarlett

In the last reading, Rubin referred to children who, through problems in interacting with other children, are without playmates. In the present paper, Scarlett uses the term 'social isolates' for such children. Taking small groups of three- and four-year-old children, Scarlett studied the interaction patterns and behaviours of social isolates, compared with those of a matched group of non-isolates. Using observational techniques, the behaviours of the children and their teachers were coded according to a detailed set of categories encompassing different types of social behaviour. Analysis of the data produced a clear set of results, that revealed specific differences between the behaviour of isolates and non-isolates. A finding of particular interest concerns the extent to which isolates contribute to their isolation through their own, unacceptable behaviours. As Scarlett points out, while not enough is yet known about the development of isolation in such children, this sort of finding does provide some information about how to alleviate the problems of children who find themselves socially isolated.

In every group of preschool children at play one can observe considerable individual variation in the amount of interaction with others. However, a few children seem to fall outside this range of expected variation; they stand out because of the paucity of their social contacts. The focus of this study was on preschool children who rarely interact with peers (i.e. who are socially isolated from peers) but who are considered to fall within a normal range of intelligence and emotional stability. These children are of interest in their own right. In addition the fact that they fall within a normal range of intelligence and emotional stability allows for a focus upon what factors – other than basic skills in thinking and communicating – are required for the development of early peer relations.

The central aims of this study were to describe how isolates as compared to non-isolates behave during nursery-school free-play sessions, how they are treated by peers and teachers, and how isolates and non-isolates react to changes in group size and structure. The goal of describing social isolates was adopted in part because there have been very few descriptive studies of infrequently interacting preschoolers and because isolates were thought to have been characterized in the literature in global and sometimes misleading ways. Terms such as 'shy', 'apathetic', 'withdrawn', 'passive', 'immature' and 'dependent' have been used to describe such children but without adequately specifying their behavioural referents. Although all of these terms may apply to social isolates, the terms are at such a high level of abstraction as to imply a wide variety of possible behaviours and behaviour patterns, many of which may not be typical or representative of socially isolated young children. Also describing the behaviour and treatment of isolates was intended to contribute to a description base necessary for eventually accounting for social isolation from peers.

The comparison of isolates and non-isolates was intended in part to specify the relation (if any) between the way young children behave towards peers and the way they are treated by peers. In the literature, the few descriptive studies of preschoolers' social behaviour do not provide a consistent picture of how behaviour patterns relate or fail to relate to peer sociability. For example, Beaver (1932) found no relation between the character of preschoolers' treatment of peers and treatment by peers whereas Kohn (1966) found that ' . . . the child gets what he puts out'.

In addition to the above, an attempt was made to describe and compare isolates' and non-isolates' behaviour with peers in different situations. There are no reported studies indicating how infrequently interacting children behave with peers in situations other than in classroom free-play sessions, despite evidence that the response patterns of preschoolers vary across situations (cf. Rose, Blank and Spalter, 1975). Also, the unstructured nature of the classroom free-play situation makes it inadequate for describing how isolates interact when they do interact. In the study to be reported, isolates and non-isolates were observed in small groups under conditions thought to encourage interaction.

The study to be reported also compared the spontaneous treatment of isolates and non-isolates by peers and teachers. There have been several studies which demonstrate that training or conditioning by adults has at least short-term effects upon isolates' rate of peer interaction (cf. Alleen *et al.*, 1964). However, it is unclear what long-term effect, if any, these procedures have. Observing peers' and teachers' spontaneous behaviour towards isolates and non-isolates was intended to indicate whether peers and teachers normally treat isolates differently than they treat non-isolates as well as indicate ways that peers and teachers may foster or inhibit the development of peer sociability.

EXPECTATIONS

Comparing isolates' and non-isolates' behaviour was expected to support the view that isolates contribute to their own isolation by making themselves less attractive, by requiring more direction from peers than peers can or wish to give, and by being less responsive to peers' positive approaches. Isolates were not expected to foster their isolation by physically distancing themselves from peers, by being overly aggressive or rejecting with peers, or by being overly dependent and 'tied to teachers' apron strings'.

Comparing how isolates and non-isolates interact was expected to reveal a variety of specific types of behaviour crucial to supporting interaction between preschoolers (e.g. attempting to structure peers, offering help). The comparison was also expected to suggest that other positive social behaviours are not crucial to whether and how young children foster peer relations (e.g. showing approval or affection).

Peers were expected to foster isolation mainly by ignoring isolates' positive approaches rather than by being rejecting or aggressive towards isolates. Overall, teachers were not expected to treat isolates and non-isolates differently – indicating that social isolation is neither fostered nor inhibited by teachers.

The comparison of children's behaviour in class free-play sessions and in the small structured play groups was expected to show that the change to a small structured group is more likely to foster interaction between isolates and non-isolates than between non-isolate children.

METHOD

Subjects and sampling procedure

Eleven isolates (six boys and five girls) were chosen from six different schools. Each isolate was matched with a classmate of the same sex and within three months of being the same age who was considered average with respect to frequency of interaction with peers. The age range for the entire sample was 42–59 months. The mean age for both groups was 48 months. All of the children had been attending school for at least three months prior to being observed. Teachers considered the isolates normal (i.e. without severe emotional problems) and as physically attractive as the non-isolates and there were no consistent differences in ethnicity between the two groups. All of the measures were used to describe both the isolates' and matched non-isolates' behaviour and treatment.

Measuring isolates', matched non-isolates', and randomly selected classmates' rate of peer interaction in class provided checks to insure that the isolates were indeed children who rarely interact with their classmates and that the matched non-isolates were average with respect to rate of peer interaction. Administering the Peabody Picture Vocabulary Test to isolates and matched non-isolates provided a check to insure that the two target groups did not differ in verbal ability or general intelligence.

Categories for describing

Four different sets of category systems were employed to characterize the behaviour and treatment of the isolates and matched non-isolates (i.e. the target children). The different sets were necessary to answer different questions pertaining to social isolation and peer sociability.

A set of categories (53 in all) describing specific individual social behaviours (e.g. asking another for help, hitting a peer without provocation) was used to answer questions about how isolates interact when they do interact and how they are treated by peers. Several of these categories were modifications of categories constructed by Shapiro and Ogilvie (1974). Prior to the collection of data, these 53 categories were grouped into 12 general categories that are better suited to answer questions about how preschoolers foster or inhibit their relations with peers. The 12 general categories of social behaviour also made possible statistical analysis of descriptions of peer interactions. The categories were as follows:

(1) Fostering understanding (e.g. asking a peer what he is doing).
(2) Seeking approval, affection, or sympathy (e.g. announcing with pride some accomplishment).
(3) Showing approval, affection, or sympathy (e.g. giving a hug).
(4) Structuring a peer (e.g. directing the activity of a peer, initiating a play sequence with a peer).
(5) Expressing positive affect towards a peer (e.g. by laughing).
(6) Offering help, information, guidance.
(7) Seeking help, information, guidance.
(8) Autonomy behaviours (e.g. expressing personal wishes, defining personal property, defending oneself from peer aggression).
(9) Following another's suggestion, direction, or initiation of a play sequence.
(10) Imitating (following another without the other suggesting, directing, or initiating a joint play sequence).
(11) Rejecting or being aggressive towards another (e.g. unprovoked hitting, ridiculing a peer).
(12) Being unresponsive or insensitive (e.g. not responding to a peer's positive approach, withdrawing from peer aggression).

The 53 specific categories were further grouped into positive and negative approaches and responses to provide global measures of how children interacted when they did interact. Negative individual social behaviours included unresponsive and insensitive behaviour as well as rejecting and aggressive behaviour.

A modification of Parten's (1932) categories allowed for a characterization of the organization and social participation of children's behaviour over a period of time. They were as follows:

(1) Unoccupied activity (e.g. aimless wandering).
(2) Onlooker activity (watching peers without interacting and without playing).
(3) Independent play (playing apart from peers in ways different from peers).
(4) Parallel play (playing next to a peer or peers in similar ways but without being engaged with peers).
(5) Associative play (playing and being engaged with one or more peers but without continually affecting or being affected by a peer).
(6) Integrative play (playing and being engaged with one or more peers in such a way that a child simultaneously and continuously affects and is affected by a peer).
(7) Conversation (extended talking with one or more peers that is both friendly and not part of a play sequence).
(8) Fighting (e.g. struggling over possession of a toy).
(9) Adult engaged (being engaged with an adult but not a peer when the adult does not inhibit the child's choosing to play alone or with a peer).

Categories describing how children space themselves from others were taken from a study by McGrew and McGrew (1972). They were as follows:

(1) Solitary spacing (when a child is clearly not within touching distance of a peer or teacher).
(2) Proximal to adult only (when a child is within touching distance of one or more adults but no peers).
(3) Proximal to one other child (when a child is within touching distance of only one peer, with or without an adult present).
(4) Proximal to more than one other child (when a child is within touching distance of more than one peer, with or without an adult present).

Prior to analysing data, descriptions of the content of children's play were categorized using the following set of categories:

(1) Imaginative – dramatic (e.g. dress-up, playing Batman).
(2) Gross motor (e.g. tricycling).
(3) Block-building.
(4) Sand or water play.
(5) Table construction (e.g. cutting and pasting).
(6) Puzzles and board games.
(7) Music, painting, dance.
(8) Listen to music or other read.
(9) Read.
(10) Other.

Teachers' behaviour with the target children was described using nine categories thought to describe possible ways teachers foster or inhibit interaction between children. The categories were as follows:

(1) Suggests line of activity not requiring or making peer interaction likely.
(2) Suggests line of activity requiring or making peer interaction likely.
(3) Approves child's non-interactive play.
(4) Reprimands (disapproves of) or limits child's non-interactive play.
(5) Reprimands or limits child's interactive play.
(6) Initiates play or conversation with the child or initiates individual instruction.
(7) Initiates group instruction which includes the child.
(8) Responds to child's request for help.
(9) Offers child help.

Procedure for observing in the classroom

Each isolate and matched non-isolate was observed for 180 20-second 'scorable' units during free-play sessions. A scorable unit was defined as a unit in which one of the categories of spacing applied plus at least one other type of category. Included as non-scorable units were periods of eating, dressing, recovering from physical hurt, and those periods when there was some environmental constraint preventing a child from interacting with a peer (as when a teacher read to a group).

After each scorable unit, a record was made of (1) which of the 53 specific categories of individual social behaviours were applicable, (2) which category of social participation best described the child's behaviour during most of the unit, (3) how a child spaced himself from others during most of the unit, (4) the content of the child's play during most of the unit, and (5) which categories for describing teachers' behaviour were applicable. Each child was observed for no longer than five consecutive minutes and for no more than 20 minutes per day (to avoid biasing results by observing a child on an atypical day).

The small group sessions. Each isolate was videotaped playing with two randomly selected classmates (a boy and a girl), and each matched non-isolate was videotaped playing with two different randomly selected classmates (a boy and a girl) during two 20-minute play sessions. Each session was divided into four five-minute periods or trials in which the children had the opportunity to play with a different toy independently or while engaged with another.

The sessions were videotaped using an 8.5mm wide angle lens usually making it possible to include all three children in the picture.

Interjudge agreement. The author and a second judge (with no prior knowledge of the study and without knowledge of the isolate/non-isolate classification of a particular child) tested the reliability of the categories using only printed instructions. Six isolates and four matched non-isolates (chosen randomly) were observed by both judges in the classroom for a total of 452 units of joint observation. Reliability for the videotaped small group sessions was obtained by scoring one tape from each of five isolates and their five matched non-isolates (chosen randomly) for a total of 600 units of joint observation. For the categories of individual social behaviours, interjudge agreement was assessed only on the 12 general categories plus the global categories distinguishing positive and negative approaches and responses.

After collapsing two of the categories of spacing, there was better than 76 per cent interjudge agreement on all categories except for the general categories of individual social behaviours. The per cent agreement for these categories when observing classroom behaviour was too low for results to be reported. In observing the small group sessions, per cent agreement was still low (61 per cent overall). Nevertheless, the results of using these categories in the small groups sessions will be reported on because the number and distribution of judge's scores was approximately the same.

RESULTS*

Most of the results are based on standard analyses of variance. When the assumption of a normal distribution was not warranted, a test for significance of F was used; the probability was based on 500 permutations of the sample data.

The behaviour and treatment of isolates and non-isolates in class

In class, isolates and non-isolates differed significantly on total amount of peer-oriented behaviour; isolates directed far fewer individual social behaviours towards peers than did non-isolates $(F\ (1/20)\ =28.91,\ P < 0.01)$ and peers directed far fewer individual social behaviours towards isolates than they did toward the matched non-isolates $(F\ (1/20) = 14.67, P < 0.01)$.

There were no significant differences between the target groups in their treatment of peers as characterized by the global measures describing social behaviour (e.g. percentage of individual social behaviours that were approaches.) Most of the individual social behaviours by the target groups and their classmates were positive, and most were approaches. However, peers had a significantly higher percentage score for negative behaviours (e.g. being unresponsive, unprovoked hitting) when engaged with isolates $(F\ (1/20) = P < 0.05)$.

The results on measures of social participation and organization were as expected. Isolates were unoccupied more than were non-isolates $(F\ (1/20) = 9.71, P < 0.01)$ and engaged more in onlooker activity $(F\ (1/20) = 20.33, P < 0.01)$. Both groups spent approximately half their class time in independent or parallel play. Non-isolates engaged more in associative play $(F\ (1/20) = 23.14,$

---

* For an appendix on the statistics quoted in this book, see p. 308.

$P < 0.01$) and integrative play (F (1/20) = 9.24, $P < 0.01$). Both groups spent very little time conversing or fighting with peers and very little time engaged only with teacher (approximately one per cent for both groups).

There was no expectation that isolates would be spatially withdrawn from peers. The results were mixed. In class, both isolates and non-isolates spent the majority of their time in proximity to one or more peers and very little time in proximity to an adult only. However, isolates spent significantly more time in solitary spacing than did non-isolates (F (1/20) = 12.09, $P < 0.01$).

When playing, non-isolates engaged in imaginative – dramatic play more than did isolates (F (1/20) = 9.28, $P < 0.01$). There were no other ways that isolates and non-isolates differed significantly in their choice of play content.

Isolates and non-isolates did not differ in their behaviour towards teachers. Both groups rarely interacted with teachers, and when they did interact, it was usually either to foster understanding (e.g. 'Teacher, after I build this I'm going outside') or seek approval (e.g. 'Teacher, look what I've built!').

Teachers rarely approached either group, and when they did, they did not differ significantly on the individual measures describing teachers' behaviour.

The behaviour and treatment of isolates and non-isolates in small group sessions

As expected, during the small group sessions isolates directed significantly fewer individual social behaviours towards peers than did non-isolates (F (1/20) = 8.38, $P < 0.01$), and peers directed significantly fewer individual social behaviours towards isolates than towards the matched non-isolates (F (1/20) = 5.26, $P < 0.05$).

When interacting with others, the character of isolates' behaviour towards peers did not differ greatly from the character of matched non-isolates' behaviour towards peers. This was surprising given the assumption that there are several types of social behaviour crucial to fostering interaction between young children. The only significant difference was that isolates structured peers less than did non-isolates (F (1/20) = 14.97, $P < 0.01$). Peers differed in their treatment of isolates and non-isolates only by their following non-isolates more than they followed isolates (F (1/20) = 12.82, $P < 0.01$).

During the small group sessions, as in class, isolates spent significantly more time in onlooker activity (F (1/20) = 68.56, $P < 0.01$), significantly less time in associative play (F (1/20) = 12.38, $P < 0.01$) and significantly less time in integrative play than did non-isolates (F (1/20) = 9.25, $P < 0.01$). Both groups spent very little time being unoccupied, conversing or fighting with peers, or being engaged only with an adult. All of these results were expected.

The effect of changing from class to the small group on the behaviour and treatment of isolates and non-isolates

As expected, in the small group sessions as compared to class, isolates but not matched non-isolates directed more individual social behaviours towards peers, $(F (1/20) = 4.94, P < 0.05)$ and were the targets of more individual social behaviours by peers $(F (1/20) = 4.94, P < 0.05)$.

Also as expected, isolates but not matched non-isolates spent significantly less time unoccupied in the small group than in class $(F (1/20) = 7.62, P < 0.05)$. Contrary to expectation, there was no significant change in per cent onlooker activity for either target group. Furthermore, there were no significant changes in how the target children interacted when they did interact (as measured by positive and negative approaches and responses).

DISCUSSION

The behaviour of isolates

The results support the expectation that infrequently interacting preschoolers share a particular pattern of behaving, a pattern not captured by any single label such as 'shy' or 'apathetic'. In particular, these children differ from interacting preschoolers by their (1) spending less time playing and more time watching peers, (2) rarely trying to influence or structure how peers behave, even when interacting with them, (3) spending less of their class time when playing engaged in imaginative – dramatic play, and (4) being more likely to interact with peers when in more structured and small groups.

These results also support the view that isolates actively contribute to their own isolation. Isolates' playing less than do non-isolates may be the single most important way they render themselves less attractive or less available as social partners. From the results presented here as well as previous research (cf. Mueller *et al.*, 1977) it is clear that young children's interactions with one another are almost always supported by some play object, game, or play activity. When a young child is unoccupied or watching peers without playing, he is not providing his peers with possible grounds for initiating interaction.

The most consistent way isolates differed from non-isolates was in the amount of time spent watching peers without interacting. From informal observations it appears that watching peers may have served different functions for different children. Some of the isolates while watching peers were mostly stationary and held slightly apprehensive facial expressions, as though they were wary of peers. Other isolates in watching peers gave no indication of being wary. On the contrary, their expression was more one of curiosity, and when a group of peers moved away to play in a different location, these children often followed to maintain a good view. The significance, if any, of these two modes of watching peers for the eventual development of peer relations by isolates remains to be investigated.

Isolates may also contribute to their own isolation by requiring more direction from peers than peers can or wish to give. When interacting, non-isolates usually attempted to structure one another. Their relationships did not usually consist of a leader (one who does most of the structuring) and a follower. Pilot work has suggested that when isolates do interact with other children they are more likely to be playing either with dominant older siblings or with classmates who are unusual for how frequently they try to structure others. Therefore, the fact that isolates rarely interact at school may be partially attributable to their adopting the role of follower in a social situation with far less leadership from others than most situations familiar to isolates.

The fact that isolates, when playing, were less likely to be engaged in imaginative – dramatic play than were non-isolates suggests that this type of play may require skills pertinent to interacting with peers, skills which isolates either lack or feel uncomfortable exhibiting in class.

The finding that isolates' but not non-isolates' total amount of peer-oriented behaviour increased significantly in the small structured groups suggests that isolates' sociableness is more situationally determined that non-isolates' sociableness. It also supports the view that isolates are more apt to interact with peers when they are encouraged to play.

The treatment of isolates

The results do not provide a clear picture of whether and how peers may inhibit interaction with isolates. In class, peers did behave more negatively towards isolates. However, since the category 'negative' covered a variety of behaviours (e.g. not responding to another's positive approach, hitting another without provocation), the most that can be said is that peers may be less satisfying as play partners when engaged with isolates than when engaged with non-isolates. In the small group sessions, peers may also have been less satisfying as play partners by their not following isolates and thereby not reinforcing whatever lines of activity were offered by isolates.

The low frequency of interaction between isolates and teachers as well as the finding that the character of teacher's treatment of isolates was similar to that of the matched non-isolates indicates that teachers may have little effect on whether or not a child becomes or remains isolated. This generalization is consistent with the teachers' own reports that they did not treat isolates differently from non-isolates. Special treatment by teachers was most often reserved for disruptive – uncooperative children.

Implications for how young children foster peer relations

The results indicate that out of the several common ways that individuals can reinforce contact with one another, only a few (relating to the fostering of joint play) seem significant for the fostering of early peer relations. Specifically, the results indicate that young children's attempts to structure one another are especially important in developing peer relations. Other types of reinforcers (e.g. helping, showing approval, giving or expressing affection) are not crucial to fostering early peer relations since isolates and non-isolates were equally likely to emit such reinforcers when interacting with peers.

The findings, then, suggest that Kohn's principle 'The child gets what he puts out' requires modification. On very general measures of interaction (e.g. rate of interaction, whether interaction is positive or negative), Kohn's principle appears adequate. However, when describing preschoolers' interactions at a more specific level, it appears that young children cannot be expected to develop peer relations simply by acting positively towards peers; their positive social behaviour must consist of at least a certain percentage of attempts to influence or structure how peers behave, and perhaps occasionally they must be willing and capable of engaging in imaginative – dramatic play.

The following protocol of two non-isolated nursery school children playing together illustrates the above points on how preschoolers usually foster and maintain interaction with one another. The protocol is a segment from one of the videotaped small group sessions.

Example 1: B and *H* are playing with Sesame Street dolls. *H* has the Ernie doll driving a toy truck. A toy mailbox is off to one side. *B* has the Bert doll start to walk; he says to *H*:

B: Pretend you're rolling him home (i.e. *B* asks *H* to have Ernie give Bert a ride in the truck).

H: No.

B: (*B* walks Bert over to the mailbox) Pretend the mailbox fell (*B* has the mailbox tip over onto Bert. Meanwhile, *H* stops what he is doing and comes over to *B*).

H: Pretend he . . .

B: (interrupting *H*), Pretend somebody trapped him (i.e. trapped Bert in the mailbox). Aaah! Get me out of here! (speaking for Bert).

B: Pretend there's a magic button (*B* points to the top of the mailbox). And pretend he pushed the magic button (*B* has Bert fly out of the mailbox). Aaah – help! (*B* has Bert get into the truck).

H: Pretend he got off.

B: Pretend he (Ernie in his truck) gave him (Bert) a ride home.

H: (*H* takes the truck from *B*) Pretend he touched the secret button (*H* has the truck touch the mailbox, and then *H* puts the mailbox on top of him, Bert in the truck). Oh God, I can't see! (speaking for Bert).

In this example, *B* and *H* interact around an imaginative – dramatic play sequence. They rarely look at each other, and the majority of their individual social behaviours are attempts to structure how the other should construe the make-believe situation.

Towards explaining social isolation from peers

The results from this study provide clues as to possible ways that social isolation from peers is fostered or maintained by isolates' own behaviour, by how isolates are treated at school, and by situational variables. However, a full explanation of how children become isolated from peers should include at least two other kinds of information, namely, information comparing how isolates and non-isolates construe or understand peers and information pertaining to home correlates of social isolation from peers.

There is no evidence from this study or from the literature that suggests that isolates are more egocentric and less knowledgeable about peers than non-isolates. Nevertheless, it may be that the way isolates behave with peers is in part a function of a peculiar way in which they construe peers (e.g. as generally hostile).

One of the main assumptions underlying the present study was that to some extent peer relations develop in parallel to parent – child or sibling – child relations. However, the assumption of parallel development does not negate the necessity of investigating what influences parents and siblings may have on whether or not young children become isolated from peers. As previously indicated, some of the findings suggest that isolates behave in class in ways appropriate to fostering or maintaining relationships at home and with non-agemates. An investigation of home correlates of social isolation from peers may provide then some interesting findings suggesting ways that families reinforce behaviour patterns that inhibit the development of peer relations.

4.

Nicknames

Jane Morgan, Christopher O'Neill, and Rom Harré

This reading consists of two short extracts from a book devoted to the study of nicknames used by schoolchildren. The reading provides an illustration of an alternative means of studying children's social behaviours, as seen through the development and use of appropriate names for individual children. The first extract, entitled 'The Practical Uses of Insult', reveals the skilful way in which children may use names to manipulate the behaviour of others, and to influence their own social standing amongst their peers. The second extract, entitled 'Name-givers', considers the question of where nicknames come from. Clearly there are a number of sources, some originating from adults, others from children. However as the authors of the reading point out, the namegiver usually enjoys a relatively high status, and, if a child, may be the leader of a group. In a prefatory note to their book, the authors express the view that 'social psychology . . . should entertain as well as instruct'. This reading clearly reflects this philosophy.

THE PRACTICAL USES OF INSULT

We have had occasion to notice the use that nicknames are put to as inciters of rage, as weapons with which to tease and irritate people. In the following piece of fiction we have as good an example as real life can provide of the introduction of the nickname into the unfolding of a challenging conversational form.

> Joby and Snap, out for an evening loiter, come across the neighbourhood bully, Gus Wilson:
> 'How do, Gus.'
> 'Now then, Joby. Where you off to?'
> 'Oh, nowhere. Where are you going?'
> 'Same place. I see you've got Copperknob with you. Ey, Copperknob, made any good lies up lately?'
> 'What's up with you?' Snap said . . .
> 'Has your uncle shot any more planes lately?' Gus said.

'I never said that', Snap said.
'Garn, you did. You said he'd shot down three planes in Spain.'
'I never did say that.'
'Are you calling me a liar, Gingernut?'
'You're calling me one.'
'That's different.'

The name game

Nicknames, we have stated, differ from their official counterparts in two main aspects: they are labels attached in the course of existence rather than at its outset, and they are usually bestowed by peers in a variety of *informal* social situations.

Translating this into school terms means they are the names of the playground, the walk home, the teacherless classroom. Nicholas comments:

> *Adult*: Does Mark (an inveterate name-caller) use them to you in class? Would he say ' "Brainchild" can I borrow a pencil?' or something?
> *Nicholas*: At play-time sometimes, when we are staying in to do a job for Miss, or sometimes if we are doing an assembly, if we have got permission to stay in and get on with our lines, sometimes he'll do it then.
> *Adult*: I see. Does he play chase or something in the playground and call people these nicknames to get them to chase him?
> *Nicholas*: No. We usually play football and he calls lots of people names there. If he wants people to chase him he'll ask them.

Think back to your own schooling – that playground ... a whirl of skirts and grubby knickers, muddy shoes and socks, groups of 'Mothers and Fathers', games of 'Off ground tig', handstands, and always at least one person wailing with injured knees. Nicknames are part of this world. Jane Bundy, as we quoted earlier, recalls her first encounter with the phenomenon: 'But Jane wasn't enough for the social jungle of the school. From the age of about six the delights of "Bandy-Bundy", "Ginger", "Rusty" and "Freckles" all came my way. Without exception these were the names of the playground, shouted at me across the yard ...'

Children realise from a very early age, in their first quarrels, despite the 'sticks and stones' rhyme, that names can hurt. Your opponent's face crumples, he or she turns and runs howling to Mum. That warm feeling of victory imprints the potential of name-calling into a child's brain.

The lesson is learnt early and never forgotten. Nicknames are deliberately used as weapons in the playground. Weapons, too, are both defensive and offensive.

> *Adult*: What about you Maxine? They call you 'Chocolate Drop', don't they? Are they being nice, or trying to make you cross?

Maxine: They're trying to make us cross so we can chase them.
Adult: And what about Isaiah? Oh, do they call you 'Blacky' and 'Kojak'? Do
you mind?
Isaiah: I chase them.

Isaiah, particularly, used names as a way of beginning a good game of chase,
and it was an acknowledged procedure. Listen to Nicholas on the possibility of
starting a game in this manner:

Nicholas: No, I wouldn't – if you get caught, then you'll get walloped, because
if you ask someone (instead) then if you do get caught you don't get hit, but
if you call them names and that, if you finally get caught, then you get
walloped.

Though he rejected it on prudential grounds, he considered it a viable alternative to the more explicit request.

Nicknaming has become an integral part of children's antagonism in the
playground to such an extent it often forms the prelude to some games, so
much so it has become a sort of ritual – the word used, in fact, in Jane Bundy's
account:

they [nicknames] usually formed the prelude to an enjoyable game of 'Chase'
or even 'Fighting' for my taunter. The names were used as offensive weapons
to annoy and they invariably did. At first my counter-attack was spontaneous
– I disliked the names intensely – but gradually they became the tacitly
accepted ritual before 'Chase'.

As animals use a carefully stylized succession pattern of moves as a pre-
amble to formal combat, so nicknames can provide the verbal prelude to open
physical hostility amongst children. Denise W., as we have already noted in a
previous section, was 'Fleabag' to most of her peers and, if she failed to 'rise' to
the various names and comments coming her way, had her hair pulled. Adam,
who was unlucky enough to be Adam Rabitt, disliked the resultant titles of
'Furry Arms' and 'Rabbit's Teeth' to such an extent that he was contem-
plating changing his surname. We have given the actual quotation in a
previous section.

'Sticks and stones' don't actually 'break bones' – true, but they often serve as
a prelude to something equally violent, or are powerful enough in themselves
to hurt when used as small, vicious, missiles, carefully aimed and deliberately
thrown.

Retaliation

In the middle of a vitriolic argument the natural form of address seems to be
the surname, or some nasty descriptive nickname, and perhaps a form of

intermediary power is the use of both first and surname together. An incident among eight-year-olds ran as follows:

> *Simon* (to Julie, who is trying to take away a hose pipe): Stop it, stop it.
> *Gloria* (in defence of Simon): Look here *Fatso*.
> *Simon*: *Julie Pearce*.
> *Julie*: I can't help it, I'm too strong.
> *Annabel* (to Simon): Can I say something to you?
> *Simon*: Sit down.
> *Julie*: I can't [sit down].
> *Simon*: You can't have a go then. You can't speak properly. (Julie grabs the pipe from Annabel.)
> *Simon* to Annabel: Shut up, she [Julie] had it first.

(Simon appeals to the convention that the firstcomer has priority, but in fact Annabel had it first.)

Later, in a game of football:

> *Simon*: Owen is a kicker, Owen is a fouler.
> *Gloria*: Four Eyes (He does indeed wear spectacles).

Jimmie knocks over Andrew while he is running.

> *Jimmie*: You blumming twit.
> *Andrew*: Pig.

(Jimmie is indeed an exceptionally fat boy and easily the fattest in the school).

Nicola calls across the playground: 'Jimmie fatso.' Jimmie ignores this.

Operative epithets – how to be chased

Merely repeating a child's name over and over again may be all that is necessary to cause him to chase the speaker. In addition, the name may be followed by 'try and catch me' or a more provocative utterance like, 'Armadle it, the big fat shit', 'Armad, he's mad, he's mad', 'Jason's getting eggy, Jason's getting eggy', where the word 'eggy' is an Oxford word meaning that somebody is getting angry and about to attack somebody else. An operative epithet is an insulting descriptive phrase having the force of a pejorative nickname, but only of transmitting use and significance.

> *Five girls* (Alison, Nicola, Sarah, Susan, Katie, to Gordon): Cheese face, cheese face.
> *Nicola*: Chase us.
> *Gordon*: I'm not going to chase you.

The girls: Gordon, Gordon, dirty face.
Alison: White hair, Gordon is a dirty face, Old Granny Faddock. (Gordon does
have very blond hair.)

All the girls poke at him. Gordon hides behind a nearby wall, then reveals his
presence and starts to chase them. On catching Alison, the two pretend fight
and disengage.

Alison: Old Granny Faddock. (And swipes at him with a paper hanky.)
The girls shout: The boys are getting eggy, the boys are getting eggy.
Alison: Gordon, Gordon, Gordon.
    (Gordon goes off, Katie follows him. He turns round to say: 'Not playing,'
    He tells the girls: 'I don't want Katie to play, I don't need her to play.')
Alison: Only Zeena can play, he only wants Zeena.
Nicola: Do you want Rachael?
Gordon: Rachael – yeh.
    (The girls use their toilets as a safe retreat and try to get Gordon to chase
    them.)
Gordon: I'm not playing, go on, clear off.
    (Play-time ends.)*

This episode incorporates many of the aspects already mentioned. In order
to try to get Gordon to chase them, the girls start off with a somewhat
innocuous operative epithet 'cheese face' and progress to phrases based more
on his personal appearance, 'white face, dirty face', ending up with his official
nickname 'Old Granny Faddock', which, of course, he cannot let pass. Gordon
proves to be quite aware of the power he has to choose whether or not to
participate in the chasing, even to the extent of dictating which girls he lets
tease him. At a more general level, it may well be the case that the activity of
teasing can be viewed as having certain well-established rules, and it would be
the task of future research to establish what these are and how children learn
them.
    It is not only in England that operative epithets are used as missiles to throw
at people to either annoy, hurt, or simply initiate some type of game.
    From Spain it is reported that during the course of a month-long English
course run by the Jesuit Order and using English assistants the pupils, varying
in age from eight to thirteen, regularly used mild insults in a mixture of English
and Spanish to provoke the English teachers into giving chase or some sort of
mock battle. Terms of abuse included such things as:

    'You are very donkey' (From the idiomatic Spanish, *'Eres muyo burro'*).
    'You are very tonto' (stupid).
    'Chorizo.' (A subtle term of abuse. Its root meaning is 'a long Continental
    type of sausage', but it has acquired overtones somewhere between our
    English 'You silly sausage' and 'You great prick'.)

        * We owe these incident descriptions to A. Sluckin.

After the insults had been dished out, the English teachers were expected to give chase.

Achieving character by verbal hazard

Why do some people do unnecessarily dangerous and reckless things? Mountaineering, gliding, gambling and the like? Goffman has seen these activities as occurring in bounded times and places, in generalized public view, in the course of which 'character' is built up by the display of courage, coolness, competence and a certain largeness of being. In the gambling saloons of Nevada one has the bathetic end of a spectrum at the other end of which are the glories of the conquest of Everest.

Children, too, look for occasions for 'action' in which they can display and achieve 'character' and some of these occasions involve potent words. Two obvious categories of potent words whose public utterance takes nerve are secret names, such a teachers' first names or nicknames, and swear words. Both are used by the children of Oxfordshire in achieving character. These devices can best be illustrated by quoting the observers' original anecdotes.

> I taught a fourth-year class. They all knew my Christian name but did not use it. There was in the class a group of lazy and not very clever girls. [Later discussion with this participant observer revealed that the group in question were at the top of the social status ranking within the class, and thus the incident can be seen as part of their continuing testing and maintenance of their positions.] One day one of them called for attention while they were doing some writing, by saying 'Kevin!'. I looked over, acknowledging that I had heard, but giving neither a negative nor a positive emotional response. Further, I went over to help only when I had seen some people with prior claims. Thus in one way status was *not* gained because I treated being called by my Christian name no differently from being called 'Sir'. However, status may have been gained in the group because I could hear by the tone of voice that it took some courage to call out 'Kevin'. This was definitely not a set-up traditional game.

An interesting point about this incident is Kevin's cool response to the hazard. It might seem as if the teacher has to be seen to be provoked, that is, there has to be the risk of punishment or anger before the hazarding would really work in the building of character. That this is not so is confirmed by an anecdote from another school. The participant observer reports that 'the younger pupils, however, sometimes played a kind of game, by deliberately calling me by my first name in the presence of another teacher, to see how both she and I would react'. On this particular occasion the teacher did not acknowledge this, although she undoubtedly 'overheard'. Clearly the numbing non-acknowledgement by the more experienced teacher nipped the hazard in the bud, though as our first informant remarks, some character would be achieved by the mere fact of the utterance of the potent word, whether or not it provoked a response.

Who gives the nicknames? The various social forces and personal emotions unleashed by the use of nicknames are sufficiently potent to suggest that the role of name-giver is a position of considerable social influence and perhaps even of power. Sometimes we have reason to think one, and only one, individual has been responsible for the entire eke-nomenclature of his classmates and other associates. In one case we have recorded, one boy has successfully nicknamed over forty others. In one private junior (prep) school we studied, hardly any nicknames were invented and promoted by pupils, indeed they hardly used nicknames in this particular school, but those that were in use were exclusively invented by the headmaster, alone amongst the staff. There is, it seems, considerable variability as to who the name-giver is, but it is clear that whoever he or she may be it is a role of power.

Faithful to the idiographic intensive method, we turn now to an exposition in detail of some particular cases, to illustrate the types of name-giver we have noticed.

Individuals as name-givers

Nicknaming, we have established, carries with it, inevitably, a certain amount of stigma. It very often highlights abnormalities and idiosyncrasies in a given society. It also, on a smaller scale, delineates individual differences in attitudes. The boy that yells 'Cowardy Custard' after a retreating pair of heels is showing his awareness of the value of physical bravery (or the lack of it) in the playground. It may simply not have any importance to his neighbour.

In several of the different 'societies', the classes that were studied, it became obvious that just as certain roles were always occupied: the Leader, the Toughie, the Joker, etc., so, in a few, one person took on the role of the Name-giver. This elite set of the schoolyard society seem to fit a carefully designed niche.

Quite frequently the roles of leader and namer are synonymous. Of the children who took part in the primary-school survey, those selected for individual interviews were often those who had been a fount of information. Peter W. and Isaiah P. are two notables who merit attention. In both cases their list of names for others was endless. Although both took care to cover any tracks, a very similar picture emerged. Isaiah, we discover, really enjoyed his playtime, happily employed in 'flipping the girls' dresses' and leading games of Chase. His classmates put his Chase into context for us: Denise (to us, 'Fleabag' to the others), states that the first person to give her her unwanted title was not the Lollipop lady – as Isaiah and his friend had intimated – but Isaiah P. himself. He also 'started calling Denise "Fleabag" as well.' Isaiah, it appeared, relished a game of Chase and had discovered that the best method of acquiring 'chasers' was to antagonize, either by name-calling or by dress-flipping.

Isaiah, then, used names with a very specific purpose: to unify the people in his 'gang' and simultaneously, and more importantly, to provoke and alienate others.

Peter W. used the same technique and the same setting – the anarchy of the playground – but whereas Isaiah's main aim was to infuriate and lend realism to Chase, Peter's seemed to be a basic and very clear-cut division in his class and to rally peers specifically around two poles. He was mentioned by his teacher as one of the main elements in name-calling that went on out of the classroom and a more careful scrutiny of his list revealed that he, along with two others, acknowledged themselves to be 'Ice-creams'. Several coloured children, on the other hand, described themselves as 'Blackies, Nig-nogs, Enochs', etc. Peter and his friends were obviously asserting the normality and correctness of their pigmentation and ridiculing the others, who retaliated with the opposite theory. Peter was attempting on a small scale to amplify perceptions of racial difference. He can be allotted the role of name-giver, rather than his cronies, as a result of the illuminating comments of his peers. Both are dark-skinned, but react differently to him; one, Steven S., describes him in his personal list quite categorically as a 'Fatty', and 'Long-haired Monster'. The hostility beneath is perhaps because Steve has suffered in the all-too-painful-present at Peter's hands. Ali K., as we have already noted in a different context, escapes the 'Blacky'-hurling, the mild 'Ali Baba' and 'Shorty' being the nastiest names to come his way. A quick glance at the sociometric graph plotted by the teacher provides the explanation. Ali is a mate of Peter's and therefore enjoys the peace of political friendship. Peter uses his role as name-caller to segregate as firmly as possible the 'Ice-creams' from the 'Enochs'.

5.

Act-rule relations: children's concepts of social rules

Donna R. Weston and Elliot Turiel

The previous readings in this section on children's social development have been mainly concerned with aspects of children's abilities and limitations when interacting with their peers. This final reading has been selected as one example of research into a different area of children's social development – their understanding of rules that may be used to govern their social behaviour at school. Although the study involves a broader age range of children, from four to eleven years, it has been included here as the results show that even younger children can distinguish between rules whose content concerns different types of action. Thus the content of a rule can be an important influence on the extent to which children will accept it. This finding reveals a shortcoming in some previous research. In Piaget's work on moral development, for example, the children's knowledge of rules was investigated with respect to the rules of the game of marbles, and then generalized to other areas. But if content is important, then such generalization may not be justified. The reader's attention is also drawn to the present paper's finding about the influence of the school on children's acceptance of rules. Weston and Turiel found that while children may question a rule as being inappropriate, they may still be prepared to accept it if it is part of their school's policy. This suggests that children are able to distinguish between their personal evaluation of a rule's moral value, and their perceived obligation to observe the school's policy even though it contradicts their own view.

This article presents a study of children's evaluations of social rules. The research was based on a series of studies (Much and Shweder, 1978; Nucci and Turiel, 1978; Turiel, 1978b) indicating that children discriminate between different types of rules. In this study it was assumed that it is necessary to distinguish between rules and the actions to which they pertain. The central hypothesis was that children's evaluations of a social rule in an institutional context are based on their judgements about the related act.

In some of the prevalent approaches to the study of children's social judgements, rules have been treated as having a singular meaning. This assumption regarding social rules has guided analyses of children's motives for moral behaviour as well as research on moral judgements. For example, it has been proposed (Hogan, 1973; Hogan and Mills, 1976) that individuals have a natural disposition towards rule-following behaviour, the function of which is to bring order to social interactions. From this perspective, the study of moral development is equated with the study of rule-governed behaviour. Others (**e.g.** Aronfreed, 1968; Cheyne, 1971; Parke and Walters, 1976), who do not necessarily postulate an inherent rule-following disposition, also equate morality with rule-following behaviour. For these theorists, rewards and punishments determine the child's learning of rules regardless of the type of act involved. In research on the development of social judgements, particularly the work on morality, it has been assumed that children have a unitary concept of social rules (Piaget, 1932; Tapp and Kohlberg, 1971), and that with age, children progress from a view of rules as fixed to a view in which rules are understood to be alterable by general agreement or mutual consent.

Recent studies, however, have shown that children and adolescents do not have a unitary concept of social rules (Nucci, in press; Nucci and Turiel, 1978; Turiel, 1978b). It has been found that they distinguish between moral rules (e.g. those pertaining to the inflicting of harm on people or stealing) and social – conventional rules (e.g. those pertaining to forms of address, modes of greeting, or table manners). Briefly defined, social conventions are behavioural uniformities that coordinate the action of individuals participating in a social system and constitute shared knowledge of expected uniformities in social interaction (see Turiel, 1978a, 1979, for a more extensive definition). In the Nucci (in press) and Turiel (1978b) studies, it was found that subjects from 6 to 19 years of age view conventional rules as changeable, as relative to the social context, and as determined by consensus. In contrast, the same subjects did not regard moral rules as legitimized by consensus or as relative to the social context. Moral rules were evaluated on the basis of factors intrinsic to acts, such as harm inflicted on others and violation of rights.

A recent study by Nucci and Turiel (1978) with preschool children suggests that the discrimination between moral and conventional rules is based on the discriminations children made between a rule and the act to which the rule pertains. In that study, preschool children were interviewed about observed naturally occurring social transgressions. After having witnessed a transgression, the child was asked, 'What if there were no rules in the school about (observed event): would it be all right to do it then?' Over 80 per cent of the preschoolers interviewed considered social – conventional transgressions wrong only if a rule against them existed in the school, whereas moral transgressions were considered wrong even if no rule against them existed in the school. Thus, young children's judgements of certain acts as wrong are contingent on the presence of a rule in the school, whereas other acts are judged wrong regardless of the existence of a rule.

The purpose of the present study was to extend the analyses of children's discrimination between rules and acts and of their evaluations of school rules to study children of a wider age range, to examine additional types of acts, to obtain explicit evaluations of institutional policies (i.e. the presence or absence of a rule in a school) regarding those acts, and to obtain evaluations of the behaviour of an authority in response to the performance of the act. Four actions were chosen for study: a child undressing in the playground, a child hitting another child, a child leaving toys on the floor in the schoolroom, and a child refusing to share a snack with another child. The act of undressing corresponds to the social – conventional domain, whereas hitting corresponds to the moral domain. The other two acts were chosen to extend the focus in prior studies on moral and social – conventional rules to include other components. Leaving toys on the floor has conventional features, but it is also an act that has salient pragmatic features (i.e. the toys may be damaged). The act of refusing to share was chosen as an example that highlights the conflict between generosity and self-interest.

The questions posed to subjects about rules and acts were somewhat different and more extensive than those used in the Nucci and Turiel (1978) study. Rather than being asked, 'What if there were no rules in the school?' subjects were presented with hypothetical stories for each of the previously listed actions depicting two schools, one having a rule prohibiting the act, the other permitting the act. Questions about the stories were designed to elicit evaluations about the act, about the school policy, and about the response of an authority (i.e. the teacher) to compliance and noncompliance with the school policy. We were interested in determining whether children base their evaluation of social actions on the presence or absence of an explicit rule in the school. We were also interested in the extent to which children's evaluations of the rules and the actions would determine their views of an authority's responsibility for rule enforcement. It was expected that children's judgements of the specific school policies and of the authority's responsibilities would vary according to the type of action involved.

METHOD

Subjects

Sixty subjects randomly selected from five public elementary schools and one nursery school participated in the study. The subjects in each age group were of mixed ethnic and socio-economic backgrounds (black and white from the working, middle, and upper-middle class). Subjects were divided into two samples. The 40 subjects administered the act – rule relations interview comprised of four age groups with 10 subjects (five boys and five girls) each: four- to five-year-olds (*M* age = five years one month). Six- to seven-year-olds (*M* age = six years eleven months), eight- to nine-year-olds (*M* age = nine years), and ten- to eleven-year-olds (*M* age = eleven years). The other 20 subjects were equally divided between the two extreme age groups (four- to five-year-olds and ten- to eleven-year-olds) and were given the act evaluations interview. The four- to five-year-old group consisted of seven girls and three boys: the ten- to eleven-year-old group consisted of five girls and five boys.

Procedure

One sample of subjects was administered the act – rule relations interview. The interview, individually administered, consists of four hypothetical stories, each depicting schools in which a given social act is permitted or prohibited by school policy. Subjects were asked a standard series of questions about an action, a rule, and a teacher's response to the action.

Due to the nature of the act – rule relations interview, it was not possible to obtain measures of the subjects' evaluations of the four social actions independently of the school policies introduced in the stories. Consequently, a different sample of subjects was administered the act evaluations interview, in which they were asked to evaluate only the four actions.

Act – rule relations interview

The act – rule relations interview consists of four hypothetical stories, each accompanied by six standard questions. Each story describes an action on the part of a child and places it in the context of one school where a rule prohibits the action and a second school where the action is permitted. The four story themes were: a child takes all his/her clothes off on the playground at school after getting too warm from playing; a child hits and pushes another child out of a swing after discovering all the swings on the playground are occupied; a child going outside to play leaves some toys on the floor after playing with them; and a child refuses to share his/her snack crackers with a visitor, also a child, to the school who asked for some crackers because there were none remaining in the box.*

The order of presentation of the school policy (i.e. permitting or prohibiting the act) differed within the four stories. The story themes and school contexts, all presented in the same story structure, appeared in the following order: *undressing* – school prohibits, school permits; *hitting* – school permits, school prohibits; *leaving toys* – school permits, school prohibits; and *refusing to share* – school prohibits, school permits.

The method for presenting each hypothetical story and questions is illustrated by this example:

> This is (   ) who goes to Park School. (   ) has been playing outside in the play area and it's a warm day. (   ) stopped playing and decided that since he/she was hot from all that play, he/she wants to take all his/her clothes off.

* For each of these story themes we were interested in children's evaluations of the actions themselves. To avoid confounding intent or motive of the story character with amount or type of consequences, such information was left unspecified.

(   ) began to take his/her clothes off and soon had nothing on. At Park School children are not supposed to take their clothes off. That is not allowed. Here is the teacher standing over here. The teacher saw (   ) take all his/her clothes off. *Do you think the teacher will say anything? Why or why not?* The teacher came over to (   ) and said 'You must leave your clothes on. Children in this school are not allowed to take their clothes off.' *Is it OK or not OK for the teacher to say that? Why or why not?*

I know about another school in a different city. It's called Grove School. This school has different children and different teachers. At Grove School the children are allowed to take their clothes off if they want to. *Is it OK or not OK for Grove School to say the children can take their clothes off if they want to? Why or why not?* This is (   ) who goes to Grove School. (   ) has been running and playing in the play area and he/she is hot. It is a warm day, so (   ) decides he/she wants to take off his/her clothes. (   ) began to take his/her clothes off and soon had nothing on. *Was that OK or not OK for (   ) to do? Why or why not?* Here is the teacher standing over here. The teacher saw (   ) take his/her clothes off. *Do you think the teacher will say anything? Why or why not?* One time at Grove School (   ) took his/her clothes off and the teacher saw. The teacher came over and said: 'That's OK. At this school it's OK to take your clothes off if you want to. *Is is OK or not OK for the teacher to say that? Why or why not?*

As can be seen in the above example, the format for the school-permits context of each story included four standard questions, followed by probes to elicit elaborations of the evaluations. Thus, the school policy was first presented, then a child's action was described, and finally questions were asked about the teacher's reaction. The format for the contrasting school context in which a rule prohibits the action differed slightly. The school policy was not first specified. Instead, the action was described, and the subject was asked questions about the teacher's response to the action.

A series of questions were included for each story in the act – rule relations interview that were designed to determine whether the children understood the stories portraying school contexts in which the action is permitted. Response to these questions indicated that all of the children in each age group understood the stories presented.

Act evaluations interview

The act evaluations interview consists of four hypothetical stories in which the same four action themes described above were presented. In this interview, however, the actions were described in only one school context without the specification of the school policy. These stories and questions were designed to elicit evaluations about the actions in the absence of any mention of the school policy. The four stories were presented, as in the act – rule relations interview, describing the action, with one standard question: 'Is it OK or not OK for (   ) to do that? Why or why not?'

Coding of responses

The interview questions elicited positive and negative (yes/no) evaluations along with an elaboration of the reasons for the evaluation. Responses were coded in three categories: positive evaluation (yes), negative evaluation (no), and equivocal (unclear responses or absence of an evaluation).

A second judge coded 11 randomly chosen act – rule relations interview protocols. There was 90 per cent agreement between the two coders.

RESULTS

In the analyses reported, all of the comparisons of evaluations in the different stories, as well as comparisons between evaluations within a story, were based on McNemar's test (Siegel, 1956) or the normal approximation of the binomial distribution. McNemar's test was used because the comparisons were of responses by the same subjects to different questions. The findings for male and female subjects were combined, since no statistically significant sex differences were found in any of the analyses.

Act evaluations interview

The act evaluations interview provided an assessment of subjects' evaluations of each of the actions independently of presentation of any information regarding school policy. Subjects were simply presented with stories depicting the action and asked to evaluate the act. Table 1 presents the percentage of subjects evaluating each act positively or negatively. Most subjects gave a negative evaluation of each act; virtually every subject evaluated the act of hitting negatively. The only significant differences were between evaluations of hitting and each of the other acts (hitting vs. undressing, $p < .01$: hitting vs. leaving toys, $p < .02$: and hitting vs. refusing to share, $p < .01$). Significant age differences were found in the evaluations of the acts of undressing ($p < .05$) and leaving toys ($p < .05$); the five-year-old subjects were evenly divided in their evaluations of these acts, whereas almost all the eleven-year-olds gave them a negative evaluation.

Table 1 *Percentages of evaluations of actions in the act evaluations interview*

	Story			
Evaluation	Undressing	Hitting	Leaving toys	Refusing to share
Positive	20	–	20	25
Negative	60	95	45	55
Equivocal	20	5	35	20

Act – rule relations interview: evaluations of school policy

In the act – rule relations interview, subjects were presented with descriptions of schools permitting the act and with examples of children who engaged in the act in the context of the school that permitted it. Table 2 presents evaluations of the school policy permitting the act and the child's action within that school. Table 2 shows that in three of the stories (undressing, leaving toys, and refusing to share), the majority of subjects positively evaluated the school policy permitting the act. Comparisons among these three stories showed no statistically significant differences. In contrast with the other stories, the large majority of subjects evaluated negatively the school policy that permitted hitting: most subjects stated that it was not all right for a school to permit children to hit each other. The differences between evaluations of the policy permitting hitting and each of the other policies were significant: for hitting versus undressing, $\chi^2(1) = 19.36, p < .0001$; for hitting versus leaving toys, $\chi^2(1) = 17.05, p < .0001$; and for hitting versus refusing to share, $\chi^2(1) = 14.45, p < .0001$. There were no significant age differences in evaluations of any of the school policies.

The evaluations of a child who engaged in the act in the school that permitted the act (see Table 2) correspond to the evaluations of the school policy. That is, in three stories (undressing, leaving toys and refusing to share), the majority of subjects evaluated the child's action positively (there were no significant differences among those stories), whereas the majority of subjects gave a negative evaluation to the act of hitting. The differences between the evaluations of the act of hitting and each of the other acts were significant: for hitting versus undressing, $\chi^2(1) = 7.58, p < .01$; for hitting versus leaving toys, $\chi^2(1) = 4.08, p < .05$; and for hitting versus refusal to share, $\chi^2(1) = 11.53, p < .001$.

Table 2 *Percentages of responses for evaluations in the act – rule relations interview*

| | Question | | | | | |
| | Evaluation of school policy permitting the act | | | Evaluation of child's action in context of school policy permitting the act | | |
Story	Positive	Negative	Depends	Positive	Negative	Depends
Undressing	67.5	27.5	5.0	75.0	22.5	2.5
Hitting	7.5	87.5	5.0	45.0	55.0	0
Leaving toys	60.0	32.5	7.5	62.5	32.5	5.0
Refusing to share	52.5	35.0	12.5	80.0	12.5	7.5

For two stories, however, the patterns of evaluations of the performance of the act contrasted with the pattern of evaluations of the school policy permitting the act. A larger number of subjects gave a positive evaluation to the child's actions (in the school that permits the acts) of hitting ($p < .01$) and refusing to share ($\chi^2(1) = 9.39$, $P < .02$) than they had to the school policy permitting those acts (compare undressing and hitting in Table 2). On the issue of sharing, there were no age differences. On the issue of hitting, the discrepancy between the evaluation of the school policy and the evaluation of the child's action was due primarily to responses of the younger subjects (see Table 3). A greater number of the younger subjects (the four- to five and six- to seven-year-old groups) than the older subjects (the eight- to nine and ten- to eleven-year-old groups) stated that the action was all right in the context of the school policy that permitted it ($\chi^2(3) = 8.48$, $P < .05$). Thus, the younger children tended to reject the policy but accept the performance of the act in its context, whereas the older children tended to reject both the policy and the act.

Table 3 *Percentages of evaluations for each age group of hitting in the context of a school policy permitting that action*

Evaluation	Age			
	5	7	9	11
Positive	70	60	40	10
Negative	30	40	60	90

Act — rule relations interview: prediction and evaluation of teacher behaviour

After subjects were presented with a description of a child engaging in an act in the school-permits context, they were asked whether the teacher would say anything in response. In other words, subjects were asked to predict whether the teacher would express approval or disapproval, given that the action was in accordance with school policy. The frequencies presented in Table 4 show that for three actions (undressing, leaving toys, and refusing to share), the majority of subjects predicted that the teacher would not respond. In the case of the story in which one child hit another, there was an even division between those who stated that the teacher would not respond (in accordance with school policy) and those who stated that the teacher would reprimand the child (in spite of the school policy). The differences between responses to the hitting story and responses to each of the other stories were significant: for hitting versus undressing, $p < .001$; for hitting versus leaving toys, $p < .02$; and for hitting versus refusing to share, $\chi^2(1) = 4.08$, $p < .05$. There were no significant age differences in response to this question.

Table 4 *Percentages of predictions of whether teacher will respond in the context of a school policy permitting the child's action*

Prediction of reaction	Story			
	Undressing	Hitting	Leaving toys	Refusing to share
Yes	10	40	10	15
No	60	40	65	65
Equivocal	30	20	25	20

Subjects were then told that the teacher did not respond to the child's act and were asked to evaluate the teacher's failure to respond. On all four stories, the majority of subjects, across the age groups, stated that it was all right for the teacher to act in accordance with the school policy.

Subjects were also presented with stories describing children engaging in actions in a school with rules prohibiting those acts. As expected, for each story almost all the subjects predicted that the teacher would respond to the child's act with a reprimand. In turn, almost all of the subjects evaluated the teacher's reaction positively.

DISCUSSION

The results of this study demonstrate that children from five to eleven years of age discriminate between different types of rules. At all of the ages studied, children evaluated rules on the basis of their judgements regarding the actions governed by the rule. The findings showed a clear distinction between the way children judge a rule pertaining to hitting others (causing harm), on the one hand, and rules pertaining to nakedness, leaving toys on the floor, and refusing to share, on the other hand. A prohibition on hitting is treated as unalterable. According to these children, a school should not allow people to harm each other, and it should regulate such behaviour. The other three actions and rules are regarded as alterable. It is considered justifiable for a school to allow those actions to occur or to prohibit them. Apparently, children neither assume that an established school policy is always right, nor do they reject all policies that are in contradiction with their own evaluations.

Similarly, discriminations were shown by children of all ages in their predictions of an authority's response to children's transgressions. Children do not assume that an authority will simply go along with an institutional policy regardless of its content: rather, it is expected that an authority will evaluate the consequences of actions. In the undressing, leaving toys, and refusing to share stories, most subjects predicted that teachers would reprimand children engaging in those acts *only* when the acts were in violation of school policy. In the case of the hitting story, however, a greater number of subjects assumed that a teacher would reprimand a child for hitting even though the act was consistent with school policy. Knowing that the rule context permitted the act did not lead some children to shift their expectations of the teacher.

These findings show that children's judgements about social actions contribute to their view of the alterability of a given rule and to their evaluations of institutional policy. It appears that it is children's judgement of the act of hitting that leads them to reject a school policy that would permit hitting. Indeed, an analysis by Weston (1978) of some of the subjects' elaborations on their evaluations indicated that evaluations of the school policy permitting hitting were based on the judgement that it is wrong to harm people. It should also be noted that although rules pertaining to undressing, leaving toys, and refusing to share were all seen as alterable, Weston's analyses indicate that subjects conceptualized each of these actions in different ways. For instance, the rule regarding putting toys away was the only one judged on pragmatic grounds; for some subjects, toys should not be left out because they might be damaged. In contrast, social approval was never given as a reason for putting toys away, but was used by a number of subjects as the reason for not being naked in public.

The finding that a majority of subjects accepted the school policy permitting children to refuse to share their food is of particular interest, given that distributive justice has been interpreted as entailing moral judgements (Damon, 1977; Turiel, 1978a). The sharing story used in this study, however, did not deal with fairness of distribution in the allocation of resources but, instead, dealt with a willingness to give one's possessions to another person. The results indicated that many children view this type of sharing to be legitimately determined by the actor (as also found by Tisak, 1977). To determine how children evaluate rules pertaining to the allocation of resources, it would be necessary to present a story in which a school permits a child to take any desired amount of a limited resource.

It was also found that subjects' evaluations of a school policy were not always consistent with their evaluations of a child whose actions were in accordance with school policy. With regard to hitting, there were age differences in the way subjects evaluated the actions of a child who hit another child in the context of a school permitting the act. The younger subjects judged the policy to be wrong, but regarded a person's adherence to the policy as justified. The older subjects rejected the policy and also maintained that the act was wrong in spite of the stated school policy. This difference may reflect age-related changes in how children explain the causes of behaviour. It appears (see Josephson, 1977; Nucci, in press; Turiel, in press) that children begin to form stable concepts of the person at approximately eight or nine years of age and thereafter attribute internal dispositional causes to behaviour.

Prior to the formation of such concepts, children regard situational influences as the primary causes of behaviour. If our younger subjects do attribute the causes of behaviour to situational influences, then it follows that they would not give a negative evaluation of a child whose behaviour is dictated by the school policy. Similarly, if our older subjects attribute the causes of behaviour to internal dispositions, it follows that they would evaluate the child's behaviour negatively, in spite of its conformity with school policy. (Incidentally, there is reason to believe that children older than eleven years of age would not evaluate negatively a child whose behaviour is consistent with a school policy that allows hitting. During late adolescence, greater emphasis is placed on the influences of the social system on individual behaviours and dispositions. See Josephson, 1977; Turiel, 1974.) It is possible, therefore, that on the basis of their inferences regarding the causes of behaviour, adolescents separate judgements of the moral value of an act from an evaluation of the person engaging in the act.

The findings of this study are in contradiction with those approaches that do not account for children's conceptual discriminations between types of rules. For instance, in his research on moral judgements, Piaget (1932) attempted to generalize from studies of children's concepts of game rules to their concepts of moral rules. However, in a systematic analysis of children's concepts of different types of rules (Turiel, 1978b), it was found that the large majority of subjects from six to seventeen years of age treated game rules differently from moral rules; game rules were regarded as legitimately changeable from one context to another, whereas moral rules were not.

As another example, in a study by Lockhart, Abrahams, and Osherson (1977), several different rule types were classified as conventional. They classified the meaning of words as an example of a rule governed by social conventions, as well as game rules, laws of the state, rules of etiquette, and moral rules. However, children's understanding of linguistic systems may differ from their understanding of the conventions of systems of social interaction. By including children's responses to questions regarding the meaning of words, Lockhart *et al.* confounded some of their analyses of social convention. Furthermore, other analyses in that study combined responses to informational questions (e.g. origins of rules, existence of rules) with responses to evaluative questions (e.g. Should a rule exist? Should it be changed?). The necessity for separating responses to these two types of questions was demonstrated by the finding in Turiel's (1978b) study that many subjects stated, on the one hand, that a rule pertaining to stealing can be changed and, on the other hand, that the rule should not be changed. Indeed, insofar as Lockhart *et al.* analysed evaluations about social – conventional rules separately from evaluations of moral rules, they too found that children regard the former as legitimately alterable to a greater extent than the latter.

Finally, the findings of this study have implications for the study of what has been referred to as 'legal socialization' (Hogan and Mills, 1976) or 'sense of law and legal justice' (Tapp and Kohlberg, 1971). In each of these studies, the concept of law is treated as equivalent to the (unitary) concept of rule. However, it is apparent from our results that children do distinguish between types of rules, among classes of actions, and that their conceptualization of act – rule relations is based on these differentiations.

The development of language and communication

INTRODUCTION

By the time children enter school, they have a very good command of their native language. Indeed, their achievements in language development appear highly impressive when one considers some of the evidence concerning their cognitive limitations.

The speed with which children acquire and make use of complexities of their language has led to an emphasis being placed on the surprising nature of their capacities. And observation tells us that by the time children reach four or five years of age, they have indeed mastered a great deal of the language system. However, we must not exaggerate their competence at this stage, for much still remains to be acquired. While we would not wish to detract in any way from the linguistic achievements of preschool children – for they are indeed impressive – it is important to note that the development of language, and of its use to communicate with others, is by no means completed when children enter school.

Evidence for further development comes from a number of sources. Carol Chomsky (1969), for example, studied the production and comprehension of complex grammatical forms in children aged five to ten years. She found that even at nine years of age, children experienced difficulty in understanding certain sentence forms. In the case of complement constructions, for example, children were introduced to two dolls, Donald and Bozo, and asked to make the dolls act out what was said. Given the sentence: *Donald promises Bozo to do a somersault,* many children made *Bozo* do the somersault, indicating their difficulty in accurately understanding this sort of grammatical construction. Other more recent studies have also demonstrated how much is still to be achieved beyond five years of age (e.g. Bowerman, 1979; Karmiloff-Smith, 1979; Palermo and Molfese, 1972).

Most of these references are concerned with studies of the development and age of appearance of particular language forms in children's speech. The papers of this Section, however, refer more to pragmatic aspects of language, their central concern being with the way in which available language is put to use. Thus the papers examine ways in which children and adults communicate, and consider assumptions that the participants hold during the course of communication. Attention is drawn to developments that take place during the period that children spend in early education, and to some of the misconceptions that exist concerning the speech of young children. For example, preschool children's speech has been described as 'egocentric', and taken as an indication of a postulated general inability to take into account the listener's perspective (Krauss and Glucksberg, 1969). While the speech of young children (like that of adults on occasion) may have some egocentric characteristics, it would be incorrect to assume that children are radically unable to take into account their listener's knowledge of the topic they are talking about.

The readings that follow provide an indication of some of the sophisticated communicative skills that young children possess, and also point to a range of skills that is still developing. An example of the former is the ability of young children to monitor their own speech for mistakes. Examples of the latter include techniques for resolving misunderstandings that occur in conversations, and skills which will be acquired when children encounter written language and begin to learn to read. The readings also make an important point concerning a mistaken assumption that adults may hold when they communicate with young children. Because children respond to adult's questions, it is often assumed that they have therefore understood them. However, as is shown in this section, this assumption is not always valid. Consequently, if we are to become more efficient at conveying knowledge to young children, we must closely examine *our* skills and methods of communication, as well as theirs.

6.

The modification of communicative behaviour in preschool-aged children as a function of the listener's perspective

Carole L. Menig-Peterson

In this reading Menig-Peterson considers the extent to which the speech of preschool children takes into account the listener's knowledge of the situation being described. She does so by considering two aspects of their speech, produced in contexts where the listener does, versus does not, possess prior knowledge of the situation being described. These aspects are whether new elements are appropriately introduced, and whether references to objects and persons are appropriately specified. In a story about a cat, for example, when the animal is introduced for the first time, it would be appropriate to say: 'Yesterday I saw a cat,' but not: 'Yesterday I saw the cat.' The latter would be correct only if the listener had prior knowledge of the cat. Thus one of the linguistic conventions concerning new elements is that they are generally introduced with the indefinite form of the article (a or an), rather than the definite form (the). Looking at the way in which children introduce new elements into a description therefore provides an indication of the extent to which they take their listener's knowledge into account. Menig-Peterson also considers whether young children specify referents in a way appropriate to the listener's state of prior knowledge. For example pronouns (such as he, she or it) may be used only when it is clear that the listener has sufficient knowledge to identify the noun that the pronoun replaces. The sentence: 'He came up and pushed him,' is inappropriate unless the listener knows who he and him are intended to refer to, for example, because the listener has witnessed the event. Thus, the specificity of reference provides an estimate of the child's ability to consider the listener's perspective. As Menig-Peterson's results show, the speech that three- and four-year-old children produce does vary with the listener's prior knowledge, indicating that children are not always insensitive to another's perspective.

The existence of role-taking skills in young children has been the subject of considerable controversy. Many investigators (e.g. Flavell, Botkin, Fry, Wright and Jarvis, 1968; Glucksberg, Krauss and Higgins, 1975; Piaget, 1926) have found young children particularly inept at modifying their verbal communication in accordance with the perspective and needs of their listener.

Other researchers, however, have found substantial role-taking ability on the part of young children. Shatz and Gelman (1973) found that four-year-olds modified their speech when talking to different-aged listeners. However, it seems possible that their results could be due partly to imitation of the listener's speech. Maratsos (1973) also found evidence of role-taking abilities in three- and four-year-old children. The children specified referents (toys) to an experimenter who was either apparently blind or had normal vision. The children were far more explicit verbally when communicating to an apparently blind adult than when communicating with an adult who could see.

The present study was an attempt to explore in greater depth the ability of preschool-aged children to modify their communicative behaviour in a naturalistic setting as a function of different role attributes of the listener, specifically listener experience or knowledge. It was assumed that the children's role-taking competence would be more apparent in a naturalistic setting with a familiar task, and telling adults about prior events is a familiar part of children's experience. In the present study, children communicated to the same adult under two conditions of apparent listener knowledge: (*a*) when the listener was apparently naïve (or unknowledgeable) about the experiences being talked about, and (*b*) when the listener was knowledgeable about those experiences. It was predicted that the children would substantially modify their verbalizations, depending upon the degree of knowledge of the listener.

METHOD

Subjects. The participants were nine girls and nine boys averaging 45 months of age (range 42–48 months) and ten girls and eight boys averaging 57 months of age (range 54–60 months). All children were chosen from white middle-class nursery school populations.

Experimenters. Sixteen nursery school teachers of the children served as experimenters. In addition, one part of the procedure required confederates. The 16 confederates were also teachers of the children with whom they participated.

Procedure. Each child participated in four sessions, each separated by about a week: two play sessions and two interview sessions that were tape-recorded. Each child was taken to two different experimental rooms twice. In each room the child had both a play session and a subsequent interview session. Both interview sessions for each child were done by the experimenter. However, the experimenter shared only the experiences of one play session with the child.

The interview session following a play session in which the child was accompanied by the experimenter was designated the experimenter-knowledgeable condition. During the other play session the child was accompanied by the confederate, and the subsequent interview session was designated the experimenter-naïve condition. Half of the children in each age group were accompanied by the experimenter during the first play session and by the confederate in the second. For the rest of the children, the conditions were reversed.

During each play session, the child participated in four tasks (making a total of eight different tasks altogether). Two types of tasks were chosen for comparison purposes: 'story events' which were stories enacted for the child by the experimenter or confederate with toy animals and dolls, and 'participatory events' which involved the child's direct participation. An example of the latter task is a staged accident: spilling a cup of Kool-Aid which the child helped clean up. (A complete description of the tasks can be found in Peterson, 1974, pp. 124–6.) The rationale behind such a comparison was simply curiosity about whether the children would be less egocentric when talking about an event in which they had been direct rather than vicarious participants. The order of tasks during each play session was: first participatory event, two stories, and second participatory event. The two groups of tasks were given to the children in a predetermined counterbalanced order.

During each interview session, one piece of equipment from each prior play session task was present in the room to facilitate spontaneous recall by the child. In addition, the child was encouraged to talk about each task not spontaneously described by means of two or three patterned prompts. If the child did not respond to any of these, a direct request to tell about the event was made by the experimenter.

Scoring procedure. Two analyses of words were done: the transcripts were scored for the appropriate introduction or non-introduction of the referents used by the child. Everything was scored from the perspective of a naïve listener so as to have a comparable baseline across conditions.

A new element was any object or person mentioned by the child which had been part of his previous play experience in the room but had not yet been introduced into the conversation. For example, the child's first mention of the 'cup of Kool-Aid' was counted as a new element. A new element was scored as appropriately introduced if it conformed to linguistic conventions of introduction.

A reference was any object or person that needed to be named if a naïve person was to understand what was being talked about. Thus pronouns such as 'it' or 'she' were scored as non-specified if a naïve listener would be unable to understand the identity of the referent. Nouns used where a pronoun would have been confusing were seen as specified references. For example, the following sentence contains two specified and one non-specified reference: 'The dog and the cat were talking, and then he left.' It is not clear who left.

Each new element and reference was scored as pertaining to a participatory event or a story event. (For a complete description of the scoring procedure, see Peterson, 1974, pp. 132–9).

All scorings of the transcripts were done by the author. However, a randomly selected 17 per cent of the protocols were independently scored by a second scorer. The agreement on scoring for new elements was 98 per cent for appropriate introduction of the new element; however, only 80 per cent of the new elements identified by either scorer were also identified as new elements by the other scorer. On specificity of references, the agreements were 93 per cent for specificity of the reference and 75 per cent for the number of references scored by one scorer which were also scored by the second.

RESULTS

The proportion of new elements used by each child that were appropriately introduced was calculated for each type of event. Five children's data were incomplete and were dropped from the analysis, along with the data of an additional three children to equalize the number of children of each sex in each age group. The means on the proportion of new elements that were appropriately introduced for the remaining 28 children are given in Table 1.

The scores of the children were analysed by means of a mixed effects analysis of variance, with between-subject factors of age and sex, and within-subject factor of type of event and condition (naïve or knowledgeable). The proportion of new elements that were appropriately introduced was substantially higher when the experimenter was naïve rather than knowledgeable ($F(1,24) = 84.44, p < .0001$). The children seem to be appropriately differentiating their behaviour as a function of the perspective of the listener. No other F statistic was significant.

The proportion of references that each child specified was calculated for each type of event. The means on the proportions of specified references are given in Table 1. The proportion of references that were specified was analysed in a mixed effects analysis of variance, with the between-subject factors of age and sex, and the within-subject factors of type of event and condition.

There was a significant age × condition interaction ($F(1,24) = 7.22, p < .02$). A simple effect calculation indicated that the four-year-olds specified significantly more references in the naïve than in the knowledgeable condition ($F(1,24) = 12.7, p < .01$). However, the proportion of references that were specified by the three-year-olds did not differ significantly between conditions ($F(1,24) = .89, p < .50$).

Inspection of the data suggested that different patterns of talking existed in

Table 1 *Means on the proportion of new elements that were appropriately introduced and the proportion of references that were specified in each type of event in the naïve (N) and the knowledgeable (K) conditions*

Response Measure	Age	Participatory Events		Story Events	
		N	K	N	K
New elements	4	.72	.26	.76	.37
New elements	3	.67	.24	.62	.35
Referents	4	.78	.69	.90	.65
Referents	3	.82	.86	.78	.86

the two conditions. The children seemed to talk more and to need less prompting when the experimenter was assumed to be naïve as opposed to knowledgeable. Consequently, the frequencies of occurrence of references in the conversations of the children before the experimenter's intervention of requesting the child to tell about the event were also tabulated. The scores of one randomly chosen four-year-old of each sex and two randomly chosen three-year-old girls were dropped to equalize the number of children of each sex in each age group. The number of references used by the children was analysed by means of a mixed effect analysis of variance calculation, with the between-subject factors of age and sex, and within-subject factors of type of event and condition. The children volunteered significantly more references when the listener was naïve than when he was knowledgeable ($F(1,28) = 5.69$, $p < .05$). No other F statistic reached significance.

DISCUSSION

The major hypothesis that the preschool child would modify his behaviour as a result of the perspective of his listener was strongly confirmed. Several aspects of the children's communicative behaviour differed in accordance with the state of knowledge of their listener, indicating that the children were tailoring their behaviour in accordance with the listener's needs. Type of event (participatory event or story event) had no effect. The effect of age was limited to the proportion of references that were specified. Older children seemed to have more control over their usage of non-specified references.

Some of the analyses presented above involve communicative behaviour similar to that explored by Piaget in 1926. Piaget was primarily struck by the errors that were made by the children he was studying. For example, he noted that the children often did not appropriately introduce new elements which they brought into their conversations, and they made liberal use of unspecified references, incorrect pronouns, and unspecified demonstratives. It can be seen from the data above that the performance of the children was far from perfect. Nevertheless, although the children are making errors, they are still modifying their behaviour substantially as a function of the knowledge of their listener.

An unresolved problem is the paradox between the results of the current study, that by Maratsos (1973), and by Shatz and Gelman (1973), and the results of other bodies of research data, for example, that reported in Flavell *et al.* (1968) and in Glucksberg *et al.* (1975). The former group of studies consistently suggests that young children are rather competent at modifying their verbalizations in accordance with their listener's perspective, and the latter group consistently suggests the opposite. One explanation may be that the tasks used in the present study and in the studies by Maratsos and Shatz and Gelman are easier for the children to do than the tasks used by the other authors. That is, the former studies only require the children to use behaviours over which they have considerable control and that are not too cognitively difficult for them. Perhaps many of the tasks used by the latter group of authors are more appropriately a measure of cognitive abilities, rather than a measure of role-taking ability *per se*. Some support for this is suggested by Maratsos (1973), who found that increased task difficulty led to increased 'egocentric' responding.

At least part of the difference in the conclusions of different studies may also be attributable to their focus. In the present study, an investigator looking simply at the children's verbalizations to the naïve listener would have ample support for claiming that the children were making a lot of egocentric mistakes. On the other hand, by looking at how their verbal productions differed relative to different listener needs, it is clear that appropriate tailoring of the communication occurs.

7.

Self-initiated corrections in the speech of infant-school children

Sinclair Rogers

In this reading, Rogers examines the corrections that five- and six-year-old children make to their speech when talking to an adult during individual interview sessions. The study provides useful insights into children's language development. For example, the occurrence of spontaneous (i.e. self-initiated) corrections of grammatical form indicates that children do evaluate the correctness of what they say. Further, consideration of the specific types of correction made provides an indication of the development of children's knowledge of the rules of grammar. Similarly, the occurrence of corrections to the meaning of what they are saying suggests that children also monitor the accuracy or appropriateness of the information they are conveying. On some occasions children will spontaneously correct the meaning of what they have said, whereas at other times they will do so when prompted by the listener's questioning. Whether prompted or spontaneous however, these corrections to meaning imply that children play an active role in maintaining effective communication with others. Thus, contrary to what earlier reports on childhood egocentrism have suggested, it is not always left to the adult to determine a child's intentions when they are not immediately clear. At times, children themselves monitor and correct the adequacy of their communication.

INTRODUCTION

The aim of the research project reported here was to map the language development of children at infant school over the course of a year. One of the series of analyses undertaken was an examination of spontaneous corrections made by the children of their own speech. Such an examination was intended to help answer two basic questions:

(1) Do children, as they grow older, become more aware of the language they use and its effects on others?

(2) Can self-initiated corrections give any indications of the actual level of linguistic development achieved by an individual child?

Errors, slips of the tongue and correction have been used as valuable data illuminating aspects of the relation between performance and competence (Fromkin, 1973); as a resource bank for analysing the rules of interaction (Jefferson, 1974); and as means of assessing developmental changes in children's language (Peterson, Danner and Flavell, 1972). Peterson *et al.* (1972) found that children aged four and seven years readily reformulated their initial messages when explicitly requested to do so, but both failed to reformulate when confronted only with non-verbal facial expressions of non-comprehension. Only the seven-year-olds tended to reformulate their messages in response to an implicit rather than explicit verbal request for additional help. It was suggested that the younger children did understand the latter type of feedback as a request for help but did not understand what kind of help was needed. Other studies, however (Berko Gleason, 1973, Shatz and Gelman, 1973, Sachs and Devin, 1976, Rogers, in press), have shown that even young children can vary their language apparently as a function of the child's concept of the listener's age and ability to comprehend.

The organization of what and how a child says something in an interview is affected by the child's concepts of formality and appropriateness of styles in particular contexts. Udelson (1975) reports that a child's language is often less fluent but apparently more organized with an adult than with another child. This disfluency may be categorized as allowing time for additions and revisions rather than pauses. Troike (1970) illustrates how a child's delivery was made more formal, in particular the absence of pauses and contractions, by being asked by an adult to tell a story.

METHOD

Two separate groups of 30 boys and girls each aged five and six were interviewed individually three times at intervals of six months at their infant school. Each child in the five-year-old group had been in the same school for one term when they were first interviewed; and each child in the six-year-old group had been in the same school for one school year when first interviewed. At the first interview, the mean age of the five-year-old group was 5.2 years (standard deviation of 0.14) and that of the six-year-old group was 6.1 years (standard deviation 0.19). At each interview the child was asked by the male researcher to talk about a picture and then to talk about a number of topics which were related to the child's life out of school. The stimulus picture varied for each set of interviews but the format of each interview was kept as similar as possible throughout the three interviews that each child had. The speech samples contain a minimum of 50 utterances of each child collected on three separate occasions together with any questions or remarks which the interviewer interposed. The corrections of speech by the child were made without prompting from the interviewer, although sometimes he asked for a passage to be repeated which he had not heard or understood. Each child seemed to have his own pattern of approach, and the number and variety of questions asked, whilst differing from child to child, in each of the three interviews did not vary greatly.

THE CORRECTIONS

The corrections may be categorized into three main types. Type A corrections are 'self-initiated corrections' of syntax or morphology without any perceived alteration in meaning or emphasis. The child voluntarily corrects his previous own utterance by, for example, deleting a double negative, adding a preposition or transposing a misplaced object. Type B corrections are 'other-initiated corrections' of meaning made in response to a question posed by the interviewer which throws doubt on what the child has just said. The child reconsiders after prompting by the interviewer, what he (the child) has just uttered and changes the meaning of the previous utterance by juxtaposing a new utterance which generally refers back to a single nominal or part of a nominal group in the originating utterance. Type C corrections are 'self-initiated corrections' of meaning which are similar to type B except that they occur without any prompting from the interviewer.

In the following tables the interviews of the five-year-olds are numbered 5(1), 5(2) and 5(3); the interviews of the six-year-olds are numbered 6(1), 6(2) and 6(3). Table 1 gives examples of the three types of corrections together with an indication of the interview which produced the correction.

RESULTS

From Table 2 it is possible to see that the level of correction of type A, while it increases slightly with time, does not increase to any marked extent in either the five-year-old or the six-year-old group. This is consistent with the view that a child produces utterances at any given time which are well formed in relation to the state of his language development. A number of studies have shown that a child's awareness of 'mistakes' in test material depends upon his own level of competence; these figures would indicate the same thing for the monitoring of the child's own production of utterances.

Table 1 *Examples of corrections: types A – C*

Original utterance (or part of utterance)	Correction	Interview
	Type A	
(1) I hung it up the coat	I hung up the coat	5 (2)
(2) we can't go no more	we can't go any more	5 (1), 5 (3)
(3) Daddy fetched us to a party (in the context of coming home)	Daddy fetched us from a party	6 (2)
(4) he didn't wash hisself	he didn't wash himself	5 (3)
(5) they was going	they were going	5 (1)
(6) what you're doing?	what are you doing?	5 (1)
(7) me go	I go	5 (1)
(8) we're going Yarmouth	we're going to Yarmouth	6 (1)
(9) I pulled off his hat off	I pulled his hat off	6 (1)
(10) I know what them are	I know what they are	6 (2)
(11) he grew bigger	he growed bigger	5 (1)
(12) I live opposite the road	across the road	6 (2)
(13) they go	they are going	5 (3)
(14) you put down it	you put it down	6 (2)

Original utterance (or part of utterance)	Interviewer	Correction	Interview
		Type B	
(15) we went there tomorrow	I beg your pardon?	Yesterday I mean	6 (3)
(16) it's a new one	a new one?	a new old one really	5 (3)
(17) we're going to Yarmouth	how will you get there?	well we were going but …	5 (3)
(18) that's a pigeon	is it?	no it's a duck because I can see its feet	5 (2)
(19) I'm going to leave school soon	are you?	well when I'm sixteen anyway	6 (1)
		Type C	
(20) Mummy was washing and he …		Daddy I mean	6 (1)
(21) the man I was		he saw me really	6 (3)
(22) I've got a bike like that		well, it's not quite the same as that really	6 (2)
(23) my little sister Julie …		no, Karen's younger than her	6 (2)
(24) our little dog was hurt yesterday		well, it's our neighbour's dog really but …	6 (3)

Table 2 *Occurrence of corrections of types A, B and C*

Utterances with corrections expressed as a percentage of the total number of utterances	Five-year-olds			Six-year-olds		
	Time 1	Time 2	Time 3	Time 1	Time 2	Time 3
Type A	6	6	7	7	8	8
Type B	2	3	5	4	5	6
Type C	0	1	2	4	6	10

In examples of correction B the child knows himself what he has meant and seems not to realize in these cases – unless queried – that what he has said has been too compressed, refers to other unknown referents or has not been understood. On very rare occasions when queried, the child repeated his original remark unaltered. These examples have not been counted as corrections.

Corrections of the type C are made when the child himself realizes that something that he has just said is in need of correction. The incidence of these corrections is extremely low with the five-year-olds and seems to become important only with the six-year-olds. This is one of a number of indications that suggest that the six-year-old child at this stage is monitoring what he says more actively than the five-year-old, and is more aware of the effect of his words on another person: he is performing a semi-formal social role elicited by a particular kind of situation. Corrections of the type C may be linked with type B, but unlike B they are not based on feedback from the interviewer. Type C corrections, then, may be seen as occurring after the child has learned to monitor his own performance.

The younger children were much more definite about what they saw, and did not query what they had to do in the interview situation. They rarely had qualms or doubts about stating what they thought they could see, and frequently made wrong decisions. Once decided, they were confident about their judgement. As the children grew older the number of definite answers decreased, and the children seemed to become increasingly uncertain of some of the comments they made. This development was manifest in the speech of many of the older children in three main ways: (i) they used a number of *I think, it looks like, it might be*; (ii) they developed the technique of throwing a question back to the interviewer: *what is it?, it's a ... isn't it?*; and (iii) their rate of spontaneous corrections of type C increased quite considerably.

For the rest of this paper there is a consideration in more detail of corrections of the type A.

Table 3 *Corrections of type A: self-initiated corrections of syntax and their relative frequency of occurrence in order*

Sentence no. (from Table 1)	Corrections of five-year-old children	Sentence no. (from Table 1)	Corrections of six-year-old children
(8)	+ Prep	(2)	Neg + Neg → Neg
(3)	Prep (1) → Prep (2)	(7)	Obj Pro → Subj Pro
(7)	Obj Pro → Subj Pro	(14)	Vb + Prep + Obj Pro
			→ Vb + Obj Pro + Prep
(10)	Obj Pro → Subj Pro	(6)	Wh + Np + Aux + Vb
			→ Wh + Aux + NP + Vb
(12)	Prep (1) → Prep (2)	(10)	Obj Pro → Subj Pro
(5)	Agreement in Aux	(9)	– Prep
(13)	+ Aux + Progressive	(1)	– NP (the coat)
(4)	hisself → himself	(8)	+ Prep
(11)	grew → growed	(5)	Agreement in Aux
(9)	– Prep	(3)	Prep (1) → Prep (2)
(1)	– NP (the coat)	(13)	→ Aux + Progressive
		(12)	Prep (1) → Prep (2)
(6)	WH + NP + Aux + Vb ⇒ WH + Aux + NP + Vb	(11)	grew → did grow
(14)	Vb + Prep + Obj Pro ⇒ Vb + Obj Pro + Prep	(4)	hisself → himself

Table 3 presents the order of frequency of corrections of type A made by the children in the two age groups. The sentence number on the left refers to Table 1, which gives a representative example of the basic structure which is corrected. The largest group of corrections deals with various forms of the verb. The reason for this constellation of corrections concerning the verb may be that, at the children's level of development, they experience most difficulty with the multitude of rules governing the verb.

As can be seen from Table 2, corrections of type A occur at a fairly static frequency throughout the age range; but relative to the other types of correction they become less important with increase in age. The incidence of the corrections of type A varied quite considerably between the two age groups. The younger children most frequently made corrections which involved the addition or deletion of a single syntactic item, or the exchange of one morphological form of a word for another. The number of corrections of more complex structures involving a re-ordering or some other alteration to the structure of phrases was relatively low compared with the replacement of single items or alterations to individual words.

The six-year-olds made more corrections of the complex structures than they did of single words or items. A further difference was also noted: while the five-year-olds made more corrections of single items than they did of more complex structures, their use and control of these latter structures was by no means near the adult norm. The six-year-olds, however, while correcting the more complex structures, clearly indicated that they had almost completely mastered the use and control of the less complex structures. It would seem that the younger children were unable to correct their complex structures because they had not yet reached sufficient competence in them in order to provide even a minimum of monitoring of their performance.

With the growth in age there is a change in the nature of corrections of type A from being applied to simpler structures and single items to longer structures with a more complex derivation. This may reflect the overwhelming current concern of the children at a particular age, so that the study of corrections may give an indirect light on the learning process as a child acquires mastery of a particular structure or a set of rules. By the time of the last interview of the six-year-olds, corrections of type A which act on single items occur less frequently than either of the other two types of corrections. As the children approach seven years of age they seem to have achieved mastery over their production of the more simple structures. They did not need to correct themselves as much as the younger children with these structures. The picture is not the same in relation to the more complex structures; the rate of self-initiated corrections indicates a less than complete mastery and at the same time the older children seem to be more concerned with the content and meaning of what they say.

CONCLUSIONS

On the basis of evidence presented above the following conclusions are suggested.

(1) With the five-year-old children the most frequently used corrections were those affecting relatively minor changes (particularly morphology) in single items. This picture was not typical for the six-year-old child. For the older child, the rules needed to produce the corrected utterances were generally more advanced (i.e. they reflect a more complex derivation and very often are multi-based transformations) than those used entirely with spontaneity. It seems reasonable to suggest that some of the corrections may indicate the state of development of certain syntactic rules. Some of the corrections may indicate the threshold between rules acquired and used actively, and those just about to be used actively without conscious effort.

(2) A study of these corrections shows that children are actively engaged in listening to what they say, and that this active participation appears to

increase with age. The child becomes more responsible for what he says, and goes through a process of matching his performance, with its known errors, with those structures and rules he has internalized in order to generate more developed utterances.

(3) It can be seen that, as a large proportion of corrections of structure concern the verb, it is in the expansion, agreement and elaboration of this that children of this age range have most difficulty.

(4) The older the children were in the sample, the more frequently they spontaneously corrected their speech. To explain this the following reasons are postulated: (*a*) the older the child is the more aware he is of the effect his speech has on others; and (*b*) as the child becomes more able linguistically, he begins to make an objective judgement of what he says and how he says it. This conclusion supports Flavell, Botkin, Fry, Wright and Jarvis (1968), who suggest that a child's awareness that differences in perspective exist between the speaker and the listener is a process which develops with age and appears to be linked to conceptual and/or cognitive maturity.

8.

Ways of reacting to communication failure in relation to the development of the child's understanding about verbal communication

Elizabeth J. Robinson and W. Peter Robinson

The previous two readings have been concerned with aspects of children's speech when communicating with adults. Here the Robinsons look specifically at one aspect of this process, the ability to produce adequate messages. In doing this, however, they also consider what children know about the reasons for communication failure. The studies they describe make use of a referential communication game, where a message is taken to be adequate if it is sufficiently specific for a listener to know exactly what is being referred to. For example, in the context of selecting one of four pictures of a car, a bus, a lorry, and a bike, then the speaker's message: 'I've chosen the picture of a car,' is adequate, because the listener knows which picture has been selected. But if all four pictures had been of cars (e.g. one yellow, one red, one green, one blue), then the same message would not be clear, for it would not convey to the listener which car the speaker had chosen. An example of an adequate message in this case would be: 'I've chosen a picture of the blue car.' Thus messages must be tailored to fit their context. But the Robinsons and others have found that young children do not always do this. Further, if an inadequate message is produced, some children do not appreciate the reason for the failure. They will blame the listener, perhaps for not listening hard enough, rather than the speaker for failing to produce a sufficiently specific message. In addition to considering this topic experimentally, the Robinsons relate their experimental results to tape-recordings of the children talking with their mothers in their own homes. In doing this they draw attention to the importance of taking into account the different language experiences that children encounter before entering school.

INTRODUCTION

A number of recent studies have demonstrated limitations in the young child's understanding about verbal communication. Markman (1977) asked first to third-grade children to judge the adequacy of incomplete instructions to perform a trick or play a game; the younger ones were less likely than the older ones to recognize the inadequacies in the instructions. Whitehurst and Sonnenschein (1981) present a number of studies in which five-year-old child speakers were told either to describe differences between a target item and others or to describe a target item so that a listener could pick it out from others. When asked to describe differences the children produced informative messages; the 'communicate' instructions were much less effective in enabling the children to produce informative messages, unless coupled with corrective feedback which informed the child whether or not he had described differences. These authors conclude that 'the young child does not know that to communicate referentially is to describe differences' (p. 21). A conclusion quite consistent with this follows from work we have carried out using the 'Whose fault?' technique for assessing the child's understanding about inadequate messages and their role in causing communication failure, and about adequate messages and their role in achieving successful communication. This involves the child and the experimenter sending messages to each other and discussing the reasons for successful and unsuccessful communication. Experimental results using this technique have enabled us to describe a developmental sequence of understanding about various aspects of communication. This may be summarized as follows: the young child up to about five or six years does not know that a message should refer uniquely to whatever the speaker has in mind. For him it is sufficient that the message refers to this item, regardless of whether it refers to other items as well. By about seven years, the child understands the importance of the uniqueness of reference of a message, and that a message which is too general can cause communication failure (Robinson and Robinson, 1976a, b, 1977a). The ability to make comparisons between intended referent and other potential referents, although necessary for the development of the understanding, is apparently not sufficient (Robinson and Robinson, 1978c).

In order to begin to explain how the development of this understanding about communication occurs, we looked at communication failures occurring in the child's everyday life (Robinson, 1981). We analysed transcripts made by Clough (1971) and Cambourne (1971) of preschool teachers, teachers and mothers talking with the children in their care to find out how misunderstandings and non-understandings were dealt with. The most common way of dealing with an apparently inadequate message was to use a conventional means of requesting a repetition, 'Pardon?'. The next most common reaction to an inadequate message was to request more information, usually employing a 'Wh' question, e.g., 'What sort of something?' 'Trevor who?' Other ways of dealing with inadequate messages were: to make a guess, e.g. 'In a car?'; to offer alternative means; to repeat or expand the original message (in this case it is the speaker who takes the initiative in dealing with the original inadequate message, rather than the listener); or to ignore it. It was very rare for an adult to tell the child that his message had not been understood and why.

The results of an experiment (Robinson, 1981) demonstrate that the young child finds it easier to recognize a listener's non-understanding and to identify the ambiguity of the original message if the listener makes her non-understanding explicit, rather than if she merely asks a question to elicit the missing information. Children were presented with snatches of dialogue between a doll, who had lost an article of clothing, and its mother, who was supposedly asked by the doll, 'Mum, have you seen my hat/gloves/sweater, etc. please?' In four of the dialogues the mother gave what appeared to be common adult responses to a child's ambiguous message, in which her non-understanding remained implicit. She said, for example, 'Which gloves?' In a fifth, she made her problem explicit: 'I don't know which cardigan you want. You've got two cardigans. You should tell me which one.' The child subjects were asked whether the mother had understood just what was wanted, and whether the doll had said enough about what was wanted. Many children identified the mother's non-understanding only when she made it explicit. The various implicit ways of dealing with her non-understanding seemed not to inform the child that there had been a communication failure.

The commonly used ways of dealing with communication failure serve to advance the immediate purposes of the interaction. They do not explicitly draw attention to the listener's difficulty. An extended explicit specification in context should provide the child with the most transparent learning opportunity, but the explicit statement of non-understanding is potentially more helpful than any of the others in fact observed. The potential can only be realized, however, if the child has the capacity to analyse the problem further, diagnosing and coordinating the relevant information, but other things being equal, explicit statements of non-understanding should provide better learning opportunities than other adult reactions.

In the first study below we investigated whether giving the child explicit information about the inadequacies of his messages would help him to improve his messages in the immediate future, and whether it would improve his understanding about communication failure. We compared the effects on performance and understanding of three treatments: in one the experimenter as listener to the child's inadequate messages simply guessed what he had in mind; in the second she replied with the common adult response of 'Which one?'; in the third she gave detailed information about what was missing from the message. In the experiment, we were additionally able to examine the effects of the adult listener's behaviour on subsequent child listener's question-asking. Several authors have reported that younger children are less inclined than older ones to ask questions when faced with inadequate messages (Alvy, 1968, Dickson, 1974, Cosgrove and Patterson, 1977, Ironsmith and Whitehurst, 1978). Cosgrove and Patterson (1977) found that giving children 'a plan' for effective listening, which emphasized the importance of representing more information if the message was inadequate, helped kindergarten through fourth-grade children but did not help preschool children. Subsequently, Cosgrove and Patterson (1978) found that modelling was also effective. We therefore compared the effect of our three treatments on child listener's question-asking.

The second study was designed to find out whether children who, in their everyday life, receive explicit information about communication failure, do advance more quickly than those who do not, in their understanding about inadequate messages and their causal role in communication failure. Data collected under the direction of C. G. Wells provided us with a unique opportunity to make this investigation (Wells, in press).

In the Wells study, the mother-child vocal interaction of 64 children was recorded at three-monthly intervals between the ages of one and a quarter and three and a half years. Half of the children were also recorded in the home shortly before they entered infants' school at five. The sample was selected to give equal representation to both sexes, four social classes of family background, and four seasons of birth. The recordings were made by means of a radio-microphone worn by the child which transmitted to a receiver linked to a tape recorder. The tape recorder was pre-programmed to record 24 90-second samples at approximately 20-minute intervals throughout the day between 9 a.m. and 6 p.m. In the evening the tape was played back to the mother who was asked to recall the participants and activity for each of the recorded speech samples.

We were able to search transcripts of these recordings of 36 of the children for communication failures, code maternal ways of dealing with them; and relate these later to the child's understanding about communication as assessed by our 'Whose fault?' technique,

At the time of being tested with the 'Whose fault?' technique, each child was also given a description completion task and a causality task. Performance in the former allowed us to see whether or not the child was capable of performing the comparisons between referent and non-referent necessary for identifying inadequate messages in the communication evaluation game. A description completion task had previously been used by Robinson and Robinson (1978c) to show that the ability to make comparisons between referent and non-referent was necessary but not sufficient for judging the inadequacy of a too-general message. In the present study, we wanted to know whether a child failed to judge a too-general message to be inadequate because he could not perform the necessary comparisons, or whether he failed to do so despite an ability to perform these. Should the former be the case, this could account for a failure to understand about message inadequacy despite appropriate maternal information about the communication process.

Performance in the causality task enabled us to see if the child could handle distal causes. We have argued and demonstrated elsewhere (Robinson and Robinson, 1978b) that the ability to handle distal, as opposed to simply proximal, causes is a necessary but not sufficient condition for blaming the speaker and his message, as opposed to just the listener, for communication failure. We included this task for the same reason as we included the description completion task: failure in the causality task could enable us to account for poor performance in the 'Whose fault?' task despite appropriate input from the mother.

STUDY 1

METHOD

Subjects

The procedure was completed by 47 children aged between five years two months and six years five months. All were white and attended an infants' school in a middle class catchment area in Bristol, England. Four other children completed all but the final 'Whose fault?' questioning, they asked questions which disambiguated the experimenter's messages and so did not experience communication failure. These four are mentioned again in the section below on modelling. A fifth child had eye sight too poor to see the dolls' clothes adequately.

Materials and procedure

Game to assess effects of feedback on message quality. The child and the experimenter played a game which involved choosing clothes for dolls to wear. The players sat on either side of an opaque screen, and had identical dolls with sets of clothes. There were six different types of garments (sweaters, trousers, shirts, socks, shoes and scarves) and eight instances of each type. On each of six trials, the child chose one of each type of garment for his doll to wear. Each type of garment was displayed on one row of a stand, so that on any one trial the child dealt with a row of eight items. The eight examples of a type of garment different on three dimensions each of which had two values. (For example, the sweaters had wide or narrow stripes, long or no sleeves and round or V-necks.) As the child selected which of each type of garment his doll was to wear, he described it so that the experimenter could select the matching one for her doll. The stated aim was that both dolls would finally be wearing the same clothes. Care was taken to ensure that the child understood that the aim was for both dolls to be wearing *exactly* the same garment: the experimenter pointed out that all the examples of each type of garment were different and demonstrated that if the child selected a particular item then the experimenter tried to pick the matching one from her set.

Of the 282 messages given by the children, 258 did not identify uniquely the garment chosen. Following these ambiguous messages, the experimenter took one of three courses of action:

(1) For the first child, the fourth, and so on, the experimenter simply made a guess. Seventeen children given this form of feedback completed the entire procedure.

(2) For the second child, the fifth and so on, the experimenter said '*Which one?*' in a puzzled tone of voice, waited for the child's response and then chose as best she could. Thirteen of the children completed the procedure.

(3) For the third child, the sixth and so on, the experimenter made explicit what was missing. For example, she said 'Well, there are four like that, I don't know whether it's got long sleeves or short sleeves, and I don't know whether it's got stripes or squares (checks)'. Probes were repeated until the child either gave an identifying message or showed no improvement on his previous one. The experimenter made her choice when the child had supplied the missing information as best he could. Seventeen children completed this procedure.

In all cases, before the child went on to another type of garment, the child's and the experimenter's selected clothes were compared to see if they were the same. The child judged whether or not the clothes matched; this indicated understanding of the aim of the activity. No child gave signs of not understanding or not accepting the task as given.

Games to assess the child's initial and final level of understanding about communication failure. Before and after playing the game just described the child and experimenter played with a second but different matching set of girl dolls and clothes. In the initial testing for understanding about communication failure, the child had three trials as speaker, describing clothes selected for his doll as in the game described above. Following the first ambiguous message given by the child, the experimenter asked the 'Whose fault?' sequence of questions: 'We've got different blouses/skirts/cardigans. We went wrong that time. Whose fault was that, mine, yours? Why? Did you tell me properly which one to pick? Did you tell me enough so that I could choose the right one? (If the child said 'No': What should you have said?) Whose fault was it we went wrong? Why? That is, the child was asked to ascribe blame for communication failure, to give his reasons, and to judge whether his message had been adequate.

The same sequence of questions was asked in the final testing for understanding about communication failure. This time, the experimenter had three trials as speaker and on each of them gave an ambiguous message. On one trial, whichever garment the child picked up, the experimenter showed that she had chosen a different one. The 'Whose fault?' sequence of questions was asked.

Treatment of results

Quality of messages given in the game involving feedback. The quality of the descriptions given of the six boy doll's garments was measured in terms of their ambiguity of reference. Prior to the experimenter's giving one of the three forms of feedback, descriptions referred to one, two, four or eight garments, and these initial descriptions were given ambiguity scores of 0, 1, 2 or 3 respectively; these scores represent the bits of information necessary to achieve unique reference. The total ambiguity score for the six garments was calculated, a score of 0 indicating perfect performance, and a score of 18 representing maximal ambiguity. The ambiguity scores actually obtained ranged from 4 to 16. Since children selected garments in different orders, and some garments proved to be easier to describe than others, we could not calculate changes in message quality over the six trials.

Understanding about communication failure. On the basis of his answers to the 'Whose fault?' sequence of questions, each child was placed twice into one of four categories, once on the basis of his answers in the initial testing, and once on the basis of those in the final testing. These will be referred to below as the initial and final blame categories respectively. The categories were:

(1) Listener blamers. The child blamed the listener only on the grounds that the listener had chosen wrongly, and judged that the speaker had told enough about the chosen garment.

(2) Lower intermediates. The child blamed the listener only on the grounds that the listener had chosen wrongly, but judged that the speaker had not told enough about the chosen garment and identified at least one attribute missing from the message.

(3) Higher intermediates. When first asked to ascribe blame for a particular failure, the child blamed the listener on the grounds of incorrect choice, but he judged that the speaker had not told enough, identified at least one attribute missing from the message, and then blamed the speaker for the failure on the grounds that the message had been inadequate.

(4) Speaker blamers. The child blamed the speaker on the grounds that the message had been inadequate, and judged that the speaker had not told enough about the chosen garment and identified at least one attribute missing from the message.

On the basis of previous work (Robinson and Robinson, 1976a, b, 1977b), we assumed that these categories formed a developmental sequence with listener blamers being the least advanced and speaker blamers the most advanced in their understanding about communication failure.

RESULTS

Initial understanding about communication related to message quality

Over all initial blame categories, the ambiguity scores ranged from 4 to 16. All 10 of those who were speaker blamers at the outset had ambiguity scores of 10 or less; 17 of the 25 were listener blamers who at the outset had scores greater than 10. The trend in ambiguity scores across the blame categories from listener blamers to speaker blamers was tested using a non-parametric trend test based on the statistic S (Ferguson, 1965) dividing the range of scores in half. The trend was found to be significant ($z = 2.49$, $p = 0.01$), with listener blamers giving the poorer messages and speaker blamers the better. The data are presented in Table 1.

Table 1 *Number of children giving messages of different ambiguity in relation to location of blame*

	Ambiguity score	
Initial blame allocation	4–10	11–16
Listener blamers	8	17
Lower intermediates	0	7
Higher intermediates	2	3
Speaker blamers	10	0

Effects of feedback: message quality in the three feedback conditions. Since children in the different initial blame categories differed in their response to the three types of feedback, we consider the categories separately.

(1) Listener blamers. The range of ambiguity scores obtained by those who were listener blamers at the outset was from 7 to 16. All 9 of these given explicit feedback had final ambiguity scores between 7 and 11; 2 of the 10 in the guessing condition and none of the 6 in the 'Which one?' condition achieved comparable scores. Using a Mann-Witney U test, it was found that the ambiguity scores in the explicit feedback condition were lower than those in the other two conditions combined ($U = 13.5$, $p < 0.002$), and that the ambiguity scores in the guessing and 'Which one?' conditions did not differ from each other ($U = 18$, $p > 0.1$). It is possible that the listener blamers who were given explicit feedback were merely learning to say more, and so gave better messages without really understanding what they were doing; they may not have realized that the messages should uniquely identify the garment the speaker had chosen. As a test of the possibility that lower ambiguity scores were due merely to longer messages, we counted the number of irrelevant attributes mentioned by each of the initial listener

blamers (that is, attributes which did not distinguish between the eight garments of one type). The initial listener blamers in the three feedback conditions did not differ significantly in the number of irrelevant attributes mentioned (Kruskall–Wallis one-way analysis of variance by ranks, $H(z) = 2.41, p = 0.3$).

(2) Lower intermediates, higher intermediates and speaker blamers. Among the children who initially fell into these blame categories there were no differences in ambiguity scores according to feedback condition. (Kruskall–Wallis analysis of variance by ranks, $H(z) = 1.2, p = 0.8$.).

Table 2 *Advancement of understanding by listener blamers in relation to experimental treatment*

| Group | N | Advancement | |
		No	Yes
Guessing only	9	7	2
'Which one?'	6	3	3
Explicit information	9	2	7

Effects of feedback on understanding about communication. Among those who were listener blamers on initial testing (24), the trend test based on S showed explicit feedback to be associated with an increased probability of advancement of category by the post-test ($z = 2.08, p = 0.03$). Among those initially in intermediate categories there were no differences between the different feedback conditions in frequency of progress by the post-test, but there were only four cases of such progress. Two children fell into a less advanced category on final as compared with initial testing; both were intermediates initially.

Effects of modelling. On the basis of the work of Cosgrove and Patterson (1978) we expected that children who were in the 'Which one?' and explicit feedback conditions might ask more questions than those in the guessing condition in the final stage of the experiment whenever the experimenter gave inadequate messages. In that stage, the experimenter gave three inadequate messages.

For this analysis we have included the four children who did not complete the final 'Whose fault?' testing because their questions disambiguated the experimenter's messages. The proportions of children who guessed (without asking any questions) on all three occasions were not different across the three feedback conditions. Among those who asked at least one question, there was no difference overall between those in the different conditions in the number asked, although among those who were initially listener blamers, there were significantly more questions asked by those in the 'Which one?' and explicit conditions (combined) as compared with those in the guessing condition ($U = 5$,

$p = 0.05$). (Of the five listener blamers in the guessing condition who asked a question, none asked more than three; of the seven in the other two conditions, five asked four or more questions.)

There were also differences between children in the different blame categories in the type of questions asked. Those who were initially speaker blamers asked only *open* questions, e.g. 'What colour?', 'What else?' Children in the initial other blame categories quite commonly asked *closed* questions, e.g. 'Has it got long or short sleeves?'; 'Is it blue?'; Is it red with two buttons?'. The proportion of children who asked at least one open question increased significantly over the following four groups of children: final listener blamers, initial listener blamers, initial intermediates (combined), and initial speaker blamers (S test, $z = 2.73$, $p = 0.006$). None of the 12 children who were still listener blamers at the end of the experiment asked an open question; six of the ten who were speaker blamers at the outset asked at least one open question.

DISCUSSION AND CONCLUSIONS

Two of the subsidiary results of this experiment add to the evidence about relationships between the child's understanding about communication and his level of communicative performance: we found an improvement in message quality across the initial blame categories from listener blamers to speaker blamers; we also found a relationship between blame category and type of question asked in response to an ambiguous message – the least advanced children in the experiment, namely those who were still listener blamers at the final testing, never asked an open question, whereas six of the ten most advanced (speaker blamers at the outset) did ask at least one open question. In previous work we have found relationships between two other aspects of communicative performance and category of blame: only speaker blamers could deliberately withhold information to make their listener's task difficult (Robinson and Robinson, 1978a); spontaneously making comparisons during message production was more common among speaker blamers than listener blamers (Robinson and Robinson, 1978b).

The central hypothesis tested in this experiment provided clear results. The provision of explicit feedback about the ambiguity of the child's message had two observable consequences on those who were listener blamers at the initial testing: their messages improved in comparison with children in the other two feedback conditions, and they were more likely to have advanced in their understanding about message inadequacy and communication failure.

STUDY 2

The main prediction was that children would come to understand that ambiguous messages can cause communication failure earlier if their mothers had provided them with this information explicitly. In operational terms we expected to find a positive association between blaming the speaker because he did not tell properly at age six and evidence of explicit specifications of non-understanding by mothers in the samples of everyday interactions recorded at earlier points in time.

METHOD

Subjects

There were 64 children in the Wells sample who were first recorded at the age of 15 months. The Wells research team was still in contact with 32 of these children at the time our study began, so we were able to trace and test these children with no difficulty. The remaining 32 children had been dropped by the Wells team at the age of three and a half years, more than two years prior to the beginning of our study. We were successful in our attempts to trace only six of these; two of the six we were unable to include in our study because a substantial proportion of the mother–child transcripts was missing. Hence our final sample consisted of 36 children, 18 of them boys and 18 girls, and with four social classes A–D about equally represented. We coded the available transcripts of mother–child speech at ages two to three and a half years, and also the transcripts of the final preschool recordings made of the 32 children with whom the Wells' team were still in contact. The children were tested at school for their understanding about communication, as close as possible to their sixth birthday, and in all cases within one month of it.

Materials

At the first testing session, each child played three games with the experimenter, in the following order:

Description completion task. The child was shown four pairs of cards, a pair at a time. The cards bore drawings of: a man with a black spotted shirt and a man with a red spotted shirt; a man with a bowler hat (round) and a man with a top hat (square); a man with a blue flower and a man with a red flower; a man holding a blue flag up high and a man holding a blue flag down low.

'Whose fault?' communication evaluation game. Child and experimenter had identical sets of six cards, separated by an opaque screen. The cards bore drawings of: a man with a red flower; a man with a blue flower; a man with a white pointed hat; a man with a white top hat; a man holding a red flag up high; a man holding a red flag down low.

'Causality' task. Child and experimenter had sets of four cards which had the same content and which could be described in the same way, but the drawings of which differed in style; the set given to the child were amateurish line drawings, while those given to the experimenter were more professional and detailed. The cards bore: a boy riding a tricycle and holding a large red flower; a boy riding a tricycle and holding a small red flower; a boy pushing a pram and holding a large red flower; a boy pushing a pram and holding a small red flower. A set of four cards identical to those of the experimenter was given to the child at the end of the causality task, so that both players had identical cards and could play the communication game.

Procedure

Each child was tested individually at his school as close as possible to his sixth birthday. The *description completion task* was based upon the task used by Robinson and Robinson (1978c). As in that study, the child's comparison ability was tested by showing him pairs of cards and asking him to complete a description of which card the experimenter had turned face down. The experimenter began each of the four trials (one per pair of cards) by eliciting a description of each card from the child. e.g. 'This is a man with a red flower and this is a man with a blue flower'. She then turned both cards face down, and said 'I've turned over the men with ...' and waited for the child to complete the description (flowers). Then both cards were turned face up and one of them was turned face down. Again the child was asked to complete the description (blue/red flowers). On the first two trials, the experimenter herself demonstrated the task by completing the three statements herself before repeating the turnings over for the child to complete. On the third and fourth trials there was no such demonstration. We argued in the paper mentioned above that this task required the child to make comparisons equivalent to those needed when judging the adequacy of a too-general message such as 'A man with a flower' when the intended referent is a man with a red flower but the listener might also choose a man with a blue flower.

The *communication evaluation game* followed the description completion task on the assumption that this ordering would minimize the misclassification of children who gave incorrect adequacy judgements simply because they could not perform the necessary comparisons. The game followed the standard course developed in our previous work: child and experimenter, with their identical sets of cards, sat at opposite ends of a table with a screen across the middle. The stated objective of the game was for one player, the speaker, to choose a card and describe it so that the other player, the listener, could choose the matching card from his set. The experimenter introduced the game to the child by showing him the two sets of cards and telling him they were identical. The experimenter explained and then demonstrated the game, giving a good message which identified her chosen card uniquely. The child picked the correct card and then had a turn as speaker. The players contined to take turns. On some of her turns as speaker, the experimenter introduced communication failure by giving messages which referred to two cards, such as 'I've got the one I want you to pick, it's a man with a red flag,' when the child could choose the flag held up or down. Whichever card the child chose, the experimenter showed that she had been talking about the other. Frequently, the children themselves spontaneously gave messages which were too general; sometimes these resulted in the experimenter choosing the wrong card.

Whenever the listener picked wrongly (whether this be child or experimenter), the child was asked the standard 'Whose fault?' sequence of questions: 'We've got different cards, we went wrong that time. Whose fault was that, mine, yours? Why? Did I/you tell you/me properly which one to pick?' (If the child says 'No' 'What should I/you have said?') 'Whose fault was it we went wrong? Why?' The child was asked this sequence of questions following three communication failures.

Finally, the child was given a *causality task* to see if he could handle distal causes. At the end of the communication evaluation game, the child was told 'Now let's play the same game with some different cards. Here are yours. Would you like to lay them out?' and he was handed face down a bundle of four cards. The experimenter laid out her cards, and began the new game by giving the child a message which apparently described one of the cards uniquely: 'I've got a boy riding a tricycle and holding a big flower.' The child picked up his card and compared it with the experimenter's. The experimenter feigned surprise, saying 'Oh, you've got the wrong cards,' and she gathered together the child's cards and began to search for the correct set. As she was doing this, she said 'Whose fault was it we couldn't play properly that time? Why?' She gave the child the correct set of cards, and each player had a few turns at sending messages to each other. In response to this 'Whose fault?' question, the child could blame either the proximal cause of the failure, himself, who had the wrong cards, or the distal cause, the experimenter, who had given him the wrong set. We therefore considered the task to be equivalent to the causal blame attributing component of the communication evaluation game, in which the child can blame either the proximal cause, the listener, who chose wrongly, or the distal cause, the speaker, who gave an inadequate message.

Treatment of results

Description completion task. The child was considered to be successful in the task if he made no more than *one* error throughout. An error could be either completing the description in too general a way ('I've turned over all the men with flowers,' when only the man with the red flower had been turned over) or by completing it too narrowly ('I've turned over all the men with red flowers' when both men had been turned over).

Communication evaluation game. On the basis of their responses to the 'Whose fault?' sequence of questions, which was asked on three occasions, children were placed in four categories, similar to those used in the first experiment: *listener blamers* blamed only the listener for communication failure and judged all the messages to be adequate; *lower intermediates* blamed only the listener but judged at least one message to be inadequate and identified a missing attribute; *higher intermediates* judged at least one message to be inadequate as above and also blamed the speaker at least once on the grounds that the message was inadequate; *speaker blamers* always blamed the speaker on the grounds of message inadequacy, and always judged the message inadequate and identified a missing attribute.

Causality tasks. The child was considered to be successful in this task if he blamed the experimenter for the error on the grounds that it was she who had given him/her the wrong set of cards.

Coding of communication failure. As an indication that an utterance was inadequate for the listener, we took either the listener's subsequent utterance, or the speaker's next utterance following the listener's response or lack of response. Ways of dealing with inadequate utterances were coded into the following categories:

(1) What?/Pardon?/Eh?: these conventional requests for repetition were separated from others (2) since some mothers seemed to respond to their children's utterances with them almost as a matter of course. We thought that if a high proportion of the child's remarks were met with this response it could cease to have any informative value. In fact, children treated in this way generally did continue to repeat their utterances.

(2) Other conventional requests for repetition, e.g. Child: 'The tape' – Mother: '*The what?*'; Child: 'The tape' – Mother: '*Say that again.*'

(3) Repetition of utterance by listener to indicate non-understanding, e.g. Child: 'Daddy not mend his car' – Mother: '*Daddy not mend his car?*' – Child: 'No' – Mother: 'Car's not broken.'

(4) Request for more information, e.g. Child: 'Does it go in that one?' – Mother: '*Which one?*' – Child: 'This one.'

(5) Guess verbalized (correct), e.g. Child: 'This is going to come off' – Mother: 'Your slipper is going to come off?' – Child: 'Yes.'

(6) Guess verbalized (incorrect), e.g. Child: 'That's a lucky colour, Ma. That's a lucky colour' – Mother: 'What is? *Orange?*' – Child: 'No that colour is' – Mother: 'Oh.' (Correct and incorrect guesses were separated because the results of the experiment mentioned above suggested that the child finds

it easier to spot the inadequacy of a message if the listener guesses incorrectly rather than correctly.)

(7) Alternative meanings made explicit, e.g. Child: 'Not going' – Mother: 'Not going? *Not on holidays? Or the barbers?*' – Child: 'To barbers.'

(8) Reformulation/repetition by speaker, e.g. Child: 'Cake please' – Mother: 'What sort do you want?' – Child: 'cake cake' – Mother: 'Well you can help yourself. *I said which sort would you like?*'

(9) Instructions, e.g. Child: 'When Tarzan go in the jungle and he lives in a hole and he chops the trees down' – Mother: 'When what? *Say it a bit slower.* I didn't catch that' – Child: 'When Tarzan's in a hole.'

(10) 'Do you mean . . .?' or 'You mean . . .?' followed by correct guess, e.g. Child: Can I draw on it?' – Mother: 'The counting book you mean? Is that what you mean?' – Child: 'Can I draw on it?' – Mother: 'No.'

(11) Explicit statement of non-understanding, e.g. Child: 'Where put eyes?' – Mother: 'What do you mean "Where d'you put your eyes"?' – Mother: 'I don't know what you're on about.' Mother: 'What do you mean?'

Instances of these 11 types were coded separately for mother and child. Only category (11) was expected to be associated with the child's understanding about communication failure.

The earliest mother–child interaction transcripts to be coded were those made when the child was two years old. For 18 of the children, transcripts of the next six recordings were coded (that is, three-monthly recordings until the age of three and a half years) and finally a recording made shortly before the child entered school. For the remaining children one or more of the transcripts was missing: for 13 children there were seven available, for four of them there were six, and for one child there were five.

RESULTS

Description completion and causality tasks

Two of the lower intermediates failed on the description completion task; all the other children were successful. One listener blamer and one lower intermediate failed the causality test; all the others were successful. We included these two tests to provide a possible means of accounting for children who were given explicit information about communication failure but who had apparently not benefited from it: it could have been because they could not handle the necessary comparisons or causal analyses. However, since none of our listener blamers and lower intermediates had received explicit information according to the transcripts (see below), there was no need to take into account their failures on the description completing and causality tasks.

Mothers' ways of dealing with communication failures

There were only three pure listener blamers: there appeared to be no differences between them and the lower intermediates in maternal ways of dealing with communication failure, so for the purposes of analyses these two blame categories were combined. Similarly, there were only six pure speaker blamers; they were combined with the higher intermediates. Hence the groups compared in the analysis below consisted of those who always blamed the listener only, and those who blamed the speaker at least once on the grounds of message inadequacy. The mean number of each way of dealing with communication failures in the two groups is shown in Table 3.

Table 3 *Total and mean frequency of occurrence of each way of dealing with communication failure among mothers of children in different blame categories*

Way of dealing with failure	Listener blamers and lower intermediates ($N = 10$)			Speaker blamers and higher intermediates ($N = 26$)		
	Total	Mean	n^*	Total	Mean	n^*
(1) What?	97	9.7	10	340	13.0	25
(2) Repetition request	15	1.5	5	46	1.8	16
(3) Repetition to indicate non-understanding	3	0.3	3	9	0.3	8
(4) Request for more information	49	4.9	10	97	3.7	25
(5) Correct guess verbalized	23	2.3	7	63	2.4	19
(6) Incorrect guess verbalized	4	0.4	3	10	0.4	9
(7) Alternative meanings made explicit	1	0.1	1	2	0.1	2
(8) Reformulation/repetition by speaker	3	0.3	3	9	0.3	6
(9) Instruction	1	0.1	1	4	0.2	4
(10) 'Do you mean' followed by guess	1	0.1	1	4	0.2	4
(11) Explicit statement of non-understanding	0	0	0	19	0.7	16
Total	197	19.7		603	23.2	

$^*n$ is the number of children whose mothers used each way.

(1) The two groups did not differ in the total number of communication failures dealt with (Mann–Whitney $U = 116$, $z = -0.49$, $p = 0.6$).

(2) The two groups did not differ in the number of different ways used by

each mother to deal with communication failures (S test, $z = 1.59, p = 0.1$) (Ferguson, 1965).

(3) For each of the eleven ways of dealing with communication failure, there were no differences between age groups in the frequency of occurrence, with one exception: see (4) below.

(4) Explicit statements of non-understanding (11) occurred *only* among the higher intermediates and speaker blamers. As shown in Table 3, there were 19 occurrences in all; these were distributed among 16 children. While none of the 10 listener blamers and lower intermediates' mothers gave their children this kind of information, 16 of the 26 higher intermediates and speaker blamers' mothers did so on at least one occasion ($\chi^2 = 9.35$, $p < 0.01$).

Children's ways of dealing with communication failures

The total and, where appropriate, mean number of ways of dealing with communication failures by children in the two blame groups is shown in Table 4.

Table 4 *Total and mean frequency of occurrence of each way of dealing with communication failure among children in different blame categories*

	Ways of dealing with failure	Listener blamers and lower intermediates ($N = 10$)			Speaker blamers and higher intermediates ($N = 10$)		
		Total	Mean	n^*	Total	Mean	n^*
(1)	What?	61	6.1	10	199	7.6	25
(2)	Repetition request				3	0.1	3
(3)	Repetition to indicate non-understanding				3	0.1	3
(4)	Request for more information	10	1.0	5	40	1.5	17
(5)	Correct guess verbalized	3	0.3	2	20	0.8	12
(6)	Incorrect guess verbalized						
(7)	Alternative meanings made explicit						
(8)	Reformulation/repetition by speaker	1	0.1	1	9	0.3	6
(9)	Instruction						
(10)	'Do you mean?' followed by guess				4	0.1	3
(11)	Explicit statement of non-understanding				2	0.1	2
	Total	75	7.5		280	10.8	

$^*n$ is the number of children who used each way.

The blame groups differed significantly in the total number of initiatives taken, with speaker blamers and higher intermediates more frequently attempting to deal with communication failure than listener blamers and lower intermediates (S test, $z = 1.93$, $p = 0.05$). Speaker blamers and higher intermediates were more likely than listener blamers and lower intermediates to say What?/Pardon?/Eh? (S test, $z = 2.0$, $p = 0.04$). There were no significant differences in the frequency of occurrence of any of the other ways of dealing with communication failure, although it can be seen from Table 4 that only speaker blamers and higher intermediates referred explicitly to meaning; only they showed ways (10) and (11) of dealing with communication failure.

Other variables

Social class. Wells used a composite index for social class: education of each parent was given a value of 4 or 2 where 4 meant leaving at minimum legal age and 2 something higher; the Registrar General's 5 point scale from 1 to 5 (lowest) was used for occupation. Scores for each parent were combined so that 6–9 = A, 10–13 = B, 14–15 = C, 16–18 = D. Table 5 shows the distribution by social class categories A–D of the children in the two blame groups who received no explicit information about message inadequacy and speaker blamers and higher intermediates who did receive such information. There was no relationship between social class and category of blame ($z = 0.36$, $p = 0.7$) and none between social class and the giving of explicit information among speaker blamers and higher intermediates ($z = 0.05$, $p = 0.9$) .

Table 5 *Distribution by social class of children in the different blame categories given explicit information and given no explicit information*

| Social class | Listener blamers and lower intermediates | Speaker blamers and higher intermediates | |
		No explicit information	Explicit information
A	4	2	5
B	2	3	2
C	1	2	5
D	3	3	4

Level of development of child's speech. It is possible that whether or not mothers gave their children explicit information about inadequate messages was dependent upon the level of the child's language development. The mean length of structured utterances (i.e. omitting single words or phrases used by the child as single words) has been calculated by the Wells team for both child and mother on each recording session. Wells presents evidence that this measure is a good indicator of general linguistic development until about the age of three and a half years. We analysed MLU (structured) at age two and a quarter years and also at three and a half years and found no differences between children in the two blame groups not given explicit information, nor between the speaker blamers and higher intermediates who were given and not given explicit information. The same comparisons were made of mothers' speech; again no differences were found.

DISCUSSION AND CONCLUSIONS

The results showed mothers of children in the two blame groups did not differ significantly in the total number of communication failures dealt with. Neither did these mothers differ in the range of ways of dealing with communication failures. There was, however, one significant and important difference between mothers of the more and less advanced children: it was only the mothers of the more advanced children who explicitly told their children that they did not understand or did not know what the child meant. Both groups of mothers were equally likely to extract information missing from a child's utterance by asking a question, to ask the child for a repetition, to verbalize and guess, correctly or incorrectly, about what the child meant, and to preface a correct guess by saying 'Do you mean . . .' or 'You mean . . .'. We suggest that the more implicit ways of dealing with communication failure are less effective ways (and perhaps wholly ineffective) of informing the child that his listener did not understand his original utterance than is an explicit statement of non-understanding.

There were no children in the less advanced group whose mothers provided explicit information about non-understanding in the speech samples examined. This is consistent with a conclusion that such provision is a sufficient condition for the child's development, but that would be a premature inference. It should be noted that none of the more advanced children failed the tests of handling distal causes and being able to make the necessary comparisons, which we had previously found to be necessary but not sufficient for coming to understand about the role of the message in communicative effectiveness (Robinson and Robinson, 1978b, c), and these are clearly intellectual pre-requisites of such understanding. However, taken in conjunction with the observation that adults so rarely appear to explain to children how ambiguity in the message can lead to communication failure, we can suggest that as a matter of fact many children could develop the understanding earlier if they were simply afforded the explicit opportunity to learn as exemplified in this study.

Ten children in the sample had developed this understanding, whose transcripts contained no record of earlier explicit statement. Since such records occurred only once in the transcripts for the majority of the other 16 advanced children, it is certainly possible that some or all of the ten mothers had provided such information, but that the infrequent time-sampling procedure adopted had not picked up such occasions. A second possibility is that these children received explicit information from a person other than the mother and outside the home. A third possibility is that at least some of the ten children attained their advanced state of understanding about communication without having received explicit information about their listener's non-understanding. However, we were not able to detect any other differences between the behaviour of the mothers of the children in the two blame groups. But there may be ways of helping the child to understand about communication which were not apparent to us from analyses of the transcripts.

An additional result of interest is that the children who were more advanced at the age of six were already, in their preschool years, handling communication failure differently from their less advanced peers: they were more likely to attempt to deal with such failures and more likely to say 'What?' 'Pardon?' or 'Eh?' Perhaps more extended sampling would have shown further differences.

We may also note that most of the children who received explicit information about their listener's non-understanding did so on only one occasion in the transcripts. It could be that a relatively infrequent incidence of such explanations is optimal for the facilitation of early understanding. While a zero incidence offers no opportunity of learning by this means, a high frequency might be of no benefit and could be harmful. Repetition of explanations which are beyond a child's conceptual grasp are by definition futile, and frequently telling him in detail about the inadequacies of his attempts to communicate could discourage him from making attempts to communicate. They could also distract him from attending to the substance of his communicative acts; the young child is unlikely to be able to process information about both the topic and the process of communication contemporaneously.

GENERAL CONCLUSIONS

The results of both investigations provide evidence of relationships between understanding about communication and communicative performance *per se*. More central to the main purposes of the studies, both imply that informing the child explicitly about the connections between inadequate messages and communication failure helps him to understand about communication. Taken together the studies illustrate the advantages of combining controlled experiments with naturally based data. The experiment showed that understanding *could* be accelerated by providing explicit information. The analysis of naturally occurring mother–child interaction is consistent with an interpretation that this understanding *is* in fact accelerated by providing explicit information. It

will be instructive to see whether similar complementary sets of experi
and natural development data can be obtained in respect of other i
aspects of understanding about communication, such as asking questic ...i
the face of uncertainty (Cosgrove and Patterson, 1978) and attending to
differences when sending messages (Whitehurst and Sonnenschein, 1981).

It may be that the listener's use of 'I don't know what you mean' helps the
child to clarify the distinction between his intended meaning and the formulation of that meaning in a particular message. Without such a distinction
between intended meaning and message, the child cannot handle the fact that
there are a number of possible forms a message might take; he cannot understand the problem of choice of wording. A distinction between intended
meaning and message underlies understanding of message ambiguity, in that
to avoid message ambiguity the message must refer uniquely for the listener to
whatever the speaker has in mind. It may be then that children are helped to
understand about message ambiguity if it is pointed out to them when a
message has not uniquely identified the speaker's intended meaning for a
particular listener. The results of both investigations are consistent with this
suggestion.

9.

On asking children bizarre questions

Martin Hughes and Robert Grieve

One of the most frequently used methods of assessing children's knowledge, whether at home, in the classroom, or in the developmental laboratory is to ask them questions. In the question and answer process, we usually make certain assumptions. For example, when we ask a child a question, then we expect that the correct answer will be forthcoming should the child have the requisite knowledge. If the child does not have the requisite knowledge, then he may simply decline to answer the question ('I don't know'), or else proffer an answer whose incorrect nature reveals his lack of knowledge. By this means, we attempt to gauge the extent of children's abilities, and their levels of intellectual and linguistic skills. The present reading describes a study whose results constitute a challenge to our usual view of the question and answer process. When children were presented with questions intended to be unanswerable (e.g. 'Is milk bigger than water?', 'Is red heavier than yellow?'), they almost invariably provided answers. The fact is, children are well practised if not ingenious at trying to make sense of situations, and their propensity to answer questions – however bizarre – requires us to re-examine what we assume to be happening when we ask children questions.

INTRODUCTION

In the study of cognitive and linguistic development it is a commonplace procedure to ask children questions. Yet it is remarkable how little we understand of this interrogative process.

What happens when we ask a child a question? While a full answer to this question is not available, the present paper reports novel information on one aspect of the process. Namely, when presented by an adult with a question, children will locate an answer for the adult's question *even if that question is conceptually ill-formed.*

Usually, of course, when adults ask children questions, these questions are intended to be perspicuous. Their meaning, at least to an adult, is intended to be clear, and the child's answer is frequently used to gauge his cognitive/ linguistic understanding. However, it is becoming increasingly clear that the gap between questions as adults present them (intended questions), and questions as children respond to them (received questions), is wider than is often supposed (McGarrigle, Grieve and Hughes, 1978).

But how wide is this gap? One way of considering this problem is to present to children questions intended to be bizarre: i.e. unanswerable as they stand. If children demur at attempting to answer such questions, this will indicate that children consider the conceptual well-formedness of what they are asked. But if children do not demur, and attempt to answer bizarre questions, then we will need to reconsider what we think is happening when we present children with questions in studies of their cognitive/linguistic development.

In what follows, we first describe what happens when bizarre questions were presented, in an informal way, to a number of children of different ages. We then describe a study where several bizarre questions were presented in a more systematic way to two groups of children, aged five and seven years.

Informal observations

If young children are presented with bizarre questions, such as: 'One day there were two flies crawling up a wall. Which one got to the top first?', it might be expected that they will be bamboozled, or amused. But when five-year-old children were presented with this question, they replied. And their replies, for example: 'The big one,' were deadpan. (We owe this observation to G. P. T. Finn.) When we presented a different bizarre question to another child, Sally (six years, eight months), we asked 'Is red wider than yellow?' '*Yes*', she replied. 'Why?' '*Because yellow's thinner than red.*' We then presented these two questions to Jenny (five years, eight months). To the 'flies' question she replied: '*The one on the left.*' That bamboozled us, and we had to ask: 'Why?' '*Because he's the biggest.*' For the 'red wider than yellow' question, she repeated it: '*Is red whiter than yellow?*' 'No, not whiter, *wider*. Which is widest, red or yellow?' '*Red*' 'Why?' '*Because it's got more colour.*' 'What about yellow and blue – which is the widest one?' '*Blue.*' 'Why?' '*It's darker.*'

To the 'colour' questions, Jenny's responses seem based on saturation – the more highly saturated member of the pair is judged to be 'wider' because it has 'more colour', or is 'darker', than the other. (And note that the responses do not seem a function of Jenny's initial mishearing of 'wider' and 'whiter', for then we would expect her choices to have been the opposite). However responses to bizarre questions involving colour do not invariably involve appeal to their relative saturation. When Alison (six years, nine months) was asked a different bizarre question: 'Which is bigger, red or yellow?' she initially looked baffled, then looked around the room and said: '*Yellow.*' When asked why, she pointed to two objects in the room and said: '*Cos that red cushion there is smaller than that yellow curtain there.*' A similar response was given by Sarah (five years, four months), who was asked the 'red bigger than yellow' question out of doors, near a colourful boating pond. Again the child searched for and compared two differently sized objects of the specified colours.

When such bizarre questions were presented to Andrew (four years, eleven months) he replied to the 'flies' question, '. . . Which one got to the top first?' '*The first one.*' 'Why did he get to the top first?' '*Because he started first, silly.*' To the 'red wider than yellow' question he replied: '*Red,*' but would give no justification other than '*Just because.*'

Fiona (seven years, two months) gave a different response to the 'red wider than yellow' question (the 'flies' question was not presented). First she did the same as Jenny, mishearing 'wider' as 'whiter': '*Which is the whitest?*' 'No, not whiter, WIDER. Which is the widest one?' (These 'wider' questions were presented to Jenny and Fiona by the same adult, whose pronunciation of 'wider' was probably indistinct. Note that both children spontaneously re-iterated the question, presumably to provide an opportunity for the adult to confirm that they had got the question right. It is of course not clear that they misheard the question. Possibly they did hear 'wider', but supposed that 'whiter' must have been intended, especially in a question involving colours, and where 'wider' taken as 'wider' is bizarre.) '*Oh, is red "wider" than yellow? What do you mean?*' 'Which is the widest, red or yellow?' '*I don't known what you mean. Do you mean when they are written down, is red or yellow longer on the page?*'

These informal observations suggest that children do tend to provide answers to bizarre questions. However they justify or implicitly justify their responses in various ways. Sometimes they use linguistic knowledge (e.g., Sally utilizes her knowledge that 'thinner' is opposite to 'wider'); sometimes they utilize extralinguistic knowledge or knowledge of objects in the environment (big flies travel faster than flies that are not so big; or colours can be distinguished on the basis of their relative saturation; or a yellow object in the immediate environment is identified as being bigger than a red object); and sometimes an aspect of the language leads into an extralinguistic justification (e.g., Andrew's reply to 'Which fly got to the top *first*' was 'The *first* one' which '. . . started *first*'). Thus these children provide answers to these bizarre questions by importing various sorts of knowledge to the situation. While the oldest child does not conform to this pattern in one sense – she is the only child to make explicit that the meaning of the question is not immediately clear – in another sense she does, for having made explicit the obscurity in the meaning of the question, note how she immediately tries to establish one: 'I don't know what you mean. Do you mean . . .'

To consider this phenomenon further, the following study was undertaken, where larger numbers of children were asked several bizarre questions in less informal circumstances.

EXPERIMENT

Different types of bizarre questions were presented to groups of five- and seven-year-old children, in their usual school setting.

Subjects

A group of eight five-year-olds (four male, four female; mean age five years, four months, range four years, eleven months to five years, ten months), and a group of eight seven-year-olds (four male, four female; mean age seven years, seven months, range seven years, three months to seven years, eleven months) were studied. These children knew the adult experimenter, having worked with him on a different, unrelated experiment a week to ten days previously.

Materials

Four questions, each intended to be bizarre, were prepared: (1) *Is milk bigger than water?* (2) *Is red heavier than yellow?* (3) *One day there were two flies crawling up a wall. Which fly got to the top first?* (4) *One day there were two people standing at a bus-stop. When the bus came along, who got on first?*

These questions are intended to be bizarre in the sense that they do not permit direct answers. This is so for different reasons. (1) and (2) are intended to involve 'category mistakes', and a reasonable response might be to say: 'I don't know what you mean,' and request further clarification. The meaning of (3) and (4) on the other hand is perfectly clear, but a reasonable response might be to say: 'I don't know,' and request further information.

It is of course difficult to be certain that a question intended to be bizarre is received as such. For example, linguistic philosophers suggest it would be a category mistake to predicate time or place of number. But we have all heard both, not only predicated, but bellowed, of number – for example at boating lakes where small craft are rented by the hour: 'Come in, Number Four, your time is up.' Or, home decorators' manuals may describe certain combinations of colours as being 'too heavy'; and we are familiar with red, orange and yellow being described as 'warm colours', compared with 'cold colours' such as blue and green. Further, (3) and (4) perhaps become more acceptable with slight modifications – e.g. 'If several people were standing at a bus stop, when the bus came along which one would we expect to get on first?' The present questions are intended to be bizarre in the sense that they cannot be answered directly. As they stand, they require clarification of their meaning ((1) and (2)), or the provision of additional information ((3) and (4)), before they can be answered.

Procedure

Children were tested individually by the same experimenter. Adult and child sat at a table on which lay some papers, including a sheet on which the adult noted the child's responses, but there were no toys or pictures to be looked at. The adult simply said: 'Listen, is milk bigger than water?' or whatever. The questions were always presented in the order: (1), (3), (2), (4). If the child failed to give a response, or said 'Don't know,' the question was repeated once. If the child gave a response without justifying it (e.g. 'Is red heavier than yellow?' '*Yes*'), he was asked 'Why?'

RESULTS

We wish to know whether children answered these bizarre questions; how they answered them; whether there were any differences between different types of question; and whether there were any differences between children of different ages. Before summarizing on these points, we first describe the responses given.

(1) *Is milk bigger than water?*

Of the eight younger children, only one child failed to respond (he was the youngest, aged four years, eleven months). Instead he grinned at this, and every other question, saying '*I don't know*,' or '*No idea*,' or '*Don't know, never tried it before*.' (This calls to mind Brendan Behan's story (Behan, 1963) about the new assistant in a Dublin bookshop who was asked if she liked Kipling. 'How could I know,' she replied, 'when I never kippilled.') Of the remaining seven, one said they were the same, and the other six said: '*Yes*.' When asked why, most responses were either in terms of the origins of the liquids (e.g. water comes out of taps, and milk comes out of either cows or bottles), or in terms of their extension (e.g. there is more milk than water when you pour them into bottles). Only one child said that milk was bigger because it was 'heavy'.

All the older children gave a response. However there were two immediately apparent differences in the responses given. First, the older children were more likely to respond in terms of the characteristics of the liquids themselves – e.g. milk is bigger '*because it's got a colour*', or "*cos it's more creamier*', or because '*milk is heavier*', or '*because it's more thicker*'.

We will refer to this distinction in terms of the extent to which the children *import context* into their replies. While five of the younger children import context into their replies, talking about where the liquids originate, or what happens when they are poured into containers, only two of the older children do so. Rather than importing additional context, the older children are more likely to remain with the objects referred to in the question, commenting on inherent characteristics such as their colour, texture, or weight.

But the more obvious difference between the younger and older children is that the latter tend to qualify their responses in some way, using phrases such as 'I think' (e.g. '*I think milk's bigger than water*') or, more frequently, by replying with questions, which range from: '*Eh?*' to '*Milk is heavier, isn't it?*' or '*Is it because it's more thicker?*' or '*Milk, I think. "Bigger" did you say?*' Six of the older children gave what we will call 'qualified responses' of this sort, but none of the younger children did so.

(2) *Is red heavier than yellow?*

Seven five-year-olds gave replies as did all of the seven-year-olds. An interesting response in the younger group was initially obscure: 'Is red heavier than yellow?' '*Yes.*' '*Why?*' '*Because there's much more red than yellow.*' '*Why?*' '*Because there's water in it.*' 'There's water in what?' '*The paint.*' The explanation becomes clear from another child: '*Yellow is a little. Yellow's got a little plastic box and the red paint's got a big plastic box.*' In school, the children use powdered paint which is mixed with water in plastic containers. So if there is more red than yellow, red *is* heavier! (So much for intentions; and so much for category mistakes.)

Only one of the younger children responded in terms of the characteristics of the colours themselves, rather than the characteristics of the paints which may be mixed using these colours: '*Red's heavier than yellow.*' (Why?) '*Yellow's not bright and red is.*' This sort of response was quite common in the older children: red is heavier '*Because it's darker*' (twice), or '*Cos it's more darker,*' or because '*Red's a darker colour than yellow*' (twice).

So there is again a difference between the groups in the extent to which they import context: the older children tend not to, confining their justifications to a difference between the colours themselves (such as saturation), while the younger children do tend to import additional context, concerned with a situation such as mixing paints from such colours, and referring to attributes such as the size, weight and water content of the containers.

The consistency with which the children responded to this presented colour question in terms of saturation merits further inquiry. Possibly, saturation is a more important characteristic of colours than brightness or hue with young children (R. N. Campbell, personal communication). In the present study, the children's recourse to saturation in response to the presented colour question is certainly very consistent.

There is also a difference in the extent to which the groups qualify their responses, but the distinction is not so marked as in (1). One of the older children says: '*I think red's just as heavy as yellow*', one says: '*Yes, I think so,*' and one is explicit in his question-as-answer: '*Red . . . Was it "heavier"?*'

The reduction in the extent to which the older children qualify their responses may be due to an order effect – recall that question (2) was in fact the third question, presented, and the children may be learning that when their replies, initially given in a tentative manner, are accepted by the adult, there is no need to continue to qualify them.

(3) *Which fly got to the top first?*

All children answered this question, save the youngest child. Four of the five-year-olds initially said they did not know, but then replied when the question was repeated.

Differences between the groups, in terms of imported context and qualification of response, are not now apparent. One of the younger children imported context, saying that the fly who reached the top first was: '*The first one. 'Cos that was the one leading the other one, taking the other one up.*' One of the older children did likewise, saying: '*The left one.*' (Why?) '*He flew up.*' (And the other one?) '*He crawled up.*'

Otherwise children from both groups replied in terms of the situation described in the question, and responses concerned characteristics of the fly who arrived first: '*The biggest one. Because he got the longest legs,*' or because '*He went more faster,*' or because he was the one who '*thought of it first,*' or because '*He started first,*' or because he was '*the one that had been drinking milk ... Milk makes you stronger.*' (Note that (3) was presented just after (1)). Alternatively, responses concerned the relative location of the two flies; the one who got to the top first was: '*The one nearest the top,*' or the one who was '*nearly at the top.*' Thus appeal was mostly made to the fly's size, length of legs, or strength; to his speed; to his time of departure; or to his place of departure. Importing other factors into the situation was rare.

There was also no qualification of responses, in either group. The 'I think it was the big one,' or 'Was it the big one?' types of response were not observed.

(4) *Who got on (the bus) first?*

The youngest child remained amused. All other children gave a response. As with (3), there was no qualification of responses.

Two of the younger children imported context, saying that the person who got on first was '*The one who was taking the other one,*' or '*The mummy* (taking the child),' as did one of the older children, saying that the stronger person got on first because he had been drinking milk, and was stronger than the other one who had been drinking water. (Note this child's use of elements from a previous question, (1). Here, with question (4), the elements do not work well, for we have to conjure up a primaeval struggle at the bus-stop. But they do work well in her answer to the 'flies' question (3), where the stronger one got to the top first. This phenomenon – importing as context elements from previous questions – may have occurred elsewhere, though not so clearly. For example, to what extent do the judgements that red is heavier than yellow because of relative water content in the paints arise from the fact that the children have previously been dealing with water in question (1): where it comes from, how it is used (poured into containers), and so on?).

However there was a difference between the two groups, related to their appeal to a rule which might be expected to hold in the circumstances of the question – namely, rules of queuing. For example, the person who got on first was '*The one there first,*' or '*The one who got there first. The one at the front of the line,*' or this rule was over-ridden by another concerning good manners: '*The lady*' (Why?) '*Because ladies should go first before men.*' This sort of response was utilized by only two of the younger children, but by five of the older ones. The remainder replied in terms of the person who was '*Nearest the bus,* or who '*Saw the bus come first.*'

These observations are summarized in Table 1, which shows the number of responses given to the four questions, whether these responses were qualified, and whether context was imported to the situation in the ways indicated above (the maximum entry in any cell is 8).

Table 1 *Responses to bizarre questions*

| | Five-year-olds | | | Seven-year-olds | | |
Question	Responses given	Responses qualified	Context imported	Responses given	Responses qualified	Context imported
(1) Milk	7	0	5	8	6	2
(2) Red	7	0	4	8	3	1
Total	14	0	9	16	9	3
(3) Flies	7	0	1	8	0	1
(4) Bus-stop	7	0	2	8	0	1
Total	14	0	3	16	0	2
Totals	28	0	12	32	9	5

DISCUSSION

The results are reasonably clear. When presented with questions intended to be bizarre – questions which cannot be answered directly without clarification of meaning (CM questions) or provision of further information (PI questions) – young children almost invariably provide replies. Younger five-year-old children frequently do so by importing additional context to the situation, expecially with CM questions, but older seven-year-old children are less likely to do this, tending instead to remain with characteristics of the elements referred to in the questions, or appealing to rules which might be expected to apply in the situation to which the question refers. The other major difference between the groups is that while the older children frequently qualify their responses in some way, indicating uncertainty, the younger children never do so. The result of this paper, that young children answer questions even if these questions are bizarre, confirms the previously mentioned finding of G.P.T. Finn. It is also akin to results detectable in the data of other studies.

For example, in a study of three- and four-year-olds' understanding of prepositions, Wales (1974) presented children with a toy doll and a toy house, and instructed them to: 'Put the doll *in/on/at* the house.' To estimate whether the children had any response bias, Wales also presented this instruction without any preposition, namely: 'Put the doll the house.' The great majority of children made a response to this anomalous instruction, failures to respond being very infrequent (4 per cent). It can also be noted that this result is not restricted to children from but one culture, speaking but one language – Wales's study was conducted with Scottish children speaking English, Indian children speaking Tamil, and Bornean children speaking Lun-Bawang. Children also respond to sentences made anomalous, not through deletion of an element as in Wales's study, but through substitution of a nonsense-term for a term in the language. Carey (1978) asked three- and four-year-old children to play a game where they had to give a puppet *more*, or *less*, tea to drink. When she asked the children to give the puppet *tiv* tea to drink, over half the children responded to this anomalous request without comment – some children gave additional tea, some reduced the amount of tea, some stirred the tea, some pretended to drink the tea themselves, and so forth. Children will also respond to questions where the meaning of terms may be to them obscure. In a study of young children's understanding of homonyms (words with the same sound, but different meanings, as in *key* and *quay*, Campbell and Bowe (1977) found that three- and four-year-olds would attempt to interpret such homonyms, even though their interpretations mights be grotesque in relation to the rest of the context. For example, if the children knew the *key*, but not the *quay*, sense of the homonym, the term might be grotesque in relation to the rest of the context. For example, if the the context. Thus the child might envisage someone visiting the seaside, going for a walk along a key, seeing a rubber boy floating in the water, and so on.

These observations on the data of other studies extend the present result. Young children not only provide answers to questions that are bizarre: they do the same for questions whose terms' intended meaning may be obscure (Campbell and Bowe, 1977), and for questions which are anomalous in various ways (Carey, 1978, Wales, 1974).

Why young children do this is not clear. It may be a characteristic of the exchange of discourse that, other things being equal (e.g. where conversational maxims such as those considered by Grice (1975) may be supposed to apply), the participants at least try to afford each other's utterances meaning, or at least suppose that each other's utterances are intended to have meaning. The task in discourse is thus not so much to *decide whether* the other's utterances have meaning, but to *identify what* his meanings are. This characteristic of human discourse may be fundamental, and can be observed in mothers 'communicating' with their infants long before the child is capable of understanding language, far less producing it (Bruner, 1974; Trevarthen, 1974).

But if we do not know why children provide answers for bizarre questions, the present paper indicates that this is what children usually do. That they do so, for the sort of bizarre questions presented here, either in terms of the information presented in the question, or by importing additional context into the situation, suggests that the child does assume that the questions are intended to have meaning, and that his task is to identify meaning in what has been said to him.

The observation that children seek to interpret questions that are bizarre, seems at first sight an extraordinary finding. Yet we wonder whether it is as extraordinary as it appears. Perhaps making something of whatever information is presented to him, or that information supplemented by imported information, is what the child has to do most, if not all, of the time. Recall that he must be well used to such a task, for when he is younger and still acquiring the language, the meaning of much of what is said to him cannot be immediately transparent. We know that when language is still being acquired, the young child derives meaning not simply from aspects of the language itself, but also from his knowledge of the extralinguistic contexts to which the language refers – his knowledge of objects in the environment, how these customarily are, or should be, related, and so on (Grieve, Hoogenraad and Murray, 1977). We have suggested elsewhere that the young child's early comprehension of language should be viewed as a process concerned with how, from the child's point of view, such elements of linguistic and extra-linguistic context interact (Hoogenraad, Grieve, Baldwin and Campbell, 1978). What the present paper suggests is that later cognitive and linguistic development might well be viewed in a similar light. Thus presenting five- and seven-year-olds with bizarre questions may simply simulate what he has been used to at an earlier age; and his interpretation of these bizarre questions may simply represent the child's practice of a familiar, well-established skill.

Thus the child's propensity to answer questions, even if they are intended to be unanswerable, may not be as startling as might at first be supposed. Nevertheless, the fact that the child will attempt to locate an answer to whatever question he is presented with has significant implications for what we think is happening when we attempt to gauge the young child's cognitive/linguistic abilities by means of the question and answer process.

Psychologists and linguists – and all others who rely on questioning young children – can no longer treat the child as merely a passive recipient of questions and instructions, but must instead start to view the child as someone who is actively trying to make sense of the situation he is in – however bizarre it may seem.

10.

Text and context in early language comprehension*

Robin N. Campbell and Theresa Bowe Macdonald

The previous reading showed that children may treat nonsensical questions seriously and struggle to find some basis on which to answer them. The authors, Hughes and Grieve, took this as evidence that children have a general tendency to try to make sense of what is said to them, however odd it may seem.

There can be no doubt that this tendency is a very strong one. We should also recognize, however, that there are at least some circumstances in which the effort to make sense seems to be abandoned. In the next reading, Campbell and Macdonald describe a study concerning words that sound the same but have two distinct meanings like 'branch' (branch of a tree or branch of a bank) or 'hair' and 'hare'. When Campbell and Macdonald told children stories containing the less familiar members of such pairs of terms (e.g. 'hare'), one third of the children based their interpretations on the more familiar meanings (e.g. 'hair'), with grotesque results, which did not seem to trouble them. We must therefore acknowledge that, alongside the desire to make sense of things, there may also be observed in children a certain capacity to accept and tolerate the nonsensical.

Campbell and Macdonald interpret their results in terms of the relation between text and context. By 'text' they mean the actual words – spoken or written – which are being interpreted. By 'context' they mean any other knowledge used by the person who is constructing the interpretation. It is, of course, context which enables us to decide which of two possible senses of a word is the 'right' one – the one which the speaker or author intended.

Children are generally much influenced by context and highly skilled at using it. Campbell and Macdonald's results remind us, however, that their success in doing so is not unvarying. And when they fail to make good use of context, they may go wildly wrong.

Understanding is a mysterious process in which the information carried by an utterance or inscription – by units of *text* – is adapted to and integrated with the listener's knowledge based on prior discourse and the current situation – a complex structure which we will refer to, rather globally, as a *context*. The outcome of this process is, generally, the reception of what we shall call a

* This paper is closely based on Campbell and Bowe, 1977.

message. The process of adaptation involves the fitting of both text to context and context to text. For the text may guide the listener's attention to elements of his current situation or to aspects of his world knowledge not so far implicated by the preceding discourse, thus modifying the context. Equally, the context may enable the listener to decide between competing interpretations of the text or, indeed, to provide an interpretation of a defective text containing illegible, impossible or unknown elements. Of course, texts are themselves characterized by considerable redundancy, at all linguistics levels, and this redundancy will enable a competent listener to guess the values of illegible, ambiguous or unknown elements with a high probability of success – even without the assistance of context. Thus a listener may be able to make a guess at the intended message on the basis of the text alone. We shall refer to such guesses as *textual projections*. On the other hand, contexts may provide strong indications that a certain message is about to be communicated (think of the mumbling foreigner advancing towards you with oustretched hand). In such cases the 'listener' may be able to guess the intended message on the basis of context alone. We shall refer to this sort of guess as a *contextual projection*.

It therefore appears that in ordinary language comprehension text and context carry out complementary functions and that the processes of textual and contextual projection are symmetrical and interdependent.*

In this paper, we shall be concerned with the understanding of spoken texts containing *ambiguous* words, or *homophones* as they are sometimes called. To make use of an example from Donaldson (1978, p. 17) a child, who is asked by his teacher to 'sit there for the *present*', has been presented with an utterance containing such an element, the homophone *present*. Now it may be that the child knows only one meaning for *present* – 'gift' – or it may be that the second meaning, though known to him, is one that comes less readily to mind, through lack of use. In either case, textual projection will lead him to expect a gift. On the other hand he may be sufficiently apprised of the ways of schools and teachers to know that he is merely being told where to sit: in this case, contextual projection will have carried the day and secured a valid interpretation. In the anecdote recounted by Donaldson, the inappropriate textual projection prevailed and a grave disappointment resulted.

However, when we examine the experimental literature dealing with language comprehension in young children, it seems that if there is any asymmetry in the relationship between the processes of textual and contextual projection, it is *textual* projection that plays a secondary role. For example, a number of studies with quantifiers (Donaldson and Lloyd, 1975; Donaldson and McGarrigle, 1974), relational terms (Donaldson and Balfour, 1968;

---

* This general view of the nature of understanding is hardly original. The first two essays in Ziff (1972) constitute a lengthier and more persuasive presentation of a roughly similar view.

Carey, 1978) and prepositions (Clark, 1973; Hoogenraad *et al.*, 1978) provide striking instances of misunderstanding in preschool children, which are best explained *not* by supposing that the child has assigned wrong values to these terms in analysing the texts containing them, but by supposing that the results of such analyses are insufficient to determine a message and, hence, a response. Consequently, the child is thrown back on the resources of contextual projection, (commonly slender in these experiments) or, failing that, of various standby procedures and response biases in order to produce his response. Moreover, McGarrigle and Donaldson (1976) have argued that in situations such as the number conservation tasks explored by them, where the results of textual and contextual projection conflict (in their terms, where text and context are 'uncoupled'), it is contextual projection which prevails, the results of textual projection being set aside or, at least, distorted.

The dynamical picture which this body of work suggests is one in which the child's knowledge of the context and his expectancies based on that knowledge set inflexible prior limits to the values that may be assigned to texts or elements of texts. The process of comprehension is therefore only partially adaptive and functions accurately only when the value that the speaker *intends* should be assigned to his text falls within these limits. There is thus no significant adjustment of context to text. We shall refer to instances of misunderstanding that arise in this way as cases of *context-based* misunderstanding.

The work that we will present here consists of some observations and an exploratory study which provide evidence that, under certain circumstances, the child's comprehension may exhibit an opposite asymmetry to the one we have just discussed, in which the results of contextual projection are ignored or set aside when they conflict with the results of textual projection. We shall call instances of misunderstanding that arise from *this* sort of process *text-based* misunderstanding. After presenting our results we will discuss, very briefly, the possibility of reconciling our findings with those of the scholars cited above – with whom we are not in disagreement.

Our attention was first drawn to this phenomenon of text-based misunderstanding several years ago when we encountered some very striking responses in a study of botanical vocabulary. These came from three children interviewed in succession under more or less the same circumstances. After 10–15 minutes of interview in which the elements of their botanical vocabularies were elicited and their ranges of application discussed we showed the children a picture of some pine cones on a twig and asked, 'what are these things?' The children's responses and the ensuing discussion are given below:

Observation 1: Michelle (four years, six months)

> *Interviewer*: What are these funny things?
> *Child*: Cones.

Interviewer: Cones. That's funny. Where d'you find cones?
Child: (No response).
Interviewer: Where d'you get cones?
Child: Off-off the cafe.
Interviewer: Off the cafe? What cafe?
Child: (No response).
Interviewer: A cafe that you go to?
Child: Uh-huh.
Interviewer: Whereabouts?
Child: Causewayhead.
Interviewer: Causewayhead? Do they have cones there?
Child: Uh-huh and wafers.
Interviewer: Aaaah! Ice-cream cones.
Interviewer: But these are not ice-cream cones, are they?
Child: No.
Interviewer: What kinds of cones are they?
Child: They're brown cones.
Interviewer: Can you eat them?
Child: No.
Interviewer: Why not?
Child: Because they would poison you and make you dead.

Observation 2: Gillian (four years, three months)

Interviewer: What are these things?
Child: Cones.
Interviewer: Where d'you get cones?
Child: In the shop.
Interviewer: What shop?
Child: Daddy's shop (an ice-cream shop).

Observation 3: Becky (three years, nine months)

Interviewer: What are these things?
Child: Things to go in your hair.
Interviewer: Where do you find things like that?
Child: I don't know.
Interviewer: (Repeated).
   What are these things?
Child: Comb. Comb your hair.

Now, of course, of the various meanings the word *cone* can take in English, undoubtedly 'ice-cream cone' is the one most familiar to young children. The most plausible explanation of the first two observations is then that textual projection of 'Where do you find/get cones?' attaches such a high probability to the meaning 'ice-cream cone' that the information obtainable from contextual projection is ignored, overruled or simply not extracted.

In the case of the third observation a simpler explanation is possible. It could be that this child has observed (at the time of original learning, perhaps) that pine cones exhibit a strong functional similarity to combs, at the same time assimilating the phonetic form (ko:n) to (ko:m). If we allow this assumption, there is no contextual inconsistency attaching to her answer. The cones are simply being identified by means of their mistakenly supposed human function, just as berries might be (correctly) identified by remarking that they are 'things to eat'. The oddity of this observation is then (under this explanation) traced back to an idiosyncratic assimilation at the time of original learning. If we reject this *ad hoc* explanation and look for one along the lines of the explanation offered for the first two observations, then we are little better off, since the story we must tell is an exceedingly unlikely one, namely, that the pine cones elicit the form (ko:m) as a response but that this is too faint or obscure to be retrieved. The link from (ko:m) to 'things to go in your hair' is next excited, being stronger than the link to 'things you find in the woods' – that is to say, favoured by textual projection – and the response produced. Although this type of observation is unreplicable (except by pure luck) we have negative evidence that suggests it is the simpler sort of explanation which is correct. In an attempt to replicate the first type of observation with 14 children of mean age three years, ten months (range three years, two months to five years), and using five ambiguous words (bat, hair/hare, cone, letter, bulb) as 'targets', we obtained 70 responses to questions of the same type as 'Where do you get/find cones?'. In no case did any child produce a response fitting our second, complex explanation of *Observation 3*. On the other hand there were many responses that showed idiosyncratic assimilation, e.g. bats were called *frogs*, *mice*, *owls*; hares were called *kangaroos*; cones were called *flowers* and bulbs (that is, e.g. daffodil bulbs) were called *mushrooms* and *apples*. It therefore seems unlikely that we need to consider this remarkable explanation of *Observation 3* further and that it is the first, simpler explanation which is correct.

In an attempt to show further evidence of text-based misunderstanding at work we carried out another experiment using a sample of 24 children from a local playgroup. The sample contained 14 girls and ten boys, and consisted of three groups of eight children (mean ages three years, eight months, four years, three months and four years, nine months). In this study the children were told the following story:

> One morning, Jane and her Mummy went to see Jane's auntie who works in the post office. She would like to work in the big post office but she works in a *branch*.(1) When they got home it was lunchtime. 'We must set the table,' said Jane's Mummy. 'Can you put the *leaf* up and put the tablecloth on?'(2) That afternoon, Jane and her Mummy and Daddy went for a picnic in the car. As they were driving along they saw a *hare* run across a field.(3) They stopped the car and got out to look but the *hare* had gone. The field was full of corn and they

saw a little mouse sitting on one of the *ears*.(4) Then they got back into the car and drove to the seaside. When they got there they went for a walk along the *quay*.(5) They saw a big *buoy* with orange and white stripes floating in the water. 'What's that *buoy* made of?' asked Jane. 'The *buoy's* made of rubber and full of air,' said her Mummy.(6) The sea was rather rough so they went for a walk in a wood full of fir trees. Underneath the trees were lots of *cones*. They had fallen from the branches.(7) At the far side of the wood was a castle. 'Look at this castle,' said Jane's Daddy. 'The oldest *wing* is over 500 years old.'(8) They went into the castle. It was very dark inside and there were *bats* flying around.(9) Soon they got back into the car to go home. They got held up behind a lot of other cars, all going very slowly. 'I hope we get out of this *jam* soon,' said Jane's Daddy.(10)

The italicized words are all, once again, ambiguous and are used here in their unfamiliar, secondary senses. At the points (1)–(10) in the course of the story the child was questioned in such a way as to establish his understanding of the text containing the ambiguous word. Children were first of all encouraged to draw, or to complete a picture, by drawing 'the hare running across the field' (in this case a drawing of a field was provided) or the like. In each case an interpretation which followed the primary, familiar meaning of the word would be judged as fantastic or grotesque by an adult. That is, a text-based comprehension process is always inadequate and leads to misunderstanding. The children's responses were examined and classified as follows:

(1) *Secondary responses.* These were correct (adult-like) interpretations based on knowledge of the secondary meaning of the word.
(2) *Primary responses.* These were incorrect and grotesque text-based interpretations based upon the primary meaning, e.g.

Observation 4: Caroline (three years, eleven months)

(a) *Interviewer*: Can you draw the hare running across?
Child: (Draws mass of hair).
Interviewer: What does a hare look like?
Child: (Touches hair).
Interviewer: Do you think it would be running across a field?
Child: Yes.
Interviewer: They went for a walk along the quay ... Can you
    draw the quay?
Child: (Drawing obscure).
(b) *Interviewer*: What sort of thing is a quay?
What's a quay for?
Child: For opening doors.
Interviewer: D'you think they could walk along a quay?
Child: (Nods).

Observation 5: Elizabeth (four years, four months)

> *Interviewer*: Can you draw the hare for me?
> *Child*: I can't draw hair.
> *Interviewer*: Why can't you draw it?
> *Child*: Too little.
> *Interviewer*: Why do you think a hare was running across a field?
> *Child*: Don't know.
> *Interviewer*: Have you ever seen a hare run across a field?
> *Child*: (Nods).
> *Interviewer*: What did the hare look like?
> *Child*: Don't know.
> *Interviewer*: What sort of thing is a hare?
> *Child*: (No response).
> *Interviewer*: Where do you normally see hares?
> *Child*: On your head.
> *Interviewer*: D'you think it was a hair from your head running across
>   a field?
> *Child*: Yes.
> *Interviewer*: That's a bit funny, isn't it?
> *Child*: (Nods).

Some representative (and amusing) drawings are shown in Fig. 1.

Responses to the word *buoy* all fell into this category, suggesting that there is no conflict with context in this case. That is, young children may not regard is as odd that a boy should have orange and white stripes, be made of rubber and full of air! Some support for this view is provided by the following case:

Observation 6: Alastair (four years, eight months)

> *Interviewer*: Can you draw the big rubber buoy?
> *Child*: Yeah. There's his body. (Draws – see Fig. 1)
> *Interviewer*: What was the buoy made of?
> *Child*: Rubber.
> *Interviewer*: Do you often get buoys made of rubber?
> *Child*: Yeah. So'm I made of rubber, And there's bones inside there.

(3) *Inventions*. These were contextually-consistent interpretations *not* based on knowledge of the secondary meaning of the word, e.g.:

Observation 7: Lisa (four years)

> *Interviewer*: What did Jane have to do?
> *Child*: Put the tablecloth on.
> *Interviewer*: What did she have to do before she put the tablecloth on?

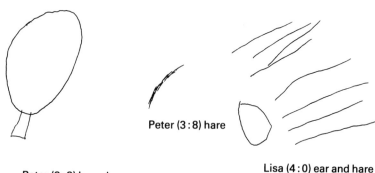

Peter (3:8) branch

Peter (3:8) hare

Lisa (4:0) ear and hare

Andrew (4:10) ear (of corn)

Lisa (4:4) buoy

Alastair (4:8) buoy

Donna (4:7) wing (of castle)

Figure 1

Child: Don't know.
Interviewer: I think she had to put the leaf up.
Child: She put the leaf up.
Interviewer: Do you know what the leaf of the table is?
Child: (No response).
Interviewer: Which bit is that?
Child: The cloth.

(4) *Don't know.* These were uninformative responses of the usual sorts, e.g. *I don't know, I can't remember, no response*, etc.

(5) *Unclassifiable.* There were also interesting subcategories of types (2) and (3), called *blends.* A *primary blend* occurs when the child's interpretation, though text-based, shows some moderating influence of contextual projection, e.g.:

Observation 8: Donna (four years, seven months)

> *Interviewer:* Do you think you could draw the castle?
> *Child:* (Draws – see Fig. 1).
> *Interviewer:* Can you draw the old wing as well?
> *Child:* (No response).
> *Interviewer:* The castle in the story has an old wing.
> *Child:* (Draws).
> *Interviewer:* What do you think the wing was for?
> *Child:* (No response).
> *Interviewer:* Do castles generally have wings?
> *Child:* (Nods).
> *Interviewer:* And what are the wings for?
> *Child:* (No response).
> *Interviewer:* What do you think that wing's made of?
> *Child:* (No response).
> *Interviewer:* (Repeats question).
> *Child:* Wood.
> *Interviewer:* What's the rest of the castle made of?
> *Child:* Stone.
> *Interviewer:* Why's the wing made of wood?
> *Child:* (No response).
> *Interviewer:* Are there lots of rooms in the castle?
> *Child:* (Nods).
> *Interviewer:* How about the wing? Does that have lots of rooms?
> *Child:* (Shakes head)
> *Interviewer:* Why not?
> *Child:* (No response).
> *Interviewer:* What else has wings as well as a castle?
> *Child:* A bird and a bat.
> *Interviewer:* Do you think it's the same sort of wing as the castle had?
> *Child:* (No response).
> *Interviewer:* What sort of wing do you think the castle had?
> *Child:* Wooden.
> *Interviewer:* What are a bird's wings made of?
> *Child:* Feathers.
> *Interviewer:* What are a bat's wings made of?
> *Child:* (No response).

The point about this observation is that Donna insists that the wing should be made of wood rather than feathers, showing (presumably) awareness that it is impossible for a stone building to sprout such an organ from its flanks!

Inventive blends, on the other hand, are contextually consistent but show the influence of the primary meaning of the word, that is, of textual projection. Examples of this kind of response are relatively abundant, e.g. 'snake' and 'grass' as an interpretation for *the hare running across the field*, 'mud' and 'sand' for the traffic *jam*.

This analysis left rather a large number of unclassifiable responses. However, in many cases we could narrow down the possibilities to just two categories. For example, it was quite often the case that a response was evidently either a *secondary* or *invention* but that it was impossible to say which (this occurred particularly with words where the secondary interpretation was guessable with high probability, e.g. *branch, leaf*). Minimally ambiguous cases like these were allocated half to one category and half to the other. The residue of cases formed the fifth category of *unclassifiable* responses. The results of this classification are shown in Table 1.

Table 1 *Incidence of response types by age groups*

	Response types				
Age groups	(1) Secondary	(2) Primary	(3) Invention	(4) Don't know	(5) Unclassifiable
Mean age: four years, nine months	32%	17%	24%	19%	8%
Mean age: four years, three months	18%	40%	11%	27%	4%
Mean age: three years, eight months	23%	33%	8%	13%	23%
All groups	25%	31%	15%	19%	10%

As expected, there are a good many cases (31 per cent) of *primary* responses, confirming the existence of text-based comprehension processes in children of this age. Of course, this figure, although high, is by no means overwhelming: a good many children managed to integrate text and context adaptively. Moreover, there were a small number of cases, increasing across the age-groupings, of successful interpretation which involved *inventive* resolution of the conflict between text and context. An important qualification must be made about such *inventions*: we cannot conclude from a successful invention that the child has learned anything new about the meaning of the word. A good example of this is given below:

Observation 9: Nerissa (three years, eight months)

> *Interviewer*: Where is it that Jane's auntie works?
> *Child*: In the post office.
> *Interviewer*: What sort of post office?
> *Child*: (No response).
> *Interviewer*: Did she work in the big post office?
> *Child*: (Shakes head).
> *Interviewer*: What sort of post office did she work in?
> *Child*: A little one.
> *Interviewer*: It says in the story that she works in a branch. Is that right?
> *Child*: (Shakes head).
> *Interviewer*: Why is that not right?
> *Child*: (No response).
> *Interviewer*: Do you think she could work in a branch?
> *Child*: (Shakes head).
> *Interviewer*: Why not?
> *Child*: Because all her things would fall out.
> *Interviewer*: What would it fall out of?
> *Child*: The branches.
> *Interviewer*: Where are the branches?
> *Child*: On the tree.

Notice that, although Nerissa (a) makes a contextually plausible response and (b) recognizes that a *primary* response is impossible, there is no evidence that she has attached any new value to *branch* as a result of this experience. That is, although there *is* fitting of text to context here, this assimilation is global and not articulated to the extent that the impossible element (*branch*) acquires a new value.

Our discussion of these results will be brief, since our goal here has been simply to establish the existence of a certain sort of misunderstanding. It seems to us that we have shown that young children will, under some circumstances, be guided by their knowledge of words to mistaken interpretations which are strongly in conflict with the current context and with their knowledge of the world. If we consider this type of misunderstanding along with the more familiar sort where contextual projection leads them to a message which is inconsistent with the text, it may be concluded that what is characteristic of the young child is a difficulty in integrating the two processes of textual and contextual projection, *on the relatively rare occasions when they yield conflicting results*. It is important to grasp the point that in our demonstrations, just as in those by the other scholars referred to above, it is only by contrivance that the child's comprehension is made to fail. In general, it may be very efficient to favour the stronger projection, be it textual or contextual. After all, there must be many occasions in the life of a child when his contextual expectations are weak or absent and where he *must* be guided by his understanding of our words.

Equally there will be many occasions where our words are *not* understood and he must be guided by contextual projection. A child who stopped short of inferring a message whenever the information available to him from textual or contextual projection was deficient or conflicting would require frequent instruction and supporting explanation. It is plain that young children are *not* like this. Rather, they enthusiastically construct messages in the most un-promising circumstances. Accordingly, the sorts of misunderstanding that we and the other scholars referred to earlier have uncovered are perhaps to be regarded as the inevitable consequence of what is, from the point of view of parent or teacher, an extraordinarily efficient system of communication.

11.

Talking with children: the complementary roles of parents and teachers

Gordon Wells

During the last ten years, Wells and his colleagues have collected a large amount of data on aspects of children's language from home and school settings. They have been particularly interested in studying children in conversation with adults, and at times with other children. In this reading, Wells discusses some of his findings, and provides some examples of the many conversations that have been recorded. The reading is of particular interest because it reveals differences between talk at home and talk at school. At home, children frequently initiate conversations, many of which arise from the interest of the moment. In contrast, at school the teacher is the most frequent initiator of discussions, and the topic chosen usually reflects the need to convey specific information according to some general curriculum. While teachers need to continue using their existing techniques, Wells suggests that they should also devote time to encouraging children to talk in the more spontaneous ways with which they are familiar. The need to complement home talk in this way is particularly important for those children who do not settle immediately to the convention of school talk (e.g. question and answer routines), and who may encounter language difficulties unless provided with other more open-ended opportunities for conversing with others.

At about the age of five, all children in our culture reach an important milestone in their development, as they move from the familiar and supportive environment of their home into the larger unknown world of school. During the next ten years the aim of those who teach them will be to induct them into the skills, knowledge and values of the wider culture, and to help them to achieve independence and responsibility in the use of their individual talents, both contributing to, and receiving from, the social, intellectual and material resources of the society of which they are becoming members. However, some children benefit from their schooling much more than others, and it has frequently been argued that a major cause of differential success is the difference between children in their ability to meet the linguistic expectations of the classroom as a result of their preschool linguistic experience at home.

Certainly, language must play a large part in the ease or difficulty with which children make the transition from home to school. For the many differences between the two environments – in size, in organization patterns and routines, in the goals that are set and in the means that children are expected to use in achieving them – impinge most strongly on the child's moment-by-moment experience through the differences in styles of linguistic interaction that characterize them. The greater the difference, the more likely it is that the child will experience a sense of disorientation, which may manifest itself in behaviour that is assessed as lack of ability or unwillingness to learn. Once labelled in this way, it may then become progressively more difficult for such children to overcome their initial disadvantage and reach the levels of achievement of which they are potentially capable.

In spite of much theorizing on this subject, however, there has been very little systematic study of the actual experience of children making this crucial transition, apart from the studies of Bernstein (1973) and Tough (1977), which have observed children in quasi-experimental situations in school and then either inferred the characteristics of home experience which preceded the performance in school or drawn obliquely upon questionnaire information. The Bristol study, 'Language at Home and at School' is probably unique in following a representative sample of children through the preschool years and into the infant school, recording regular samples of their spontaneous use of language in these two settings. In this paper, I shall try to describe some of the main characteristics of children's experience of talk at home and at school, as we have observed it in the recordings we have made, and I shall consider some of the implications of the differences that emerge from a comparison between them for the ease with which children make the transition.

TALK AT HOME

If one asked parents the question 'Why should children talk?', one would probably receive an answer such as that given by one particular mother: 'It's natural. They want to join in and be like other people. They just learn from listening to and talking to other people.' And in many ways, 'naturalness' describes what we have observed. Despite wide variations in the kinds of home in which they are growing up, there is remarkable uniformity in the sequence in which children learn the main components of language and even in the rate at which this learning takes place. There are differences between children, of course, both in the age at which they begin to talk and in the stage they have reached on entry to school, but these are relatively insignificant when compared with the amount that all children learn in these early years. All but a very small minority of children reach the age of schooling with a vocabulary of several thousand words, control of the basic grammar of the language of their community, and an ability to deploy these resources in conversations arising from the many and varied situations that occur in their everyday lives. Of all the children that we have studied, there is only one of whom this claim cannot be made with confidence, and even he is by no means limited to 'a basically non-logical mode of expressive behaviour', as Bereiter (1966) would have us believe to be typical of vast numbers of children. It seems, therefore, that the child's predisposition to learn whatever language he is exposed to, together with some minimum experience of language in use, is sufficient for the child to acquire a basic linguistic competence before he goes to school.

However, there are important differences between children, particularly when looked at from the point of view of the transition to school, and these concern the uses they habitually make of their linguistic resources; the things they talk about, and the ways in which they talk about them (Halliday, 1968). Learning one's native language is not simply a matter of learning vocabulary and grammar, but rather of learning to construct shared meanings as part of collaborative activities in which the words and sentences both refer to the shared situation and reflect a particular orientation to it. As Bernstein (1971) has argued, through the aspects of common experience that parents choose to talk about, and the particular relations that are given prominence in the form of their utterances, they present to their children a particular view of the world and their place within it. For example, if objects are constantly referred to in terms of ownership, and prohibitions and permissions are justified in terms of proprietorial rights, the child will be quick to learn the grammatical markers of possession (Wells, 1974) and over time will acquire an orientation to 'property' that is very different from that of the child whose parents encourage an exploratory attitude to objects, only prohibiting an interest in particular objects when there is a risk of danger.

Differences of orientation resulting from parental emphasis are particularly common between the sexes, boys and girls being subtly directed towards different interests through the situations in which their parents choose to initiate conversations with them. In a comparison we made of conversations initiated with three-year-olds, we found that over half the conversations with girls were in relation to household activities where the children were frequently 'helping' to carry out the task (a ratio of 2:1 compared with the boys), whereas a far greater proportion of conversations with boys were in situations where the children were engaged in exploratory play, with or without the active participation of the adult (a ratio of 3·5:1). Surprisingly enough, there were not such marked differences between boys and girls in the conversation that they initiated at this age, but by the time children start school, there are quite strong differences between boys and girls in the topics that they most frequently talk about – differences that are at least partly the result of their earlier experiences at home.

There are differences, too, in the ways in which language contributes to the structuring of experience. Everything that happens in a child's daily life is a potential subject for the sort of talk that facilitates attention, interpretation and evaluation, but parents differ in the use they make of these opportunities. In some homes, events are taken very much for granted, each one receiving the same sort of passing comment, whereas in other homes there is a much greater selectivity, some events being discussed in considerable detail and connections made with the wider context in which they occur. As a result of such different experiences, the internal models of the world that children are constructing take on their particular shapes and textures and come to be more fully developed in some areas than others.

In the following episodes we can see these subtle shaping processes in action as particular events are explored through talk. In the first example, James (aged three and a half years) has just come in from playing outside, and he is standing at the door, taking his boots off. He draws his mother's attention to a bird, and his mother takes up his interest, explaining the bird's nest-building activities.

Mother (helping James to change): There we are ... There – one slipper on.
James: I can see a bird.
Mother: A what love?
James (watching bird in garden): See a bird.
Mother: Is there? Outside? (whispers).
James: Yes. (whispers).
James (points to bird): See. (whispers).
Mother: Is he eating anything? (whispers).
James: No. (whispers).
Mother: Where? (whispers throughout).
Mother: Oh yes he's getting – Do you know what he's doing?
James: No. (whispers).
Mother: He's going to the ... the ... paper sack to try to pick out some pieces –
Oh he's got some food there.
And I expect he'll pick out some pieces of thread from the sack to go and make his nest ... up ... underneath the roof, James.
Wait a minute and I'll – OK wait a mo' wait a mo' James.
James: That bird's gone. (whispers).
Mother: Has it gone now?
James: Yes. (whispers).
Mother: Oh.
Take those long trousers off because they're ... a bit muddy in there.
James: Yes he's gone.

Here we see a mother naturally entering into her child's interest and directing it through the fuller meaning she gives to what they are looking at together.

In the second example, Wendy (aged three and a half years) is playing at the kitchen sink.

Wendy: I'm going to play with the water again, Mummy (climbs onto a chair at the sink). Is that all right?
(Mother returns to kitchen).
Wendy: I'm washing this for you, Mummy.
Mother: You're being very helpful this morning, Wendy (appreciatively).
Er. Yes (doubtfully). Don't make it TOO bubbly love (comes to investigate).
Have you put some more –? (Refers to wash-up liquid)
No (= don't do that).
'Cos Mummy's just wiped up all that, lovey.
And I told you I didn't want to get it too wet . . .
Didn't I?
Wendy: I want to play –
Mother: Er – no (wipes draining board again).
There we are.
Now try NOT to get all the water over there, love . . .
Please (continues to wipe and put away dishes. Wendy blows bubbles through a straw).
Wendy: See those bubbles! Come and see those bubbles.
Mother: Just a minute love.
And I'll come right away.

This time the child's interest doesn't entirely fit in with Mother's plans, but the mother accepts the child's intentions before setting the restraining conditions on how the activity can be carried out.

Finally, Jacqueline at the much younger age of two and a quarter years brings a book to show to her mother.

Jacqueline: Look at those balls, Mum I show you (holds out book).
Mother: Show me what, darling?
Jacqueline: I show you all the balls. I show you balls.
Mother: You're showing me the balls in your book, are you?
Let me see then.
Where?
Jacqueline: Balls (shows the picture).
Mother: What's this? (asks about other picture).
Jacqueline: That's a doggy.
Mother: What's this?
Jacqueline: That's a pussy cat.
Mother: And who's this?
Jacqueline: That's Lulu.
Mother: Hasn't she got a lovely kitten?
Jacqueline: Lulu's putting the – Pussy cat's.
Mother: Lulu's putting the pussy cat's hat on, yes.
Jacqueline: Lulu's – pussy cat's – Lulu's – putting pussy cat's hat on.

Mother's questions here are first to check that she has understood the child's intentions correctly and then to invite her to go on talking about the pictures.

We can see here how the mother guesses Jacqueline's meaning intention and provides her with the complete form, which Jacqueline is then able to say herself.

In all these examples of 'home-talk' we can see a number of important qualities that characterize the sort of conversational experience which leads to effective use of language by children:

1. A warm responsiveness to the child's interests and a recognition of the child as an autonomous individual with valid purposes and ways of seeing things.
2. Negotiation of meaning and purpose in the joint construction of an inter-subjective reality.
3. An invitation to the child to consider the immediate present in a wider framework of intention and consequence, feelings and principles.

Such conversations also have, albeit loosely and sometimes imperfectly, a reciprocity and cohesion which results from both participants attempting to understand the meaning intended by the other and to express their own meanings in ways which will be understood against the background of shared information that has either been made explicit or can be taken for granted.

There are a number of further characteristics which distinguish such talk from that which is most typical of schools. Firstly most of the conversations are initiated by the child (70 per cent was the figure we found in one analysis); secondly, it is sporadic, arising spontaneously from the interest of the moment, and it is almost completely lacking in a didactic pressure to teach particular facts or skills; and thirdly, it ranges widely over the whole of the family's shared experience, both inside and outside the home.

TALK AT SCHOOL

All the children quoted above are making excellent progress at school. Jacqueline, indeed has made such good progress that she has been moved into the junior school well before her seventh birthday, and James is the most advanced reader of the children we have been following up in the project 'Children Learning to Read'. The following extract, which shows how confidently Jacqueline is coping with the routines of school life, is taken from a recording made when she had been in school less than a term. She has just drawn a picture of Jack Frost, and is about to dictate a story to go with it.

> *Teacher*: What're we going to write here today?
> *Jacqueline*: This . is . a – (Jacqueline dictates to teacher).
> *Boy*: Jack.
> *Jacqueline*: No.

Teacher: What's his name?
(Jacqueline plays with teacher's pendant).
Jacqueline: Jack Frost.
Teacher: Jack Frost.
Jacqueline: Here . is . Jack Frrro – (Jacqueline dictates to teacher;
  teacher writing).
Teacher: Jack.
  What's Jack Frost doing?
Jacqueline: Frosting the grass.
Teacher: He . is . frosting .
  He's frosting the grass.
Jacqueline: With – (continues to dictate).
Teacher: With – oh with whom?
Jacqueline: His wand.
Teacher: With his wand (sounding surprised).
  What's he doing to you?
(Jacqueline looks at her fingers).
Jacqueline: Nibbling my toes and my – and fingers.
Teacher: He's nibbling?
Jacqueline: Yeah.
Teacher: Nibbling? Right.
Jacqueline: My . toes –
Teacher (writing): Nibbling –
Jacqueline: – and my –
Teacher: – my –
Jacqueline (holds up her fingers): – fingers.
Teacher: And my –? What else did you say?
Jacqueline: Chin.
Teacher: Chin.
  Oh you're going to write –
  Have to write this line very little, won't you?
  Now . d'you remember how you do it?
Jacqueline: Yeah.
Teacher: That line goes along there (shows Jacqueline which direction
  to write).
Jacqueline: Yeah (= Yes, I know).
Teacher: Do you want me to put the dots for you or can you do it without
  the dots?
Jacqueline: I can do it without the dots (with assurance).

The final story, which was written with great concentration, read as follows:

Here is Jack Frost.
He is frosting the grass with his wand.
He is nibbling my toes, my fingers and my chin.

From Jacqueline's point of view, it seems that the answer to our question 'Why should children talk?' is that it is both enjoyable and interesting. She has confidence, because her experience has led her to form expectations that people will take her seriously as a conversational partner and will be interested in what she has to say. And indeed, watching her with her teacher, it seems that her expectations are justified.

Not all children make the transition to school so easily, however, and some, lacking confidence and fluency, may be so tongue-tied and monosyllabic that they give the impression of being almost without language altogether. Teachers certainly have the impression that many children enter school with a 'linguistic deficit', and those who are unwilling or unable to respond to the linguistic demands of the classroom apparently lend support to this impression. How serious, then, is the problem? Certainly there are children who have little or no command of English on entry to school, but these are, almost without exception, children of non-English speaking parents: their problem is not lack of language, but lack of English, and they need the special provision of appropriate second language teaching. These children apart, the number of children of English-speaking parents who have not acquired a basic command of English by the age of five is very small indeed. However, the particular dialect of English they have learnt, or the uses they habitually make of language, may be different from those most valued in school, and as a result, they may find it difficult to communicate successfully with strange adults, who are unfamiliar with their expectations.

Differences resulting from non-standard dialects need not be a handicap, for they rarely cause serious misunderstanding; and as Labov (1970) and others have demonstrated, they are in no sense linguistically inferior to the standard dialect. Differences in habitual use of language, on the other hand, can have much more serious consequences, because behaviour resulting from difference can so easily be mistaken for deficiency. The following example, recorded at the end of Rosie's first month in school, is a good example of the sort of difficulties than can occur.

A small group of children are looking at colour slides of India. The teacher has selected a slide, looked at it through the viewer, and passed it to Rosie.

> *Teacher*: They're Indian ladies, and what else?
> (Rosie looks through viewer).
> *Rosie*: I can see something.
> *Teacher*: What can you see?
> *Rosie*: And they're going in the sand.
> *Teacher* (fails to understand): Mm?
> *Rosie* (hands viewer to teacher): You have a look.
> *Teacher* (hands viewer back to Rosie): Well you have a look and you tell me.
>   I've seen it already.
>   I want to see if you can see.
> (Rosie looks through the viewer).
> *Rosie*: Oh they're going in the sand.
>   They're going in the sand.

(Teacher doesn't hear as she is attending to other children).
Teacher: What's behind the men?
   Can you see the men in the red coats?
(Rosie still looking).
Teacher: Can you see the men in the red coats?
   What is behind those men?
Teacher: Can you see?
(Rosie nods).
Teacher: What is it?
Rosie: They're walking in .
Teacher: Pardon?
Rosie: They're walking.
Teacher: They're walking, yes.
   But what's walking behind them?
   Something very big.
Rosie: A horse.
Teacher: It's much bigger than a horse.
   It's much bigger than a horse.
   It's big and grey and it's got a long nose that we call a trunk.
   (mimes a long trunk).
Rosie: Trunk (imitating).
Teacher: Can you see what it is?
   What is it?
Rosie: (nods).
Child: (unintelligible).
Teacher: No that's what his nose is.
   Its nose is called a trunk.
   Can you see what the animal is?
Rosie: N – no (= I can't guess).
Teacher: It's much bigger than a horse.
   Let's give it to Darren and see if Darren knows.
(Darren looks. Rosie puts her thumb in her mouth. Teacher looks for
more pictures in books).
Teacher: There's a picture of the animal that was walking behind the men –
   with the red coats on.
   What's that? (shows picture to Rosie).
Rosie: The soldiers.
Teacher: Mm?
Rosie: Soldiers
Darren: Elephant } simultaneously.
Teacher (points to the elephant): What's that?
Rosie: An elephant.

The complete episode lasts almost five minutes and one hardly knows who is most deserving of sympathy – child or teacher. The teacher, apparently assuming that Rosie can produce the desired answer, gives her as many clues as possible, but all to no avail, for Rosie consistently adopts strategies unhelpful to the task as posed by the teacher, such as inviting the teacher to look, and describing only the people in the picture. Given her final response, it is difficult to know if she knew the word 'elephant'; but whether she did or not, she clearly did not perceive the task as one where she was required to produce this word or to admit her ignorance and ask for information.

It is interesting to contrast this episode with a somewhat similar conversation between Rosie and her mother that arose in the course of doing the housework. Here again a question was asked to which Rosie did not know the answer, but once her mother had realized this, she provided the answer herself and Rosie echoed it with enthusiasm.

> *Rosie*: Mum I've washed all up there.
> (Rosie has cleaned the front room).
> *Mother*: Have you?
>   There's a *good* girl.
> *Rosie*: Yes.
>   Oh there ain't no bits in there.
> *Mother*: We got to make the beds later on.
> *Rosie*: Eh?
> *Mother*: Make the beds.
> *Rosie*: Come on then.
> *Mother*: Not yet.
> *Rosie*: What in a minute?
> *Mother*: Yeah in a minute?
> *Rosie*: What – what time clock have we got to do it?
> *Mother*: I don't know.
>   I'll see how –
>   Got to wash up first.
>   What's the time by the clock?
> *Rosie*: Uh?
> *Mother* (pointing to the position of the hands on the clock): What's the time?
>   Now what number's that?
> *Rosie*: Number two.
> *Mother*: No it's not.
>   What is it?
>   It's a one and a nought.
> *Rosie*: One and a nought.
> *Mother*: Yeah.
>   What's one and a nought?
> *Rosie*: (No response).
> *Mother*: What is it?
> *Rosie*: (That's one).
> *Mother*: Yeah.
>   What is it?
> *Rosie*: One.
>   One and a nought.
> *Mother*: What's one and a nought?
> *Rosie*: Um that.
> *Mother*: Ten!

Rosie: Ten (imitates).
Mother: Ten to ten.
Rosie: Ten to ten (imitates with enthusiasm).
Rosie: Shall we wash them because they're not clean enough?
   (reference to the clock).
Mother: (shakes her head).
Rosie: On that other side he ain't (in justification).
Mother: Well you can't wash him inside.
   He'll break.
Rosie: Would he?
Mother: Mm (= yes).
Rosie: If – if – if we wash him inside w – wou – wouldn't – w – w – would that
   thing wouldn't go round?
Rosie: On the numbers?
Mother: (No response).
Rosie (comparing clock with the clock on recording box): He got –
   He got one.
   And he got one.

The point of making this comparison, however, is not to claim that Rosie's mother is more effective as a teacher, or even as a conversation partner, for in most ways she is not. What is brought out by the comparison is the relatively greater control of the language system that Rosie displays at home, and particularly when she initiates the interchanges. One must conclude, therefore, that Rosie's failure to meet the linguistic demands of her teacher is not an absolute lack of language skills, as one might suppose if one simply met her at school, but rather that her poor performance is in part due to the nature of the demands made on her in school, particularly their remoteness from direct, personal involvement in a shared or self-initiated activity.

It has become fashionable to lay the blame for the sort of ineptitude that Rosie displays in the school episode above on the inadequacies of the home environment, and in some cases this may be appropriate, at least in part. Rosie is indeed one of the least linguistically mature children in our sample, and her home, although a place of much warmth and concern for the children's happiness, is not one where the sort of conversation that was illustrated in the first section of this paper is at all frequent. Nevertheless, as we have just seen, even such children may have linguistic abilities that are not called forth by the particular range of demands that are made on them in school, and so it is their deficiencies rather than their abilities which are most salient to their teachers. Such children are doubly unfortunate, and there is no doubt that there are substantial numbers of them. However, any suggestion that working class children *as a whole* are 'disadvantaged', in any absolute or irrevocable sense, because their home experience leads them to use language differently, is certainly not appropriate. A comparison of 40 children from our study (Wells, 1977) drawn from the full social spectrum, showed that there were no clear-cut differences between classes in the use of language, such as those found by Dr Tough (1977) in her study of groups selected to represent the extremes of social class. Of the three children whose 'home-talk' was illustrated earlier, two were from working-class homes (Jacqueline and James), and neither showed any signs of linguistic disadvantage either on entry to school or later.

As well as being inaccurate, such sweeping assertions about the inadequacies of homes have the additional disadvantage of distracting teachers from their obligation to examine their own role in helping children to make a success of the transition from home to school. We have seen an example which illustrates how some children fail to meet the linguistic demands of schools. But are the demands themselves entirely appropriate, either to the children who are entering school or to the longer-term aims of education that are espoused by the majority of teachers?

In order to pursue this question further, let us next consider some typical examples of classroom interaction selected from the observations we have been making of children during their first month in school.

In the first extract, the teacher has read *Little Black Sambo* and is recapitulating the main points of the story with the whole class:

> *Teacher*: He would feel fat, wouldn't he, after eating all those?
> *Children*: Yes.
> *First child*: He would burst.
> *Teacher*: He would burst, yes.
>   What did the first tiger take off Little Black Sambo?
> *First child*: Shirt.
> *Second child*: His coat.
> *Teacher*: His coat that his mummy had made.
>   Do you remember when his mummy made it?
>   What colour was it?
> *Children*: Red.
> *Teacher*: Red, yes.
>   What did the second tiger take?
> *Children*: Trousers.
> *Teacher*: His trousers.
>   What did the third tiger take?
> *Children*: Shoes.
> *Teacher*: Was he pleased to take the shoes?
> *Children*: Yes }
>   No }
> *Teacher*: Why not?
> *First child*: Because he had 40 feet.
> *Teacher*: He said – what did he say to him?
> *Second child*: I've got four feet and you've ...
> *Teacher*: I've got four feet and you've got –?
> *Children*: Two.
> *Teacher*: You haven't got enough shoes for me.

In this second extract, the teacher has arranged a small group to do number work: counting beads and threading them on to a string with number labels. Penny is working faster than the other members of the group:

> *Penny* (threading coloured beads on to a string to match number cards):
>   I'm winning.
> *Teacher*: I'll come and see if they're right.
> *Penny*: One two three four five six seven.
> *Teacher* (checks Penny's work): That's right.
>   What's after seven?
> *Penny*: Eight.
> *Teacher*: Eight.
>   Can you find another eight? (telling Penny to find a number card with 8 on).
> *Penny*: Can you see a number eight? (picks a card with 8 in green).
> *Teacher*: I can see one two three four number eight.
> *Teacher*: That's right.
>   What colour have you got to find this time?
> *Penny*: Blue.
> *Teacher*: Blue.

The third extract once again comes from a session involving the whole class, following the reading of *Elmer the Elephant*. In the course of a discussion of some of the pictures, Stella volunteers a personal anecdote:

> *Teacher*: Can you see what that elephant's got on the end of his trunk?
> *Children*: (laugh).
> *Teacher*: What is it?
> *Children*: A blower.
> *Teacher*: A blower – a party blower.
>   It is funny, isn't it?
> *Stella*: My – my – my brother brought one home from a party.
> *Teacher*: Did he?
>   What does it do as well as blowing?
> *Stella*: Um.
> *First child*: (inaudible).
> *Teacher*: Sh! (signals she wants Stella to answer).
>   What does it do?
> *Stella*: Mm – the thing rolls out (makes an appropriate gesture).
> *Teacher*: Yes the thing rolls down and rolls up again, doesn't it?
>   But what does it do as well as unrolling and rolling up?
> *Stella*: Um.
> *Teacher*: Does it do anything else?
> *First child*: Squeaks.
> *Teacher*: Sh! (signals for Stella to answer).
>   Does Adrian's squeak? –
>   Adrian's blower squeak?
> *Stella*: (nods).

Teacher: Does it?
  They usually squeak and they often have a little feather on it too, don't they? (intonation of finality).
Children: Yes (chanted).
Teacher: Well I think that's a lovely story.
  It's one of my favourite ones.

The first thing that strikes one about these episodes – unless one already takes it for granted – is the very high proportion of teacher utterances that are questions, and of these what a very small proportion are questions to which the teachers do not already know the answer. Even when the form of the question seems to invite a variety of answers, there is often only *one* that is really acceptable to the teacher, and it is not uncommon to see children gazing at the teacher's face in an effort to guess what is in her mind, down to the precise word. It almost seems from these examples that teachers believe the answer to the question about why children should talk to be because teachers ask them questions.

However, as we saw in the examples of 'home talk', one of the chief characteristics of effective conversation is a reciprocity in the shared construction of meaning. Questions do occur but to nothing like the same extent as in the school examples and – more importantly – when they do occur they are asked equally by child and adult, and almost always because the asker is seeking information which he believes the hearer can supply. Many teacher-directed questions, on the other hand, show very little evidence of reciprocity: the asker already possesses the requested information and seems, as often as not, to direct the question to the pupil who is least likely to know the answer. It is true that some children will already have had some experience of questions of this sort in specific contexts such as identifying objects in picture books, or learning nursery rhymes by heart. But what about those children who are not at all familiar with the rules of this particular language game? They will, of course, eventually have to learn them in order to fit in at higher levels of education where the 'closed question' and the 'Teacher Initiation – Pupil Response – Teacher Feedback' routine have been shown to be the norm (Barnes, 1971; Sinclair and Coulthard, 1975). But in the shorter term the bewildering experience of being judged according to their ability to play a game whose rules are completely unfamiliar to them may persuade them once and for all that school is an alien institution and the activities that take place there are both irrelevant to their model of social interaction and destructive of the self-confidence that they have built up in their ability to talk within the rules that operate at home.

Even in the longer term, is the style of interaction exemplified in the 'school-talk' above conducive to the generally agreed aims of education? How far does it contribute to the independent, active and enquiring attitude that is essential if pupils are, as Barnes (1976) puts it, to convert 'school' knowledge into 'action' knowledge, and make it the basis for further learning? What preparation does it provide for the reciprocal negotiation of meaning that every adult needs to be able to engage in, in his many dealings with other people in social groups, at work and in his contacts with bureaucracy? Just as the young child's internal model of reality is shaped by the salience that is given to different aspects of experience in his conversations with his parents, so does the pupil's model of reality continue to be shaped by those orientations to knowledge and those styles of inter-personal interaction that are given salience in the transactions of the classroom. That being so, the domination of school-talk by the teacher-evaluator, and the constant pressure on the pupil to produce correct verbal responses as acceptable tokens of the thought processes that the curriculum is designed to encourage, can hardly be the most effective way to achieve the goals that are set.

This is not to argue, however, that infant schools should attempt to replicate the style of interaction that typifies the best sort of home. Even if there were agreement on what is the best sort of home, such an aim would be neither appropriate nor feasible. Although both home and school have an educational function, the school complements the informality of the home by introducing the child to more formal ways of acquiring and utilizing knowledge, and its organization draws upon the skills of highly trained and expensive professionals. I do not, therefore, intend to suggest that teachers can substantially change the imbalance between their own and pupils' share of pupil–teacher interaction (not at least without a prohibitively expensive increase in the teacher–pupil ratio), nor do I wish to suggest that teachers should give up asking questions. What I do wish to suggest is that they should be much more flexible in their style of interaction, selecting the type of teacher–pupil talk that is best suited to the purpose of the particular activity that the pupils are engaged in.

TALK IN RELATION TO TASKS

Since most of what goes on in the classroom is designed to contribute to some part of the overall curriculum, it may be helpful to think of most of the activities that children engage in in terms of *tasks*, each task having a *goal* with respect to some area of the curriculum that provides its *content*. For example, Penny's activity of bead-threading (p. 139) is just such a task. The goal of this task is to produce a sequence of groups of beads that matches the numbers and colours on the instruction cards; the content is foundation work for mathematics. Naturally particular tasks may be relevant to more than one area of the curriculum, and there are a variety of ways of dividing the curriculum into content areas depending on the purpose of the division. However, for this discussion I should like to make a broad distinction between four broad areas:

skills, knowledge, values and creative activities, and I shall argue that the sorts of goals that are set, and the procedures that are appropriate for attaining them, differ according to which of the content areas is involved.

Language enters into tasks to varying extents, sometimes as no more than a relatively unimportant procedure, as for example when the child needs to ask a neighbour for some object that is required to complete a task that is being carried out individually, and sometimes as the goal of the task itself, as for example in individual writing or in class discussion. In general, except where language skills provide the content of the task, the degree to which language is central is least in the area of skills and it increases towards the creative activities end of the continuum, except where the creative activities are essentially non-linguistic. However, when a task of any kind involves talk between teacher and child, the style of talk that occurs carries messages about the inter-personal relationship between them and about the teacher's orientation to the content of the task as well as messages about the task itself.

From this point of view perhaps the most important dimension on which tasks differ is the extent to which the goal of the task is determined in advance.

The goal of an addition task, for example, is normally entirely predetermined: $2 + 2 = 4$, and no other outcome is acceptable, once the procedure of addition has been fully grasped. The creation of a picture or imaginary story, on the other hand, has an almost entirely undetermined goal, although procedural criteria of internal consistency and practical skills in manipulating brush or pencil may be relevant in assessing the way in which the goal is realized, once this has been finally decided. Between these two extremes, there are varying degrees of constraint on the form that the outcome of a task may take, and on the procedures that are appropriate in arriving at it. However, the decision as to where a particular task falls along this continuum is very much in the hands of the teacher, through the way in which she presents the task and the style of talk she adopts in her own contribution to its achievement.

With this rough sketch of a framework for thinking about tasks, we are now in a better position to consider the kinds of talk that are appropriate to tasks of different kinds. Let us start with a type of task where the strategy of 'closed' questioning *is* appropriate. The first example is taken from a study of language in the infant school carried out by Margaret Hocking (1977). The task involves the concepts of 'older' and 'younger', and the procedure suggested is a comparison of pairs of children with respect to their month of birth. The teacher is calling the children to her, two at a time. Here she is talking to Sarah and Lawrence:

> *Teacher*: Right, which is the oldest?
> *Sarah*: I am.
> *Teacher*: Let's see which is the eldest of you two?
> *Lawrence*: Sarah.

Teacher (to Sarah): Now your birthday came in January.
   You were seven in January.
   What were you Sarah?
Sarah: Seven.
Teacher: Who's the eldest?
Lawrence: Me.
Teacher (to Sarah): Who do you think is the eldest?
Sarah: (inaudible).
Teacher: You think Lawrence is the eldest, do you?
Sarah: Yes.
Teacher: Now think about it.
   Yours was January.
   Lawrence came in February.
   Which is the eldest?
Sarah: Lawrence, I think.
Teacher: Well who came first?
Sarah: I did.
Teacher: Then I think you are probably the eldest, don't you?
   You go at the top then.
   Put it on the top one.
(Sarah puts her name at the top of the ladder).
Lawrence: I'm the second.
(Lawrence places his name underneath).

The second example comes from a study being carried out by Jan Adams, as part of our research programme, in which the aim is to compare the teaching styles of parents and teachers. The child is given a collection of picture-cards of familiar objects, including the members of a family, items of clothing, toys, foods, etc. The task presented to the child is that of grouping the pictures of things that go together, but no constraint is put upon the criteria that may be used in forming groups. The teacher's (or parent's) role is to help the child to apply whatever criterion he chooses in a consistent manner, and to discuss the criterion where this is helpful. In this example we see Rosie, the child quoted earlier, carrying out the task with her teacher.

Teacher: Let's have a good look at some of the pictures.
   Can you tell me what's here?
   Can you tell me some of the things that are here?
Rosie: That's a swing.
Teacher: Which one is a swing?
   This one? (points to picture of swing).
Rosie: (nods).
Teacher: What do you do to a swing?
Rosie: Sit on it.
Teacher: Can you find some other things that you can sit on?
Rosie: Yes.

Teacher: Have a look and see if you can find some other things that you sit
   on and we'll put all of those together with the swing.
Rosie: Ain't nothing else.
Teacher: What about these? (points to several pictures).
Rosie: There's a bike (picks up bike).
Teacher: Can you sit on a bike?
Rosie: (nods).
Teacher: Put it with the swing then.

   Both of these examples (together with the earlier example of Penny threading
beads) have a number of features in common. Firstly, they are taken from tasks
which have clearly understood goals with respect to content, on the border
between skills and knowledge; both also involve clearcut procedures – comparison of birth-date in the first, and classification according to a chosen
criterion in the second – in order to achieve those goals. Secondly, because they
are based on particular items of publicly available knowledge, they fall at the
end of the continuum where the outcome is relatively pre-determined, and
applications of the procedures can be appropriately described as right or
wrong. Thirdly, the teacher is using these particular instances as exemplars of
very general principles; and fourthly, implicit in the task-related dialogue, is
the expectation that the child will internalize the procedure embodied in the
question-and-answer sequence, so that he will eventually be able to operate
such procedures alone, with the aid of a similar internal dialogue. The relationship between teacher and pupils on these tasks might therefore be aptly
described as that between master and apprentice, and the dialogue as a means
of increasing the pupils' awareness of the appropriate procedures for manipulating available information to achieve an agreed goal. However, these goals
are essentially instrumental, since they concern skills that should eventually
function as procedures in higher order tasks.
   If we now turn to the sort of task represented by the discussion of *Elmer the
Elephant*, we can see that it is of a very different kind. Here the point of
departure is the shared class experience of listening to the story of *Elmer the
Elephant*, and the particular task we are concerned with is initiated by Stella's
spontaneous contribution, sparked off by mention of the party blower. The
goal that one might expect the teacher to have in mind is for the child to
develop the personal information she has volunteered in response to the story.
With such a goal, the outcome certainly cannot be pre-determined, nor can the
particular procedure adopted be treated as an exemplar of a more general
principle (except perhaps of the very vaguely-defined procedure of recounting
personal experience fluently). Since the child's experience is personal, the
teacher is no more of an authority than the child, and so the relationship
should not be that of master and apprentice, but rather that of collaborators.
In practice, however, the episode turns into the familiar task of 'guess what's in
teacher's mind' – not just once, but twice. It would not be surprising if Stella

quickly learned never to offer information unless actually called upon to do so.

What style of interaction, then, would be appropriate for a task of this kind? Put like that, it is difficult to answer without being prescriptive. But one might expect the teacher contribution to take the form of an invitation to continue or a suggestion to focus on a particular aspect of the topic introduced. Questions, if they were used, might be expected to take the form of asking for examples or specific additional detail or of requests for justification of the accuracy or relevance of the contribution – 'How do you know?', 'Why are you telling us this?'.

A search through all our recordings yielded only one where episodes of this kind occurred, and it is perhaps significant that it should have been Jacqueline's teacher who provided it. In the following example, she was preparing to read a story about frost, and she wanted to be sure that the children were familiar with the relevant ideas.

Teacher: When I woke up this morning –
I don't know who looked out of the window when they woke up this morning?
(Children raise hands).
Teacher: Only – only one two three.
Oh four of you.
Now who can put their hand up and tell me what they saw out of the window this morning?
Jacquy?
Jacquy: Ice.
Teacher: Ice.
Ice.
Whereabouts was the ice? (waggles her fingers).
Jacquy: On the grass.
Teacher: On the grass.
Jacquy: On – and on our car.
Teacher: That's right.
It's not . it's . ice –
But what do we call it?
It's little tiny bits of ice.
First child: I call it . . .
I call it Jack Frost.
Teacher: Frost really, isn't it?
Frost.
What did it make the grass look like? (waves hands horizontally in the air).
Jacquy: White.
Teacher: White.
All white?
Or was there some green as well?
First child: Some green.
Jacquy: White and green.
Teacher: White and green.

Second child: Mine –
  Mine was all over the –
Third child: The leaves white.
Teacher (To third child): The leaves were white.
  (To second child): Yours was all over the grass, was it?
Fourth child: So was mine.
Teacher: So was yours?
Ian: I had –
  I had a taste of grass.
Teacher: And – (is about to continue then decides to pick up Ian's contribution).
  Did you?
(Several children talk).
Teacher: (holds up finger to concentrate on Ian's contribution).
  Ian said he had a little taste of it.
  (To Ian): Did it taste of anything?
Jacquy: Yeah.
Teacher: What did it taste of?
Jacquy: Taste cold.
Teacher (pressing fingers of both hands together): Tastes cold.
  Who knows what ice is?
  It's something that's frozen.
  Ice is made out of something that's frozen.
Second child: Well I have that in my drink at home.
Jacquy: Cold.
Teacher (pointing to second child): That's right.
  You have it in your drink at home.
Teacher: And how does mummy make it?
Children: By water.
Teacher: That's right!
  Ice is WATER that's frozen hard. (Pressing fingers together).
Teacher (Pointing to Ian who had tasted ice): So that's why it wouldn't really
  taste very Ian –
  You're right Jacquy.
  It would taste – ? (No answer from Jacquy).
  Cold, wouldn't it? (Touching her lip).
  Cold.
Teacher (Pointing to Jacquy): And you said you had it on your windows.
  Is that right?
(Jacquy nods).
(Several other children also speak).
Child: And me.
Teacher: What did it do on the windows of the car?
Jacquy: Didn't do nothing.
Teacher: It didn't do anything.
Child: You couldn't see out the back window.
Jacquy: No.
Teacher: You couldn't see out of the window, no.
Jacquy: It's very dangerous.

Jacquy: Out the back window you couldn't. 'Cause there is a wire at the back window.
Teacher: Oh and it makes –
It heats up the back window so the frost disappears?
Jacquy: Yeah.
Teacher: Well then this is a little poem about a man called Mister Jack Frost.
(Taking book).
Children: Ooh!
(Children laugh).
Teacher: And Mister Jack Frost is the one that comes and creeps down . . . .
And puts all the frost on our windows and on the grass.
You listen.

The preceding example falls within the content area of knowledge – knowledge about frost and its relation to water. The teacher is drawing upon the children's experience, but she has a clear idea in advance of the facts that should be established before she starts to read the story. The interaction strategy of asking questions about the children's observations and then generalizing from them seems entirely appropriate, therefore, to the task that she had set, once Jacqueline's first response had been accepted and refined to establish the topic for discussion.

However, to find an example of exploratory talk where the outcome was not determined in advance, I had to turn to a class discussion of 'The Pobble who has no Toes' in one of the recordings analysed in Margaret Hocking's study. The teacher's purpose in this case was specifically to encourage the children to make a personal response to the poem, whilst still remaining faithful to the meaning of the text.

Teacher: Shall we just read that bit again?
'His Aunt Jemima made him drink lavender water tinged with pink.'
First child: What's lavender water taste like?
Teacher: I don't know.
I've never tasted it.
Have you?
Second child: We have a drink and it's pink and it's strawberry.
And the first time I had it I didn't like it so the next time I put sugar in and I liked it.
Teacher: Do you think you would like lavender water?
Children: No.
Teacher: Why not?
Third child: Because when mummy tells me would you like lavender water I says no thank you.
Teacher: I wonder why you wouldn't like it though.
Child: I expect it tastes horrid.
Child: Like sea water.
Child: Nasty.
Child: Salty.

Teacher: You think it would be salty?
     What do you usually do with lavender water?
Child: I don't know.
     I don't know what it is.
Teacher: It's a perfume.
     Lavender water is a scent that ladies put on.
Child: Ugh!
Teacher: It wouldn't be very nice, would it, to drink?
Child: Maybe that's why his toes came off.
Teacher: Maybe that did make his toes come off.
     He certainly lost them.
Teacher: What about the things he ate?
     Would you like them?
     'Eggs and buttercups fried with fish?'
Children: No.
Child: I like the fish and eggs.
Teacher: What about the buttercups?
⎧ *Child*: I wouldn't like them.
⎨ *Child*: I don't like fish.
⎩ *Child*: I don't like flowers and that.
Teacher: You don't like flowers.
     Don't you normally eat flowers?
Children: No.
Child: Don't you eat cabbage?
     And cabbage is a flower.
Child: Yes and you eat cauliflowers.
Child: You'd not eat flowers that bloom.
Teacher: The things that are green.
     The flowers that are green, yes.
Child: Can we eat the grass?
Children: No.
Child: But the grass is green.
Teacher: We don't eat the grass but some animals do.
Child: The cows eat it.
Child: Cows.
Child: Guinea pigs.
Teacher: That's right.
     They like it.

The whole discussion is in this style: the children contributing ideas from their own experience and the teacher helping them to maintain the thread, by picking up the most relevant aspect of each child contribution and using it to extend the exploration. Naturally, there are a number of digressions, such as the discussion of herbivores above, but in the process, as Hocking points out, the children are learning the beginning of the critical method in an interaction which, significantly, is child-initiated and mainly child-sustained.

It *is* possible, therefore, to develop a style of interaction which is relatively undetermined and open to pupil contributions, yet at the same time appropriate to the chosen task. And because it can embrace spontaneous pupil contributions, it is surely the most effective way of complementing the talk of the home, by building on the foundations that have already been laid in the free-ranging, child-initiated conversations that have been the experience of the vast majority of children before they come to school. At the same time, such talk looks forward to the larger goals of formal education, by introducing the criteria of conformity to experience, internal consistency and relevance, in relation to curricular tasks selected by the teacher.

Since these are the qualities that one would expect teachers to be endeavouring to develop in children's talk, why is it that this style of interaction is so rare in children's first experience of school? A number of explanations might be suggested. The most obvious is that teachers do not, after all, place as much value on these qualities as their public pronouncements would have us believe; at heart they are only concerned to train skills and to drum in facts. However, I do not believe that this is, in fact, the case. More probable, it seems, is that they do value such qualities but in a rather diffuse way that does not fully inform their moment-by-moment interactions in the classroom. Other pressures, such as the desire to be seen to be efficient, and to keep to a well-prepared programme of work, take on a greater priority, and control of the class – or the loss of control that is feared if children are allowed to take the initiative in task-related talk – assumes an over-riding importance. It is certainly true that a high proportion of children's spontaneous contributions to class or group discussion are in varying degrees irrelevant to the immediate task, and thirty or more children all wanting to develop their own line of thought pose a serious threat to the teacher's control over the discussion. But before we accept this explanation at face value, we should stop to ask 'Irrelevant to whom?' Not to the child, presumably, since he is prepared to speak out in front of his peers, and struggle to make his meaning clear. The irrelevance must, therefore, be in the mind of the teacher, who has planned in advance the course that the children's learning should take. But what is relevant to the teacher may be irrelevant to the child, unless he is helped to relate his personal experience to the task in hand, and teacher's control may be bought at the expense of the full and active involvement of the child.

Relevance in talk is only a particular case of matching means to ends, procedures to goals, and in many spheres of activity children have already achieved considerable competence of this sort, particularly where the goal is self-chosen. What makes talk a special case, however, is that it is a reciprocal activity, in which both participants have to be prepared to negotiate their meanings towards the attainment of a shared goal. Relevance in talk is thus essentially a matter for negotiation. But it is through such negotiation of meaning that language is first acquired, with parents helping children to match utterances to the understanding they both have of a shared situation. By the time they come to school, children already have some understanding of relevance in talk, as can be seen in the conversations that they themselves initiate. What schools should provide, therefore, is the opportunity to develop and extend these conversational skills by putting them to use in the exploration of the new ideas and experiences that the more formal curriculum provides. However, this is only possible if at least some curricular tasks adopt a style of interaction which is truly reciprocal, and where the goal of the task is sufficiently open-ended for the relevance of the children's contributions to be negotiated as the talk proceeds. Only in this way will children develop the confidence and skill to use talk as a means of understanding and controlling the world in which they live. Our problem as teachers is to learn how to maintain the supportive responsiveness of parents, whilst at the same time complementing it with a clear sense of the skills and knowledge that we wish to make available.

12.

Into print: reading and language growth

Jessie F. Reid

The readings in this section have been mainly concerned with children's use of spoken language when communicating with others. However, when children enter school, they are also expected to develop written language skills as they learn to read and write. Extending language skills to the written code is by no means straightforward. When children start learning to read, many have little idea of the general nature and purposes of written language. They must understand something of these before they can make sense of the details of the code. Secondly they must come to see that in written English the correspondence between letters and sounds is complex and not one-to-one. They must be enabled to organize their grasp of these complex relationships in the most helpful ways and to integrate it with their implicit linguistic knowledge in the search for meaning. The third area where important new learning must take place is that of syntax. Sentence structures in written language can differ in many ways from those found commonly in speech, and word recognition alone will not guarantee that such structures are understood by young readers who meet them for the first time.

In the present paper, difficulties that children may meet in all three areas are considered and illustrated by carefully chosen examples. The reading is of value both for the way in which it views the difficulties in a psycholinguistic framework and for the thoughtful suggestions it makes as to how they may be overcome.

There are two fairly direct ways of seeing how reading theory and practice have changed over the last 20 years. One way is to look at lists of publications and see how dramatically the number has increased. Another way – and a striking one – is to examine the indexes of some standard books on the psychology and teaching of reading. If we compare the indexes of two books from the forties and fifties, say Gates (1947) and Anderson and Dearborn (1952), with those of three from the sixties and seventies, say Goodman (1968), Clay (1972a) and Gibson and Levin (1975), the most arresting contrast is to be found in the amount of space allotted to items like language, speech, syntax, sentence patterns, prediction, context, and concepts of print. While all of these topics figure prominently in the indexes to more recent works, some of them do not occur at all in the earlier ones. By contrast, references to visual perception, discrimination, eye movements, association, Gestalt theory, and word shape, which were common in earlier discussions, have diminished. In other words, research on and thinking about reading has altered, not just in volume but also in content and focus.

The change is often described as consisting in a shift of thought towards classifying reading and writing as new kinds of language learning, rather than new kinds of perceptual and motor skill. But to put it in this way does not fully express the crucial nature of the change. Reading has always been thought of as connected in one way or another with speech. What has altered, and what has caused our view of reading to alter, is our understanding of the nature of language itself and of language acquisition. This change has in its turn affected the ways in which we view the development of literacy in children, and its relationship to the oral language learning which has preceded it.

To illustrate the change, I want to use the case of a girl whom I shall call Clare. When she was about seven and a half years old and already a good reader, Clare came to me with a commercially-produced version of the story of *The Sleeping Beauty*, declaring that she could not read it. She was obviously surprised and somewhat upset, for the book had the large colourful pictures and bold clear print that are standard in books for 'young readers'. When I asked her to tell me what was wrong, she answered: 'I can read the words, but I don't know what they mean.' Further questioning revealed that one of the sentences which had defeated her ran thus: 'The princess's father and mother invited her fairy godmothers, seven in all, to come to her christening.' It became clear, when I asked Clare to read the sentence aloud, that she could indeed 'read the words', and that she knew the meaning of 'invited' and 'christening'; her puzzlement came entirely from three of the simplest words in the sentence – the words 'seven in all.' Indeed, the obstacle presented by this phrase was so great that she had to be encouraged to read past it, and her voice showed that it caused her totally to lose hold of the sense.

Traditional views of the nature of reading acquisition would most likely have classified Clare's problem as a failure in 'comprehension'; which in one sense it was. But in so doing, they would have implied that it was not really a basic *reading* problem at all. For these traditional views were based on the notion that the central activity in learning to read consists in 'word-recognition'. The recognition could be of overall shape (whatever that is) or of letter patterns. But the process of extracting meaning from written sentences was seen as a process of identifying written words, whose meanings (learned by 'association' from speech) were then strung together in a simple additive manner. Failure to 'comprehend' was thus a failure to grasp, or attend to, word meaning. A look at a well-known textbook on the psychology of reading, such as Anderson and Dearborn (1952) will confirm the prevalence of this view – a view which we now know to be seriously mistaken. The comprehension of language does not work that way. And to some degree Clare, aged seven, sensed this. She was concerned not with word meaning but with *sentence* meaning – with what the words collectively meant – even though her ability to talk about sentence meaning was too limited to express this adequately.

The belief that 'word recognition' lay at the heart of learning to read meant that the efforts of those who composed early materials went mainly into making this one task easier. But even during the first half of the present century, one or two notable exceptions to the prevailing orthodoxy on word recognition appeared. There were several exponents of the 'sentence method' (e.g. Jagger, 1929), and even earlier, there was the remarkable E. B. Huey (1908) who attacked the 'insidious thought of reading as word-pronouncing' (p. 350). Both these writers had views on reading which were much in advance of their time, views which are only now finding adequate theoretical foundations in the accounts of language and language acquisition which have emerged over the last 25 years. These accounts have enabled us to look in quite new ways at the process of acquiring written language. We see, as we did not see before, the nature of the extensions of language learning which literacy entails.

In looking for a phrase which might distil the essence of what follows, I was reminded of a saying attributed to Professor Simon Lawrie. He was the first holder of the Chair of Education in the University of Edinburgh, and is recorded as having once said that the prime task of the teacher is 'to put herself into the attitude of ignorance of the learner'. A conscious attempt of this kind to adopt the mental stance of someone else is what Piaget would call an act of decentration. It is often not an easy thing to do, but I believe Lawrie's view – that teachers (and researchers) are called upon to try – is profoundly true.

In the late fifties and mid-sixties I undertook a number of studies in which I – in an effort to improve my own decentration – interviewed five-year-olds about learning to read and write (Reid, 1958; 1966). I wanted to find out how the experience appeared to them and how they could talk about it. For the purposes of this discussion I shall first discuss the 1966 study, which provided the insights which I now want to examine.

As I listened to the children's spontaneous comments and their answers to my questions, I began to see how much I had not previously understood. I realized for the first time that there were children who did not know what reading consisted in – who had no concept of marks which stood for speech. I found for instance a child who thought she was 'past reading'. 'We finished it yesterday,' she assured me very firmly. Questioned further, she said 'Yes, we read all the pages.' When I asked her what was in the book that she had finished yesterday, she replied, 'If that one was the same and that one was not the same.' She had been working through exercises in 'visual discrimination' which did not involve any written words at all.

I also found children apparently totally ignorant of the simplest functions of writing – of names on buses, or addresses on letters. In other words, the 'attitude of ignorance' of these children was one where they needed to be helped to discover what a writing system was – indeed that such a thing existed – and that it served useful, even essential, purposes in everyday communication. That was where these children had to begin.

The work I did then was replicated and expanded, first by John Downing (1970) and later by others, with similar results. As well as finding puzzlement and ignorance about the existence and functions of written language, I and others found some very marked gaps and confusions in children's vocabulary for talking about print, even though they were actually trying to cope with a reading primer. They called letters 'numbers' or 'words'; they called words 'names' or 'the writing'; they called sentences 'stories'. They referred to individual letters as (say) 'h for horse'; some thought that 'big' letters (i.e. capitals) were 'for big animals', or that they made 'a different sort of word'. Some children called sounding 'spelling' or *vice versa*. Some said things like 'I'll write a house' and 'I'll draw my name', and indeed showed, when they tried to write, that they did not realize one of the distinctive features of written symbols – namely, that orientation mattered. It was clear that these children lacked the necessary conceptual grasp of the nature of our written language system and also the vocabulary to talk about it, either to themselves or to anyone else.

There are of course children who come to school with a good understanding of these matters (Clark, 1976). But there are many who do not, and I am now quite sure that for them the activity of reading can remain totally mysterious. It is not, after all, an activity like riding a bicycle or baking a cake, where the onlooker sees what the cyclist or the baker is doing, and where the intentions and purposes are clear. Before the actual learning of the code begins, the child must see something of the nature and aims of the task.

Work of a kind which paralleled and complemented the foregoing studies was done by Marie Clay. In 1972 she produced a test of concepts of print called 'Sand' (this being the title of the story which ran through the test material). The concepts covered by the test were in many respects the same as those with which Downing and I had been concerned. In a previous study of early reading behaviour, Clay (1969) made several observations which related closely to our interest in the child's conception of 'a word'. In particular, she noted the importance for a child of 'pointing' while reading aloud. Many teachers frown on the practice, but Clay pointed out that the child was using movement to help him make a correct word-for-word match between the words he uttered and the print on the page. This establishing of the 'print-speech match' is an important process, because as Clay showed it can lead to self-correction by children as they read, and to important discoveries about word-boundaries, which are not marked in speech. (For an extended discussion of this topic, see Downing, 1979).

All these ideas have given a new dimension to the notion of reading readiness. They have led to the conviction, now more and more widely held, that the most relevant preparation for reading alphabetic writing consists not in practising visual discrimination with pictures and diagrams but in being helped to see what written alphabetic language looks like, to learn the conventions by which it is set out, and to discover how it is used. We are also coming to see that, in step with their growing understanding of print, children must become more aware of how their spoken language sounds and how it works.

Several publications since 1970 have embodied these notions of preparation. The principles underlying *Breakthrough to Literacy* give them a prominent place. They are the basis of much of the early work in *Link-up* (Reid and Low, 1972), and in Kit 1 of *Letter Links* (Reid and Donaldson, 1978). Downing and Thackray's book on reading readiness (Downing and Thackray, 1971) acknowledges their importance, pointing out that readiness is now more than ever to be seen as something we can induce and not just wait for. And important confirming evidence comes from a longitudinal study of early reading progress by Gordon Wells and Bridie Raban (Wells and Raban, 1978). They found the best predictor of attainment in reading at age seven to be the child's understanding of concepts of written language on entry to school. While it is true that a correlation does not by itself show a direct causal link, early understanding of concepts of print appears to contribute powerfully to progress in learning to read and write. This conclusion is supported by much evidence from the individual studies already described (Clark, 1976; Downing, 1970; Reid, 1966).

How can this important conceptual basis for learning the written code be further developed when the teaching of reading is begun? In terms of widespread classroom practice, it was probably the 'language-experience' approach to literacy which began the move away from emphasis on mere code-learning. In this approach, the teacher takes off from children's own utterances – things they want to communicate – and puts these into writing which the children can then 'read back'. While Huey refers to it (1908, p. 339) its origins are a little obscure. It was in fairly wide use in the United States during the sixties (Spitzer, 1967), and became familiar to many people in Britain through the writings of Sylvia Ashton Warner (1966). However, the fact that it is not listed in the index to Hunter Diack's excellent survey *In Spite of the Alphabet* (Diack, 1965) suggests that its use in Britain was not yet widespread by that date.

The language-experience approach represents an advance which even its early users may not have fully realized. Firstly, it begins where the child is, and shows the transformation of speech into writing actually taking place. It therefore provides an opportunity for teacher and child to talk about this process, and for the teacher to point out those important features of written language (such as separate words, letters, lines, arrangement of text on a page, left-to-right conventions) with which the child must come to feel at home.

But the language-experience approach does something more. It places written language in meaningful situations, and shows it expressing information which the children have decided they want to convey. In the first years of the 'new wave' of studies of oral language acquisition, the primacy of meaning for children learning to comprehend and use oral language was initially neglected, because of a preoccupation with syntax and grammar (see below). It was not until the early seventies that a turning point was reached, a point marked by a paper by Macnamara (1972). His contention – that children first learn about meaning, as embodied in events, situations and sensed purposes, and then learn to fit language to these meanings – shed further light on the strange nature of written language for the novice. Written language is language in a new code – 'language by eye' instead of 'language by ear'. But it is also, as met in books, a language without situation, without a speaker, without an immediate purpose. It is what Margaret Donaldson (1978) has called 'dis-embedded'. It is language pared down to the words alone, with no support from intonation, gesture, or facial expression. Robert Louis Stevenson (1879) called it 'the silent, inexpressive type'. Children must, he says, 'confront the silent, inexpressive type alone, like pioneers'. This acute piece of observation, buried in one of his *Essays of Travel*, shows a rare insight into the nature of learning to read.

There is a fashion today to describe the act of reading a book as 'having a dialogue with the text'. Now whatever reading a book may be, it is not a dialogue. Rather, it is listening with the mind to a monologue, delivered by an absent and most probably unknown author. The print is fixed and unchanging. It does not add one word in answer to a question or a comment. This is not to say that reading is a passive activity. But it does mean that the child learning to read has to learn a new way of reacting to a verbal message.

A language-experience approach, however, can greatly ease the transition the child has to make. It builds on the child's intention and wish to com-municate, and so provides an important bridge between the immediacy and vividness of conversation and the static remoteness of print. I have already referred to *Breakthrough to Literacy*, which can be seen as a development and a formalization of language-experience techniques. Observation of children working with the materials (Reid, 1975) showed that they came to understand the communicative function of written language very well. It was clear that the teacher's role in reading and responding to what the children had composed was a powerful element in this learning process.

Three other bridges exist, all easily accessible. One is found in the use by the teacher of written communication in the classroom – not labels on objects like tables or doors, but real messages – notices, notes to other teachers, sentences under children's paintings. Another is the reading aloud of stories, making it clear that the print on the paper, and not the pictures, is the key to the words that are uttered. The third is the use of public print – perhaps the most 'embedded' of all written language which children can encounter, apart from the writing they themselves have been involved in generating. Children can, with help, become easily aware of such things as street signs or advertisements and can understand their purposes very well. Public print can also be successfully integrated into many classroom activities and into early reading material (cf. Reid and Low, 1972).

There is yet a third outcome of the language-experience approach which recent thinking has justified. When sentences are dictated by children, it follows that they contain not only vocabulary the children know, but sentence structures which conform to the children's speech patterns. Concern with the sentence patterns that appear in the texts which young children are given to read has developed along with a changing view of language acquisition. As long as language growth was seen as mainly consisting in the acquisition of vocabulary, then early books were judged acceptable if the vocabulary reflected the words children 'knew'. The meaning was thought of as the sum of the word meanings. We now realize that much more is involved. Clare's problem, we must remember, was not with vocabulary. It was to discover how certain words were *related* to one another – how they were to be combined to produce meaning. These structural relations among words in a phrase or sentence are what we call *syntax*, and it is to the role of syntax in reading that I now want to turn.

The recognition that young children beginning to read are dealing not just with words but with the syntax and grammar of written texts – and hence with phrase and sentence meaning – was another major change in our thinking about how they should be helped. It opened new avenues in reading research and teaching methods, it altered the construction of early reading materials, and it added yet another dimension to the concept of 'readiness'. It also clarified greatly the notion of 'readability'. The new studies of language acquisition made it clear that children learning to speak acquired general rules from the language they heard adults speaking. They gradually acquired a grasp of the way words must be ordered, combined and inflected to convey meaning. The children arrived at this knowledge without any direct teaching and they made many mistakes on the way. But some of these very mistakes (like saying 'bringed' instead of 'brought') were seen as evidence that 'rule-forming' was at work. Certain features of language structure – for example, the correct word order in questions – were sometimes relatively late in being learned. A child of around four might well say 'What they are doing?' (Menyuk, 1969). Yet by the age of five, children were seen as having an extensive grasp of basic sentence structure. They were therefore coming to the task of reading with powerful equipment to which reading theory and practice had paid little or no attention. We now began to realize that they must be given a chance to put it to use.

How was this to be done? The answer seemed to be that the early texts which they were given to read should be of a kind which allowed them to make use of their syntactic knowledge as well as their knowledge of vocabulary and their general understanding of their world. As we have seen, text constructed in the course of language-experience activities achieves this end (unless of course the teacher alters it as she writes it down). But what about reading schemes or other early books, to which children must fairly quickly move?

The unnatural and stilted nature of sentences in primers based on word methods or on early 'phonic' methods had been noticed a long time before. They ranked high among the faults mentioned by Huey (1908). However, a general change in the style of basal reading texts was slow to come.

It is often the case that evidence appears before there is a theory to explain it. When this happens, the evidence may have to wait for years to find recognition, even from the person who discovered it. In 1958 I published a study of a group of five-year-olds in their first year of learning to read, in which I interviewed them and also gave them some experimental reading tasks. The results (Reid, 1958) opened my eyes to many things. Unlike the children in the study described above, who were from less privileged homes, this group of middle-class children were more able to give accounts of how they set about trying to read something. Some of them were remarkably articulate about certain sources of confusion and difficulty. When questioned more closely about these, the children attributed almost all of the difficulty to 'more difficult words' or 'harder words'. Pressed for examples, the spoke of 'long words you can't spell and you just have to remember them' (like 'except'), of letters that 'don't say anything' (as in 'right'), of 'words not good for sounding' or 'not sounded that way' or where 'you'd expect it to be something else' (like 'one'). The difficulties at the surface of their consciousness, about which they could speak when questioned, were all to do with words, with rules for 'sounding' which did not apply, with expectations not fulfilled.

The preoccupation with words and sounds which this group showed seems to mirror very well the preoccupation noted earlier as running through writings on reading method up to the 1950s. This is not surprising. The teacher who concentrates on words and sounds is implicitly telling the children that these are what 'reading' is about. But one of the reading experiments which I conducted with these same children suggested that although individual words were the main focus of conscious attention and effort, they were not the sole determiners of what the children actually did when they were reading a sentence. I gave them two sets of four sentences, with a large common vocabulary, but so constructed that the second set was more advanced than the first in syntax and concepts. An example from the first set was: 'Can you give me more words to read?'; an example from the second set was: 'We must not give up when work is hard.' In another pair, 'I can see his face in the darkness' was contrasted with 'Darkness was upon the face of the deep.' The children all read the eight sentences in the same order, because I wanted to find out what happened when they met, in a more puzzling context, words they had read correctly, or had been helped to read, in the easier one.

I found that the best readers could read both versions. Some of the average readers however, could read the first set but not the second. Moreover they refused, or misread, words which they had read correctly a few moments earlier. When asked why these were difficult, they said things like, 'Hard words you've never seen before.' Words described in this way included 'his', 'to', 'deep', 'face', 'more', 'not' and 'darkness.' Quite apart from the fact that these were words already identified, they were almost all likely to be part of the sight vocabulary of middle-class children near the end of their first year at school, as these children were. It was obvious then, that 'word recognition' could not be the whole basis of their success or failure. Something which at the time I called simply 'difficult context' was influencing their recognition of apparently very 'easy' words. The children, however, showed no awareness of this at all. At the time this study was done, a great wave of interest in the role of syntax in early reading was building up in North America; but I did not yet know about it. So I did not fully realize how my findings demonstrated one of the crucial links – and one of the crucial divisions – between spoken and written language.

Four years later Ruth Strickland (1962) published a monograph on the relationship of children's oral language to the language in basal readers. It is interesting to reflect that a gap of over 50 years separates it from the publication by E. B. Huey of *The Psychology and Pedagogy of Reading* (Huey, 1908). Her study was a major influence in bringing reading theory into line with thinking on language acquisition. In it, she made a comparison, in terms of the sentence structures used, between a large body of transcripts of the speech of kindergarten children and sentences sampled from four widely-used basal readers. Her analysis laid bare the great poverty and rigidity of the language in these books when viewed alongside the flexibility and variety of the sentences in children's speech. She raised the question whether the books from which children learn should perhaps contain language which resembles much more closely, in sentence structure, the ways the children speak.

A close look at her data showed that there were actually two kinds of mismatch between the books and the speech samples. The early reading books were indeed rigid and bare in comparison with children's speech; but in addition they contained quite a number of sentence patterns which the children's speech samples did not contain, sometimes because they were things that one writes but does not say. I therefore decided to use her speech data as the basis for an analysis of four schemes in wide use in Britain (Reid, 1970), looking particularly at this second kind of 'mismatch'. The results served to specify very clearly the main ways in which the language of these early reading books was, in the words of E. B. Huey ' ... totally unlike anything a child would naturally say ...' (Huey, 1908). And the matter at issue was not vocabulary: it was *syntax* – the ways in which words are ordered and related to one another to convey meaning.

To begin with, much of the language of the primers did not reflect the ways in which 'function' or 'grammatical' words (e.g. 'to', 'but', 'so'), as opposed to 'content' words, play their part in giving a sentence flow, coherence, and sense. There were many instances of adverbial phrases (like 'in school' or 'by the fire') appearing in positions where children would not put them and therefore would not expect them (e.g. A child would not say: 'By the fire sat a dog'). Many of the sentences were what Hocker (1963) called 'hortatory' – exhortations to 'look', 'see', 'come', etc., in which it was often unclear whether the speaker was one of the characters or the author of the book. Two instances of the confusing nature of this kind of writing, taken from my own records, are worth quoting at this point.

In the first instance, a child reading: 'Come here, Tip' said: 'It says "Come here Tip" and it says he's coming along here.'

In other words, the child interpreted the 'command' to Tip as a statement *about* Tip. In the second instance, a child reading: 'See the boats, John,' at the foot of a page, turned the page saying: 'Now we'll see what John says.' But the following page merely continues to exhort John to see the boats! This is a splendid example of a child interpreting a piece of text as a real item of dialogue, something which would require a reply, and anticipating that the text would conform to one of the ways she knew dialogue worked.

The arguments, then, for a radical change in the language of early readers were powerful. But many people continued to doubt whether the emphasis on sentence structures was well founded. How could we know that 'implicit knowledge' in this area was transferred to reading?

The most convincing demonstration that children's implicit knowledge of basic rules of syntax does transfer to the task of making sense of print has come from the study of early reading errors. Goodman, to whom we owe much of the impetus in this movement, called his method not the study of errors but the 'analysis of miscues' (Goodman, 1969). This choice of wording conveys the central emphasis – that many of the errors of the beginner are 'guesses' which show the child attempting to use linguistic knowledge as 'cues' to construct 'hypotheses' about meaning. Following Goodman's first study (Goodman, 1967) evidence on the errors of beginning readers came from studies by Clay (1969) and by Weber (1970). These showed that a high proportion of substitution errors fitted the preceding syntax, and that they often consisted of supplying the correct part of speech even if the sense was wrong. These high proportions could be found, moreover, in the reading of children who were not progressing very well. That is to say, children with limited word-identification skills were drawing on some of the deep implicit knowledge which guided their comprehension and production of speech.

There is now a school of thought, represented by Goodman and by Smith (1978), which looks on the construction of meaning and the use of syntactic knowledge as the principal components in reading from the very start, and proposes a radical change in how beginners are taught. It is argued that learning to read should proceed merely 'by reading'. Children should learn on 'real books' with a good story line and reasonably varied vocabulary and sentence forms. They should, according to this view, begin by having the story read to them, and then, on successive re-readings of it, supply more and more of the text themselves. Even if their first 'readings' bear little relation, at a word level, to the text, these are to be accepted. Two accounts of this method at work can be found in McKenzie (1977), and in Meek (1982).

In some places, Goodman and Smith appear to argue that any attention to the details of the code is misplaced and unnecessary (Goodman, 1981; Smith, 1978). Smith argues this on largely theoretical grounds, while Goodman (who like Smith plays down the importance of word identification) holds this view in the face of the massive body of evidence he has himself collected about 'miscues'. Yet these miscues are, in the last analysis, wrong hypotheses not corrected by checking the words on the page.

Both writers are at pains not just to stress the primacy of meaning, but to argue that reading need not be different in its nature from listening to speech. But it is inescapably different, in many ways. Some of these have already been examined in this paper. And it is these differences which argue for, rather than against, some deliberate attention to the code – though not for attention to the code in isolation from other kinds of cue. Rather they argue for modes of teaching and learning which will strengthen children's ability to switch rapidly from one kind of cue to another and to integrate them to good effect.

This very process of integration was charted by Biemiller (1970) in a longitudinal study of the reading of first-grade children. Some of the children were seen to move fairly quickly from an early reliance on prediction, producing many 'response errors', to a stage of 'non-response errors' – a stage where they fell silent when puzzled and tried to draw on their phonic knowledge. It was these children who made the best progress, eventually reaching a third stage where they made use of cues of both kinds while making many fewer errors overall. These are important findings. No one would want to deny that a skilled reader 'predicts' meaning – in some sense of that term – and economizes on cues in scanning print. But there is a world of difference between this smooth and efficient processing and the tentative 'guesses' of the beginner. In between the two states there lies a long learning period – a period in which many things have to happen. One of these things is that 'word recognition' has to become assured, quick, and in many cases context-free.

Children between the ages of seven and eleven move in their reading into fiction and 'content area' texts which contain varying blends of narrative and information. (Consider, for instance, geography as opposed to history.) In making this move they leave behind the simple syntax and supportive illustrations of their early books and encounter some of the richness and variety of written registers – the different forms which written language takes to fit differing purposes. But with this richness and variety come new kinds of difficulty, stemming not just from vocabulary but from syntax, organization, style, and – let us not forget – from new and *unexpected* content. For while it is true that expectations support our reading, it is equally true that unless a book can surprise us or tell us things we did not previously know, there is little point in our reading it.

To cope with new ideas and new language forms, good word recognition may well not be enough (as we saw in the case of Clare), but it is most assuredly necessary. If Clare had not been able to recognize all of the words in her puzzling sentence, she would probably have attributed her problem (as did the boys in my first study) to 'difficult words', and she might thus not have realized that it was a problem about meaning. Furthermore, she would have been less ready to be taught about the syntactic forms that were unfamiliar to her. Greater attention can be paid to syntactic pattern when word recognition skills are well developed.

How does efficient word recognition develop? The literature on this question is vast, and I have already touched on the theoretical accounts that were orthodox until quite recently. How should we now view this aspect of reading growth and its place in the whole complex process?

Let us look at the way we now see the task from the children's point of view. What they have to do is to build up a picture (or, if you like, a model) of the way the words in their language are written down – that is, of the orthography. They must do this not just so as to be able to write words, but also to be able to read them with increasing certainty. It is, as we have seen, not enough to entertain hypotheses about what the text says: these hypotheses must also be confirmed or disconfirmed. And this decision-making, which modern writers such as Goodman and Smith stress so much, can only come from confident knowledge of the ways in which letter patterns can – or cannot – function. To build up their internal model, children need to be given correct information about the ways in which, in the case of English, 26 letters are used to represent around 44 phonemes. Teachers have for a long time referred to this area of learning as 'phonics', and have seen it as a confused and confusing mass of 'rules' and 'exceptions' which they have tried, in varying ways, to structure and simplify. The trouble is that simplifying may distort to the point where the true picture is totally obscured.

I want to suggest a somewhat different approach. I believe that as children begin to learn the details of the written code, they urgently need to learn two important general facts about the system. One is that letters sometimes function singly, and sometimes in groups (e.g. 't' and 'h' function singly, but also as the digraph 'th'). The other is that both single letters and letter groups can have more than one sound value (e.g. 'a' sounds differently in 'cat', 'was', 'make', and 'any').

It is vital that children realize these two facts at an early stage, and that the teacher acknowledges them. Otherwise, children will assuredly begin to build their picture of the system on a 'one-letter-one-sound' model, while constantly meeting words which do not fit into it. A five-year-old child in one of my studies talked of words that were 'funny – not the same letters as you say them in'. Questioned further, he gave as an instance 'me', which he thought should have 'two e's', or be written 'mE'. Another said confidently, trying to read 'how': 'I'll sound it and then I'll get it – huh/o/wuh/.' When this did not work, his resources were at an end. Children are perfectly capable, at the age of five, of dealing with choices – with the idea that if one solution does not make sense, they can try something else; all they need is correct information about what the choices are. Complicated rules, with lists of exceptions, can be put aside.

For the early reader, then, the decision as to whether a word has been correctly identified must be based on some fusion of judgements about sense and judgements about letter pattern. Later, however, word recognition has to become more confident and self-contained, because it in turn becomes the basis on which other problems – about syntax and about sentence meaning – have to be dealt with.

In an illuminating discussion of the growth of confident word recognition in reading, Ehri (1978) makes use of the notion that each word in our mental word-store has for us a 'linguistic identity'. This identity is compounded of how the word sounds, how we pronounce it, how it is constructed (e.g., whether it has a suffix), how it functions syntactically, and what it can mean. She suggests that when we learn to recognize the word in print, we add its 'graphic identity' to this complex interwoven image (as distinct, that is, from merely attaching it to the sound). She points out that growth in word recognition can therefore best take place through meeting printed words in meaningful contexts, since these allow the learner to build round each new written form a rich aggregate of knowledge about its linguistic properties.

Finally, a stage is reached where the word is instantly recognizable without contextual support of any kind. But while it makes good sense to think of form, syntax and meaning as all helping to establish word recognition, the other side of the interaction is equally important. What of the situation where syntax and meaning are the source of difficulty? For the early reader, as we have seen, the effect can be to block word identification. Later, as in the case of Clare, this does not necessarily happen. Clare 'could read the words'. But how prevalent are difficulties of the kind she found?

It is not difficult to show experimentally some of the areas where problems other than those of word recognition can exist for children beyond the beginning reader stage. In 1972 I conducted an experiment with reading tasks at different levels of syntactic difficulty (Reid, 1972). The children had to read sentences and answer a literal question on each one. For instance, one group read: 'Tom walked in front of Dick and carried a flag.' The other group read: 'Tom walked in front of Dick. Tom carried a flag.' Both groups were then asked: '*Who carried the flag?*' While the question was easy for the second group, 36 per cent of the first group thought the flag was carried by Dick. Many other items in the test gave similar results. (See also the work of Carol Chomsky, 1969.) If syntactic features of even this simple kind can be so misleading, we must conclude that they should be discussed and taught. But if children are to learn to understand these structures, then they must read and identify the words on the page. The order and identity of the word string must be clear. Guessing and paraphrasing will only serve to blur the distinctions they must learn to make (Donaldson and Reid, 1982).

Looking at language structures in this close way involves children in becoming more aware of language form (as distinct from the total meaning) than they have formerly been in their use of speech. This kind of awareness has come to be known either as 'metalinguistic' or as 'linguistic' awareness – signifying that it is directed at the language *as a system*. Its relevance for reading progress is now a topic of lively interest and concern (see for instance Downing, 1979).

In the field of spoken language, linguistic awareness and the ability to talk about it have now taken their place alongside the many other linguistic capacities to be studied. It is clear, however, that 'linguistic awareness' can be defined in more than one way. Indeed if we stretch the meaning of 'awareness' far enough it can be viewed as a developing continuum, starting soon after birth. But what we are concerned with here is the state where in Courtney Cazden's words (Cazden, 1974), 'language becomes opaque', becomes something you contemplate, think about, talk about, instead of just seeing through it to what it means. Such awareness can be directed to the speech of others or to the language of a story heard or read – that is, to speech received; it can be directed to one's own speech or one's own writing – to language produced; and it can be directed to different features of the language – to the phonology of speech or the orthography of writing, to grammar and syntax, to vocabulary, to intonation. Children engaged in verse-speaking or drama, or playing any language game which requires them to attend to the sound or the form of what they say or hear, are having their linguistic awareness fostered in one of these ways.

Here, we are chiefly concerned with awareness of specific features of syntax and grammar – with the kind of knowledge of sentence structure and its meaning which was not available to those children in my experiment (Reid, 1972) who thought that Dick was carrying the flag. The particular syntactic pattern, described as a 'deletion' (in this case of the subject of the verb 'carried'), was something they had not learned to handle. But even more may be involved than surface syntax. Compare the two sentences in the further example (see Donaldson and Reid, 1982).

Tom followed Dick carrying a flag.
Tom saw Dick carrying a flag.

In the first, the flag-carrier is Tom; in the second it is Dick. Here however, the surface syntactic forms are identical. What the children must come to know this time is that 'perception verbs' ('saw', 'watched', 'heard', etc.) follow different syntactic rules from other verbs when the subject of a subsequent verb is not named. An interesting study of the way children learn to handle these rules can be found in Goodluck and Roeper (1978). It is worth noting that while the second sentence in the above example is something children would readily say, the first is not. It is a more literary form than the second.

The case for planned teaching about language structures found in books is therefore very strong. 'English' schemes aim their language work largely at vocabulary and at writing skills, while the 'comprehension' tasks they contain, though making demands on reading skills, do not actually serve to extend children's knowledge so much as to test them on what they already know.

Progress in reading can be seen, then, as having a fourfold nature. It involves the development of new concepts, and the learning of new terms, relating to the nature and purpose of written language. It involves the acquisition of a visual code for speech and of principles and strategies needed to understand and use it. It involves the transfer of implicit knowledge about syntax to this new medium, followed by a great expansion of syntactic under-standing to cope with the language of books. And it involves developing new attitudes to language whereby conscious attention to structure takes its place alongside attention to total meaning, and the text is seen as a self-contained source of communication.

In contrast to the limited, code-oriented views which it is superseding, such a view offers much more scope for coherent and thoughtful teaching, in which the achievement of literacy is treated as a many-sided extension of linguistic and mental growth.

Intellectual development

INTRODUCTION

Until recently, it was common to emphasize the intellectual limitations of preschool children. Their performance on a range of tasks including conservation, classification, and perspective-taking made their thinking seem considerably egocentric and their cognitive skills surprisingly restricted.

Recent work has called for some modification of this view. In particular it has thrown light on the importance of context and on the extent of children's sensitivity to contextual cues.

Among the best known of all Piagetian tests are those which deal with conservation of number, length, weight and so on. Piaget's basic finding is that a child may judge two arrays equal in, say, number when they *look* equal – when, for instance, two rows of objects are laid out in one-to-one correspondence – but may judge the same arrays unequal a moment later after the experimenter has made an irrelevant change such as pushing the objects in one row closer together. For a long time this finding was taken as evidence of a basic incomprehension of number, this being held to be symptomatic of more widespread cognitive limitations. It has recently emerged, however, that what might seem like a minor modification of the task makes a substantial difference to the results. If the irrelevant change is made not by the deliberate act of an adult experimenter, but in some seemingly accidental or incidental way – for instance by the intervention of a naughty teddy bear – then the number of young children who continue to judge that the arrays are still equal after the change rises significantly (McGarrigle and Donaldson, 1974; Light *et al.*, 1979; Dockrell *et al.*, 1980). Why should this be? One possibility is that some of the difficulties which children experience in the standard Piagetian test arise from the fact that they are sensitive not only to the words of the question they are asked, but also to the context in which the words are uttered. That is, in deciding how to interpret the question, they may attend to what the adult *does* as well as to what he says. Thus when the adult has deliberately altered the length of one of the rows they may conclude that length is what he now wants to talk about. In other words, they are demonstrating a considerable measure of social sensitivity and have not understood that this is not immediately appropriate in dealing with a formal intellectual task. (It is worth pointing out that when we set them such tasks we never tell them that they are supposed to attend to our words alone.)

While we believe that this interpretation of the research findings will prove basically correct, it should be noted that the issues are still being actively debated and further evidence has recently been gathered (see Donaldson, 1982, for a review). In any event, however, the findings about modifications to the conservation task are by no means the only ones which reveal the importance of having regard to context in assessing young children's intellectual abilities. The present section contains a number of readings which, taken together, indicate that in contexts which make sense to them and which allow them to deploy the skills they possess, preschool children are highly competent. They can conserve, classify, measure, memorize, reason, and appreciate perspectives other than their own with considerable degrees of success. Yet this does not mean that on entry to school children are intellectually fully accomplished. For although young children do exhibit such skills, their thinking is still context dependent. That is, although able to deploy their intellectual skills in some contexts, they are not yet able to deploy them in any context. The ability to think and reason independently of context has still to undergo much further development.

Nevertheless, in investigating contexts in which children do reveal their intellectual skills, many of the readings in this section reflect a recent and important change in emphasis. Rather than revealing children's intellectual weaknesses, recent research has concentrated on establishing children's strengths (see Donaldson, 1978, Gelman 1978). This has led to a more balanced view of the intellectual development of young children – a result of considerable importance within early childhood education. Knowledge of the skills that young children already possess on entry to school, and the ways in which these skills have yet to develop, provides a different perspective on what has to be learned in school. Skills typically taught in school, particularly reading and number skills, can now be seen as the development and extension of skills already present. For example, if arithmetic is viewed as an extension of informal knowledge of number that children bring to school, then their transition to the learning of formal arithmetic may be made easier to negotiate.

Further, the recognition that children bring a range of considerable intellectual skills to school may provide a better understanding of children who fail in school, or who find the transition to formal schooling more than usually difficult. Such children's lack of success may not be simply attributable to a lack of intellectual abilities. Rather, such children may have failed to realize the nature and purpose of school activities. They may not, for example, have realized that written language is a means of representing and recording what people say, or that arithmetic symbols are a means of representing objects and actions carried out on objects in the everyday environment.

It is therefore important to ensure that the implications of recent work investigating young children's thinking are fully recognized. The readings that follow provide an indication of the range of evidence now available which contributes to a better understanding of the nature of young children's minds.

13.

Interpreting inclusion: A contribution to the study of the child's cognitive and linguistic development

James McGarrigle, Robert Grieve and Martin Hughes

The development of classification skills in children is a topic of interest to psychologists and educators, as classification forms the basis of a range of school learning activities. One particular set of problems (class inclusion problems) investigates the ability to compare classes with their constituent subclasses. For example, given a bunch of primulas and daisies, when do children know that there are more flowers than primulas, and that there are more flowers than daisies? That is, when do children appreciate that any class (here, the bunch of flowers) is greater than any subclass (primulas or daisies) included within it? Until recently, it was supposed that children could not solve such problems until about seven or eight years of age and, in some contexts, not until considerably older. As the present reading indicates, it can be seen that if children understand what comparison the adult is requiring them to make, most four-year-olds can handle inclusion problems successfully.

In Piaget's inclusion problem, the child is required to compare a whole with one of its parts (Inhelder and Piaget, 1964; Piaget, 1952). For example, the child is shown a number of wooden beads, most of which are brown, but two of which are white, and asked whether there are more wooden beads or more brown beads. Piaget reports that younger children, aged below seven or eight years, typically reply that there are more brown beads. This, together with justifications they may provide (e.g. that there are more brown beads 'because there's only two white ones'), indicates that instead of comparing part with whole (the brown beads with all the wooden beads) they in fact compare the two parts (the brown beads with the white ones). Older children, aged seven or eight years, reply that there are more wooden beads, indicating that they have appropriately compared part with whole.

According to Piaget, younger children fail on this problem because their cognitive structures lack the operational characteristic of reversibility required for simultaneous comparison of part and whole. That is, the young child cannot decompose the whole to obtain the part, and at the same time reverse this operation to recompose the whole for comparison with the part. Thus in Piaget's view the younger 'pre-operational' child cannot make the simultaneous comparison of part with whole, and is instead limited to comparing one part with another when presented with inclusion problems.

Although there is little doubt that younger children *do* typically compare one part with another in inclusion tasks, Piaget's claim that this is inevitable seems open to question, for there is evidence that the performance of younger children may improve when certain aspects of the inclusion task are varied: for example, when changes are made to the characteristics of the array (Isen, Riley, Tucker, and Trabasso, 1975; Tatarsky, 1974; Trabasso, Isen, Dolecki, McLanahan, Riley and Tucker, 1978; Wohlwill, 1968); or when changes are made to the form of the inclusion question (Kalil, Youssef and Lerner, 1974; Markman, 1973; Markman and Seibert, 1976; Shipley, 1974; Winer, 1974); or when changes are made to the method of task presentation (Jennings, 1970; Winer and Kronberg, 1974; Wohlwill, 1968). In addition, several studies have found that performance on inclusion tasks may improve when training procedures are employed to overcome initially incorrect responses (Ahr and Youniss, 1970; Brainerd, 1974; Grieve, 1971; Kohnstamm, 1963; Sheppard, 1973).

If younger children can simultaneously compare part with whole in certain forms of task presentation, then their failure to do so in standard presentations of inclusion problems needs to be explained. Recently, attempts have been made to characterize the information-processing strategies the child adopts on receipt of inclusion problems (Isen *et al.*, 1975; Klahr and Wallace, 1972; Meadows, 1977; Wilkinson, 1976), and these models have drawn attention to difficulties the child may experience (for example those associated with identifying, counting and comparing class and subclass). However in adopting some information-processing strategy, the child operates on certain assumptions about what the task requires (see Hayes, 1972, on inclusion, and Braine and Shanks, 1965a, b, on conservation). In relation to inclusion, it has been proposed that in standard presentations of the task, the perceptual characteristics of the array may encourage the young child to adopt the erroneous assumption that the task requires comparison of one part of the array with another part, rather than one part of the array with the whole (Wohlwill, 1968). That is, in standard presentations, the array typically consists of two subclasses whose distinction is perceptually salient (e.g. the brown and white beads), and this may encourage the young child to assume that the task requires comparison of these distinct constituents. This suggests that if improvements in performance are to be obtained, this assumption needs to be discouraged.

Experiment 1 attempts to do this by presenting arrays which contain more than one salient feature. The materials used are model farmyard animals (cows), each of which can vary according to its *colour* (black or white) and its *posture* (standing up or lain sleeping on its side). With these materials the child can be asked to compare a class defined in terms of one salient feature (e.g., colour) with an included subclass defined in terms of the other feature (posture). If, as intended, this form of task presentation does discourage the child's assumption that the task involves comparison of salient subclasses, then it should result in higher performance compared with a more standard form of task presentation.

EXPERIMENT 1

SUBJECTS

Forty-eight children (24 male and 24 female) of mean age four years, eight months (range three years, three months to five years, three months), drawn from nursery schools in Edinburgh participated.

METHOD

Each child was presented with three inclusion problems. In the standard form of the task (Problem 1A) the array consisted of four model cows, one white and three black, all standing, and the question involved reference to the salient distinction between subclasses of black and white cows (i.e. 'Are there more black cows or more cows?'). In the alternative tasks, the child was asked to compare sets defined in terms of different salient features. For Problem 1B, the array consisted as before of one white and three black cows, but all the cows were lain 'sleeping' on their sides, and the child was asked to compare the black cows with the sleeping cows. For problem 1C, the array consisted of four cows, but now all were white, with one standing while the other three lay sleeping on their sides; and here the child was asked to compare the sleeping cows with the white cows.

The children were individually tested by the same experimenter, who first presented the material (four white cows and three black cows), and asked the child to point to and name the 'cows', the 'black cows', and the 'white cows'. When placed on its side, an animal was said to be sleeping, and the child was also asked to point out the experimenter's arranged instances of 'sleeping cows'. When the child was familiar with the materials and their referent expressions, the materials were removed to a box out of the child's view. The arrays and problems were then presented to the child one at a time, material excess to any problem being concealed in the box. Order of presentation of problems was varied systematically across the group, and order of presentation of terms within problems was balanced. The arrays and problems appear in Table 1.

RESULTS AND DISCUSSION

The number and proportion of children who responded correctly to the three problems are given in Table 1. It can be seen that about a third of the children responded correctly on 1A, just over half responded correctly on 1B, and half responded correctly on 1C. Comparing these levels of performance, performance on 1B and 1C is not significantly different (sign test, $p = 0.596$), but performance on both 1B and 1C is is significantly better than on 1A ($p = 0.032$ for 1A–1B; and $p = 0.056$ for 1A–1C).

Table 1 *Material and results in Experiment 1 (N = 48)*

Problem	Array	Question	Subjects correct	Proportion
1A	W B B B	Are there more black cows or more cows?	15	.31
1B	⌇ B B B	Are there more black cows or more sleeping cows?	25	.52
1C	W ⌇ ⌇ ⌇	Are there more sleeping cows or more white cows?	24	.50

These results show that performance on the alternative 1B and 1C presentations is significantly better than on the standard 1A presentation. Thus, it seems that, as intended, the alternative presentations have been to some extent effective in discouraging the typical assumption that the inclusion task requires comparison of subclasses.

However, it is not clear from this experiment precisely which aspects of these alternative presentations are responsible for the improvement in performance. The three problems used here differ in more than one respect, for not only is the array different for each problem, but in each case different expressions are used to refer to the class and subclass. Either of these factors might by itself have been responsible for the observed changes in performance. Consequently the next experiment uses more systematic variations in the form of the array and the wording of the question in order to determine the extent to which these factors were responsible for the effect observed in Experiment 1.

EXPERIMENT 2

SUBJECTS

Forty-eight children (26 male and 22 female) of mean age six years (range four years, nine months to six years, nine months), drawn from primary schools in Edinburgh participated.

METHOD

The materials consisted of one white and three black cows, arranged in standing or sleeping position. The four tasks required comparison between the black cows and the standing/sleeping cows. The arrays and questions employed appear in Table 2. The children were tested individually by the same experimenter, and as in Experiment 1, the experimenter first ensured that the child was familiar with the materials and their referent expressions before presenting the inclusion tasks. Order of presentation of problems was balanced across the group, as was order of mention of terms in the problems.

RESULTS AND DISCUSSION

There are several findings to be considered here. First, performance on 2A and 2C is not significantly different (sign test, $p = 0.387$). Thus when the question is kept constant and the only change concerns the way the materials have been arranged, the different arrangement of materials does not by itself have a significant effect.

Second, performance on 2B is better than on 2A, but the improvement is not significant ($p = 0.227$). In contrast, performance on 2D is significantly better than on 2C ($p = 0.013$). Thus, altering the form of the question from 2A to 2B has had no effect, while significant improvement has resulted from the alteration from 2C to 2D. While these alterations are similar in terms of question form ('cows' qualified by 'standing up' in 2B and by 'sleeping' in 2D), they differ in that the questions refer to arrays which are differently arranged.

Taken together, these two findings indicate that changes in the wording of the question, or in the form of the array, may not by themselves have a significant effect on performance. Rather, it is the interaction between these two factors which seems of importance. The challenge to the child's assumption that the inclusion task requires comparison of subclasses may not prove effective without both the introduction of a second salient feature (here accomplished by means of the unusual 'sleeping' posture of the animals) and a form of question which defines the sets for comparison in terms of the different salient features. In the present study, significant improvement results when both these factors are present (2D), but not in presentations with only one factor present (2B, where only the question is changed; and 2C, which alters only the arrangement of materials).

The third main finding that deserves attention is that while these changes may result in some degree of improvement in performance, a considerable proportion of children still do not succeed on the task. (This also occurred in Experiment 1). One argument here, on a Piagetian view, is that this is to be expected: since younger children are being asked to compare sets, one of which is included in the other, then of course they will fail. An alternative view, however, would argue that situations which introduce the sorts of questions and arrays typically found in inclusion tasks are generally difficult for young children, regardless of whether or not the sets to be compared are included. That is, the child's difficulties in such situations may be associated more with the process of arriving at which sets are to be compared, rather than with making comparisons between sets that are included. On this view, it would be expected that young children would have difficulties when asked to compare sets which are *not* included. In contrast, the Piagetian view would not predict difficulties in comparing nonincluded sets. These two predictions are examined in the next experiment, where the child is asked to make comparisons between nonincluded sets.

Table 2 *Material and results in Experiment 2 (N = 48)*

Problem	Array	Question	Subjects correct	Proportion
2A	B B B W	Are there more black cows or more cows?	14	.29
2B	B B B W	Are there more black cows or more standing-up cows?	18	.38
2C	ᗺ ᗺ ᗺ ⋝	Are there more black cows or more cows?	12	.25
2D	ᗺ ᗺ ᗺ ⋝	Are there more black cows or more sleeping cows?	23	.48

EXPERIMENT 3

SUBJECTS

Thirty-six children (21 male and 15 female) of mean age five years, four months (range four years, ten months to five years, ten months) drawn from primary schools in Edinburgh participated.

METHOD

Model farmyard animals, one white and three black horses, and two black and two white cows, were arranged facing each other across a section of model farmyard wall. The cows faced the horses in one-to-one correspondence, and the black cows were always opposite black horses. The arrangement is shown in Figure 1.

The children were tested individually by the same experimenter. Materials were arranged in front of the child who sat in the position shown in Figure 1. To control for possible position preferences, the horses appeared to the left for half the children, and to the right from the remainder. When the children were asked to name the different kinds and colours of animals, no child failed to provide accurate descriptions. The children were then presented with the three problems shown in Table 3, order of presentation of questions and order of mention of terms within questions being balanced across the group.

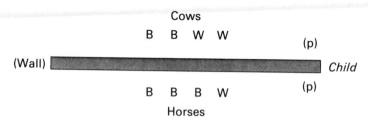

Figure 1: *Arrangement of material in Experiment 3*

On presentation of a question, the experimenter would point to the appropriate sides of the array in turn; thus for Problem 3A: 'Are there more black horses here (pointing to the horses' side of the wall) or more cows here (pointing to the cows' side of the wall)?' In an attempt to avoid limiting the child's scope for interpreting the referents of the terms in the questions, the experimenter did not point directly at any individual horse or cow, but rather pointed to the positions (*p*) indicated in Figure 1. The child's responses and any supporting verbalizations were noted by the experimenter.

RESULTS AND DISCUSSION

Table 3 shows the number and proportion of children who responded correctly on each problem. Problem 3A was answered correctly by few children, while about half the group gave correct answers to 3B and 3C. It is clear that

Table 3 *Material and results in Experiment 3* (N = 36)

Problem	Question	Subjects correct	Proportion
3A	Are there more black horses or more cows?	5	.14
3B	Are there more white cows or more horses?	21	.58
3C	Are there more horses or more cows?	18	.50

children do have difficulties when asked to make this kind of comparison, even though the sets to be compared are not included.

The surprisingly low level of performance on these tasks in itself requires consideration, for it shows that young children have an unexpected degree of difficulty in arriving at the sets to be compared. The discussion which follows is based primarily on the spontaneous comments which accompanied the children's responses (children were not required to justify their responses). It should be regarded as tentative, and more intensive study of this kind of problem is clearly required.

In Problem 3A the child was asked: 'Are there more black horses or more cows?' Few children gave the correct answer; most incorrectly answered that there were more black horses. Spontaneous comments (e.g., 'There's more black horses 'cos there's only two black cows') suggest that instead of comparing the black horses with all the cows as requested, many children in fact compared the black horses with the black cows. To arrive at this comparison it is possible that the children were simply failing to restrict the scope of the adjective 'black' to the first term in the question ('horses') as intended, and also applied it to the subsequent term in the question, 'cows'. (This calls to mind textbook examples of phrase-structure ambiguity: for example, does 'old men and women' refer to old men and old women, or does it refer to old men and all women whether young or old?) It should also be noted that it is not immediately clear that these children responded on the basis of the relative *number* of black horses and black cows; they may have responded on the basis of the relative *proportion* of black animals in each set. In other words, they may have been responding as if to the question: 'Are more of the horses black or more of the cows black?' This is not implausible: there is evidence from other studies that young children's judgements of 'more' may be based on factors such as length, density and fullness, as well as number (e.g. Donaldson and Lloyd, 1974; Donaldson and McGarrigle, 1974; McGarrigle and Donaldson, 1975).

Other supporting comments to the 'more black horses' response in 3A are equally revealing. Some children replied that there were more black horses 'because there's only one white', or 'and there's only one white horse', or 'cos three are black and one horse is white', or 'cos there's three black horses and only one white'. Thus a question calling for comparison *between* sets of black horses and cows at times seems to have involved the child making comparison *within* one of these sets, the black horses with the white horse. (Also note the similarity in performance between the present task and a standard class inclusion task. In the present task the child is asked to compare black horses and *cows*, while in a typical inclusion task he would be asked, say, to compare black horses and *horses*. Nevertheless, his response to both questions is the same: he compares the black horses with the *white horse*. This response occurs independently of whether or not the sets to be compared are included).

With 3B ('Are there more white cows or more horses?') just over half the children correctly replied that there were more horses. However, it is possible that some of this apparent success is spurious, for the supporting comments of some subjects who replied 'More horses' suggest that they were in fact comparing the white cows with the *black* horses. Thus, the child's reply may not always mean what it appears to mean; here, the reply 'horses' ranges over the three black horses, not over all four horses as might be supposed. While the extent of such spurious success is not clear, it suggests that the child's difficulties with these comparative tasks may be greater than apparent success rates indicate. In addition, it indicates that considerable attention must be devoted to methodology in further study in this area.

Children who replied incorrectly in 3B that there were more white cows seem to have been comparing the white cows with the white horse (e.g. 'There's more white cows cos there's only one white horse'). Failure to restrict the scope of the adjectival modifier, and judgements based on the numerosity or relative proportion of sets (compare 'Are there more white cows or more white horses?' with 'Are more of the cows white or more of the horses white?'), could again account for this sort of incorrect response.

The remaining problem, 3C ('Are there more horses or more cows?') was not expected to cause difficulty, yet only half the children correctly replied that they were 'the same'. Of the 18 children who gave incorrect replies, one responded that there were more cows because 'they're so fat and take a lot of room up'. Size of animal was not mentioned by any other child. The remaining 17 incorrect responses were that there were more horses, and the children's spontaneous comments indicated that they were comparing the black horses with the white horse. This kind of response is very similar to that found in 3A and in standard inclusion tasks, and suggests again the readiness of some children to assume that the task involves a comparison of perceptually distinct subsets. It should also be noted that, as in 3B, the response 'horses' given here appears to range over the three black horses, rather than over all four horses as might be supposed.

It is clear from the present experiment that young children have difficulty answering questions which require comparison of nonincluded sets. In particular, their spontaneous comments indicate that their difficulties do not lie in actually calculating which of two sets is the larger, but rather in determining precisely which sets are to be compared. Almost invariably the children who 'failed' on these problems were in fact performing a task different from that intended, and indeed, for each problem there was considerable variation in what the children actually did. While we cannot be certain from the present study precisely why the children performed in this way, various factors (such as failure to restrict the scope of adjectival modifiers, comparison on the basis of relative proportions within sets, and the child's assumptions about the nature of the task) are suggested for further inquiry.

As well as being of interest in their own right, the present findings throw a new perspective on the child's performance in class inclusion tasks. The problems used here were similar to the inclusion problems used in Experiments 1 and 2, both in terms of the arrays (classes consisting of subclasses distinguishable by a salient feature) and in terms of the questions asked (comparison between sets defined for the most part with reference to the salient feature). Moreover, performance on the present tasks was frequently similar to that found in standard class inclusion tasks, particularly for Problems 3A and 3C, where many children responded to a question asking for comparison between two sets by comparing salient subclasses within one of these sets. These findings strongly suggest that the child's difficulties with class inclusion tasks do not arise merely because the sets to be compared are included, but rather that they are instances of a more general set of difficulties which occur whether or not the task involves included sets. This in turn suggests that if the child's ability to solve inclusion problems is to be gauged with any accuracy, there is a need to find ways of presenting the inclusion task which minimize the sort of difficulties revealed by Experiments 1–3. This is pursued in Experiment 4.

EXPERIMENT 4

In this study, young children were presented with inclusion problems using the array shown in Figure 2. Here a toy teddy is placed in a starting position at the left of the array, which consists of four red steps to the teddy's chair and a further two white steps to the teddy's table.

With this array, the inclusion task remains constant, and involved comparison of the red steps with all the steps. However, the presence of additional materials allows the task to be presented in a number of different ways. For example, the child can be asked whether it is further (for Teddy) to go to the chair or further to go to the table, a formulation involving comparisons of lengths, or distances, one of which is included in the other. This is analogous to a formulation used by Piaget when he presented the problem of the brown and

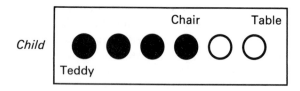

Figure 2: *Arrangement of material in Experiment 4*

wooden beads in terms of 'necklaces': the child was asked which would be longer, a necklace made of brown beads or a necklace made of wooden beads (Piaget, 1952, Chapter VII). (Piaget reports that this formulation produced results similar to those found with more standard presentations. He also reports instances where the child was presented with two identical sets of beads, and asked to compare a necklace made from the wooden beads of one set with a necklace made from the brown beads of the other set. According to Piaget, the younger ('pre-operational') children also failed on this version of the task (p. 169). However, this problem is not a class inclusion problem; rather, it is analogous to the comparison of nonincluded sets studied in Experiment 3. Therefore Piaget's conclusion: 'It thus seems to be the relationship of inclusion that is the stumbling block for these children' (p. 171) is not in fact justified by his own data).

This 'further' formulation makes no direct reference to the sets of steps, and can be compared with formulations which do. For example, the child can be asked whether there are more steps to go to the chair or more steps to go to the table. Or, the question can involve reference to the perceptually salient distinction between the sets of red and white steps, asking whether there are more red steps to go to the chair or more steps to go to the table.

These different ways of expressing the inclusion problem are compared in Experiment 4. In addition, this experiment examines whether the 'further' formulation, which might be expected to prove most effective in conveying the intended task to the child, can facilitate performance on subsequent presentation of the formulations which involve reference to the steps.

SUBJECTS

Children were drawn from nursery schools in Edinburgh. The experimental group consisted of 32 children (17 male and 15 female) of mean age four years, eight months (range three years, seven months to five years, three months). The control group consisted of 24 children (15 male and 9 female) of mean age four years, eight months (range three years, four months to five years, three months).

METHOD

The material consisted of a small three-inch-high toy teddy bear, and an appropriately sized table and chair. The 'steps' were one-and-three-quarter-inch diameter plastic discs, four red and two white. The children were tested individually by the same experimenter, who first introduced the child to 'Teddy', 'Teddy's chair', 'Teddy's table', and 'Teddy's steps'. The experimenter then arranged the materials as shown in Figure 2, and demonstrated Teddy's journeys to the table and to the chair. Finally, the experimenter explained that Teddy '. . . wakes up in the morning and wants to go to his table or his chair. Will you help him? He wants to know . . .' (presentation of questions).

Following these preliminaries, the questions shown in Table 4 were presented to the child. For each question, Teddy was placed in a 'start' position next to the child. In order to ensure a reasonable interval between each problem, Teddy also engaged in irrelevant activities (playing, hiding, etc.) between questions. Responses and supporting comments were noted. In the absence of a scoreable response, the question was repeated once. A scoreable response was defined as one which mentioned, or pointed to, either the table or the chair.

In the experimental group, the order of presentation of problems was $4A_1$ followed by $4B_1$, or $4B_1$ followed by $4A_1$ (balanced across the group); then $4C$; then $4A_2$ and $4B_2$, or $4B_2$ followed by $4A_2$ (balanced). Half the children received $4A_2$ and $4B_2$ in the same order as $4A_1$ and $4B_1$, and half in the reverse order. Order of mention of terms in the questions was balanced across the group.

Lest performance on these problems improved simply as a function of repetition of inclusion questions, the control group was presented with $4A_1$ and $4B_1$, in balanced order, then with their repetitions $4A_2$ and $4B_2$, in balanced order. For the control group, order of mention of terms in the questions was balanced as in the experimental group.

RESULTS AND DISCUSSION

The number and proportion of correct responses to the problems presented to the experimental and control groups appear in Table 4.

Results on B presentations are always better than on A presentations. Thus, performance is better on $4B_1$ than on $4A_1$ in the experimental group (sign test, $p = 0.025$), and in the control group ($p = 0.073$). This remains so when the problems are re-presented; performance on $4B_2$ is better than on $4A_2$ both in the experimental group ($p = 0.004$) and in the control group ($p = 0.020$). Thus performance is always better on questions which do not refer to the salient distinction between subclasses (B presentations) than on questions which do (A presentations).

In the experimental group, performance on 4C is also better than on $4A_1$ ($p = 0.006$). In addition, presentation of 4C facilitates performance on subsequent re-presentations of both $4A_1$ and $4B_1$. Thus performance on $4A_2$ is higher than on $4A_1$ ($p = 0.062$), and performance on $4B_2$ is higher than on $4B_1$ ($p = 0.033$). This is not merely due to the same problems having been re-presented, for re-presentation of 4A and 4B does not result in changes in performance in the control group ($p = 0.344$ for $4A_2-4A_1$; and $p = 0.500$ for $4B_2-4B_1$).

Thus when the task involves a question which refers to the salient distinction between subclasses, performance is comparatively low (A presentations, both groups). But when the question makes no reference to the distinction which is salient, performance is significantly better (B presentations, both groups). When the question does not directly refer to the sets of steps (4C), performance is also significantly better; and presentation of this (4C) task facilitates re-presentations of both A and B tasks.

It should be noted that relatively high success rates were obtained in the present study. That is, B tasks (both groups) were answered correctly by about two thirds of the three- to five-year-old children, as was the C task in the

Table 4 *Material and results in Experiment 4*

Problem	Question	Experimental group ($N = 32$)		Control group ($N = 24$)	
		Subjects correct	Proportion	Subjects correct	Proportion
$4A_1$	Are there more red steps to go to the chair or more steps to go to the table?	12	.38	9	.38
$4B_1$	Are there more steps to go to the chair or more steps to go to the table?	21	.66	15	.63
4C	Is it further to go to the chair or further to go to the table?	23	.72	(Not presented)	
$4A_2$	Repetition of A_1: more red steps to chair or more steps to table?	17	.53	7	.29
$4B_2$	Repetition of B_1: more steps to chair or more steps to table?	28	.88	14	.58

experimental group. Further, the facilitative effect of the C task in the experimental group results in just over half the children succeeding with the more standard inclusion problem in $4A_2$, and in nearly all the children succeeding with $4B_2$. These high success rates, compared with the significantly lower success rates found with the more standard inclusion problem ($4A_1$ in the experimental group, $4A_1$ and $4A_2$ in the control group), suggest that traditional ways of presenting inclusion problems may seriously misrepresent the young child's cognitive abilities. The present finding, that a large proportion of three- to five-year-olds can succeed on inclusion problems, runs counter to Piaget's claim that young children do not have the ability to complete inclusion problems correctly.

Another main finding of this study is that a significant proportion of subjects were facilitated in tasks 4A and 4B by presentation of task 4C. These improvements in performance on A and B tasks cannot be due merely to linguistic or perceptual factors, since the same questions were presented in the same situation; nor can they be due merely to question repetition, as the control group results establish. Instead it would seem that what has changed in the child's assumptions, or presuppositions, about how such questions are to be understood. Thus the 'further' presentation not only proved most effective in conveying the intended task to the child; in addition it had a substantial effect on the child's interpretation of subsequent presentations of the task. This again shows the need to consider the child's assumptions about the task in accounting for his performance.

Finally, the present experiment confirms the main finding of Experiment 2, that it is the *interaction* between the array and the instructions which is crucial in determining the child's performance on inclusion tasks. Here, performance is low when the question refers to the salient distinction in the array (A presentations). However, when the distinction remains in the array but is not referred to in the question (B presentations), performance improves.

GENERAL DISCUSSION

This work draws attention to the fact that linguistic and perceptual aspects of presented tasks cannot be considered in isolation from what the child thinks the task is about. The child's assumptions, or presuppositions, about the task, and the role this factor plays in the child's interpretation of task instructions, is of fundamental importance. For example, in Experiment 3 some children appear to have been responding as if they had over-extended the scope of the adjectival modifier (where this referred to the salient distinction in the array), but it is not clear if such children were simply making linguistic errors, or if their assumptions about the task determined the way in which they processed the instructions. The latter explanation seems more likely in view of the facilitative effects in Experiment 4, where the child's assumptions about the task appear to play an important part in determining how he arrives at the task he actually performs.

The present studies therefore emphasize that if we wish to learn why the child arrives at the tasks he completes, such inquiry must consider not only the array and/or the form of the question the child is presented with, but how these interact in determining the child's assumptions, or interact with the child's presuppositions, about the nature of the task to be completed.

In conclusion, it can be noted that the studies reported here achieve several ends. By showing that the young child can succeed on inclusion problems, they identify a need to specify an interpretation of the child's typical behaviour in standard presentations of the problem alternative to that of Piaget. In giving an account of why young children fail to complete inclusion problems as customarily presented, and in describing how young children may also fail to complete comparisons of nonincluded sets, they emphasize the need to distinguish received tasks, those the child in fact completes, from intended tasks, those the adult intends the child to complete. They also identify factors of importance in determining the nature of the task the child receives, indicating the need to consider how the child's interpretation of the task he is presented with may be affected by interactions between characteristics of the array, the question and the child himself, particularly his assumptions about task requirements.

14.
The child's understanding of number

Rochel Gelman and C. Randy Gallistel

If a child below six years of age is shown a row of six buttons, and a row of six coins set out in one-to-one correspondence with the buttons, then the child will agree that the two rows have the same number of objects. If the row of buttons is then spread out so that it becomes longer than the row of coins, the child will usually say that there are more buttons than coins. This sort of finding, which can be reliably obtained with children aged below about six years, has been held to show that young children lack appreciation of invariance and do not conserve number. That is, they do not appreciate that the number of objects in a set remains the same despite a change in the way the set is arranged. In recent years, however, the conclusion that young children cannot conserve number has come increasingly under challenge. In the present reading, Gelman and Gallistel describe what children seem to know about number and counting operations from age two years. The development of number knowledge and counting skills involves complex interactions and coordinations between several component skills — conceptual, verbal and gestural. Gelman and Gallistel describe something of how these processes develop in two-, three- and four-year-old children, showing that preschoolers do not totally lack appreciation of invariance of number, and are by no means as ignorant of counting procedures as was once thought.

INTRODUCTION

The magic experiment

The 'magic' paradigm was designed initially as a test of the preschooler's ability to reason about number. In particular, the question was whether young children differentiate between two categories of transformations that can be performed on a set. Gelman sought to determine if young children treated addition and subtraction as number-relevant transformations and substitution and spatial displacement of items as number-irrelevant transformations. She employed a two-phase procedure: The first phase established an expectancy for number; the second recorded the child's reaction to surreptitiously performed ('magic') transformations of the expected arrays. In the first phase children were shown two plates containing different numbers of small plastic toys. For example, one plate might hold two mice and the other three mice, or one might hold three mice and the other five mice. The experimenter designated one of these 'the winner' by simply pointing to it – making no reference to number. The other plate was designated 'the loser'. Phase I then became an identification game. The plates were covered with cans and shuffled. If the child appeared to be keeping track of the covered winner, as one is able to in a shell game, the shuffling continued until the child appeared to have lost track. When the shuffling stopped, the child was asked to guess where the winner was and then uncover that plate to see if he was right. If he had guessed incorrectly and recognized that he had, that is, if he said that the uncovered plate was the loser, he was immediately allowed to uncover the other plate. When the other plate was uncovered, he was again asked if it was the winner. The experimenter provided immediate feedback about the child's identifications. If a child erroneously identified a loser as the winner, for example, the experiment said, 'No, that's the loser,' and covered and shuffled the plates again. Whenever the child correctly identified the winner plate, the experimenter gave him verbal confirmation and a prize before recovering and reshuffling the plates. Note that the feedback from experimenter to child was based on the child's correct or incorrect identification of a plate after he had uncovered it, not on his guesses. Each uncovering of a plate was counted as a trial. Thus, when a child uncovered the loser plate, correctly identified it as such, and then uncovered the winner plate, the sequence counted as two trials. The purpose of running what was basically an identification experiment in the ostensible form of a shell game was twofold: First, the game-like nature of the task was extremely effective in engaging the young child's interest. Second, it built up a strong expectation about which display would be the winner and which the loser. This first phase of the experiment continued for at least 11 trials. On three of these trials, the child was asked to justify his identification. This served to determine what the child considered to be the definitive properties of the sets.

The second phase of the experiment began when the experimenter surreptitiously altered the winner set. In some experiments, the experimenter altered the spatial arrangement of the set, making it longer and less dense or shorter and more dense. In other experiments, the experimenter altered the colour or identity of one of the elements. And in still other experiments, the size of the set was changed by adding or subtracting one or more elements.

From the child's standpoint, Phase II was just a continuation of Phase I until he discovered that neither plate contained a set that was identical to what had been the winner set. Again the child was asked to identify each plate as winner or loser. When the child had uncovered the altered winner plate, the experimenter asked a series of questions: Had anything happened? If so, what? How many objects were now on the plates? How many objects used to be on the plates? Could the game go on? Did the game need fixing? If so, how could it be fixed? If the child said that the game had to be fixed and that he needed certain items to fix it, he was given a handful of items that included the ones he had asked for plus several others.

Everything the child said was tape-recorded for later transcription. The experimenter also rated the degree of the child's surprise in Phase II on a three-point rating scale and made notes about any striking aspect of the child's behaviour, such as search behaviour.

The experiment was very effective at bringing out spontaneous counting and talk about number. The children talked about and used number not only at the end of Phase II, when they were asked to do so, but throughout the experiment. They frequently counted the items on the plates or stated their number, even when no questions had been asked; and they frequently counted the prizes they had won. The counting behaviour observed at the beginning of the experiment was all the more remarkable in that the experimenter took pains to avoid mentioning number during the first phase of the experiment. The counting that occurred throughout the magic experiment – both before and after children were asked questions about number – forms the data base for our initial inferences about the nature of the child's counting process. These sequences were already present in the transcripts of protocols from the magic experiments. Most of the transcripts were made before we became interested in the analysis of counting, and all of them were made by transcribers who knew nothing of our interest in counting behaviour. Therefore the transcribers are unlikely to have biased the transcripts.

The choice of protocols

In choosing the set of transcripts to use for our counting analyses we were guided by two considerations. First, we wanted to consider counting sequences generated by two-, three- and four-year-olds under the same experimental conditions. Children from each of these age groups had participated in magic experiments that displayed sets of two and three items in Phase I and then confronted children with the effect of either removing one item from the three-item array or displacing (so as to shorten or lengthen) the three-item array. Second, we wanted to consider the effect of set size. In a recent magic experiment, Gelman (1977) showed three- and five-item arrays to three- and four-year-olds in Phase I. Phase II displayed the effect of removing two items from the five-item array or displacing the items of the five-item array. Thus, subjects saw as many as eight items (three plus five) in this experiment – the largest number of items so far employed in Gelman's magic experiments.

The above considerations led us to focus on two sets of magic experiments: (1) those that employed two- and three-item arrays and compared the effects of subtraction and displacement; and (2) those that employed three- and five-item arrays and compared the effects of subtraction and displacement. Henceforth, we refer to these subtraction experiments as the $[(2 \text{ } vs. \text{ } 3)-1]$ and

[(3 *vs.* 5)−2] experiments. In both subtraction and displacement conditions, the items in the arrays were identical one to the other (for example, green toy mice) and arranged in linear displays.

The definition of a count sequence

For purposes of data analysis we identified a count sequence primarily on the basis of a child having used tag items from two well-known lists – the number words and the letters of the alphabet. A child did not have to use these tags in the conventional order, but he did have to use them.

The reader might be surprised to see that in this case we are relying on the use of conventional verbal tags. Previously, we pointed out that the ability to count should not be considered to be the same thing as the ability to use a culture's conventional count words in the conventional order. So why are we now restricting our analysis to count words and letters of the alphabet? The answer comes from the nature of our data base. If we had asked the children to count, we might consider for our analyses any behaviour that followed the request, though we would be well advised to exclude certain obviously irrelevant behaviours (such as requests to go to the bathroom). But we did not ask children to count. This leaves us with the problem of knowing how to identify the beginning of a count sequence. Our guess that children were counting came from the observation that they, on their own, used strings of number words or letters. Thus, for these analyses, we decided to use the child's verbal behaviour to index a count sequence. Note that despite our decision to rely on verbal behaviours and therefore, from our point of view, to be con-servative in our definition of a count sequence, we do follow one of our caveats, namely that the child need not use tags in the conventional order. Thus, we analyse sequences like; two, six; ten, two, six; and one, eight, five for what they might show about the child's ability to use counting principles.

RESULTS

Evidence for the one-one principle

A particular count sequence was scored as evidence for the use of the one-one principle if it had the same number of different verbal tags as the number of items in a given array. Thus, if a child said two different number words or letters of the alphabet when confronted with a two-item array, he was scored as having demonstrated the use of the one-one principle on that trial. Likewise, if a child said three different number words when viewing a three-item array, the count sequence was so scored. Thus the child who said 'two, six' or '*A, B*' when confronted with a two-item array was scored as correct (that is, correctly using the one-one principle), just as was the child who said 'one, two'. Further, a child who said 'one, four' on one trial and 'four, one' on a later trial was scored as correct for both trials. In other words, consistency with respect to order over trials was not a criterion. The one-one analysis simply addressed the question of whether children used as many different tag words as there were items in an array.

Table 1 summarizes the results of the analysis for the one-one principle in the spontaneous count sequences recorded in the [(2 *vs.* 3)–1] and [(3 *vs.* 5)–2] magic experiments. No effort is made to break down the results according to set size within a given experiment, because the children made errors on so few of the trials.

We consider first the results for the [(2 *vs.* 3)–1] experiment, for which we have data for two-year-olds as well as for three- and four-year-olds. Note that the younger the child, the greater the tendency to count. This observation is a replication of other findings (Beckmann, 1924; Descoeudres, 1921; Gelman, 1972b). What is noteworthy in this case is that the finding is extended to cover two-year-olds.

Errors in one-one correspondence seldom occur. Even the two-year-old's sequences are 80 per cent error free. This is not to say that the youngest children counted as adults do. Many in fact did so, but five of the two-year-olds used their own lists of tags (for example, one, thirteen, nineteen; two, six; one, four, three; *A*, *B*). Whatever tags they use, two-year-olds show a remarkable tendency to say one number word for each item in an array.

Not surprisingly, the older preschoolers make even fewer errors on sets of two and three items than the two-year-olds do. Furthermore, the data from the [(3 *vs.* 5)–2] experiment show that children as young as three years of age honour the one-one rule for sets of three and five items. For these set sizes, 88 per cent of the three-year-old count sequences and 82 per cent of the four-year-old count sequences met the one-one criteria. Thus we conclude that children of preschool age follow the one-one principle for counting – at least with respect to small sets.

Some errors that violated the one-one principle did occur. They fall into three categories, and the tendency to make errors of different types interacts with set size and age. Partitioning errors, that is, skipping an item or tagging it more than once, were observed in the (3 *vs.* 5) sequences and were made somewhat more often by three-year-olds than by four-year-olds. No such errors occurred in the (2 *vs.* 3) experiments. The effect of set size on this kind of one-one error seems straightforward. The more items the child has to count, the more likely it is that he will fail at some point to keep already counted items separate from to-be-counted items. Increasing set size still further should increase the tendency to make partitioning errors. We do not want to dwell too much on the increase in partitioning errors from set sizes of two and three to set sizes of three and five, however, for the tendency to make such errors was slight. We conclude that children are able to conduct step-by-step partitioning of sets for the purpose of counting.

Occasionally a two-year-old in the [(2 *vs.* 3)–1] experiment made a tag-

Table 1 *Use of the one-one principle in spontaneous counting*

Age group and experiment	N	Number of counters	Number of count sequences	Number of sequences with one-one errors	Errors by type				
					Partitioning	Tagging	Coordination	Other	
Two-year-olds									
[(2 *vs.* 3)−1]	16	14	56	11	0	6	4	1	
Three-year-olds									
[(2 *vs.* 3)−1]	32	25	69	9	0	0	8	1	
[(3 *vs.* 5)−2]	24	20	159	19	9	0	10	0	
Four-year-olds									
[(2 *vs.* 3)−1]	32	16	25	0	0	0	0	0	
[(3 *vs.* 5)−2]	24	19	150	23	3	1	19	0	

duplication error, assigning the same tag to different items (for example, one, four, four). The virtual absence of tagging errors in the three- and four-year-old sequences suggests that by the age of three children have learned enough count words to be able to give unique tags to as many as five items.

As Table 1 shows, the most common type of error in applying the one-one principle had to do with coordination. Such errors occurred in both the [(2 *vs.* 3)–1] and the [(3 *vs.* 5)–2] experiments at all age levels. They involved failing to count the last item in an array or using still another tag after all the items in the array had been tagged. In other words, a count of one too many or one too few was scored as a coordination error. One might argue that such errors are really partitioning errors. Perhaps the child misses the last item because he stops transferring to-be-counted items too soon. Perhaps the child who counts a nonexistent item is slow to recognize that he has transferred all the items to the already counted category. Given (*a*) that the one-too-many errors occur as frequently as the one-too-few errors, (*b*) that such errors occur across age groups and set sizes, and (*c*) that other partitioning errors do not necessarily accompany such errors, we are inclined to view these errors as a special class. They bring to mind the preschool children in various Russian studies (such as Luria, 1961), who did not know exactly when to stop a verbal accompaniment of a motor response. In other words, it is as if the children who make the one-too-many or one-too-few error have yet to perfect their ability to stop two coordinated processes at the same time. Their stop rules may be faulty. We know of no way to be sure of this hypothesis with regard to the data in Table 1. One reason we subsequently collected videotape data was to support our decision to classify the one-too-many and one-too-few errors as coordination errors rather than as partitioning errors.

The use of idiosyncratic lists was not ubiquitous. Such a tendency showed up only in the two-year-olds, and even in this group number words were the prevalent items on the idiosyncratic lists. By three years of age, the children completely restricted their lists to number words and typically used them in the conventional order. Thus, nearly all of the evidence for the one-one principle involves the overt use of the English number words as tags. Yes, children watch *Sesame Street*. But exposure to a given experience does not guarantee that, in Piagetian terms, it will be assimilated. We agree with Piaget that cognitive structures guide the organism's tendency to assimilate a given input from the environment. Therefore the fact that children assimilate the use of one-to-one correspondences between objects and number words leads us to postulate the one-one principle as a component of the cognitive structure underlying the development of counting behaviour.

The one-one principle in the counting process can be stated as follows: In enumerating (counting) a set, one and only one numeron* must be assigned to

---

* Gelman and Gallistel (1978, pp. 76, 77) introduce the terms 'numeron' and 'numerlog' as follows: 'The use of unique tags to mark or tick off the items in a collection is intrinsic to the

each item in the set. Since even our youngest subjects used count words as tags, we reformulate this principle as follows: For the child as young as two and a half years, enumeration already involves assigning one and only one numerlog to each item in the array. In other words, the child knows, although perhaps not consciously, that numerlogs are to be used as numerons.

Evidence for the stable-order principle

Counting involves more than the ability to assign arbitrary tags to the items in an array. Even if the child uses numerlogs to do this, he does not necessarily know the counting procedure. He must demonstrate the use of at least one additional principle – the stable-order principle. That is, there must be evidence that he uses tags (numerons) in a repeatable order.

To assess the degree of adherence to this principle, we analysed the same protocols that we analysed in connection with the one-one principle. We judged a child to be following the stable-order principle if when enumerating objects he (*a*) used the conventional sequence of count words, (*b*) used another standard sequence of terms (such as the alphabet), or (*c*) *consistently* used one nonstandard sequence. To meet this last criterion, a child had to count at least twice and to use the same nonstandard sequence across trials. The following protocol contains an example.

D. S., age two years, six months, during the surprise phase saw a rearranged three-item array as well as the original two-item array from Phase I. Eventually, the experimenter pointed to the two-item array and asked D. S. about quantity.

> How many on this (the two-item) plate? *Um-m, one, two.* How many on this (the three-item) plate? *One, two, six!* You want to do that again? *Ya, one, two, six!* Oh! Is that how many were on at the beginning of the game? *Ya.*

Table 2 summarizes the extent to which data from the (2 *vs.* 3) and (3 *vs.* 5) experiments can be taken to show the working of a stable-order principle in the control of the counting procedure. The table shows the number of subjects who counted, the number who always met the stable-order criteria, and the number

---

counting process. Further, the tags must be used in a fixed order. Finally, the tags must have an arbitrary status; they cannot be the names or descriptions of the items in the collection being counted. The set of count words meets these criteria, but then so do other sets of tags. One obvious candidate is the alphabet, and it is noteworthy that many languages have used the alphabet as count words (Greek and Hebrew, for example). But the tags need not even be verbal. They may be any of a host of entities, including short-term memory bins. Recognition of this fact leads us to introduce some terminology in order to be able to refer separately to the general category of possible count tags and the sub-set of such tags which constitute the traditional count words. We call the former numerons; the latter numerlogs. Numerons are any distinct and arbitrary tags that a mind (human or nonhuman) uses in enumerating a set of objects. Numerlogs are the count words of a language.'

Table 2 *Use of the stable-order principle in spontaneous counting*

| Age group and experiment | N | Counters | Category of stable-order score (number of subjects) | | |
			Always use stable order	Are shaky on order*	Show no stable order
Two-year-olds					
[(2 *vs.* 3)–1]	16	14	9	2	3
Three-year-olds					
[(2 *vs.* 3)–1]	32	25	23	1	1
[(3 *vs.* 5)–2]	24	20	17	3	0
Four-year-olds					
[(2 *vs.* 3)–1]	32	16	16	0	0
[(3 *vs.* 5)–2]	24	19	19	0	0

* Correct on at least 60 per cent of trials.

who met the stable-order criteria on at least 60 per cent of their count sequences. Subjects in this last group are credited with a *shaky* execution of the principle. The table also shows the number of children who gave no evidence of following a stable-order rule. We found very few children of any age who could not be credited with some inclination to use the stable-order principle. Of the 14 two-year-old children whose protocols were analysed, 11 showed at least some grasp of this principle. And the three- and four-year-olds continued to honour the principle as set sizes increased up to five.

Readers may begin to wonder if we find *any* serious errors in the counting behaviour of young children. They should remember that when we grant a counting principle – in this case the stable-order principle – we do not assume the flawless use of that principle. Our basic evidence for granting the stable-order principle comes from looking at the conditions under which very young children can accurately estimate number. Most very young children (two to three years of age) can accurately estimate only very small sets (sets of no more than two to five items). These set sizes correspond closely to the range within which children use a sequence of numerlogs with a stable order. But we know that larger set sizes present difficulty for young children. Their accuracy at abstracting numerosity falls off as the set size increases. It is possible that their ability to follow the stable-order principle likewise falls off. As we will see later in the chapter, their use of this principle falls off only to a limited degree.

It is possible to argue that the children whose behaviour is represented in Table 2 were not following a stable-order principle but were just repeating what they had had occasion to memorize. Several features of the data militate against this argument. For one thing, children did not have to use the conventional numerlog list to be scored as having the stable-order principle. We are particularly impressed with the occasional child who uses the alphabet in place of the conventional number-word sequence. The spontaneous use of a non-numerical sequence suggests to us that young children have a cognitive principle in search of an appropriate list, a principle ready to assimilate whatever usable list becomes available. It is the two-year-old who uses the alphabet when counting. Does anyone seriously maintain that adult speech to two-year-olds includes such forms as 'Now, Billy, I want you to (*a*) pick up your toys, (*b*) find your storybook, and (*c*) come and sit on my lap.' Gelman has never encountered such an example in her protocols of speech between adults and two-year-olds (Gelman and Shatz, 1977) – even where the adults are academics. To us, the spontaneous use of the alphabet emphasizes the extent to which the child's behaviour is guided by certain principles rather than by situation-specific rote learning. Although rote learning is necessary before the children can use the standard numerlog sequence, we suggest that children fasten on it precisely because it conforms to the stable-order principle of counting. How else to explain the idiosyncratic but stable lists of number words?

Anyone who watches young children count will surely notice the following features. Children practice counting toys, steps, cracks, or whatever – without being told to do so. Children appear to be aware that their counting sequences are unstable or unorthodox; evidence of this awareness is their tendency to correct themselves. Witness the behaviours of M. F. and A. B.

M. F., age four years, five months, participated in the [(3 *vs*. 5)–2] experiment. The following exchange occurred in Phase 1.

> *Experimenter*: Why does that (the three-item plate) lose?
> *M. F.*: Cause it's one, two, three.
> *Experimenter*: Why does that (the five-item plate) win?
> *M. F.*: Because one, two, three, four, five, six. Mm-m. One, two, three, four, five.
> (M. F. had counted the last item twice and then, without any input from the experimenter, recounted correctly. She immediately proceeded to count again.)
> *M. F.*: One, two, three, four. No, one, two, three, four, five. 'Cause it's five.

A. B., age three years, six months, participated in an undergraduate's project on language acquisition. During the course of a long interview, she encountered a display of eight items and began counting.

> *A. B.*: One, two, three, four, eight, ten, eleben. No, try dat again. One, two, three, four, five, ten, eleben. No, try dat again. One! two! three-ee-four, five, ten, eleben. No.
> (This pattern of self-correction continued for many attempts and ended with the following count, which may or may not have been error free).
> *A. B.*: One, two, three, four, five, six, seven, eleven! Whew!

Such rehearsals are characteristic of early language-learners – learners who are assumed to be practising a rule just learned (Weir, 1962). They are also characteristic of the sensori-motor patterns of Jacqueline, Lucienne, and Laurent, Piaget's children. Developmental psychologists consider these examples to be instances of knowledge structures that guide assimilation of environmental stimuli. We see no reason not to claim similar examples as evidence of the presence of the stable-order principle.

Thus, we interpret the data in Table 2 as evidence of an underlying counting principle. We of course do not claim that children have innate knowledge of the number-word sequence. This list obviously needs to be learned; but it begins to appear that the learning is facilitated and guided by an already present cognitive principle.

We have stated the stable-order principle as follows: Numerons used in counting must be used in the same order in any one count as in any other count. Given the data presented in Table 2 we can reformulate the principle to say the following: For the child as young as two and a half years, enumeration already involves assigning numerlogs in the same order in any one count sequence as in any other count sequence, at least for sets of two to five items.

Evidence for the cardinal principle

Counting involves more than the unique tagging of items and the use of a repeatable list of tags. Because of the special status assigned to the final tag in a given tagging sequence, counting allows one to determine how many items a set contains. The final tag, unlike any of the preceding tags, is taken to represent a property of a set as a whole, namely its cardinal number. This role of counting in the definition of numerosity leads us to consider the cardinal principle a component of the counting process.

Before we go on, it is important to make clear what we are and are not doing by incorporating the cardinal principle into our definition of the counting procedure. We know that the counting procedure can yield a representation of the cardinal numerosity of the set. We also assume that a young child who arrives at such a representation may be using this procedure. Indeed whenever the evidence indicates that a child has singled out the last tag in a particular count sequence, we say that he has used the cardinal principle. We do not assume that counting is the only way individuals might arrive at a representation of the cardinal numerosity of a set. Nor do we assume that a child who uses the counting procedure to establish such a representation has a full appreciation of all the properties of cardinal number.

There are several set-theoretic definitions of cardinal number. All these definitions involve the application of the one-one principle in the comparison of more than one set. In general, when the elements of two different sets can be placed in one-to-one correspondence, the two sets are said to have the same cardinal number. Other sets that can be placed in one-to-one correspondence with these sets also have the same cardinal number. Note that here the definition of cardinal number is bound to the definition of equivalence. For the moment, we remain neutral on the issue of whether the definition of equivalence of sets of different objects and the definition of cardinal number are so intricately tied together. We simply point out that it *is* possible to ask 'How many things are hers?' in reference to a single set. And the counting procedure is well suited to answering such a question.

We alluded above to the behavioural criteria by which we infer the use of the cardinal principle, namely an indication that the child treated the last tag in a sequence differently from earlier tags in that sequence. Specifically, we judge a child to have followed the cardinal principle if he met at least one of four criteria. Two of these criteria involve behaviour that we take to provide *direct* evidence for the use of the cardinal principle. To meet the first of these direct criteria, the child counted (correctly or incorrectly) the number of items in the array and repeated the last tag: for example, 'two, sixteen; sixteen'; 'one, two, three; three!'

As in this second example, the repetition of the last tag was sometimes given emphatic stress. This led us to consider whether children sometimes used exaggerated stress for the final word in a count without repeating that word. Finding that some did, we decided to include this stress as our second direct criterion. We recognize that the children we observed use the intonation patterns of English and that therefore some stress is to be expected on the final word of many sequences. In these count sequences, however, the preschoolers often exaggerate the stress on the final word well beyond the bounds of ordinary intonation patterns, giving the impression of a shout or a scream. Only such exaggerated stresses were counted as evidence of the cardinal principle according to the second criterion. The transcribers of the protocols were not primed to look for stress; presumably they noted only those cases that were exaggerated. In any case, for now we include this second criterion, keeping in mind the need to obtain evidence of its validity before using it in further studies.

It is interesting to note that Bereiter (1968, p. 14) advises teachers of young children that 'the last number counted should be given special emphasis, both with voice and touch, following which the adult should present a statement and question on this order: Five crayons! ... How many crayons?' Such a teaching method incorporates both of our direct criteria for evidence about the cardinal principle. We infer that Bereiter, too, has observed young children using both criteria.

We also judged the presence of the cardinal principle by two *indirect* criteria, both of which concerned number words that were not immediately preceded by count sequences. A child met the first of these criteria if he assigned numerlogs to each of the items in the set on one trial, for example 'one, two, three' and shifted to a simple indication of numerosity of the same set without overt counting on a later trial. The children could meet this criterion by using their own idiosyncratic lists of numerlogs. Thus if a child said 'one, two, six' on first encountering a three-item array and later said 'six' to describe the same array, he was scored as having used the cardinal principle by this criterion.

Children met the second indirect criterion if they assigned the correct value to the set without counting aloud. We did not score children as having used the cardinal principle if they simply stated an incorrect value. To do so would amount to claiming that the child who says number words out of the blue understands the cardinal principle.

In a way, by using these two indirect criteria we are reifying our hypothesis that correct estimates of numerosity are almost always based on counting, whether covert or overt. Critics might object that stating the correct numerical value of a set should not be taken as evidence for the cardinal principle of counting since the estimate may not have been obtained by counting. It could be argued that the child simply forms an association between the perception of say, three objects and the word *three*. As is evident from Table 3 the ability to simply state the numerosity of a given set without overt counting is a later development, suggesting to us that it is based on the development of covert skills (compare Gelman and Tucker, 1975). However, in our presentation of the data, we keep separate the direct and indirect criteria, so that the reader who is sceptical may draw his own conclusions.

Table 3 shows the number of children who met the various cardinal criteria, either separately or in combination, at least once. We had some difficulty with the question of how many times we should require a child to show this principle. The basic problem is that we were not asking our subjects any particular question that might elicit the use of this principle. Furthermore, the

Table 3 *Use of the cardinal principle in spontaneous counting*

Age group and experiments	N	Number who stated a cardinal numerosity for set	Cardinal criteria (number of subjects)			
			Direct	Indirect	Both	Neither
Two-year-olds						
[(2 *vs.* 3)–1]	16	16	5	5	4	2
Three-year-olds						
[(2 *vs.* 3)–1]	32	31	5	10	16	0
[(3 *vs.* 5)–2]	24	24	4	5	15	0
Four-year-olds						
[(2 *vs.* 3)–1]	32	29	0	21	5	3
[(3 *vs.* 5)–2]	24	22	2	5	15	0

criterion that requires the counting first and simply labelling later seems unlikely to be met more than once. For these reasons we decided to use an at-least-once rule for the cardinal principle.

As Table 3 shows, the cardinal principle is clearly used by children as young as two and a half. Note that indirect indications of the use of the cardinal principle increase with age: 64 per cent of the two-year-olds, 83 per cent of the three-year-olds, and 100 per cent of the four-year-olds who applied the cardinal principle met the indirect criteria.

One fact that Table 3 does not reveal is that only the youngest subjects were credited with the cardinal principle solely on the basis of the stress criterion. This fact could be taken to mean that we should drop this criterion, in which case two of our youngest subjects would move to the 'Neither' column of the table. Alternatively, it could be taken to mean that the stress criterion indexes the beginning stages of the acquisition of the cardinal principle. If this is true, we should see children using stress patterns to index cardinal number at about the time they master a given set size. Accordingly, we might expect older children to satisfy the indirect criteria for set sizes they have already mastered and the direct criteria for set sizes they are just mastering. Further, a close inspection of carefully collected count sequences might reveal the restricted use of the stress criterion for set sizes just within the range of the child's competence. Even if we decide to exclude the stress criterion, it remains true that three-fourths of our youngest subjects show evidence of possessing the cardinal principle.

The data from the $[(3 \ vs. \ 5)-2]$ experiment also indicate that three- and four-year-olds show clear evidence of being able to apply the cardinal principle. Very few children in these age groups met only the direct criteria. Of those who did, there were none who met only the stress criterion. This result is perhaps unfortunate, for it leaves us unable to resolve the question of the validity of the stress criterion as an index of the emergence of the cardinal principle. We will have to wait until we consider how children of this age perform with still larger set sizes.

On the basis of the results in Table 3 we conclude that the cardinal principle is present even in the youngest children we have studied, two-and-a-half-year-olds. We also find that the ability to give the last tag in a sequence a special status is manifested in diverse ways, suggesting that full competence with this principle may emerge by passing through a number of steps.

The cardinal principle may be stated as follows: The final numeron assigned to the last object in the set represents a property of the set – its cardinal number. Our findings allow us to reformulate this principle as it applies to young children, as follows: For the child as young as two and a half years, enumeration already involves the realization that the last numerlog in a set – at least in a small set – represents the cardinal number of the set.

Table 4 *Combinations of the three how-to-count principles in spontaneous counting*

Age group and experiment	N	Combination used (percentage of subjects)					
		All three perfect	All three, one shaky	One-one and stable-order	Stable-order and cardinal	Cardinal alone	No reference to number
Two-year-olds							
[(2 *vs.* 3)–1]	16	38	25	13	0	25	0
Three-year-olds							
[(2 *vs.* 3)–1]	32	38	34	3	3	19	3
[(3 *vs.* 5)–2]	24	33	50	0	0	17	0
Four-year-olds							
[(2 *vs.* 3)–1]	32	41	0	9	0	41	9
[(3 *vs.* 5)–2]	24	54	21	4	0	17	4

Evidence for the combined use of the how-to-count principles

Having analysed the magic experiment protocols from the standpoint of each of the three principles in the child's counting process, we now examine how well the children combined these three principles into an integrated counting procedure. Table 4 presents the percentage of children in each age group who manifested each possible combination of principles. Considering first the results of the [(2 *vs.* 3)−1] experiment, we find that approximately 40 per cent of the children at each age level received perfect scores on all three principles. A closer consideration of the results in Table 4 leads us to conclude that the vast majority of children utilize or try to utilize all three principles.

First, there are the children who used all three principles but not consistently across the count trials. We gave such children credit for *shaky* mastery of the principles. We feel justified in adding these children, at the very least, to the pool of those who showed evidence of using all three principles. But including only these children and those with perfect scores would yield a peculiar result, namely, that two- and three-year-olds are better at counting than are four-year-olds. Only 41 per cent of the four-year-olds, as opposed to 63 per cent of the two-year-olds and 72 per cent of the three-year-olds, fall in these two groups. Note that in the [(2 *vs.* 3)−1] experiment no four-year-olds appear in the 'all three but at least one shaky' category. If they show evidence for all three principles, they do so unfailingly. But if four-year-olds are so good at following the principles, why are only 41 per cent scored as having all three? We think this puzzling result is an artifact of our scoring criteria. Some children received credit for showing only the cardinal principle. These children did not count aloud but simply stated the numerlogs that represented the numerical value of the arrays. Since they did not count overtly, we could not score them in the one-one and stable-order analyses. This group included 41 per cent of our four-year-old subjects. Should we assume that they lacked the ability to use the one-one and stable-order principles? We think not. For one thing, almost all of the four-year-olds correctly counted their prizes at the end of Phase I, and none had received fewer than five prizes. So they counted larger set sizes than those being discussed here. Why then, did they not count the smaller arrays? Recall that four-year-olds are less inclined than younger children to count small set sizes overtly. Only with larger set sizes are four-year-olds consistently observed to count aloud. These facts lead us to conclude that children who simply label, rather than counting, set sizes of two and three have progressed beyond the need to count overtly in order to represent such small numerosities. Accordingly, we suggest that they be considered to possess all three counting principles. If we grant them all three principles, we find that 88 per cent of the two-year-olds, 91 per cent of the three-year-olds, and 82 per cent of the four-year-olds are able to successfully coordinate the three how-to-count principles when faced with arrays of two or three items. The reader who is disturbed by our assumption that children who demonstrate only the cardinal principle also possess the one-one and stable-order principles will be reassured by our later finding that children who label small sets count larger ones correctly.

The fact that so many children can be credited with having all three principles makes it difficult to investigate the relative difficulty of the principles. The percentages in the remaining cells are small but do give us a hint. Children in these cells are most likely to use the combination of the one-one and stable-order principles. That is, they are most likely to show evidence of being able to count the number of items in an array without being able to assign a cardinal value to that array. This evidence suggests that the ability to apply the cardinal principle lags behind the ability to apply the one-one and stable-order principles.

The scores from the [(3 *vs.* 5)−2] experiment also indicate that children are able to use the three principles in concert. The three- and four-year-old subjects differ in one notable way: The three-year-olds are more likely to be shaky in their use of at least one of the three principles.

A comparison of the results of the two experiments (see Table 4) is informative in two ways. First, four-year-olds count aloud more with the larger set sizes than with the smaller set sizes. This observation is reflected in the fact that very few four-year-olds demonstrate only the cardinal principle with the larger sets. Second, the [(3 *vs.* 5)−2] experiment brings out some shaky counters in the four-year-old group. Thus, as expected, set size increases both the tendency to count aloud and the tendency to err while doing so.

SUMMARY OF THE STUDY ANALYSES

Our analysis of the data from Gelman's magic experiments shows that young children follow the three basic how-to-count principles of our counting model – at least when dealing with homogeneous, linearly arranged sets of no more than five items. Children make relatively few errors on the various principles. The one-one errors that occur tend to be either partitioning errors or co-ordination errors. Coordination errors (overcounting or undercounting) occur for all set sizes; partitioning errors (skipping or double counting) seem to be restricted to the larger of the set sizes we used. Tagging errors (using the same tag more than once) are almost nonexistent. Together these findings suggest the following conclusions: that preschoolers have available a list of tags long enough to allow them to follow the one-one principle; that they have some difficulty coordinating the selection of tags with the step-by-step partitioning of items (thus the tendency to select one too few or one too many tags); and that increasing the set size increases their difficulty in keeping track of the difference between counted and to-be-counted items. If these interpretations are correct, what might we expect when children confront still larger set sizes? We predict that partitioning errors will become more common and that coordination errors will continue to appear. Together these errors may initially seem to account for children's inability to count larger set sizes. On closer inspection, however, we find that their unstable ability to coordinate the components of the one-one principle accounts for more of the difficulty. We also predict that tagging errors will begin to appear. As we have already suggested, one major difficulty children will confront when counting larger arrays will be the need to have as many unique tags as there are items to tag. Larger sets should make this straightforward problem of list learning more prominent. It will be interesting to monitor the way children deal with this problem. They may repeat tags, 'one, two, three, four, four'; recycle a list, 'one, two, six, eight, one, two, six, eight'; introduce illegal tags, 'one, two, three, cow'; or even limit their count to as many items as they have tags. We make no predictions here but simply point to the variety of interesting errors they might make in trying to apply the one-one principle in the face of the limitations of their stably ordered lists of tags.

It is worthwhile to look more closely at the question of what constitutes a coordination error. We have scored a coordination error when children assigned one too many or one too few tags to the items in an array. Upon reflection, we see that this is a gross index. We have no way of telling whether a child who made such an error omitted a tag for (or double-counted) the first or the last item in the array. At the beginning of a count such an error would indicate trouble starting the process; at the end of a count it would signal trouble in stopping the process. A difference clearly exists between starting and stopping a complex motor-verbal sequence. The evidence suggests that the latter is generally more difficult (Luria, 1961). We would feel more at ease with our decision to classify these errors as coordination errors if we found that in counting, too, it is harder for the young child to stop than start. This is not to say that we should find no starting errors. Indeed, if coordinating the components of the one-one principle is a problem for young children, they should make *some* errors at the beginning of a count. Since we cannot retrieve the relevant information from audiotape transcripts, the answers to these questions must wait for the analysis of our videotape data.

We have other reasons for moving to videotape. Anyone who watches young children count notices the ubiquitous use of pointing. We have mentioned how pointing might aid the child in the coordination of the tagging and partitioning components of the one-one principle. But by choosing to point, the child further complicates the task before him. Now he has to coordinate pointing with the other components. He may miss an object that he intends to point to, point to an item more than once or never, point to a space, and so on. Furthermore, he has to start and stop the pointing procedure at the same time as he starts and stops the tagging and partitioning procedures. (Note that we are still talking only about the one-one principle. And some think that counting is a trivial skill!) At any rate, to study the role of pointing, we obviously need videotape data. Such considerations led to Gelman's decision to videotape all further data collections concerning counting.

In our analysis of the use of the stable-order principle, we noted that our older subjects typically used the conventional number-word list but that the two-year-olds showed some tendency to use idiosyncratic lists – even for set sizes of two and three. We anticipate that when older children are asked to deal with larger set sizes they will use lists that begin with the conventional sequence but shift over to idiosyncratic sequences, such as 'one, two, three, four, five, eight, ten, nineteen'.

Three findings from the cardinal principle analyses stand out: First, older subjects give mostly indirect evidence of the use of the cardinal principle, stating the numerlog that represents the cardinal numerosity of the set without counting out loud to get it. If there is indeed a developmental tendency to shift from tagging each item with a numerlog and repeating or emphasizing the last one to simply stating the last one, we should find a similar trend within an age group as set size increases. That is, a child who gives only indirect evidence of using the cardinal principle in counting sets of five or fewer items might give more direct evidence when dealing with a set of seven items. Second, we credited children with possession of the cardinal principle if they placed unusual stress on the last tag in their list. The tendency to do this was more prevalent in the youngest children, suggesting that it is an early index of an emerging understanding of the special status of the last tag in a count list. It is also possible that this stress is the easiest way for the child to signal his knowledge that the last tag should be treated differently. Before we continue to include this criterion in scoring for the use of the cardinal principle we should look for evidence that it is used by older children. Again, research with larger set sizes is required. If the use of stress is an early developmental index of the child's understanding of cardinal number, then older children might return to it when counting larger set sizes.

Finally, the tables contain a hint that the child's ability to apply the cardinal principle emerges somewhat later than his ability to apply the one-one and stable-order principles. It is as if the child needs to practice tagging a given set size before he can focus on the last tag on the list. Such a line of argument suggests that children should be less likely to meet the criteria for the cardinal principle when counting larger sets. In other words, when we introduce larger sets we should find more subjects than we have found so far who use the one-one and stable-order principles without the cardinal principle.

15.

What is difficult about learning arithmetic?

Martin Hughes

In the previous reading by Gelman and Gallistel, it was shown that preschool children have more knowledge of the principles of number and counting operations than was previously supposed. Why then do some children find it so difficult to master arithmetic when they enter school? In the present reading, Hughes discusses the arithmetic system and describes some novel studies on the child's understanding and use of arithmetic symbols, statements, and operations. Part of the power of the arithmetic system is that it is highly abstract, and not tied to particular contexts. But as Hughes shows, it may be so abstract that young children may fail to realize that arithmetic symbols have anything to do with particular contexts. Thus they fail to appreciate that arithmetic symbols can be used to represent objects, and arithmetic symbols and statements can be used to represent operations carried out on objects. Children's difficulties with what Hughes calls 'the formal code of arithmetic' are well illustrated in the original studies that are described in the reading.

> 'Maths is like learning a foreign language, Marcie. No matter what you say, it's going to be wrong anyway.'
>
> 'Peanuts'

As our society becomes more and more dependent on high levels of computer-based technology, it becomes increasingly important that children should grow up with a basic competence and familiarity with numbers, and that they should feel at home in the world of calculation and computation. Of course, there are many children who easily develop a facility with numbers. Yet there are also many children who share the sentiments of the Peanuts character above, and who approach numerical problems with a mixture of confusion and helplessness. Some of these children manage to scrape by in school, by picking up a collection of techniques, tricks and rules of thumb. These may suffice to get them through the exams, but they may be only hazily understood. Other children do not even manage this, and remain almost totally at sea.

Why do children find arithmetic so difficult? Why does it seem like a foreign language to so many of them? For some years now one of the standard responses from educationalists to such questions is that formal arithmetic has been imposed on children long before they were conceptually ready for such learning. This position has often been justified by appealing to the work of Jean Piaget and his colleagues in Geneva.

THE PIAGETIAN EXPLANATION

Piaget's explanation of young children's difficulties with number can be found in various books and articles published over a period of some thirty years. However, one particularly influential article of his appeared in *Scientific American* in 1953. The first two paragraphs of this article are worth quoting in full:

> It is a great mistake to suppose that a child acquires the notion of number and other mathematical concepts just from teaching. On the contrary, to a remarkable degree he develops them himself, independently and spontaneously. When adults try to impose mathematical concepts on a child prematurely, his learning is merely verbal; true understanding of them comes only with his mental growth.

> This can easily be shown by a simple experiment. A child of five or six may readily be taught by his parents to name the numbers from one to ten. If ten stones are laid in a row, he can count them correctly. But if the stones are rearranged in a more complex pattern or piled up, he no longer can count them with consistent accuracy. Although the child knows the names of the numbers, he has not yet grasped the essential idea of number: namely, that the number of objects in a group remains the same, is 'conserved', no matter how they are shuffled or arranged.

These paragraphs contain several characteristically Piagetian ideas. We find here, for example, the belief that teaching children before they are conceptually 'ready' is likely to produce only superficial learning: that true learning comes only with the child's mental growth, and that mathematical concepts cannot be taught. There is also the underlying implication that learning mathematics is not essentially difficult, for it is something which children can for the most part acquire 'independently and spontaneously'.

At the centre of Piaget's argument, however, is the idea of conservation. Piaget maintains that if children cannot conserve number – that is, if they appear not to understand that the number of objects in a group remains the same however the objects are arranged – then they are not yet ready to start on school arithmetic. Indeed, Piaget suggests that teachers should mistrust any apparent ability – such as counting – that young children bring with them to school: if the children cannot conserve then this apparent knowledge is likely to be 'merely verbal' parrot-style learning.

Many of these ideas have now become widely accepted within early mathematics education. For example, the idea that mathematical concepts are acquired through the child's mental growth – and in particular through activities involving concrete objects – is taken as virtually axiomatic by most nursery and infant school teachers. The majority of infant school mathematics schemes start off with very concrete activities, such as matching objects on a one-to-one basis, or sorting them into sets. These activities are intended to develop the young child's general concept of number, as measured by a Piagetian conservation test. It is only when children seem to have grasped the idea of number conservation that they are considered ready to start on addition and subtraction.

NEW EVIDENCE ON THE ABILITIES OF THE PRESCHOOL CHILD

If children arrive at school as limited in their concept of number as Piaget suggests, then it is clearly undesirable to proceed as if they were more advanced. However, while Piaget's ideas have become increasingly influential within early childhood education, they have been attracting increasing amounts of criticism within developmental psychology (Donaldson, 1978; Gelman and Gallistel, 1978). In particular, there is now a considerable amount of evidence that children starting school are by no means as limited in their number concepts as Piagetian theory maintains.

Much of this evidence is concerned with Piaget's claim that children starting school do not, on the whole, understand the idea that number is conserved when a collection of objects is displaced or rearranged. In order to understand these criticisms, we need to consider the nature of the conservation task itself. In what is generally regarded as the 'standard' number conservation procedure, a young child is confronted with two identical rows of objects placed in one-to-one correspondence (Piaget, 1952). Virtually all children will agree at this stage that the two rows contain the same number of objects. The critical part of the task comes next. The adult displaces one of the rows so that it is now longer (or shorter) than the other, and asks the child if the two rows still contain the same number of objects. Piaget found that children younger than six or seven years will not, as a rule, conserve their judgements, but will incorrectly say that one row now contains more objects than the other. It is only when children reach the age of six or seven years that they will regularly conserve; that is, they will reply that the rows still contain the same number of objects despite the displacement.

There is widespread agreement that young children do in fact respond to the standard number conservation task in the way Piaget describes. However, it is increasingly being questioned whether this standard procedure is really testing what it claims to test. Several studies have now compared the standard procedure – in which the adult displaces one of the rows in a deliberate manner – with alternative procedures in which the displacement is either 'accidental' or 'incidental' (McGarrigle and Donaldson, 1974; Light *et al.*, 1979; Neilson and Dockrell, 1981). In each of these studies, significantly more children gave the right answer with the alternative procedure than with the standard procedure. It seems that some children may fail on the standard conservation task yet still have a good understanding of number conservation.

More direct evidence that young children have coherent number concepts comes from the work of Rochel Gelman and her associates in America (Gelman, 1972; Gelman and Gallistel, 1978; Gelman and Tucker, 1975). Much of Gelman's evidence comes from studies using an ingenious 'magic' game. In this game, children develop an expectancy that a particular array will contain, for example, three objects. The array is then surreptitiously altered in one of two ways. In one condition objects are added to or taken from the array, while in the second condition the objects are simply rearranged. In both cases, the reaction of the children to the change in the array is carefully noted.

On the basis of her magic studies, Gelman claims that children as young as three years understand the *invariance* of small number arrays (three objects or less). That is, they seem to understand that displacing the objects in an array does not affect its numerosity in the way that adding or subtracting objects does. While this is not quite the same thing as Piaget's idea of conservation (see Silverman *et al.*, 1979 for further discussion of this point), it does seem that Piagetian theory cannot easily account for Gelman's findings.

Gelman also claims that many three- and four-year-old children understand the idea of addition and subtraction. In the course of a 'magic' game children who notice that objects have been removed from an array can usually say that more objects must be added if the game is to be 'fixed' (i.e. restored to its original condition), and they can often say how many objects need to be added to do this. Again, such a claim does not fit easily with Piaget's own belief that children below six or seven years do not really understand addition or subtraction (Piaget, 1952, p. 190).

Gelman's claim that preschool children understand addition and subtraction is based on somewhat indirect evidence: her children were not actually asked to carry out additions or subtractions. More direct evidence comes from a study I have recently carried out in Edinburgh (Hughes, 1981). In this study, 60 children aged between three and five years were given simple addition and subtraction problems in a variety of different forms. In one task the children watched as bricks were added to or taken from a box, and they were then asked how many bricks were now in the box. For example, they might know there were three bricks in the box to begin with, and might see two bricks being taken out but not see what was left. Their task was to work out that only one brick remained. Like Gelman, I found that if the numbers involved were small (one, two, three or zero) then the children performed surprisingly well (83 per cent correct). The children also performed well (62 per cent correct) when simple additions and subtractions were presented in a hypothetical form (e.g. 'If there were three children in a sweetshop and two went out, how many children would be left in the shop?'). Just over a quarter of the children could also carry out similar additions and subtractions when the numbers involved were slightly larger (five, six, seven and eight).

Such findings give strong support to Gelman's claim that preschool children have 'a coherent set of principles for reasoning about number', particularly if the numbers involved are small. Most children who are approaching school age, it would seem, understand the invariance of number, and can carry out simple additions and subtractions, when the numbers involved are small. Moreover, a sizeable proportion of children have similar competence with slightly larger numbers. While the abilities involved are obviously not as sophisticated as those possessed by older children or adults, they still reveal a striking degree of competence in very young children.

THE NATURE OF SCHOOL ARITHMETIC

If these conclusions are correct, then we need to think again about why young children may find difficulty with school arithmetic. The Piagetian explanation is that children are being introduced to formal arithmetic too early, at an age when they lack a coherent concept of number. It now seems that children starting school are not so incompetent with number as Piaget has made out. But if this is so, there is even more of a puzzle: if children are more competent at the outset, why do so many still have difficulty learning school arithmetic?

Some clues to this problem come from the study of addition and subtraction mentioned above (Hughes, 1981). As well as the tasks already described – involving bricks in boxes and children in sweetshops – the children were also asked 'school arithmetic' questions such as 'What does one and two make?' Most children found these questions extremely difficult: overall, only about 10 per cent of such questions were answered correctly. Similar difficulties arose when the questions were phrased slightly differently – e.g. 'How many is one and two?', or 'What is one and two more?' It seems, in other words, that while most children approaching school age know that one brick added to two bricks makes three bricks, very few can answer questions involving 'one and two'.

At first sight this result does not seem too surprising. Questions involving 'one and two' do feel intuitively harder than those involving 'one brick and two bricks'. But what exactly does this 'hardness' consist of?

The first point to make is that questions like 'What does one and two make?' are totally unfamiliar to most preschool children. According to Corran and Walkerdine (1981), such a use of language occurs very rarely in conversations between four-year-olds and their mothers at home. When number words such as 'one' and 'two' do occur, they almost invariably refer to objects: 'one cup', 'two spoons', and so on. Corran and Walkerdine argue that questions like 'What does one and two make?' are part of a very restricted form of discourse – which I will call the *formal code of arithmetic*. Unlike ordinary language, this formal code will not be acquired simply through the child's participation in everyday conversations, but will have to be learned in the more formal setting of school. Rather surprisingly, some preschool children seem to be aware of this fact. One four-year-old in the study who was asked what one and two made replied that she could not answer questions like that because she 'didn't go to school yet'.

The second point to make about the formal code of arithmetic is that statements in the code are *context-free*. They make no reference to any particular objects or entities: they are not about anything specific. Yet this property is precisely what makes arithmetic such a powerful tool for thinking and problem-solving. The formal code of arithmetic is essentially a representational device in which words such as 'one' and 'two' can represent, or stand for, a whole range of objects: one brick, two houses, and so on. The quantity is what matters: the nature of the objects is irrelevant. Statements like 'one and two makes three' get their power from this very great generality. They are not about anything in particular, yet they are relevant to just about everything.

It seems, however, that the context-free nature of arithmetic statements is the source of much of children's difficulty with them. In the following dialogue, Ram (four years, seven months) makes his puzzlement quite explicit:

> *Adult*: What's three and one more? How many is three and one more?
> *Child*: Three and what? One what? Letter – I mean number?
> (We had earlier been playing a game with magnetic numbers and Ram is presumably referring to them here)
> *Adult*: How many is three and one more?
> *Child*: One more what?
> *Adult*: Just one more, you know?
> *Child*: I *don't* know (disgruntled).

These observations provide a new perspective on the difficulties facing young children when they first encounter formal arithmetic. The problem is not that young children are completely lacking in their number concepts, for we have already seen that this is not so. Rather the problem is that they are encountering a novel code, or representation system, which may well be like a foreign language to them. Pursuing this analogy further, what they need are procedures for *translating* between this new language and the modes of representation which they already have. In other words, the problem is one of creating links between the novel, formal language of arithmetic and their existing number knowledge.

One question of obvious importance is whether young children can create these links for themselves, or whether they need to be helped. The study described earlier (Hughes, 1981) suggests that most preschool children do not spontaneously translate formal code questions, such as 'What does one and two make?', into a more concrete form. When asked these questions 'out of the blue', they usually replied by naming a number, such as 'six', which bore no obvious relationship to the question being asked. Very few children appeared to be reasoning along the following lines: 'Well I don't know what one and two makes, but I do know that one brick and two bricks makes three bricks, so maybe the answer's three.' Naturally, one would not expect preschool children to verbalize the problem in exactly this way, but their thinking might have proceeded along such lines.

At first sight this might seem to be an unlikely thing for a young child to do. However a group of young children did something very similar in a study carried out by Bob Grieve and myself (Hughes and Grieve, 1980). In this study children aged five and seven years were asked questions like 'Is red bigger than yellow?' We wanted to see how young children would react when asked questions which, to us, seemed quite bizarre. To our surprise, we found that virtually all the children treated these questions seriously and constructed sensible meanings for them. One tactic they often used was to translate the questions into a specific context. For example, one child looked round the room and then replied that yellow was bigger than red 'because that red cushion there is smaller than that yellow curtain there'.

If children spontaneously translate unusual questions involving colour into specific contexts, then it is reasonable to suppose that they might be encouraged to do the same with unusual questions involving number. In an attempt to facilitate this process I presented preschool children with formal code questions either immediately before or immediately after questions about particular objects. Even with this procedure, though, the children rarely translated between the two types of question. The following dialogue with Amanda (three years, eleven months) was typical of this approach:

> *Adult*: How many is two and one?
> *Child*: (long pause: no response).
> *Adult*: Well, how many bricks is two bricks and one brick?
> *Child*: Three.
> *Adult*: OK . . . so how many's two and one?
> *Child*: (pause) Four? (hesitantly).
> *Adult*: How many is one brick and one more brick?
> *Child*: Two bricks.
> *Adult*: So how many is one and one?
> *Child*: One, maybe.

Amanda clearly sees no connection between the formal code questions and the questions concerned with bricks. Indeed, she seems to be using a strategy of giving a *different* response to the formal code questions. It is as if she is thinking 'Well I don't understand this question but I know it's not the same as the previous one, so I'll try a different answer.'

I have also tried another approach which emphasizes what is common to a whole series of addition questions about specific objects. This approach, however, was equally unsuccessful. The child in the following example is Patrick (four years, one month).

> *Adult*: How many is two and one more?
> *Child*: Four.
> *Adult*: Well, how many is two *lollypops* and one more?
> *Child*: Three.
> *Adult*: How many is two *elephants* and one more?
> *Child*: Three.
> *Adult*: How many is two *giraffes* and one more?
> *Child*: Three.
> *Adult*: So how many is *two* and one more?
> *Child*: (looks adult straight in the eye) Six.

It is interesting that children find questions involving colour words easier to translate into specific contexts than those involving number words. This may reflect some universal property of number as an abstract system, or it may be a particular property of our own number words, such as 'one' and 'two'. There are some cultures, for example, where the connection between the number words and the number being represented is made more directly. Menninger (1969) describes an early Indian system in which the word for 'one' was the same as the word for 'moon'; the word for 'two' the same as that for 'eyes'; that for 'four' the same as that for 'brother' (in Indian mythology Rama has three brothers); the word for 'seven' the same as that for 'head' (the head has seven openings) and so on. It is possible that young children would find it much easier to learn formal arithmetic if our own number system contained similar links between number words and concrete objects.

WRITTEN ARITHMETICAL SYMBOLISM

So far we have been concerned with formal arithmetic in its spoken form: that is, when it is expressed in verbal statements like 'one and two makes three' or 'three take away two makes one'. But these same statements can of course be represented in written form, such as:

$1 + 2 = 3$

or

$3 - 2 = 1$

The age at which children are introduced to this kind of written symbolism varies from country to country and from school to school. The children whose work is shown in Figure 1 below attended a socially-mixed school in Edinburgh, run by the local authority. Towards the end of their first year in school (age five to six years) the children are introduced to simple additions like those shown in Figure 1A. By the end of their second year in school (age six to seven years), they can produce the more complex additions and subtractions shown in Figure 1B.

Our interest in what the children were doing in their workbooks grew out of a study of their spontaneous written representations of simple number concepts. In this study, carried out by Miranda Jones and myself, we wanted to know how children would represent on paper, without any prompting from us, basic arithmetical concepts such as cardinal number (the number of objects in a group), addition and subtraction. In particular, we wanted to see whether they would use the conventional symbolism (1, 2, 3, +, −, =, etc.) which they

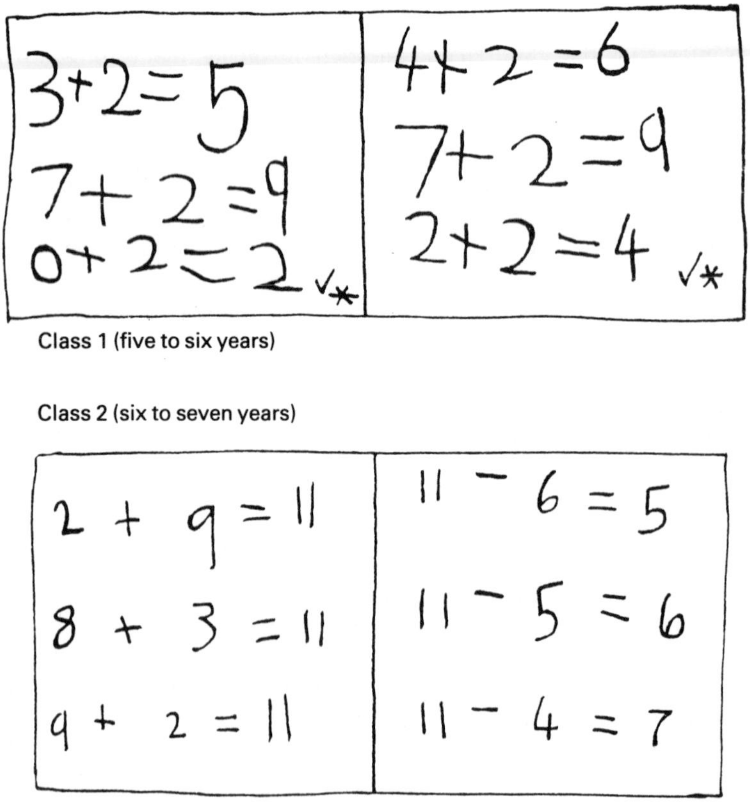

Class 1 (five to six years)

Class 2 (six to seven years)

Figure 1: *Pages from children's workbooks*

had been taught and which they used in their workbooks, or whether they would use their own more idiosyncratic methods.

A group of 72 children between five and seven years of age were given three tasks in random order. In the *cardinal number* task, a group of bricks numbering between one and six was placed on a table. The child was given paper and pencil and asked to show how many bricks were on the table. In this task the children were also asked to represent zero: i.e., to show there were no bricks on the table. In the other two tasks, the *complete operations* and the *transformation* tasks, the children were asked to produce paper and pencil representations of simple additions and subtractions. In the *complete operations* task, the child was asked to show, for example, that there were originally three bricks on the table, that one brick was then taken away, and that two bricks were left. In the *transformation* task, the child was asked to show that a specified number of bricks had been added to or taken away from a large pile of bricks of unknown number.

The children's responses were extremely interesting. On the whole the *cardinal number* task provided few difficulties, with almost all the children providing an accurate representation of the number of bricks on the table. The most frequent response (45 per cent overall) was simply to draw the required number of bricks, with the next most frequent (38 per cent) being to write conventional numerals (1, 2, 3 ...). Several children drew single vertical strokes or tallies for each brick, while others drew vague blob-like shapes. Some children, interestingly enough, drew the appropriate number of some different object – like one girl who said 'I'll draw houses' and drew three houses to represent three bricks (see Figure 2 for examples of these responses).

The two tasks which involved representing addition and subtraction proved very much harder. In the *complete operations* task, no child in any age group was able to produce an adequate representation of any of the operations, with the commonest response (69 per cent) being simply to represent the final number of bricks on the table. We had expected this task might be difficult because it required the child to represent three different quantities (the initial amount, the transformation, and the final amount). For this reason we had also included the *transformation* task, in which the child was only required to represent a single transformation – what had been done to the pile. Surprisingly enough, the *transformation* task proved just as difficult as the *complete operations* task. Most of the children (69 per cent of all responses) correctly represented the number of bricks which were added or subtracted, but very few represented whether an addition or subtraction had taken place. Only 11 children managed to differentiate between addition and subtraction in their responses, and only four of these did so in a way which might have been understood by anyone else. One seven-year-old wrote 'took 1 away' or 'add 3', while a six-year-old drew the added bricks superimposed on the pile and the subtracted bricks inside the box (see Figure 3). A five-year-old drew a hand adding bricks to the pile, while

Daniel (5:11)

Leigh (6:11)

Kashif (7:4)

Emma (5:2)

Pamela (5:1)

Figure 2: *Responses to cardinal number task*

subtracted bricks were drawn being put into the box (see Figure 3). Finally, another five-year-old drew the bricks which were added but drew dashes to show those which had been removed.

Some children went to ingenious lengths in their attempts to represent additions and subtractions. For example, one seven-year-old represented bricks that were added with the appropriate number of British soldiers marching from left to right, while bricks that were subtracted were represented by Japanese soldiers marching from right to left (see Figure 3). Other children attempted to represent movement by drawing arrows or hands (see Figure 4) but these attempts almost invariably failed to convey what had happened.

The most surprising finding from the two addition and subtraction tasks however, was that *not a single child used the conventional operator signs + and − to*

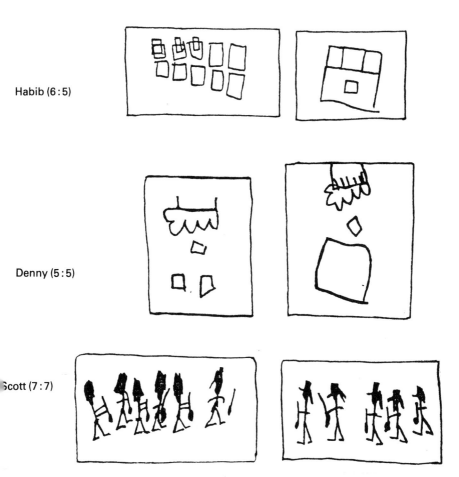

Figure 3: *Attempts to discriminate between addition and subtraction*

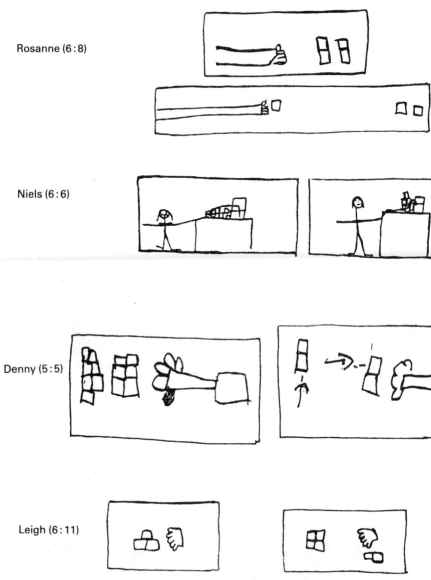

Figure 4: *Attempts to show movement in representing addition and subtraction*

represent addition or subtraction. We know from the children's workbooks (Figure 1) that operator signs were being used regularly – in some cases daily – by the children from age five years upwards, yet not one child thought of solving the difficult problem of representing addition and subtraction by using these signs.

This total reluctance to use operator signs, together with the similar, but less extreme reluctance to use numerals, suggests that what the children are doing in their school workbooks may be a wholly self-contained activity, which few of them see as being relevant to the tasks they are being asked to perform. In other words, many children do not seem to realize that the arithmetical symbols which they use in their workbooks can also be used to represent quantities of objects or operations on these quantities. If this conclusion is correct, then there appears to be a serious deficiency in many children's understanding of the nature and utility of written arithmetical symbolism.

LEARNING ARITHMETIC – A NEW FRAMEWORK

It seems that if we are to make much progress in understanding why children have difficulty with arithmetic then we need a framework something like the one shown below.

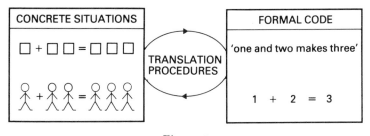

Figure 5

This figure illustrates schematically the fact that a simple arithmetical statement like 'one and two makes three' can be represented in two different forms. On the left hand side we have various concrete realizations of this addition, involving physical objects such as bricks, children in a sweetshop and so on. On the right hand side we have the same addition expressed in the formal code, both in its spoken form: 'one and two makes three', and in its writen form: $1 + 2 = 3$. Linking the two forms of representation are what I have called *translation procedures*. These are perhaps the most important part of the picture.

Now being competent at arithmetic has two important components. At the most obvious level, it means being able to operate solely within the formal code, to carry out arithmetical calculations and computations free from any concrete realizations. This aspect of arithmetical competence was emphasized most strongly by traditional teaching methods, and is what people nowadays have in mind when they talk of going 'back to basics'. But there is more to arithmetical competence than that. As the progressivists quite rightly pointed out, we do not want children simply to churn out arithmetical statements by rote: we want them to *understand* what they are doing, what the arithmetical statements mean. Unfortunately, many progressivists, taking their lead from Piaget, have taken this to mean an overemphasis on concrete experience, and a corresponding devaluation of operating with the formal code. In other words, the traditionalists have emphasized the right hand side of Figure 5 at the expense of the left, while the progressivists have emphasised the left at the expense of the right.

The framework presented here suggests the beginnings of a way out of the 'progressivist versus traditionalist' dilemma. This framework not only puts a more equal emphasis on *both* modes of representation, but also gives particular importance to the links between them. These links are important in learning the formal code, but they are also used in solving arithmetic problems long after the code has been acquired. Many problems, for example, come in concrete form and have to be translated into their appropriate formal representation before they can be solved. At the same time, we often have to translate formal problems into concrete realizations in order to understand them fully, or to check that a particular solution is reasonable. A truly competent user of arithmetic should not only be able to operate within the formal code of arithmetic, but should also be able to make fluent translations between formal and concrete representations of the same problem.

On this analysis, the ability to translate between different modes of representation is of central importance in arithmetical competence. Yet much of the work described earlier suggests that this is precisely what children find difficult. We have seen that few preschool children will spontaneously translate questions asked in the formal code into concrete situations which they can understand – even when, like Amanda and Patrick, these formal questions are asked immediately before or after questions referring to concrete situations. Clearly, translation involving numbers does not come easily to very young children. But neither does it seem to have been grasped by older children in primary school. Despite being able to cover page after page of their workbooks with addition and subtraction sums, many children were still reluctant to represent concrete events by arithmetical symbols. Being able to manipulate the formal code does not, it would seem, guarantee that the user understands the kind of code that it is.

HOW CAN WE HELP?

An important implication of this argument is that learning arithmetic is by no means a natural and effortless process. On the contrary, in asking young children to master a novel context-free code we are requiring them to do something which runs very much counter to their 'natural' mode of thinking. Not only that, we are asking them to move in two directions at once. On the one hand, we are trying to free their thinking from the concrete, to introduce them to the power and usefulness of a context-free mode of thought. But at the same time we want to avoid doing this in a way that severs all links with the concrete, for these links are essential for understanding the representational nature of the formal code.

We must accept, then, that in introducing young children to formal arithmetic we are demanding a great deal of them. But how can the task be made easier? What principles and techniques can we offer which might make the process more successful?

Some procedures that might assist children are emerging from a study I have recently carried out. The aim of this study was to introduce arithmetical symbols to four-year-old preschool children, through the use of simple games. My purpose in doing this was two-fold. I wanted to see whether such an enterprise was possible, whether very young children could grasp the idea of using symbols at all. But I was also concerned about how the symbols were introduced: I wanted to find a way of introducing them which was not only enjoyable to the child but which provided a clear rationale as to why the symbols were being used, and why they might be helpful to the child.

This point may become clearer when I describe the games. The basic set-up involves a number of identical tins containing different numbers of 'sweets' (in fact, bricks wrapped up in silver paper). The child is shown that one tin contains one sweet, another contains two sweets, and so on. The lids are put back on and the tins shuffled round. The child is asked to guess which tin has one sweet in, and so on. After a few turns of guessing in this way, the adult introduces a set of plastic numerals, with magnets on the back, and suggests the child sticks them on the tins to help distinguish between them. Most of the chldren I have worked with respond readily to this suggestion. Some children respond in the way an adult might, by sticking the number 1 on the tin with one sweet in, the number 2 on the tin with two in, and so on. Other children, interestingly enough, often use the magnetic numbers in one-to-one corres-pondence with the sweets: they stick one number – it doesn't matter which – on the tin containing one sweet, two numbers on the tin containing two sweets and so on. Whatever form of response they use, almost all the children seem to appreciate that this helps them distinguish the tins. As Craig (four years, three months) put it: 'It's easy now, 'cos we put the numbers on!'.

Once children can use the magnetic numbers to represent the number of sweets, the game can be extended to introduce operator signs + and −. In one version, for example, the child shuts his eyes while the adult puts some more 'sweets' in one of the tins. However, the adult leaves behind a message on the lid of the tin to show what he has done. For example, he might put on + 1 to show he has added one more sweet.

The following dialogue comes from a game with Thomas (four years, no months). We started with the number 1 on the tin and one sweet inside. I explained that if I then put one more sweet in the tin I would leave the signs + and 1 on the lid; if I put in two more sweets, I would leave + 2 and so on. While Thomas's eyes were shut I put one more sweet in the tin and added the signs + 1. The tin now had 1 + 1 on the lid.

> *Child*: (guesses with eyes shut) Three!
> *Adult*: Open your eyes.
> *Child*: (notices 1 + 1 on tin) I said three! (he seems to realize his guess was wrong).
> *Adult*: How many sweets have I put in?
> *Child*: Two ... (pause) ... one to begin with (points to 1 on left hand side) and then you put in two (points to 1 on right hand side).
> *Adult*: No I didn't.
> *Child*: You put in one more.
> *Adult*: I put in one more.
> *Child*: Which makes two!
> (Thomas replaces the 1 + 1 with 2, and hides his eyes again. I put in two more sweets and put + 2 on the tin: the tin now has 2 + 2 on the lid)
> *Adult*: Open your eyes. How many have I put in this time?
> *Child*: (looks at 2 + 2 on tin) That means three ... 'cos you started with two and then you put in one ... two (puzzles over + 2).
> *Adult*: I put in two more, didn't I?
> *Child*: You put in two more, so it makes four!

While Thomas is not totally fluent at reading and interpreting the message on the tins, he seems to have grasped some of the ideas involved. He appears to understand that a message left behind in this way can tell us about events that have happened in the past: he is also on the verge, it seems, of mastering the convention that such messages are conventionally read from left to right. It is also interesting to note how he is detaching himself from thinking about the sweets and is instead thinking in terms of numbers. In the dialogue above, Thomas does not once refer to 'sweets', but instead uses terms like 'you started with two', 'you put in two more' and 'so it makes four'.

Thomas is clearly a long way from being competent at arithmetic. Nevertheless, games like these are important in demonstrating two points. First, they show that even before they go to school, children can begin to grasp the beginnings of arithmetical symbolism, provided we are careful to introduce the symbols in appropriate ways. But more importantly perhaps, the games are showing young children the usefulness of arithmetical symbols. They are demonstrating that there are situations where numbers – and operator signs – do indeed make life easier, where there is a rationale for using them, and where there is a purpose for making translations between symbols on the one hand and concrete objects and events on the other. If we can continue to keep this principle at the forefront of our teaching throughout school, then we may be able to make learning arithmetic a much easier process.

16.

Spontaneous measurement by young children

Peter E. Bryant and H. Kopytynska

The ability to make what are called 'transitive inferences' is fundamental to an under-standing of measurement. For example, given a yellow stick (A) and a blue stick (B), the child can establish through direct comparison that the yellow stick is longer than the blue one – i.e. A > B. Now given the same blue stick (B), and a red stick (C), the child can establish that the blue stick is longer than the red one – i.e. B > C. However from this information, can the child make the transitive inference that the yellow stick (A) must be longer than the red stick (C), without comparing these two directly? Some investigators hold that children cannot reason transitively, nor measure adequately, until about eight years of age. Others hold that such abilities are evident from age four years. In the present reading, Bryant and Kopytynska briefly describe several studies in which five- and six-year-old children are observed to use measurement spontaneously to solve comparison problems. The results of these studies suggest that children can reason transitively and measure adequately in simple situations, at least from age five years.

Whether or not the young child can make transitive inferences (A > B, B > C ∴ A > C) is still a controversial issue. Bryant and Trabasso (1971) have claimed that he can, provided that he remembers the necessary information, but this claim has been disputed (de Boysson-Bardies and O'Regan, 1973; Youniss and Furth, 1973). Youniss and Furth's main argument is that it is one thing to show that a child can make inferences, but quite another to demon-strate that he puts these inferences to any effect. They cite the measurement experiment of Piaget, Inhelder and Szeminska (1960) as evidence that the child does not make inferences spontaneously to solve problems. Here children had been shown a tower of bricks on a table and asked to build one as big on the floor. A stick the same height as the first tower was available: the question was whether the child would use this as a measure to equate the towers, thus making an inference (A = B, B = C ∴ A = C). Children below eight years old did not measure with the stick, and it was concluded that they had no idea of measurement. We here report experiments which lead to the opposite con-clusion.

An alternative interpretation to Piaget's is that children do understand that it is possible to use intervening measures, but did not in this case realize that a direct comparison of the two towers by eye might be unreliable and thus that some measurement was needed. We decided to test this notion in three experiments in which, as the two quantities to be compared were invisible, it was very obvious that a direct comparison was not viable. We predicted that here children would measure.

Our experimental test involved four trials; in each the child was given two identical looking black wooden blocks (eight inches high, three inches wide) side by side on a table. Each had a hole in the top, the complete depth of which could not be seen: the hole was either six or four inches. In two of the four trials the holes were the same (six inch with six inch, four inch with four inch): in the other two one hole was six inch, the other four inch.

Between the two blocks lay a ten-inch long stick: its central two-inch portion was yellow while the surrounding four inch at either end was red, so that the yellow portion was uncovered when placed in a four-inch hole and covered in a six-inch hole.

In each trial the child was asked to find out whether the two holes were the same and, if not, which was the deeper. We wanted to know if the child would spontaneously use the stick as a measure to make this comparison. If he did not on any trial he was given a prompt to use the stick as a measure.

In Experiment 1, 20 five-year-olds and 20 six-year-olds were also told on each trial to use the stick though they were not told how. In Experiment 2 the same number of five- and six-year-olds were told nothing about the stick. In Experiment 3 the same number of five-year-olds were given the same task as in Experiment 2, except that the entrance to the two holes was widened and painted white, to see if this would distract the child from measuring. (The depth of the holes was still invisible).

Also in each experiment each child was given a pre- and post-test version of Piaget *et al.*'s measurement task, which was exactly the same except that it was miniaturized, with a toy table and towers and sticks which were either six or four inches.

All the children failed both traditional tower measuring tests in all three experiments. Many of them were, however, successful in our hole measuring task. As Table 1 shows, the majority of children used the stick as a measure without any prompting, and most of their judgements were correct. A substantial number of children were never prompted and were correct on every trial. There were no significant differences between age groups or experiments. We conclude that young children do have an idea of measuring.

In Experiment 4 we tested our idea that a crucial factor is whether or not a child realizes that a direct comparison will be unreliable with 40 five-year-olds and 40 six-year-olds. Half had to compare holes in Perspex boxes. To make direct comparisons of the visible holes unlikely we changed the depth of the

Table 1 *Performance in the four experiments*

	Experiment 1		Experiment 2		Experiment 3		Experiment 4 Wooden box		Experiment 4 Perspex box	
	5 years	6 years	5 years	6 years	5 years	6 years	5 years	6 years	5 years	6 years
Mean age (years and months)	5.6	6.6	5.6	6.5	5.8	6.4	5.5	6.6	5.7	6.8
No. of children (out of 20) measuring on every trial with no prompting	17	19	15	14	16	16	11	16	7	14
No. of children never prompted and correct on all four trials	10	15	10	9	11	10	8	7	2	7
Mean no. (of four) of correct judgements by those children never prompted	3.41	3.79	3.53	3.43	3.38	3.50	2.84	2.91	3.07	3.44

holes in this experiment to six and five and a half inch and we placed the blocks on different tables in both conditions. Otherwise the procedure was the same as before.

The prediction was that Perspex boxes, by encouraging direct comparisons, would lead to less measurement. Although the results (Table 1) provide some partial support for this prediction, the difference was not significant. Many children still measured even in this experiment.

Whatever is the importance of the child's appreciation of the precariousness of direct comparisons, we have established, contrary to all preceding evidence, that young children can spontaneously use intervening measures. This result has some educational significance and since the measuring must have involved inferences it is strong support for the claim that young children make, and benefit from making, transitive inferences.

17.

Methods for observing developmental change in memory

Ann L. Brown and Judy S. DeLoache

In this reading, Brown and DeLoache ask how developmental change might be studied, and discuss the matter with particular reference to the Russian investigator Istomina's studies of three- to seven-year-old children's memory. On method, Brown and DeLoache endorse the view that experimental investigation needs to be supplemented by ethnographic study. Put simply this means that, before trying to test specific hypotheses on children's abilities experimentally, we should first observe and try to understand children and their culture. Istomina's studies of the development of memory provide a good illustration of the point. Children aged three to seven years are far better at remembering items to be purchased in a shopping game than words to be remembered in a 'lesson'. As Brown and DeLoache observe, we should therefore 'extend the realm of our investigations from the laboratory into the real world'. However, we need well-controlled experiments too.

We would like to emphasize that in order to construct a realistic picture of the child's competencies, it is sometimes necessary to use methods other than traditional experimentation. We sometimes gain our most interesting information from informally observing, questioning, and playing with children, particularly the very young. Indeed, without these methods we would have even less information about cognitive development below five years of age than we now do. We do not wish to denigrate experimentation. In fact, it is our bias that to confirm a hypothesized developmental trend, it is almost always necessary to devise a tightly controlled experimental test. However, we plead for other approaches because of the predominance of laboratory experimental methods in our field.

Although we realize that calls for an increased concern with ecological validity are becoming commonplace, and to some wearisome, we support the movement in the area of the development of cognitive skills. Our estimates of a child's competencies are sometimes dramatically changed if we consider them in naturally occurring situations. If, therefore, we are in the business of delineating the cognitive competencies of the four-year-old, we will have a distorted picture if we see the four-year-old only in a laboratory setting. Of course, the four-year-old's laboratory performance is informative, but it is only one side of the picture. We also need to consider the other side, how our four-year-old functions in the world around him, outside the confines of the laboratory. This argument probably holds for any population, including the rat, but it gains more credence the younger and less compliant the laboratory game player.

For these reasons we advocate a three-pronged research plan similar to that described by Cole and Scribner (1975) for cross-cultural research comparisons. The basic theme is an interweaving of experimental and ethnographic research to investigate a particular activity in a range of situations, from the naturally occurring to the experimental. Such a strategy seems ideally suited for comparative research with groups that differ not in terms of national origin or degree of formal schooling but in age or school success within our society.

First, one should investigate the subject's understanding of the experiment or task and his role as subject. Before reaching any conclusions about competency one should become thoroughly familiar with the task demands and how these appear to the child. We must know whether the child is familiar with the materials and the response demands, whether he can understand the instructions, and whether the point of the experiment seems reasonable to him. In short, is the leading activity that is envisaged by the experimenter (e.g., deliberate retention as goal) also countenanced by the child? As a second approach, Cole and Scribner (1975) suggest that we should 'experiment with the experiment.' Instead of repeating one fixed paradigm across ages, we should work with many different variations of a paradigm, variations suited to the interests and abilities of the children studied. The third strategy is to investigate the same process in a range of situations, including the naturally occurring context of the culture – for example, early childhood.

Cole and Scribner's plea is similar to that made by Soviet developmental psychologists (Brown, 1978; Meacham, 1977). They emphasize that cognitive activities develop and change within a sociohistorical cultural context and that the nature of these acculturation processes influences the activities, motives, focus, and type of cognitive competence displayed by the individual. Therefore, it must be profitable to view the memory of the developing child in relation to the ecology of childhood.

We know of few studies that exemplify this approach; in fact, to illustrate it we turn to some research conducted 'long ago and far away'. Almost 30 years ago Istomina (1975) published a study in the Soviet Union on the development of voluntary memory in children between three and seven years. We describe this experiment in some detail because it is an excellent example of our argument that assessment of children's memory capacity and metacognitive skills is influenced by the artificiality of many laboratory tasks, which the child may not fully understand or be fully engaged in.

One of the most interesting features of Istomina's experiment was a comparison between children's memory for lists of words in a relatively standard list-learning situation versus their memory for comparable lists embedded in a meaningful (to the child) activity. Istomina's reason for contrasting these two conditions was 'that the development of retention and recall as internal, purposeful acts takes place initially as part of a broader, articulated, and meaningful activity (since it is only within the context of such activity that the specific acts of remembering and recall can have any meaning for a child)' (pp. 8–9). A game that made sense to the child and aroused a desire to participate should provide motivation for the child to set memory goals for himself and to discover various mnemonics. The child should be more likely to adopt the goal of remembering and to seek strategies to help him remember if he is highly motivated to perform some task in which memory plays an essential role.

Istomina set children the task of remembering a list of items to be bought at a play store. The store was set up in their preschool and equipped with a cash register, scale, play money, and a variety of items 'for sale', including toys, food, clothing, and the like. One at a time, the children were recruited to go on a shopping errand. The teacher would slowly name five items for the child to buy and send him to the store in the next room. An assistant at the store recorded how many items the child recalled and observed the accompanying activity. In a control condition, the experimenter called each child for a 'lesson', and instructed him to listen attentively so he could later recall all the words. The list of words was of comparable length, meaning, and difficulty to the list of store items. In both situations, the experimenter prompted the child to remember as much as he could, asking if he could remember any more if he had forgotton anything. Recall was clearly superior in the game situation, indeed almost twice as high at the younger ages. When remembering is an intrinsic part of some meaningful activity, we obtain a higher estimate of young children's memory capabilities (Murphy and Brown, 1975).

We do not know exactly why recall is higher in a meaningful activity, but Istomina (1975) suggests several possibilities. For one thing, the children are more motivated to remember: They want to play the game properly, and at some point most of the older children realize that this means remembering their shopping lists. Istomina argues that although the youngest children know what it means to remember ' . . . this is not enough: they must not only know what remembering is by itself but also be able to see it as an end result, an objective to which activity must be directed, i.e. to grasp it as a goal' (p. 59). The goal of remembering is more salient in the game situation, so children are more likely to adopt it as their own goal. This is in contrast to the typical learning situation in which we are often uncertain that the child shares the experimenter's goal.

Once the child can set remembering as a conscious goal, he then starts searching for more effective ways to carry it out. Istomina's naturalistic situation produced a delightful set of protocols detailing individual children's emergent procedures for remembering. Many of her subjects seem to have discovered spontaneously most of the mnemonic strategies developmental psychologists have identified. The strategies adopted and the way in which they are used become increasingly complex and sophisticated with age.

Three-year-old Valerik barely waited for the list of items to be read before rushing off to the store. The three-year-old's view of the game seemed to be limited to going to the store and returning with items but did not seem to include the notion of bringing back the specific items on the list. Four-year-old Igor listened attentively to the shopping list and then tried to carry out his errand as quickly as possible. He even seemed to try to avoid distractions, refusing to stop and talk when on his way to the store. Very few four-year-olds showed more specific mnemonic behaviours, but between four and five a qualitative shift seemed to occur, and all the older subjects seemed to make active attempts to remember. Many five- and six-year-olds actively rehearsed: They were often observed moving their lips, repeating the words over to themselves as the experimenter read them and as they walked to the store.

Many of the older children showed strong executive control and seemed to be monitoring their own memory states and even checking themselves to determine how well they remembered.

> *Slava M.* (five years, six months) listened silently as the list was read, looking at the experimenter tensely, and after a slight pause asked him to repeat the list one more time. He did not recall the list immediately, frowning, shrugging his shoulders, and saying: 'Wait a minute, I'll get it, hold on . . .' (p. 26).
>
> *Dima F.* (six years, six months) listened to the list, muttering silently, and then repeated it almost as if to himself. He quickly recalled three items, then paused, screwed up his eyes, and said, with concern: 'Oh! What else was there? Nope, I can't remember what else I have to buy . . .' (p. 26).
>
> *Alik K.* (five years, eight months) listened to the message to the end and then quickly went off to the store. However, halfway there he turned back. 'I can only remember endive. What else was there?' he asked the experimenter (p. 27).

Alochka also returned from the store to ask the experimenter for the items she had forgotten. Clearly, these children must have been testing themselves on their way to the store. Finally, the oldest children (six to seven years old) displayed more sophisticated strategies such as trying to form logical connections between the items on their lists, often rearranging the order of the words based on their meaning.

Istomina's (1975) work is fascinating not only for the information it provides about young children's memory processes but also for the methodological point it emphasizes. The best situation in which to study very early memory development is in a natural context in which the child is likely to understand the task and be motivated to perform it. The young child's performance on laboratory tasks is often markedly inferior to his performance in a game setting. Although this variable is crucially important when studying very young children, the same general point is applicable to other ages as well. Subjects of any age, even adults, are likely to perform better in a meaningful task in which they are actively engaged. Thus, if we want accurate, generalizable information about development, we should extend the realm of our investigations from the laboratory into the real world. However, a vital aspect of this approach is that we must investigate the same process in both situations; we must look at the process in a natural activity that is meaningful to the subject and suited to his abilities, and we must also use well-controlled experiments to test particular hypotheses about the process. Experiments themselves can be engineered to provide controlled observations and exciting activities for children.

18.

Children's reasoning

Margaret Donaldson

Can young children reason deductively? That is, from a given set of premises, can they draw the conclusion that these premises warrant? In experimental tests of this question, the answer has frequently been in the negative. And yet, as Donaldson points out in the present reading, evidence that children as young as four years old can reason deductively may be obtained in observations of their spontaneous reasoning, particularly as they listen to stories. The fact is, it is difficult to devise experimental procedures which allow the reasoning abilities of young children to be revealed. However, as the present reading also makes clear, while difficult, the task is not impossible.

Piaget has not been alone in claiming that young children are incapable of inferences which, to an adult, seem elementary. From a type of psychological theory utterly opposed to his own, precisely the same conclusion has been drawn. One of the most eminent of the associationist – or behaviourist – psychologists, Clark Hull, claimed that the essence of reasoning lies in the putting together of two 'behaviour segments' in some novel way, never actually performed before, so as to reach a goal. Serious objections can be raised to this way of defining reasoning but let us accept it for the moment and look at what happens if we study children's thinking in a way guided by the Hullian conception.

When Hull spoke of the joining of two 'behaviour segments' he spoke against a background of studies of rats learning to run mazes – studies of a kind so popular with the behaviourists. A 'behaviour segment' was then exemplified by the running from one point in the maze to another.

The claim was as follows: suppose you arrange the maze as in the diagram below. Now suppose that a rat learns to run from A to B to get a small reward; and from A to C to get an equally small reward; and from C to D to get a much bigger reward (all of these bits of learning taking place on separate occasions). If you then place him at point A and he chooses the path A → C → D, instead of the path A → B, he must be *reasoning* that you can get to D that way, for he has never actually *been* from A to D that way before.

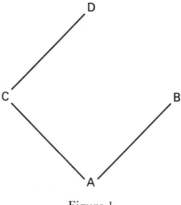

Figure 1

Of course, there is a 50/50 chance of taking that road randomly, with no reasoning at all. But if a large number of rats were all to take it, that would be evidence of rodent reasoning.

In fact this evidence has not been obtained. Rats don't, apparently, figure things out in this way.

More strangely, evidence has been obtained which makes it look as if children under the age of seven don't either.

Two followers of Clark Hull, Howard and Tracy Kendler (1967) devised a test for children that was explicitly based on Hullian principles. However, it did not involve running a maze. Instead the children were given the task of learning to operate a machine so as to get a toy. In order to succeed they had to go through a two-stage sequence corresponding to the segments of the maze. The children were trained on each stage separately. The stages consisted merely of pressing the correct one of two buttons to get a marble; and of inserting a marble into a small hole to release the toy.

The Kendlers found that the children could learn the separate bits readily enough. Given the task of getting a marble by pressing the button they could get the marble; given the task of getting a toy when the marble was handed to them, they could use the marble. (All they had to do was put it in a hole.) But they did not for the most part 'integrate', to use the Kendlers' terminology. They did not press the button to get the marble and then proceed without further help to use the marble to get the toy. So the Kendlers concluded that they were incapable, like the rats, of deductive reasoning. This work was done in the 1960s. No wonder Chomsky could so readily convince people of the need to postulate a highly specific device for the acquisition of language.

On the other hand, the Kendlers' results are bound to seem deeply puzzling to anyone who has watched children playing in a nursery or listened to their conversation, and who really brings the two kinds of data together in his mind.

Here is a striking example of the kind of reasoning of which children seem to be capable if one observes their spontaneous behaviour, by contrast with their behaviour when they are being tested.

This exchange happened to be tape-recorded, so it can be quoted very accurately. It took place shortly after the death of Donald Campbell when he was trying to break the world water speed record, and some months after a visit by a research worker called Robin Campbell to the school where the conversation took place. The speakers were a little girl of five and another research worker.

> *Child*: 'Is that Mr Campbell who came here – *dead?*'
> (Dramatic stress on the word 'dead'.)
> *Research worker*: 'No, I'm quite sure he isn't dead.'
> (Much surprised.)
> *Child*: 'Well, there must be two Mr Campbells then, because Mr Campbell's dead, under the water.'

This child has put together, if not two 'behaviour segments', two quite distinct pieces of information: *Mr Campbell who came here is not dead* and *Mr Campbell is dead*, and has drawn a valid conclusion, which she states as a necessary consequence: '. . . there *must be* two Mr Campbells then . . .'. Her reasoning involves the understanding that the existence of a living person is incompatible with the death of that same person. So if Mr Campbell is dead and Mr Campbell is alive, there simply must be two of them!

How can it be that children of five are capable of reasoning like this, yet can fail to 'integrate' two very simple bits of separately learned behaviour in a task such as the Kendlers used?

The mystery at first appears to deepen when we learn, from Michael Cole and his colleagues (Cole, Gay, Glick and Sharp, 1971) that adults in an African culture apparently cannot do the Kendlers' task either. But it lessens, on the other hand, when we learn that a task was devised which was strictly analogous to the Kendlers' one but much easier for the African adults to handle.

Instead of the button-pressing machine, Cole used a locked box and two differently coloured match-boxes, one of which contained a key that would open the box. Notice that there are still two behaviour segments ('open the right match-box to get the key' and 'use the key to open the box') so the task seems formally to be the same. But psychologically it is quite different. Now the subject is dealing not with a strange machine but with familiar meaningful objects; and it is clear to him what he is meant to do. It then turns out that the difficulty of 'integration' is greatly reduced.

Recent work by Simon Hewson (1978) is of great interest here for it shows that, for young children too, the difficulty lies not in the inferential processes which the task demands, but in certain perplexing features of the apparatus and the procedure. When these are changed in ways which do not at all affect the inferential nature of the problem, then five-year-old children solve the problem as well as college students did in the Kendlers' own experiments.

Hewson made two crucial changes. First, he replaced the button-pressing mechanism in the side panels by drawers in these panels which the child could open and shut. This took away the mystery from the first stage of training. Then he helped the child to understand that there was no 'magic' about the specific marble which, during the second stage of training, the experimenter handed to him so that he could pop it in the hole and get the reward. A child understands nothing, after all, about how a marble put into a hole can open a little door. How is he to know that any other marble of similar size will do just as well? Yet he must assume this if he is to solve the problem. Hewson made the functional equivalence of different marbles clear by playing a 'swapping game' with the children.

These two modifications together produced a jump in success rates from 30 per cent to 90 per cent for five-year-olds and from 35 per cent to 72.5 per cent for four-year-olds. For three-year-olds, for reasons that are still in need of clarification, no improvement – rather a slight drop in performance – resulted from the change.

We may conclude, then, that children experience very real difficulty when faced with the Kendler apparatus; but this difficulty cannot be taken as proof that they are incapable of deductive reasoning.

With this conclusion in mind, let us see now how children behave in a very different type of situation.

It is highly informative to listen to the comments children make and the questions they ask when they listen to stories. In this situation a rich harvest of evidence of reasoning may be reaped.

Here are a few examples:

'What a lot of things he's taking! He wouldn't have ... he's only got two hands and he wouldn't have space for his two hands to carry all these things.'
  (*Premises*: (1) Peter has more to carry than two hands can carry; (2) Peter has only two hands. *Conclusion*: It is not possible for Peter to carry all that he is represented as carrying. Implied criticism of the story.)

'She must have eaten all her food on the other day.'
  (*Premises*: (1) Houses normally have food in them; (2) This house has no food. *Conclusion*: The food must have been all eaten up.)

'But how can it be [that they are getting married]? You have to have a man too.' (The book contains an illustration of a wedding in which the man looks rather like a woman. The child thinks it is a picture of two women.)
  (*Premises*: (1) You need a man for a wedding; (2) There is no man in the picture. *Conclusion*: It can't be a wedding.)

'I think you have missed a page. You didn't say that he cut out the leather.'
(*Premises*: (1) There is a page on which the story tells of cutting out leather;
(2) No reference has been made to cutting out leather. *Conclusion*: A page has been missed.)

Child: 'You're not looking.'
Teacher: 'Pardon?'
Child: 'Why are you not reading it?'
Teacher: 'Because I know it.'
(*Premises*: (1) When you read a book you look at it; (2) The teacher is not looking at the book. *Conclusion*: She is not reading the book.)

It is impossible to take account of this evidence and at the same time to maintain that children under the age of six or seven are incapable of reasoning deductively. So if sometimes – as in certain experimental situations – they do not appear to reason deductively, we must look more closely at what is happening. If we cannot get children to reason when we contrive experiments, whereas we can observe them reasoning spontaneously, then we must ask why.

It turns out, however, that in spite of the findings of Piaget and the Kendlers and some others, it is not impossible to get children to reason in the contrived circumstances of an experiment. It is harder but it is not impossible.

Barbara Wallington (1974) conducted a series of experiments where the task was to find a toy in one – or more than one – of a set of boxes which might or might not have stars on the lids. She designed her studies with great care and a desire to give children every chance to grasp what it was that she wanted of them. The results were revealing.

The children were given information which they could use to guide their search. For instance, they might be told: 'If there is a star on the box, then there is a wee animal in the box,' or: 'If there is no star, then there is a wee animal in the box.' After hearing a statement of this kind, they were asked to predict which boxes would contain a toy and to check whether they were right.

The pattern of the children's choices and the nature of their answers when they were asked why they had made the choices showed very clearly that many of them were engaging in processes of strict reasoning in the sense that they were using the experimenter's statement as a basis from which to deduce conclusions. They very rarely drew all the conclusions which would be judged correct by the canons of traditional formal logic – but neither did a group of adults to whom the same task was given. The older children (and 'older' in this case means between four years, three months and four years, eleven months) frequently responded in just the same way as the adults, taking 'if there is a star . . .' to mean 'if *and only if* there is a star . . .' and reasoning accordingly. Some of the children were also able to give explanations very like those of the adults, using such expressions as: *it must be, it has to be*. Here are two examples, by way of illustration: 'When there's no star, there's supposed to be a wee animal in the box.' 'It must be in there [box with no star] if it's not in there [starred box].' In this last case the given statement had been: 'If there is a star, then there is no wee animal.'

Notice that these justifications were made after the children had indicated which boxes they were choosing but before they had been allowed to open them.

From children under four years, such responses as these were relatively uncommon. But even the youngest children did not behave randomly. They tended to have systematic search strategies, even if these were as primitive and unrelated to the experimenter's words as starting with a box at one end and working along the row.

Further evidence that, even in experimental situations, children can sometimes give proof of their ability to reason is now being obtained. Peter Bryant and Paul Harris have each independently looked at the child's ability to engage in the kind of inference which is concerned with transitive relations such as 'equal to' or 'greater than'. (This is yet another form of inference which Piaget regards as criterial for operational thought and which, therefore, according to his theory, is not normally to be found in children under age seven.)

Harris and his colleagues (personal communication) showed four-year-old children two strips of paper placed about three feet apart. The strips differed in length by about a quarter of an inch – too small a difference to be perceptible. Thus when the children were asked which strip was longer approximately half their judgements were correct, this being, of course, the result that would be expected by chance alone. Then a third strip of paper, equal in length to one of the other two, was produced; and it was briefly placed alongside each of the others in turn. The question was then repeated. And now most of the children gave the correct answer. This seems to show clearly that they were capable of understanding measurement, which is to say that they were able to make inferences of the form: if A equals B and if B is longer than C, then A must be longer than C.

Bryant and Kopytynska (1976) have reached conclusions similar to those of Harris about the ability of young children to make measurements.*

Let us take stock. From the evidence we have been considering, it emerges that children are not so limited in ability to reason deductively as Piaget – and others – have claimed. This ability shows itself most markedly in some aspects of their spontaneous behaviour – and we have seen that it reveals itself with great clarity in the comments they make while listening to stories. But it can be demonstrated also in the contrived situation of an experiment from about the age of four, if not sooner, even though many experiments have failed to elicit it.

---

* See Paper 16 in this book.

19.

Intuitive and analytic thinking

Jerome S. Bruner

In this reading, written some 20 years ago, Bruner contrasts analytic and intuitive thought. The former is seen as a deliberate, detached activity, the latter as more immediate, and less formal. As Bruner is quick to observe, this is not to say that the two modes of thought are opposed: while different, they are essentially complementary. Intuitive thought, often primary, frequently needs to be subsequently checked by analytic procedures. Unfortunately, primary intuitive thought, since informal and often far from detached, may well be undervalued in the relative formality of school learning. How can we encourage intuitive thought – not of the careless, self-indulgent variety, but of the plausible, adventurous, and, at times, inspired variety? In the present reading, Bruner discusses this problem, with reference to both 'artistic' and 'scientific' pursuits. 'The warm praises that scientists lavish on those of their colleagues who earn the label "intuitive" is major evidence that intuition is a valuable commodity and one we should endeavour to foster in our students.' Given the current concern with how to encourage analytic thought in children, it is timely to recall Bruner's advice on the importance of intuitive thinking.

Much has previously been said about the importance of a student's intuitive, in contrast to his formal, understanding of the subjects he encounters. The emphasis in much of school learning and student examining is upon explicit formulations, upon the ability of the student to reproduce verbal or numerical formulae. It is not clear, in the absence of research, whether this emphasis is inimical to the later development of good intuitive understanding – indeed, it is even unclear what constitutes intuitive understanding. Yet we can distinguish between inarticulate genius and articulate idiocy – the first represented by the student who, by his operations and conclusions, reveals a deep grasp of a subject but not much ability to 'say how it goes', in contrast to the student who is full of seemingly appropriate words but has no matching ability to use the ideas for which the words presumably stand. A careful examination of the nature of intuitive thinking might be of great aid to those charged with curriculum construction and teaching.

Mathematicians, physicists, biologists, and others stress the value of intuitive thinking in their respective areas. In mathematics, for example, intuition is used with two rather different meanings. On the one hand, an individual is said to think intuitively when, having worked for a long time on a problem, he rather suddenly achieves the solution, one for which he has yet to provide a formal proof. On the other hand, an individual is said to be a good intuitive mathematician if, when others come to him with questions, he can make quickly very good guesses whether something is so, or which of several approaches to a problem will prove fruitful.

The development of effectiveness in intuitive thinking is an objective of many of the most highly regarded teachers in mathematics and science. The point has been repeatedly made that in the high school plane geometry is typically taught with excessive emphasis upon techniques, formal proofs, and the like, that much more attention needs to be given to the development of students who have a good intuitive feel for geometry, students who are skillful in discovering proofs, not just in checking the validity of or remembering proofs with which they have been presented. There has been very little done, for example, on the use of diagrams as geometrical experiments as in Hilbert and Cohn's *Geometry and the Imagination*, in which visual proof substitutes for formal proof where possible. Similarly, in physics, Newtonian mechanics is typically taught deductively and analytically. In the judgement of many physicists, at least, there is too little attention to the development of intuitive understanding. Indeed, some have suggested that improving the use of intuitive thinking by teachers is as much a problem as improving its use by students.

Yet, as it has been observed, it is wrong to look at intuition as 'all à la mode and no pie'. The good intuiter may have been born with something special, but his effectiveness rests upon a solid knowledge of the subject, a familiarity that gives intuition something to work with. Certainly there are some experiments on learning that indicate the importance of a high degree of mastery of materials in order to operate effectively with them intuitively.

Those concerned with the improvement of curricula in physics and mathematics particularly have often cited as one of their important aims the use of procedures that will contribute to the improvement of intuitive thinking. In their attempts to design such procedures, there has been a question of the kind of systematic psychological knowledge that would be of help. Unfortunately, little systematic knowledge is available about the nature of intuitive thinking or the variables that influence it. What seems most appropriate at this point, therefore, is an attempt to outline the kinds of research which, if even only partially carried out, would begin to provide information useful to those concerned with the improvement of particular courses or, more generally, of the curriculum as a whole. What kinds of questions do we need the answers to?

Questions about the nature of intuitive thinking seem to centre upon two large issues: what intuitive thinking is, and what affects it.

One can say many more concrete things about analytic thinking than about intuitive thinking. Analytic thinking characteristically proceeds a step at a time. Steps are explicit and usually can be adequately reported by the thinker to another individual. Such thinking proceeds with relatively full awareness of the information and operations involved. It may involve careful and deductive reasoning, often using mathematics or logic and an explicit plan of attack. Or it may involve a step-by-step process of induction and experiment, utilizing principles of research design and statistical analysis.

In contrast to analytic thinking, intuitive thinking characteristically does not advance in careful, well-defined steps. Indeed, it tends to involve man-oeuvres based seemingly on an implicit perception of the total problem. The thinker arrives at an answer, which may be right or wrong, with little if any awareness of the process by which he reached it. He rarely can provide an adequate account of how he obtained his answer, and he may be unaware of just what aspects of the problem situation he was responding to. Usually intuitive thinking rests on familiarity with the domain of knowledge involved and with its structure, which makes it possible for the thinker to leap about, skipping steps and employing short cuts in a manner that requires a later rechecking of conclusions by more analytic means, whether deductive or inductive.

The complementary nature of intuitive and analytic thinking should, we think, be recognized. Through intuitive thinking the individual may often arrive at solutions to problems which he would not achieve at all, or at best more slowly, through analytic thinking. Once achieved by intuitive methods, they should if possible be checked by analytic methods, while at the same time being respected as worthy hypotheses for such checking. Indeed, the intuitive thinker may even invent or discover problems that the analyst would not. But it may be the analyst who gives these problems the proper formalism. Unfortunately, the formalism of school learning has somehow devalued intuition. It is the very strong conviction of men who have been designing curricula, in mathematics and the sciences particularly, over the last several years that much more work is needed to discover how we may develop the intuitive gifts of our students from the earliest grades onwards. For, as we have seen, it may be of the first importance to establish an intuitive understanding of materials before we expose our students to more traditional and formal methods of deduction and proof.

As to the nature of intuitive thinking, what is it? It is quite clear that it is not easy either to recognize a particular problem-solving episode as intuitive or, indeed, to identify intuitive ability as such. Precise definition in terms of observable behaviour is not readily within our reach at the present time. Obviously, research on the topic cannot be delayed until such time as a pure and unambiguous definition of intuitive thinking is possible, along with precise techniques for identifying intuition when it occurs. Such refinement is the goal of research, not its starting place. It suffices as a start to ask whether we are able to identify certain problem-solving episodes as more intuitive than others. Or, alternatively, we may ask if we can learn to agree in classifying a person's style or preferred mode of working as characteristically more analytic or inductive, on the one hand, or more intuitive, and, indeed, if we can find some way to classify tasks as ones that require each of those styles of attack. It is certainly clear that it is important not to confuse intuitive and other kinds of thinking with such evaluative notions as effectiveness and ineffectiveness: the analytic, the inductive, and the intuitive can be either. Nor should we distinguish them in terms of whether they produce novel or familiar outcomes, for again this is not the important distinction.

For a working definition of intuition, we do well to begin with Webster: 'immediate apprehension or cognition.' 'Immediate' in this context is contrasted with 'mediated' – apprehension or cognition that depends on the intervention of formal methods of analysis and proof. Intuition implies the act of grasping the meaning, significance, or structure of a problem or situation without explicit reliance on the analytic apparatus of one's craft. The rightness or wrongness of an intuition is finally decided not by intuition itself but by the usual methods of proof. It is the intuitive mode, however, that yields hypotheses quickly, that hits on combinations of ideas before their worth is known. In the end, intuition by itself yields a tentative ordering of a body of knowledge that, while it may generate a feeling that the ordering of facts is self-evident, aids principally by giving us a basis for moving ahead in our testing of reality.

Obviously, some intuitive leaps are 'good' and some are 'bad' in terms of how they turn out. Some men are good intuiters, others should be warned off. What the underlying heuristic of the good intuiter is, is not known but is eminently worthy of study. And what is involved in transforming explicit techniques into implicit ones that can be used almost automatically is a subject that is also full of conjecture. Unquestionably, experience and familiarity with a subject help – but the help is only for some. Those of us who teach graduate students making their first assault on a frontier of knowledge are often struck by our immediate reactions to their ideas, sensing that they are good or impossible or trivial before ever we know why we think so. Often we turn out to be right; sometimes we are victims of too much familiarity with past efforts. In either case, the intuition may be weeks or months ahead of the demonstration of our wisdom or foolhardiness. At the Universtiy of Buffalo there is a collection of successive drafts of poems written by leading contemporary poets. One is struck in examining them by the immediate sense one gets of the rightness of a revision a poet has made – but it is often difficult or impossible to say why the revision is better than the original, difficult for the reader and the poet alike.

It is certainly clear that procedures or instruments are needed to characterize and measure intuitive thinking, and that the development of such instruments should be pursued vigorously. We cannot foresee at this stage what the research tools will be in this field. Can one rely, for example, upon the subject's willingness to talk as he works, to reveal the nature of the alternatives he is considering, whether he is proceeding by intuitive leaps or by a step-by-step analysis or by empirical induction? Or will smaller-scale experimental approaches be suitable? Can group measurement procedures involving pencil and paper tests be used to provide a measure? All of these deserve a try.

What variables seem to affect intuitive thinking? There must surely be predisposing factors that are correlated with individual differences in the use of intuition, factors, even, that will predispose a person to think intuitively in one area and not in another. With respect to such factors, we can only raise a series of conjectures. Is the development of intuitive thinking in students more likely if their teachers think intuitively? Perhaps simple imitation is involved, or perhaps more complex processes of identification. It seems unlikely that a student would develop or have confidence in his intuitive methods of thinking if he never saw them used effectively by his elders. The teacher who is willing to guess at answers to questions asked by the class and then subjects his guesses to critical analysis may be more apt to build those habits into his students than would a teacher who analyses everything for the class in advance. Does the providing of varied experience in a particular field increase effectiveness in intuitive thinking in that field? Individuals who have extensive familiarity with a subject appear more often to leap intuitively into a decision or to a solution of a problem – one which later proves to be appropriate. The specialist in internal medicine, for example, may, upon seeing a patient for the first time, ask a few questions, examine the patient briefly, and then make an accurate diagnosis. The risk, of course, is that his method may lead to some big errors as well – bigger than those that result from the more painstaking, step-by-step analysis used by the young intern diagnosing the same case. Perhaps under these circumstances intuition consists in using a limited set of cues, because the thinker knows what things are structurally related to what other things. This is not to say that 'clinical' prediction is better or worse than actuarial prediction, only that it is different and that both are useful.

In this connection we may ask whether, in teaching, emphasis upon the structure or connectedness of knowledge increases facility in intuitive thinking. Those concerned with the improvement of the teaching of mathematics often emphasize the importance of developing in the student an understanding of the structure or order of mathematics. The same is true for physics. Implicit in this emphasis, it appears, is the belief that such understanding of structure enables the student, among other things, to increase his effectiveness in dealing intuitively with problems.

What is the effect on intuitive thinking of teaching various so-called heuristic procedures? A heuristic procedure, as we have noted, is in essence a non-rigorous method of achieving solutions of problems. While heuristic procedure often leads to solution, it offers no guarantee of doing so. An algorithm, on the other hand, is a procedure for solving a problem which, if followed accurately, guarantees that in a finite number of steps you will find a solution to the problem, if the problem has a solution. Heuristic procedures are often available when no algorithmic procedures are known; this is one of their advantages. Moreover, even when an algorithm is available, heuristic procedures are often much faster. Will the teaching of certain heuristic procedures facilitate intuitive thinking? For example, should students be taught explicitly, 'When you cannot see how to proceed with the problem, try to think of a simpler problem that is similar to it; then use the method for solving the simpler problem as a plan for solving the more complicated problem'? Or should the student be led to learn such a technique without actually verbalizing it to himself in that way? It is possible, of course, that the ancient proverb about the caterpillar who could not walk when he tried to say how he did it may apply here. The student who becomes obsessively aware of the heuristic rules he uses to make his intuitive leaps may reduce the process to an analytic one. On the other hand, it is difficult to believe that general heuristic rules – the use of analogy, the appeal to symmetry, the examination of limiting conditions, the visualization of the solution – when they have been used frequently will be anything but a support to intuitive thinking.

Should students be encouraged to guess, in the interest of learning, eventually how to make intelligent conjectures? Possibly there are certain kinds of situations where guessing is desirable and where it may facilitate the development of intuitive thinking to some reasonable degree. There may, indeed, be a kind of guessing that requires careful cultivation. Yet, in many classes in school, guessing is heavily penalized and is associated somehow with laziness. Certainly one would not like to educate students to do nothing but guess, for guessing should always be followed up by as much verification and confirmation as necessary; but too stringent a penalty on guessing may restrain thinking of any sort and keep it plodding rather than permitting it to make occasional leaps. May it not be better for students to guess than to be struck dumb when they cannot immediately give the right answer? It is plain that a student should be given some training in recognizing the plausibility of guesses. Very often we are forced, in science and in life generally, to act on the basis of incomplete knowledge; we are forced to guess. According to statistical decision theory, actions based on inadequate data must take account of both probability and costs. What we should teach students to recognize, probably, is when the cost of not guessing is too high, as well as when guessing itself is too costly. We tend to do the latter much better than the former. Should we give our students practice not only in making educated guesses but also in recognizing the characteristics of plausible guesses provided by others – knowing that an answer at least is of the right order of magnitude, or that it is possible rather than impossible? It is our feeling that perhaps a student would be given considerable advantage in his thinking, generally, if he learned that there were alternatives that could be chosen that lay somewhere between truth and complete silence. But let us not confuse ourselves by failing to recognize that there are two kinds of self-confidence – one a trait of personality, and another that comes from knowledge of a subject. It is no particular credit to the educator to help build the first without building the second. The objective of education is not the production of self-confident fools.

Yet it seems likely that effective intuitive thinking is fostered by the development of self-confidence and courage in the student. A person who thinks intuitively may often achieve correct solutions, but he may also be proved wrong when he checks or when others check on him. Such thinking, therefore, requires a willingness to make honest mistakes in the effort to solve problems. One who is insecure, who lacks confidence in himself, may be unwilling to run such risks.

Observations suggest that in business, as the novelty or importance of situations requiring decisions increases, the tendency to think analytically also increases. Perhaps when the student sees the consequences of error as too grave and the consequences of success as too chancy, he will freeze into analytic procedures even though they may not be appropriate. On these grounds, one may wonder whether the present system of rewards and punishments as seen by pupils in school actually tends to inhibit the use of intuitive thinking. The assignment of grades in school typically emphasizes the acquisition of factual knowledge, primarily because that is what is most easily evaluated; moreover, it tends to emphasize the correct answer, since it is the correct answer on the straightforward examination that can be graded as 'correct'. It appears to us important that some research be undertaken to learn what would happen to the development of intuitive thinking if different bases for grading were employed.

Finally, what can be said about the conditions in which intuitive thinking is likely to be particularly effective? In which subjects will mastery be most aided by intuitive procedures followed by checking? Many kinds of problems will be best approached by some combination of intuitive and other procedures, so it is also important to know whether or not both can be developed within the same course by the same teaching methods. This suggests that we examine the mode of effective operation of intuition in different kinds of fields. One hears the most explicit talk about intuition in those fields where the formal apparatus of deduction and induction is most highly developed – in mathematics and physics. The use of the word 'intuition' by mathematicians and physicists may reflect their sense of confidence in the power and rigour of their disciplines. Others, however, may use intuition as much or more. Surely the historian, to take but one example, leans heavily upon intuitive procedures in pursuing his subject, for he must select what is relevant. He does not attempt to learn or record everything about a period; he limits himself to finding or learning predictively fruitful facts which, when combined, permit him to make intelligent guesses about what else went on. A comparison of intuitive thinking in different fields of knowledge would, we feel, be highly useful.

We have already noted in passing the intuitive confidence required of the poet and the literary critic in practising their crafts: the need to proceed in the absence of specific and agreed-upon criteria for the choice of an image or the formulation of a critique. It is difficult for a teacher, a textbook, a demonstration film, to make explicit provision for the cultivation of courage in taste. As likely as not, courageous taste rests upon confidence in one's intuitions about what is moving, what is beautiful, what is tawdry. In a culture such as ours, where there is so much pressure towards uniformity of taste in our mass media of communication, so much fear of idiosyncratic style, indeed a certain suspicion of the idea of style together, it becomes the more important to nurture confident intuition in the realm of literature and the arts. Yet one finds a virtual vacuum of research on this topic in educational literature.

The warm praise that scientists lavish on those of their colleagues who earn the label 'intuitive' is major evidence that intuition is a valuable commodity in science and one we should endeavour to foster in our students. The case for intuition in the arts and social studies is just as strong. But the pedagogic problems in fostering such a gift are severe and should not be overlooked in our eagerness to take the problem into the laboratory. For one thing, the intuitive method, as we have noted, often produces the wrong answer. It requires a sensitive teacher to distinguish an intuitive mistake – an interestingly wrong leap – from a stupid or ignorant mistake, and it requires a teacher who can give approval and correction simultaneously to the intuitive student.

20.

The use of hiding games for studying coordination of viewpoints

Martin Hughes and Margaret Donaldson

Can young children adopt a perspective other than their own? Several studies, particularly those of Piaget and Inhelder, suggest that they are unable to do so until about the age of seven years. This finding is but one aspect of Piaget's notion of the young child's 'egocentrism' – the young child's supposed inability to 'decentre' from his present perspective. In the present reading, Hughes and Donaldson show that young children are far from being invariably egocentric. This is demonstrated by gauging children's perspective-taking abilities in hide-and-seek games, a context which makes good sense to young children. The three- and four-year-olds whom Hughes and Donaldson studied know what is involved and intended in hiding games. Thus although they may never have encountered the particular situations Hughes and Donaldson here employed (hiding one toy from another), they are nevertheless able to deploy their general knowledge of what is involved in hiding and seeking. It is of interest to note that in the studies described, young children are not only able to adopt the perspective of one another – they can also adopt, and coordinate, the different perspectives of more than one other individual.

One of Piaget's best known claims is that children below the age of six or seven years are highly egocentric, and cannot take account of another person's point of view (e.g. Piaget, 1926; Piaget and Inhelder, 1969). Piaget has devised several tasks for demonstrating the egocentrism of young children, one of which is the classic mountain task (Piaget and Inhelder, 1956, Chapter 8).

The mountain task was designed to test whether young children could take another person's point of view in the literal sense of being able to calculate what that person could *see*. In a typical version of the task the child is seated before a model of three mountains, each of which is a different colour, and a doll is placed so that it is looking at the mountains from a different point of view. The child is shown a set of pictures of the mountains taken from different angles and is asked to choose the picture which shows what the doll sees. Piaget and Inhelder found that children below about eight years were unable to do this; indeed there was a powerful tendency among children below the age of six or seven to choose the picture showing their *own* point of view. This finding is extremely reliable, and has been replicated several times (e.g. Aebli, 1967; Dodwell, 1963; Garner and Plant, 1972).

Piaget and Inhelder concluded from their findings that the children's egocentrism was preventing them from working out what the doll could see: 'the children ... all really imagine that the doll's perspective is the same as their own, they all think the little man sees the mountains in the way they appear from where they themselves sit' (Piaget and Inhelder, 1956, p. 220). According to Piaget and Inhelder, the young child is unable to *decentre*: that is, he is unable to see his own viewpoint as one of a set of possible viewpoints, and to coordinate these different points of view into a single coherent system.

The child's performance on the mountain task would indeed seem to justify the conclusions of Piaget and Inhelder. However the mountain task is not the only way to test children's ability to recognize and coordinate different points of view. In the present paper we outline a different way of investigating these abilities.

In the studies described below the task is presented to the child as a hiding game. The child is asked to hide a small boy from one or more toy policemen who are 'looking for the boy'. In the first study the child has to do this by placing a small model wall between one of the policemen and the boy; in the other studies he has to hide the boy within various configurations of walls. Thus the child is not asked directly to calculate what the policemen can see. Nevertheless, the demand is implicit in the task: he cannot succeed without taking account of what the various policemen can see.

In choosing a task that in many ways resembles a game we were implicitly following the example of Peel (1967), who devised a game to investigate children's understanding of logical terms such as 'if ... then ...'. In Peel's game the experimenter and child took turns to put coloured beads or counters into a box, according to rules such as: 'If and whenever I draw a red bead you are not to draw a red counter'. Peel argued that games such as this are particularly useful for studying children's thinking skills, in that a formally complex task can be presented to children in a way that retains their interest and enjoyment. This belief also underlies the studies presented here.

STUDY 1

The task used in our first study was the most straightforward of the three. The child was seated at a low table, in the middle of which were placed a policeman, the boy and a wall. The policeman and boy were about six centimetres high, and the wall was seven centimetres high by four centimetres wide. The experimenter told the child that the policeman was looking for the boy, and that the boy wanted to hide from the policeman. The policeman and boy were then placed facing each other near the edge of the table, at P and B respectively (see Figure 1(a)), and the child was asked to '*put the wall so that the policeman cannot see the boy*'. The child had thus to place the wall so that it blocked the line PB.

The task was repeated for two more positions of the policeman and boy: first, with the line PB perpendicular to the edge of the table (Figure 1(b)), and secondly, with the line PB across the corner of the table (Figure 1(c)). We included this last position because of the claim by Piaget and Inhelder that young children find it particularly difficult to imagine a straight line across the corner of a table (Piaget and Inhelder, 1956, Chapter 6). In each case the policeman and boy always faced each other and the child could always see the policeman's face.

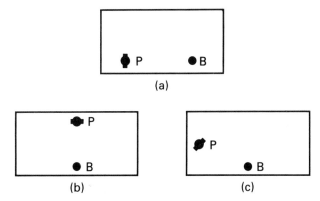

(a)

(b)   (c)

Figure 1: *Positions of policeman (P) and boy (B) in Study 1*

These three versions of the task were given to a group of ten three-year-olds (range three years, three months to three years, eleven months, mean three years, eight months) and ten four-year-olds (range four years, two months to four years, nine months, mean four years, six months). Somewhat surprisingly, the children's performance was virtually errorless, with nine out of ten children in each age group placing the wall correctly in all versions of the task. There were no differences between the various versions of the task: all children, three- and four-year-olds alike, succeeded on the 'across the corner' version.

These results already make it clear that three- and four-year-old children can perform in a non-egocentric fashion in certain situations. None of the children showed any signs of confusing their own view of the boy with the policeman's view (for example, by placing the wall between *themselves* and the boy). All the children were clearly aware that placing the wall on the line PB prevented the policeman from seeing the boy, and the fact that the boy was still clearly visible to *them* did not seem to influence their judgements. Accordingly, we decided to use the same basic idea to see if young children could coordinate two different points of view at once.

STUDY 2

In the second study we used three small dolls – two policemen and a boy – and a cross-shaped configuration of walls (see Figure 2). The children were asked to hide the boy from *both* the policemen, and thus had to keep in mind two different points of view at once.

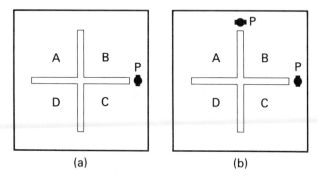

(a)   (b)

Figure 2:   *Positions of policeman (P) in Study 2*

Each child was introduced to the task very carefully to give him every chance of fully understanding the situation. The experimenter placed the boy, the walls and a single policeman on the table and told the child, as in the first study, that the policeman was looking for the boy and that the boy wanted to hide from the policeman. The experimenter then arranged the walls and the policeman as shown in Figure 2(a), so that the policeman could see into the sections marked B and C, but not into sections A and D. The boy doll was then placed in section A, and the child was asked '*Can the policeman see the boy?*' This was repeated for sections B, C and D in turn. The experimenter then moved the policeman to the opposite side, so that he could see into sections A and D, but not sections B and C. This time the child was asked '*hide the boy so that the policeman can't see him*'. If the child made any mistakes at these preliminary stages, his error was pointed out to him and the question repeated until the correct answer was given. But in fact very few mistakes were made (only 8 per cent overall).

When it was clear that the child fully understood the situation, the experimenter brought out the other policeman, saying '*Here's another policeman. He is also looking for the boy. The boy must hide from BOTH policemen*'. The two policemen were then positioned as shown in Figure 2(b), leaving only section D un-observed. The child was asked to '*hide the boy so that BOTH the policemen can't see him*'. This was repeated three times, each time leaving a different section as the only hiding place.

The task was given to 30 children aged between three years, six months and four years, eleven months, with a mean age of four years, three months. The overall success rate was again surprisingly high, with 22 children correct on all four trials, and five children correct on three out of four trials. The younger children were no less successful than the older ones, and it was clear that virtually all the children tested were able to take account of and coordinate two different points of view.

STUDY 3

In view of the ease with which the children had performed in Study 2, we decided to make the task even harder in the next study. We used two versions of the task. In the first, the wall arrangement had five sections, and the two policemen were positioned so that only one section was left unobserved (see Figure 3(a)). The child's task was again to '*hide the boy so that BOTH the policemen can't see him*'. In the second version of the task, the wall arrangement had six sections, and this time there were *three* policemen looking for the boy (see Figure 3(b)). The child was asked to '*hide the boy so that NONE of the policemen can see him*'. Each task consisted of four trials, corresponding to four different positions of the policeman. As in the previous study, both tasks were introduced to the children carefully and gradually, to give them every chance of understanding the situation.

The subjects in this study were 20 three-year-olds (range three years, one month to three years, eleven months, mean three years, six months) and 20 four-year-olds (range four years, no months to four years, nine months, mean

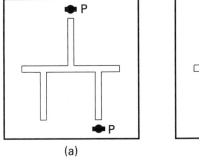
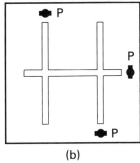

(a) (b)

Figure 3: *Typical positions of policeman (P) in Study 3*

four years, five months). None of these children had been subjects in either of the two previous studies. The children were divided into two groups, matched as far as possible for age and sex. One group performed the first version of the task, while the other group performed the second version.

Despite the increased complexity of the task, the four-year-olds still had little trouble with either version. Nine out of ten four-year-olds made no errors at all on the five-section, two-policemen task, and eight out of ten made no errors in the six-section, three-policemen task. The three-year-olds had more difficulty with the tasks, although their performance was still fairly high: six out of ten made one or no errors in the first task, and seven out of ten made one or no errors on the second task. The difference between three- and four-year-olds was significant at the 0.05 level for the first task only ($U = 23$, Mann-Whitney U test, two-tailed). As can be seen, there were no major differences between the two versions of the task. This finding was somewhat surprising as we had predicted that the three-policemen task would be harder than the two-policemen task.

Very few of the errors produced by the three-year-olds could in any sense be termed egocentric. No child confused his own view with the policemen's by consistently hiding the boy so that the boy was out of sight from the child. Indeed, two of the children who failed on the task consistently placed the boy doll in the sections *nearest* to them, so that the doll was fully visible to them as well as to the policemen. Two children chose to play a different game from the one which the experimenter had in mind; one consistently hid the boy under the table, and the other hid him in her hand! These responses – which were perfectly adequate in their own way – were somewhat reluctantly scored as incorrect. The remaining errors were mainly the occasional mistakes made in calculation by children who otherwise performed well on the task.

DISCUSSION

The level of performance found in these three studies is remarkably high. Very few of the children – three-year-olds or four-year-olds – had any difficulty either with the one-policeman task used in Study 1, or with the simpler two-policeman task used in Study 2. It was only when the task was made more complex still, in Study 3, that the three-year-olds started to make an appreciable number of errors, and even then the majority of children still performed extremely well.

These findings clearly have important implications for the notion of early childhood egocentrism, and we will return to these implications shortly. First, however, it is worth pausing to look at the children's performance on the tasks in more detail, and to consider the kinds of thinking skills they might be using.

When one watches the children perform these tasks, it often seems as though they are playing an enjoyable little game with the experimenter, somewhat like a simple form of chess. The experimenter places the policemen in position, and asks the child to hide the boy: the child responds by putting the boy within one of the sections of the walls. The experimenter then moves one of the policemen to another position, so that the boy is now visible: the child in turn replies by moving the boy to a new safe position. The experimenter moves the policemen again, the child replies again and so it goes on: move and counter-move, threat and reply. These games are obviously very enjoyable to the children and they seem to have no difficulty in understanding what to do. Indeed, the child will often respond before any instructions are given, as if he understands the rules of the game well enough and does not need reminding of what he has to do. This, as we shall see later, is an important point.

The analogy with chess is reinforced by the habit of some children who pick up the boy, move him to a section of the walls and, *without letting go of him*, look around to see if he is visible to any of the policemen. If he is, they move him to another section and try again. This is very similar to what often happens when a beginner starts to play chess: he will pick up a piece, move it to a square on the board, and without letting go, will look around to see if the piece can be captured, or if the move is otherwise unsafe. This practice soon disappears as the beginner learns to internalize the whole process instead. By analogy, it is tempting to suppose that the children who succeed on the policemen task without moving the boy from one section to another have likewise managed to internalize the process of trying each section to see which is safe.

If this is so, then it raises interesting questions about the thought processes which might be involved. Do they involve imagery – in that the child imagines the boy in a particular section and then works out if he is visible or not – or is it rather a primitive case of inference, with the child thinking along the lines:

> 'If I move him to section A, then he will be visible. I don't want this, so I won't move him to section A.'
> 'If I move him to section B, . . . etc.'?

The process could, of course, involve both imagery and inference. Indeed, it is likely that for advanced chess players, who can 'see' many moves ahead, both imagery and inferences are involved. This kind of thinking has been little studied, however, either in adults or in children, and at present we can only speculate on what might be involved.

While it remains unclear precisely what thought processes are required to succeed in our tasks, there can be little doubt that they reveal the presence of well-coordinated, 'decentred' thinking in three- and four-year-old children. In successfully coordinating the viewpoints of three different policemen at once, the children show themselves to be virtually unhampered by the constraints of egocentrism. These findings thus add further support to a growing body of evidence which shows that young children can – in certain circumstances – calculate what another person can see (see review by Flavell, 1974; also Borke, 1975*). In addition, there are findings from two further studies which support those presented here. In one study, Light (1974) gave two tasks involving hide and seek situations to a group of children around their fourth birthdays, and one of the tasks was similar to that used in Study 2. Light found that performance was high on both tasks, with well over half the children giving predominantly correct responses. In the other study, Flavell, Shipstead and Croft (1978) gave various versions of a hiding task, similar to that used in Study 1, to children aged between two and a half and three and a half years. They found that almost all the children could hide an object from a toy dog by moving the object behind a screen, but that it was significantly harder to hide the object by moving the screen. All the same, most of the three- and three-and-a-half-year-olds were able to do this latter version of the task.

There is thus substantial evidence to show that three- and four-year-olds are by no means as egocentric as Piaget has claimed. But why, in that case, do they fail on the mountain task? Why do so many children pick their own view of the mountains when asked to select the doll's view? One factor which undoubtedly influences the children's performance is the complexity of the array. The mountain task is particularly difficult in that it requires the child to perform both front/back and left/right reversals in order to work out the doll's view, and there is indeed evidence that performance improves as the array is simplified (Fishbein, Lewis and Keiffer, 1972; Flavell *et al.*, 1968). However it seems that another factor may also be involved. It could well be that in the mountain task the child has considerable difficulty in *understanding what he is supposed to do*.

Support for this idea comes from a study one of us carried out with a simplified version of the mountain task (Hughes, 1978). Instead of mountains, Hughes used three dolls of different colours each facing outwards from the corner of a triangular base. The array was positioned between the child and the experimenter, so that the child saw the face of the doll nearest him (say, a red doll) and the experimenter saw the face of a different doll, the one nearest him (say, a blue doll). Hughes found that when three- and four-year-olds were asked, in the standard manner, to select a picture showing the experimenter's view, very few could do this. However, the great majority of them could succeed when this question was preceded by questions referring to particular features of the array ('which doll's face do I see?/do you see?', etc.) and to the same features of the pictures ('which doll's face do you see in this picture?', etc.). By drawing the child's attention to these features, the preliminary questions helped him understand what was involved in the task.

In contrast, the tasks used in the present studies were extremely clear to the

---

* The next paper in this book.

children, and they immediately grasped what they were supposed to do. We were careful to introduce the tasks in ways which would help the child understand the situation, but in fact these precautions were largely unnecessary. The children understood the rules of the game at once and, as we have already seen, they often responded to each trial without any reminders from the experimenter as to what the game was about.

Why do children find these tasks so easy to grasp, compared with problems like the mountain task? We believe it is because the policemen tasks make *human sense* in a way that the mountain task does not. The motives and intentions of the characters (hiding and seeking) are entirely comprehensible, even to a child of three, and he is being asked to identify with – and indeed do something about – the plight of a boy in an entirely comprehensible situation. This ability to understand and identify with another's feelings and intentions is in many ways the exact opposite of egocentrism, and yet it now appears to be well developed in three-year-olds. Indeed, as one of us has argued at greater length (Donaldson, 1978), it seems likely that it constitutes a very fundamental human skill, the origins of which may be present even in the first few months of life.

21.

Piaget's mountains revisited: changes in the egocentric landscape

Helene Borke

A matter of concern, if not contention, in recent debates on intellectual development relates to the fact that, when the nature of the task is changed, young children will reveal abilities they were thought to lack. In the previous reading for example, it is claimed that three- to four-year-old children are far from cognitively and perceptually egocentric, for, when tested on hide and seek games, they by no means fail to adopt the perspectives of others. Such findings seriously question Piaget's interpretation of the results he obtained on his classic 'three mountains task', where children up to seven and eight years failed to represent the perspectives of others. But is this disagreement merely a result of the radically differing tasks: hide-and-seek games versus *mountains task? The present reading suggests that this is not so. 'By replicating Piaget and Inhelder's basic experimental design but substituting a more age-appropriate task, it was hypothesized that children as young as three and four years of age would demonstrate perceptual role-taking ability.' Borke used a series of arrays, including Piaget's mountains array. The difference between her studies and Piaget's original one was that her task was introduced, and realized, in ways appropriate to three- and four-year-old children. As the reading shows, Borke's hypothesis was confirmed — three- and four-year-olds can demonstrate perceptual role-taking ability, even when the basic experimental design remains the same.*

Piaget and Inhelder's (1956) mountain experiment is most frequently cited in the literature as support for the theory of early egocentrism. In this experiment, Piaget and Inhelder investigated perceptual role-taking ability in children between four and twelve years of age. The children were asked to imagine how a doll would view a mountain scene from several different positions. The subjects communicated their ability to visualize the doll's viewpoint by (a) selecting one picture from a group of pictures to show how the mountains looked to the doll from different perspectives, (b) selecting one picture and placing the doll in an appropriate position for taking an identical snapshot, or (c) arranging three cardboard replicas of the mountains to reconstruct the doll's view. Piaget and Inhelder reported that when asked to indicate what the doll saw, the four- and five-year-old subjects invariably responded by giving their own perspective. Although the six-year-old subjects appeared to show some awareness that the doll's viewpoint was different from their own, like the younger children, they were unable to reproduce the doll's view successfully. Not until nine years of age did the children demonstrate a real comprehension of the doll's perspective. Piaget and Inhelder concluded that the young child 'appears rooted in his own viewpoint in the narrowest and most restricted fashion so that he cannot imagine any perspective but his own' (p. 242).

Another possible conclusion is that the task presented to the children for communicating their perceptual role-taking skills was beyond the cognitive capabilities of most children below nine years of age (Borke, 1971, 1972, 1973). The effect of the task on the relationship between age and role-taking ability is evident in several experiments by Flavell, Botkin and Fry (1968). In one study modeled after Piaget and Inhelder's mountain experiment, a series of four geometric configurations of increasing difficulty was presented to subjects between seven and seventeen years of age. The subjects were given a duplicate set of geometric forms and asked to reconstruct the model so that it looked just the way the examiner saw it from various positions. The results showed that the youngest subjects had difficulty reproducing the examiner's view on the easiest displays and only a minority of the seventeen-year-old subjects could reconstruct the most difficult configuration correctly.

On another series of tasks designed by Flavell *et al.* to investigate role-taking ability in children between three and six years of age, the six-year-old subjects made relatively few errors. The younger children showed considerable variation in performance, but on the two easiest tasks (e.g. orienting a picture for the examiner to look at upside down and predicting which of two pictures the examiner was viewing) even the majority of the three-year-old subjects demonstrated an ability to take into account the other person's perspective. While Flavell interpreted his results as supporting Piaget's conclusions that children under six years of age are either 'wholly or almost wholly unaware of perspective differences', his data suggest that the complexity of the task may well be a critical variable in determining at what age children demonstrate role-taking ability.

Recently a number of investigators (Fishbein, Lewis and Keiffer, 1972; Hoy, 1974; Huttenlocher and Presson, 1973) studied the effects of altering both the task and the mode of responding on children's ability to reproduce another person's perspective. All of these researchers found that success in demonstrating perceptual role-taking by preschool and elementary school children varies with both the dimensions of the task and the type of response required. In two of these studies (Fishbein *et al.*, 1972; Huttenlocher and Presson, 1973), the researchers had subjects rotate a three-dimensional scene to reproduce the other person's point of view. This procedure resulted in significantly fewer errors than when children were asked to indicate another person's perspective by selecting a picture. Fishbein *et al.* reported that on the rotation task even their three- to five-year-old subjects predicted the other's perspective correctly over 90 per cent of the time.

If young children's ability to succeed on perceptual role-taking tasks is a function of both the nature of the task and the type of response required, then both of these variables should be controlled in any research investigating the ability of young children to predict another person's viewpoint. By replicating Piaget and Inhelder's basic experimental design but substituting a more age-appropriate task, it was hypothesized that children as young as three and four years of age would demonstrate perceptual role-taking ability.

METHOD

The subjects were eight three-year-old children and fourteen four-year-old children attending a child care centre sponsored by a large urban university. The majority of the subjects were the children of students. Approximately one fourth of the youngsters in each group came from the neighbouring community. White children predominated with no more than two black subjects in each age group.

The task presented to the children consisted of four three-dimensional displays. The children were first shown a practice display to orient them to the task and then three experimental displays. As each subject entered the room, he or she was seated at a table facing the practice display which consisted of a large red fire engine (see Figure 1). An exact duplicate of the fire engine appeared on a revolving turntable to the subject's left. Each youngster was then introduced to Grover, a character from *Sesame Street*, and told,

> Grover is going to play this game with us. He will drive his car along the road. Sometimes Grover likes to stop and look out of his car. Now the fire engine on this other table turns so you can look at it from any side. When Grover stops to look out of his car, I want you to turn the scene that moves so you are looking at it the same way Grover is.

The examiner then parked Grover in turn at each of the three sides which present a view different from the subject's. If a subject incorrectly predicted how the fire engine looked to Grover for any of the three positions, the examiner said, 'Sometimes it is hard to tell what Grover sees. Let's go over and look at the fire engine the way Grover sees it.' The subject was then asked to go back and 'move the turntable so that the fire engine looks the way Grover sees it'. If the children again gave an incorrect response, the examiner moved the turntable to the correct position explaining, 'this is the way Grover sees the fire engine from where he is parked'.

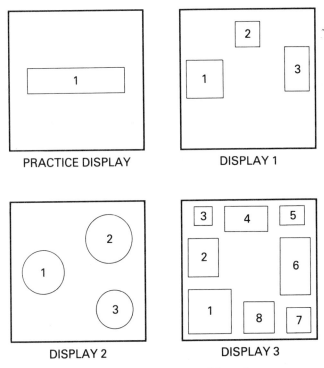

Figure 1: *Displays as viewed from above*

After completing the practice trial with the fire engine, each subject was shown the three experimental displays one at a time (see Figure 1). Display 1 consisted of a small lake with a toy sailboat (1), a miniature horse and cow (2), and a model of a house (3). Display 2 was a papier-mâché replica of Piaget and Inhelder's three mountains: the mountain with a cross on top (1), the mountain with a snow cap (2), and the mountain with a small house on top (3). Display 3 contained a wide variety of miniature people and animals in natural settings: cowboys, indians, and trees (1), a lake with ducks (2), a windmill (3), cows pulling a wagon (4), a dog and a doghouse (5), a barn with farm animals and a farmer (6), a woman feeding chickens (7), two rabbits and a pig pen with pigs (8).

The procedure for these three displays was similar to that used in the practice task except that the child was not given any further opportunity to look at the scene from Grover's point of view. If the subject gave an incorrect response, it was simply accepted and the experimenter moved Grover to the next position. For every display, Grover parked in turn at each of three sides which presented a view different from that of the subject. The sequence of stops was varied randomly for the three scenes. A subject's response was scored correct if the revolving display was turned so that it matched Grover's perception and scored egocentric if the display conformed to the subject's own view.

RESULTS

A 3 × 2 (Scene × Age) analysis of variance of the total number of correct responses revealed significant differences in the accuracy of the children's perception on the three displays (F (2, 64) = 8.32, $p <$ .001). No other effects were significant.

All subjects were highly accurate in their prediction of Grover's perception on the two scenes containing toy objects, but made significantly more errors when responding to Piaget and Inhelder's mountain scene. On Display 1 showing a lake with a sailboat, animals, and a house, the three- and four-year-old subjects rotated the duplicate scene so that it accurately reflected Grover's perspective for all three positions over 80 per cent of the time. On Display 3 containing a wide variety of different objects, the three-year-olds predicted Grover's viewpoint correctly for all three positions over 79 per cent of the time, and the four-year-olds predicted Grover's perspective correctly 93 per cent of the time. In contrast, on Piaget and Inhelder's mountain scene, the three-year-old subjects gave only 42 per cent correct responses for the three positions and the four-year-olds gave 67 per cent correct responses. There were no significant differences in the children's ability to predict Grover's perspective for any of the three positions. Of the total number of errors on all three displays, almost one third or 31 per cent were egocentric and slightly over two thirds or 69 per cent were random.

DISCUSSION

The nature of the task appears to have a significant effect on the role-taking ability of young children. The children's considerably greater success on both the simple and complex scenes containing small toy figures as compared with the three mountains suggests that one important factor affecting role-taking ability is the ease with which the subject can discriminate cues for visualizing the other person's perspective. Discrete, easily differentiated objects provide more cues for young children to identify and remember than essentially similar configurations such as Piaget and Inhelder's three mountains.

Another critical variable appears to be the way the child is expected to communicate an awareness of the other person's perspective. Having subjects revolve an exact duplicate of the experimental display to indicate the other persons's viewpoint resulted in a very low error rate on the two scenes depicting discrete objects. The four-year-olds even achieved some degree of success on Piaget and Inhelder's three mountains. This confirms the observations of other researchers (Fishbein *et al.*, 1972; Huttenlocher and Presson, 1973) that children find it much easier to communicate their awareness of another person's point of view when asked to turn an identical display than when asked to select a picture or build a model. While young children can recognize pictures of objects from a fairly early age, they seem to experience considerable difficulty when asked to make the transition from a three-dimensional display to a two-dimensional picture. Reconstructing a model of the other person's viewpoint also appears to involve conceptual skills beyond the capacity of most children under six or seven years of age. The relatively small proportion of egocentric responses to all three scenes, compared with the predominance of such responses in children under six years of age reported by Piaget and Inhelder, suggests that the more difficult it is for subjects to solve a task, the greater the likelihood that they will give their own perspective in an attempt to perform successfully in the situation.

Data from the present study and from previous investigators exploring perceptual role-taking skills in four- to six-year-olds (Fishbein *et al.*, 1972; Flavel *et al.*, 1968) raise considerable doubt about the validity of Piaget's conclusion that young children are primarily egocentric and incapable of taking the viewpoint of another person. When presented with tasks that are age appropriate, even very young subjects demonstrate perceptual role-taking ability. If one accepts the premise that the capacity to understand another person's perspective is a basic component of empathy, then the evidence indicates that the potential for empathic understanding is already present in children as young as three and four years of age.

The development of awareness and control

INTRODUCTION

The study of children's awareness of their own thought processes is not new, but interest in it has risen sharply in recent years. Psychologists now recognize that young children acquire many skills in relatively unreflecting ways. For instance, the ability to use language and the ability to think about language are by no means one and the same. Likewise the ability to remember is not to be identified with the ability to reflect on memory or on ways of remembering more successfully. The importance of studying the latter kind of skill is now widely acknowledged.

It has become common to use the term *metacognition* to refer to all those capacities which entail reflection upon one's own mental powers. Thus *metacognitive development* is the growth of conscious knowledge about thought, memory, attention, language and related processes.

This kind of development is of special significance for educators because of the demands made upon children by the traditional Western kind of schooling. Before the school years, thinking and language are for the most part spontaneous in the sense that they arise out of the children's own interests and concerns. Their thoughts in the preschool years are largely guided by their own purposes, which may shift freely from moment to moment. There are few tasks to which they are required to 'apply their minds'. As Donaldson puts it (Donaldson, 1978) the thinking of preschool children is for the most part embedded in immediate personal experience.

When school begins, however, (in the great majority of schools at least) all this changes. Children are now given things to learn whether they particularly want to or not. Of course all enlightened teachers try very hard to arouse the interest of the children in what they are learning, and happily they often succeed. However, the point is that, even if the children enjoy their studies and gain much satisfaction from them, it is still the case that new kinds of mental activity are necessarily entailed. Problems are 'set' by other people. Thinking is required to detach itself from immediate shifting personal concerns and become more disciplined and deliberate. There are instructions to be followed precisely, constraints to be accepted. There are new criteria for success and failure. Thus a quite new measure of self-control is called for; and if this is to be achieved, new kinds of self-awareness are indispensable.

Vygotsky (1962) was one of the first to recognize these facts and to appreciate their educational implications. Some have argued that all learning should spring directly from a child's own spontaneous interests. Vygotsky, on the other hand, saw in the demands for disciplined thinking and conscious control the school's special value. As he put it '. . . control of a function is the counterpart of one's consciousness of it'. And he saw 'consciousness and deliberate mastery' as the hallmark of all the higher intellectual functions of the mind.

The influence of Vygotsky's thinking has been profound and so it is fitting that the readings in this section should include an extract from his own writings. The four other readings give an indication of the nature of more recent work in this field.

22.

School instruction and mental development

Lev S. Vygotsky

As we have seen, Vygotsky considered reflective control *and* deliberate awareness *as essential factors in school learning. Indeed, he saw school instruction as serving to raise awareness, which in turn would further enhance mental development and learning. In the reading that follows Vygotsky takes up the issue concerning the relationship between mental development and school instruction. He has some particularly interesting things to say about the relation between learning to speak and learning to read. In presenting his views, Vygotsky refers to some of his own work and to that of his colleagues – particularly a series of four investigations carried out by students of the Herzen Pedagogical Institute in Leningrad. Unfortunately, full descriptions of these studies are not available to us in published form.*

In formulating our own tentative theory of the relationship between instruction and development, we take our departure from four series of investigations. Their common purpose was to uncover these complex interrelations in certain definite areas of school instruction: reading and writing, grammar, arithmetic, natural science, and social science. The specific inquiries concerned such topics as the mastering of the decimal system in relation to the development of the concept of number; the child's awareness of his operations in solving mathematical problems; the processes of constructing and solving problems by first-graders. Much interesting material came to light on the development of oral and written language during school age, the consecutive levels of understanding of figurative meaning, the influence of mastering grammatical structures on the course of mental development, the understanding of relationships in the study of social science and natural science. The investigations focused on the level of maturity of psychic functions at the beginning of schooling, and the influence of schooling on their development; on the temporal sequence of instruction and development; on the 'formal discipline' function of the various subjects of instruction. We shall discuss these issues in succession.

(1) In our first series of studies, we examined the level of development of the psychic functions requisite for learning the basic school subjects – reading and writing, arithmetic, natural science. We found that at the beginning of instruction these functions could not be considered mature, even in the children who proved able to master the curriculum very successfully. Written language is a good illustration. Why does writing come so hard to the schoolchild that at certain periods there is a lag of as much as six or eight years between his 'linguistic age' in speaking and in writing? This used to be explained by the novelty of writing: As a new function, it must repeat the developmental stages of speech; therefore the writing of an eight-year-old must resemble the speech of a two-year-old. This explanation is patently insufficient. A two-year-old uses few words and a simple syntax because his vocabulary is small and his knowledge of more complex sentence structures nonexistent; but the school-child possesses the vocabulary and the grammatical forms for writing, since they are the same as for oral speech. Nor can the difficulties of mastering the mechanics of writing account for the tremendous lag between the schoolchild's oral and written language.

Our investigation has shown that the development of writing does not repeat the developmental history of speaking. Written speech is a separate linguistic function, differing from oral speech in both structure and mode of functioning. Even its minimal development requires a high level of abstraction. It is speech in thought and image only, lacking the musical, expressive, intonational qualities of oral speech. In learning to write, the child must disengage himself from the sensory aspect of speech and replace words by images of words. Speech that is merely imagined and that requires symbolization of the sound image in written signs (i.e. a second degree of symbolization) naturally must be as much harder than oral speech for the child as algebra is harder than arithmetic. Our studies show that it is the abstract quality of written language that is the main stumbling block, not the underdevelopment of small muscles or any other mechanical obstacles.

Writing is also speech without an interlocutor, addressed to an absent or an imaginary person or to no one in particular – a situation new and strange to the child. Our studies show that he has little motivation to learn writing when we begin to teach it. He feels no need for it and has only a vague idea of its usefulness. In conversation, every sentence is prompted by a motive. Desire or need lead to request, question to answer, bewilderment to explanation. The changing motives of the interlocutors determine at every moment the turn oral speech will take. It does not have to be consciously directed – the dynamic situation takes care of that. The motives for writing are more abstract, more intellectualized, further removed from immediate needs. In written speech, we are obliged to create the situation, to represent it to ourselves. This demands detachment from the actual situation.

Writing also requires deliberate analytical action on the part of the child. In speaking, he is hardly conscious of the sounds he pronounces and quite unconscious of the mental operations he performs. In writing, he must take cognizance of the sound structure of each word, dissect it, and reproduce it in alphabetical symbols, which he must have studied and memorized before. In the same deliberate way, he must put words in a certain sequence to form a sentence. Written language demands conscious work because its relationship to inner speech is different from that of oral speech: The latter precedes inner speech in the course of development, while written speech follows inner speech and presupposes its existence (the act of writing implying a translation from inner speech). But the grammar of thought is not the same in the two cases. One might even say that the syntax of inner speech is the exact opposite of the syntax of written speech, with oral speech standing in the middle.

Inner speech is condensed, abbreviated speech. Written speech is deployed to its fullest extent, more complete than oral speech. Inner speech is almost entirely predicative because the situation, the subject of thought, is always known to the thinker. Written speech, on the contrary, must explain the situation fully in order to be intelligible. The change from maximally compact inner speech to maximally detailed written speech requires what might be called deliberate semantics – deliberate structuring of the web of meaning.

All these traits of written speech explain why its development in the school-child falls far behind that of oral speech. The discrepancy is caused by the child's proficiency in spontaneous, unconscious activity and his lack of skill in abstract, deliberate activity. As our studies showed, the psychological functions on which written speech is based have not even begun to develop in the proper sense when instruction in writing starts. It must build on barely emerging, rudimentary processes.

Similar results were obtained in the fields of arithmetic, grammar, and natural science. In every case, the requisite functions are immature when instruction begins. We shall briefly discuss the case of grammar, which presents some special features.

Grammar is a subject which seems to be of little practical use. Unlike other school subjects, it does not give the child new skills. He conjugates and declines before he enters school. The opinion has even been voiced that school instruction in grammar could be dispensed with. We can only reply that our analysis clearly showed the study of grammar to be of paramount importance for the mental development of the child.

The child does have a command of the grammar of his native tongue long before he enters school, but it is unconscious, acquired in a purely structural way, like the phonetic composition of words. If you ask a young child to produce a combination of sounds, for example *sk*, you will find that its deliberate articulation is too hard for him; yet within a structure, as in the word *Moscow*, he pronounces the same sounds with ease. The same is true of grammar. The child will use the correct case or tense within a sentence but cannot decline or conjugate a word on request. He may not acquire new grammatical or syntactic forms in school but, thanks to instruction in grammar and writing, he does become aware of what he is doing and learns to use his skills consciously. Just as the child realizes for the first time in learning to write that the word *Moscow* consists of the sounds *m-o-s-k-ow* and learns to pronounce each one separately, he also learns to construct sentences, to do consciously what he has been doing unconsciously in speaking. Grammar and writing help the child to rise to a higher level of speech development.

Thus our investigation shows that the development of the psychological foundations for instruction in basic subjects does not precede instruction but unfolds in a continuous interaction with the contributions of instruction.

(2) Our second series of investigations centred on the temporal relation between the processes of instruction and the development of the corresponding psychological functions. We found that instruction usually precedes development. The child acquires certain habits and skills in a given area before he learns to apply them consciously and deliberately. There is never complete parallelism between the course of instruction and the development of the corresponding functions.

Instruction has its own sequences and organization, it follows a curriculum and a timetable, and its rules cannot be expected to coincide with the inner laws of the developmental processes it calls to life. On the basis of our studies, we tried to plot curves of the progress of instruction and of the participating psychological functions; far from coinciding, these curves showed an exceedingly complex relationship.

For example, the different steps in learning arithmetic may be of unequal value for mental development. It often happens that three or four steps in instruction add little to the child's understanding of arithmetic, and then, with the fifth step, something clicks; the child has grasped a general principle, and his developmental curve rises markedly. For this particular child, the fifth operation was decisive, but this cannot be a general rule. The turning points at which a general principle becomes clear to the child cannot be set in advance by the curriculum. The child is not taught the decimal system as such; he is taught to write figures, to add and to multiply, to solve problems, and out of all this some general concept of the decimal system eventually emerges.

When the child learns some arithmetical operation or some scientific concept, the development of that operation or concept has only begun. Our study shows that the curve of development does not coincide with the curve of school instruction; by and large, instruction precedes development.

(3) Our third series of investigations resembles Thorndike's studies of the transfer of training, except that we experimented with subjects of school instruction and with the higher rather than the elementary functions, i.e. with subjects and functions which could be expected to be meaningfully related.

We found that intellectual development, far from following Thorndike's atomistic model, is not compartmentalized according to topics of instruction. Its course is much more unitary, and the different school subjects interact in contributing to it. While the processes of instruction follow their own logical order, they awaken and direct a system of processes in the child's mind which is hidden from direct observation and subject to its own developmental laws. To uncover these developmental processes stimulated by instruction is one of the basic tasks of the psychological study of learning.

Specifically, our experiments brought out the following interrelated facts: The psychological prerequisites for instruction in different school subjects are to a large extent the same; instruction in a given subject influences the development of the higher functions far beyond the confines of that particular subject; the main psychic functions involved in studying various subjects are interdependent – their common bases are consciousness and deliberate mastery, the principal contributions of the school years. It follows from these findings that all the basic school subjects act as formal discipline, each facilitating the learning of the others; the psychological functions stimulated by them develop in one complex process.

(4) In the fourth series of studies, we attacked a problem which has not received sufficient attention in the past but which we consider of focal importance for the study of learning and development.

Most of the psychological investigations concerned with school learning measured the level of mental development of the child by making him solve certain standardized problems. The problems he was able to solve by himself were supposed to indicate the level of his mental development at the particular time. But in this way only the completed part of the child's development can be measured, which is far from the whole story. We tried a different approach. Having found that the mental age of two children was, let us say, eight, we gave each of them harder problems than he could manage on his own and provided some slight assistance: the first step in a solution, a leading question, or some other form of help. We discovered that one child could, in cooperation, solve problems designed for twelve-year-olds, while the other could not go beyond problems intended for nine-year-olds. The discrepancy between a child's actual mental age and the level he reaches in solving problems with assistance indicates the zone of his proximal development; in our example, this zone is four for the first child and one for the second. Can we truly say that their mental development is the same? Experience has shown that the child with the larger zone of proximal development will do much better in school. This measure gives a more helpful clue than mental age does to the dynamics of intellectual progress.

Psychologists today cannot share the layman's belief that imitation is a mechanical activity and that anyone can imitate almost anything if shown how. To imitate, it is necessary to possess the means of stepping from something one knows to something new. With assistance, every child can do more than he can by himself – though only within the limits set by the state of his development. Koehler found that a chimpanzee can imitate only those intelligent acts of other apes that he could have performed on his own. Persistent training, it is true, can induce him to perform much more complicated actions, but these are carried out mechanically and have all the earmarks of meaningless habits rather than of insightful solutions. The cleverest animal is incapable of intellectual development through imitation. It can be drilled to perform specific acts, but the new habits do not result in new general abilities. In this sense, it can be said that animals are unteachable.

In the child's development, on the contrary, imitation and instruction play a major role. They bring out the specifically human qualities of the mind and lead the child to new developmental levels. In learning to speak, as in learning school subjects, imitation is indispensable. What the child can do in co-operation today he can do alone tomorrow. Therefore the only good kind of instruction is that which marches ahead of development and leads it; it must be aimed not so much at the ripe as at the ripening functions. It remains necessary to determine the lowest threshold at which instruction in, say, arithmetic may begin since a certain minimal ripeness of functions is required. But we must consider the upper threshold as well; instruction must be oriented towards the future, not the past.

For a time, our schools favoured the 'complex' system of instruction, which was believed to be adapted to the child's ways of thinking. In offering the child problems he was able to handle without help, this method failed to utilize the zone of proximal development and to lead the child to what he could not yet do. Instruction was oriented to the child's weakness rather than his strength, thus encouraging him to remain at the preschool stage of development.

For each subject of instruction there is a period when its influence is most fruitful because the child is most receptive to it. It has been called the *sensitive period* by Montessori and other educators. The term is used also in biology, for the periods in ontogenetic development when the organism is particularly responsive to influences of certain kinds. During that period an influence that has little effect earlier or later may radically affect the course of development. But the existence of an optimum time for instruction in a given subject cannot be explained in purely biological terms, at least not for such complex processes as written speech. Our investigation demonstrated the social and cultural nature of the development of the higher functions during these periods, i.e. its dependence on cooperation with adults and on instruction. Montessori's data, however, retain their significance. She found, for instance, that if a child is taught to write early, at four and a half or five years of age, he responds by 'explosive writing', an abundant and imaginative use of written speech that is never duplicated by children a few years older. This is a striking example of the strong influence that instruction can have when the corresponding functions have not yet fully matured. The existence of sensitive periods for all subjects of instruction is fully supported by the data of our studies. The school years as a whole are the optimum period for instruction in operations that require awareness and deliberate control; instruction in these operations maximally furthers the development of the higher psychological functions while they are maturing. This applies also to the development of the scientific concepts to which school instruction introduces the child.

23.

The child as psychologist

Paul L. Harris

In this reading Harris considers children's knowledge of psychological phenomena. He intends this term to include many of those abilities which other authors refer to as metacognitive abilities. Thus Harris considers aspects of development during childhood which are concerned with the child's growing awareness of himself and his cognitive and linguistic processes. In the reading, Harris points out that although the early work of Piaget included studies of children's knowledge of psychological phenomena (e.g. children's understanding of dreams), Piaget subsequently concentrated on children's knowledge of physical phenomena and events, including invariance of quantity (e.g. conservation of liquid), classification of objects according to their physical properties (e.g. colour, shape), and establishment of physical laws (e.g. equilibrium in a balance). However as Harris points out, we also need to know how children develop concepts of the way people behave, and concepts of how their own minds work. He therefore provides a brief overview of the development of some of this psychological knowledge during childhood, referring to memory, perception, language, motivation, and social behaviour. The reading is important in that it draws attention to the need to consider children's psychological knowledge, knowledge that has implications for children's performance in the classroom.

I shall try to show that the developing child is, in part, an apprentice psychologist. He is gradually acquiring psychological knowledge about why other people behave as they do. Moreover, he is acquiring insight into the way in which his own mind operates. For example he comes to understand that some things are hard to remember while other things are easy; he learns that sometimes he resists temptation, while at other times he does not. These psychological insights can be put to use by the child in order to change his own behaviour – to increase the likelihood, for example, that he will remember something or resist a temptation. I shall also point out that in certain areas psychological knowledge is difficult to acquire so that even adults have a limited insight into the way that their own minds operate.

Let me begin by looking at some of the early work which is relevant to my theme. In his early books Piaget questioned the child about certain psychological phenomena. The child's answers were especially interesting because they showed that the child has quite independent ideas of his own, ideas he has clearly not borrowed from adults. The following conversation between Piaget and a five-year-old child on the subject of dreams reveals the child's independence of mind (Piaget, 1929).

> 'Do you ever have dreams?' asks Piaget.
> 'Yes, I dreamt once that I had a hole in my hand,' replies the child.
> 'Are dreams true?'
> 'No, they are pictures we see . . .'.
> 'Are your eyes open or shut when you dream?'
> 'Shut.'
> 'Could I see your dreams?'
> 'No, you would be too far away . . .'.
> 'Is the dream inside your head or inside you?'
> 'It isn't in me because then I wouldn't see it.'
> 'And could your mother see it?'
> 'No, she isn't in the bed. Only my little sister sleeps with me.'

Piaget emphasizes in this example how the child has difficulty in distinguishing between the mental and the physical. According to the child, the dream, being visible, has some of the properties of an ordinary physical object. The child claims for example that the experimenter would be too far away to see his dream and he also locates the dream outside himself rather than inside himself. Thus the child invests a purely mental process with a physical property such as a position in the visible world.

Piaget also found that the child makes the reverse assimilation; he attributes psychological properties to a purely physical phenomenon. He showed children a metal box hanging on a string. The string had been twisted so that as it unwound, the box also turned round and round. This is the conversation which took place between Piaget and one child. The conversation shows that the child does not simply borrow his explanations from adults.

> 'Why does the box turn?' asks Piaget.
> 'Because the string is twisted.'
> 'Why does the string turn too?'
> 'Because it wants to unwind itself.'
> 'Does the string know it's twisted?'
> 'Yes.'
> 'How do you think it knows?'
> 'Because it feels that it's all twisted.'

Despite the fascination of these findings, Piaget turned away from the child's understanding of psychological phenomena to study the child's understanding of obviously physical phenomena such as the conservation of quantity, and the concepts of space, time, speed, chance and so forth – in short, all those concepts which preoccupy the physicist rather than the psychologist.

However there are I think good reasons for renewing our study of the child's psychological knowledge, even though Piaget abandoned his own investigations so many years ago. In the first place, it is reasonable to expect that there will be certain universal trends in the child's acquisition of psychological knowledge just as there are apparently universal trends in the child's understanding of physical phenomena. This universality is to be expected because the psychological world which the child encounters in different parts of the world has certain universal features just as the physical world exhibits certain universal features. Despite their cultural diversity human beings all over the world will confront the child with certain basic biological regularities. All human beings exhibit intentionality, emotion, perception, memory, and thought for example.

The second reason for renewing our study of the child's psychological knowledge is that the child is clearly at home with mentalistic explanations. The conversation that I quoted earlier shows that the child is happy to explain overt behaviour – for example the behaviour of the string – in terms of mental categories such as wanting and knowing.

The third reason for studying the child's psychological knowledge concerns the relationship between knowledge and action. Although Piaget studied the child's acquisition of important physical principles such as the principle of conservation, it is not obvious how the acquisition of this principle influences the child's day-to-day behaviour. Indeed it required Piaget's famous clinical method to unearth the fact that the young child does not believe in the principle of conservation. As I shall try to show, the acquisition of psychological knowledge by the child has important repercussions not simply on the way that the child thinks but on his everyday behaviour towards other people, his capacity to resist temptation, his play and his behaviour in the classroom. This means, I hope, that a consideration of the child as a psychologist can be used to cross some of the barriers that exist within psychology. For example the study of intellectual processes in the child or the adult is rarely linked to the study of motivation or social behaviour. In this lecture I shall ignore these traditional barriers within psychology.

Let me begin by considering the child's understanding of the ways that memory works. As adults, we know that our memory is selective. If we have just seen a television programme or read a book, we know that total recall is impossible. What we can do is to remember the gist or the main theme, forgetting inessential details. Thus Bartlett (1932) showed that if adults are asked to recall a story after various lengths of interval – a few hours, a few days, several weeks or even years – then the adult produces an increasingly condensed summary of the original story. Time often leads to some distortion of the original story but the essential features of the plot are usually preserved.

Recent research by my colleagues and myself (Harris, 1978) shows that young children behave in exactly the same way. They also produce a summary of the original story, concentrating on the important episodes. If one asks them to recall the story after a delay of a couple of weeks rather than a few minutes, they produce an even more condensed summary but still concentrate on the important parts of the story.

Do young children know that their mind works in this way? Do they recognize that certain parts of the story – the essentials – are easier to remember than other parts – the details? Some recent research shows that adults make this distinction quite easily (Brown and Smiley, 1977). Adults could predict in advance that a sentence concerned with the central plot of the story would be easier to remember than a sentence about some unimportant detail. Young childen, on the other hand, could not make this prediction. They thought that they would remember these two different types of sentence equally well. Nonetheless, if these same young children were given the story in question to remember, then they were as selective in their memory as adults. Apparently then there is a gap between what the child actually does and what he knows he does. His memory operates selectively but he does not know that it does.

Does this lack of psychological insight have any repercussions on the child's behaviour? Tentatively, we can say yes. Some recent work (Wellman, personal communication) shows that as the child gets older he exercises control over his memory by reading in a more planful and deliberate way. For example, the child does not simply read a story through from beginning to end, he is more active: he underlines parts of the text and goes back to some earlier part in order to check how it links up with some later part. This activity surely reflects, to some degree, the child's awareness that a story or an argument has an internal organization, an organization which he must recreate in his own mind if he is to remember it effectively. In contrast, the younger child can detect this organization only at an unconscious level. That is to say it influences his memory but he himself exercises no deliberate control over its influence.

In discussing the child's psychological knowledge, Flavell (1977) has pointed out that such knowledge falls roughly into two categories: general principles such as the principle that stories are easier to remember than lists of words, and local introspective knowledge. Let me give you an example of this second category of local introspective knowledge. Sometimes we are about to introduce someone only to discover that we have temporarily forgotten their name. This frustrating experience is usually called the tip of the tongue experience because the name seems to be accessible but eludes vocalization. When one forgets a name in this way one is usually quite confident that one knows the name and indeed when someone rescues us by offering the name, we immediately recognize it. This shows that, for adults at least, the tip of the tongue feeling is predictive. It allows them to say whether they have momentarily lost the word or whether they have forgotten it completely. The tip of the tongue experience, then, is a piece of private introspective knowledge which allows us to predict the workings of our own mind in a particular situation.

Wellman (1977) has recently asked children about their tip of the tongue experiences. He gave them various objects which the children had to name. If a child could not name an object correctly, the experimenter asked him to decide whether the name was on the tip of his tongue or whether he had completely forgotten it. To get the child to make this distinction, Wellman asked the child to say whether or not he would recognize the correct name if the experimenter told him it. Wellman found that although older children could make this prediction correctly, younger children were much less accurate. That is to say, they could not decide on the strength of their tip of the tongue feeling whether they had momentarily forgotten the name and would recognize it if the experimenter said it or whether they had forgotten it altogether.

Apparently, the older child is more knowledgeable not simply about what we may call general psychological laws – such as the effect of meaningful organization on memory – he also develops the ability to monitor his own current mental status and to make predictions about its likely consequences. It is as if the older child can take his own mental temperature and on the basis of that temperature is able to make a diagnosis and a prognosis concerning future mental events.

On the basis of Wellman's findings concerning the tip of the tongue feeling, one may speculate in the following way. As adults, we can recognize that there are various degrees of mental certainty. Between certain knowledge and complete ignorance, there is a considerable twilight zone of doubt and uncertainty. The existence of this mental twilight zone and its recognition by us, is helpful because it is a signal to persist, to look further, to gather more information, to ask a question and so forth. The child, on the other hand, appears to shift more abruptly from the state of ignorance to the state of knowledge. He does not readily notice the existence of the twilight zone of doubt and uncertainty. This general statement is indeed speculative but I believe it is possible to find supportive evidence. I will give two examples – one drawn from the area of perception and the other from the area of language comprehension.

We have been studying the child's ability to make simple perceptual judgements (Harris and Singleton, 1978). We showed children two sticks and asked them to point to the longer of the two. Sometimes the two sticks were close together making visual comparison easy; sometimes the sticks were far apart making visual comparison hard. The older children typically pointed to the longer stick when the two were easy to compare, but hesitated if the sticks were far apart. They would admit ignorance or say that they couldn't tell unless the sticks were moved closer together. The younger children on the other hand showed little hesitation whether the sticks were far apart or close together. My interpretation of this result is that the young child is unable to monitor his own perceptual processes like the older child. He cannot distinguish degrees of perceptual certainty just as he cannot assess the strength of a tip of the tongue experience.

We find the same insensitivity to his own mental state if we examine the young child's awareness of his comprehension of language. In an early set of studies (Piaget, 1926) Piaget explained to a group of young children how a syringe worked. Each of these children was then required to pass on this explanation to a friend of the same age. Piaget noticed two things. First of all the children typically offered explanations which were difficult to follow. For example here is the explanation of one six-year-old:

'You see there is the piston; then you pull it and it makes a squirt. Then it leaves room for the water. When you push the little piston it makes the water come out, it makes a squirt, you see ...'

His friend listened attentively to this explanation. Here is his attempt at reproduction:

'He told me that it was ... something. There was something where there was water, and then the water came out.'

Clearly this child is not much wiser about how a syringe works. Piaget noticed, however, that although the children were frequently given inadequate explanations – or, at least, explanations which they had not understood – they rarely complained or asked for more information. Instead they behaved as if they had understood perfectly, although their subsequent answers to Piaget's questions showed that this was rarely the case. Here again then, as in the case of perceptual judgements, the child appears to be insensitive to his own mental state.

Why exactly does the child not notice his lack of comprehension? Unfortunately the relevant research has not been done but we may consider two possible explanations. From several experiments we know that the young child interprets what he hears in the light of the surrounding non-verbal context. Perhaps the best analogy to this, in adult terms, is the feeling of comprehension we experience as adults when we hear a foreign language in a familiar situation. On the basis of the situation we are often able to guess what is being said. Indeed even when we are somewhat familiar with a foreign language our understanding of what is said will vary greatly depending on whether the topic of conversation is a familiar one or not. Children must rely on this contextual knowledge a great deal if they are ever to acquire the vocabulary of their mother tongue. Miller (1974) has pointed out how enormous this problem is. The average child acquires about 55,000 words during his school years. This means that he must learn about 12 new words per day. Presumably only a fraction of these words are ever explicitly defined by an adult for the child, so that the child must solve the problem by intelligent guess-work using contextual knowledge. Given that this strategy must be continuously in operation – if the child is to pick up so many new words each day – it is not surprising that he may sometimes ignore the fact that too many gaps exist in a particular sentence for comprehension to occur at all. This hypothesis implies then that the young child certainly experiences incomprehension but does not recognize it for what it is. It is too much a fact of life for him to remark upon.

Another possible explanation turns the above suggestion upsidedown. Perhaps the young child, far from relying on the non-verbal context to help him understand what is said, restricts his efforts at comprehension to the words themselves.* That is to say he does not go beyond the words to construct in his imagination a concrete analogue of what his friend is telling him about the syringe. His understanding remains entirely verbal. As a result he never encounters the feeling of incomprehension that we have when we cannot fit the implications of a particular sentence into the mental context that we have constructed up to that point.

I have dwelt on this last topic at length because it has obvious practical implications. A good pupil is one who tells his teacher when he has not understood, or one who asks questions in order to fill in the gaps in his knowledge. To the extent that we can help children to monitor their comprehension more effectively and also to signal their lack of comprehension to a teacher, we shall be able to help teachers to be more effective.

So far, the examples of psychological knowledge that I have discussed have concerned cognitive processes: memory, perception and language comprehension. However I suggested earlier that psychological knowledge influences the child's behaviour in general. I shall try to extend the argument, then, with examples from the study of motivation and social behaviour.

Adults know that a piece of behaviour can be prompted by external circumstances or by some internal reason. When there is a possibility that both are operative we cannot tell which is actually causal. An example will make this more clear. Richard Nixon eventually admitted – at least in part – his complicity in Watergate. Was this produced by a violent surge of guilt, an internal reason therefore, or alternatively by external pressures on Nixon to confess before he was proved guilty by the law? We obviously cannot be sure that guilt alone was responsible. Had Nixon confessed earlier, before the external pressures became so intense, his confession would no doubt have been taken more seriously by the American public.

This kind of reasoning operates in the following way: if an external and an internal reason exist for a piece of behaviour, you cannot be sure which of the

---

* I am grateful to Dr S. Hampson for suggesting this hypothesis to me.

two is responsible. If however one reason is clearly absent, you can confidently attribute the behaviour to the opposite reason. Thus behaviour produced in the absence of external pressure is probably attributable to internal reasons and vice versa.

Do young children engage in this rather complicated psychological analysis? From all we know of the child's naïveté in producing a causal analysis of the physical world, one might doubt it. However some recent research (Schultz and Butkowsky, 1977) shows that young children can make such an analysis. The children – a group of five-year-olds – were shown a film in which a small boy solved a puzzle and looked pleased with himself as a result. The film then continued in one of two different versions. In one version the same small boy was shown failing to solve some other puzzles. The children who saw this film concluded that the boy had solved the first puzzle because it was easy and not because of any special ability on his part. The other version of the film showed some other children failing to solve the first puzzle. The children who saw this version concluded that the boy who had solved the puzzle must have had a special ability. Here then we see exactly the same kind of weighing of external factors such as the easiness of the puzzle, in relation to internal factors such as ability or cleverness.

Does this kind of analysis influence the way that the child perceives his own behaviour and indeed alter that behaviour as a result? Some recent research suggests that children may indeed reason as follows.

'If there is an obvious external reason for my behaviour, I probably do not have any internal reason. So if the external reason is removed, there is no reason for me to continue behaving like that.'

Here is one concrete instance of this kind of reasoning (Condry, 1977; Lepper, Greene and Nisbett, 1973). Two groups of children were given some new toys to play with. One group was given an external reason for playing with the toys, namely a reward. A second group were given no such reward. Later the experimenters gave the two groups of children the same toys for a second time and watched how long the children spent playing with them. Remarkably, the children who had previously been given a reward to play with the toys spent less time playing with them than children who had received no such reward. Apparently, the provision of some external reward reduced the children's belief in their own internal reasons for playing with the toys. It was as if the rewarded children were saying to themselves 'Because I played with these toys before in order to get a reward, I am not really interested in them. So I shall not bother to play with them now.'

The implication of these results for the classroom and the nursery is quite clear: we must be careful that we do not undermine the child's intrinsic motivation by giving him an unnecessary extrinsic motivation. For my last example of psychological knowledge, I want to discuss the child's capacity for self-control or resistance to temptation. Mischel devised a simple situation in which to test self-control (Mischel, 1974). The children were shown two rewards and asked to say which one they preferred. Once they had made their choice, they were told that they could not have their reward immediately but in a little while when the experimenter came back. In the meantime, they were asked to stay in the waiting-room until the experimenter returned. If they called the experimenter back during this waiting period they would get the less preferred reward immediately. Thus the experimental question was whether the child could resist the temptation of an immediate reward and wait instead for a more attractive reward. As one might expect Mischel found that it was much more difficult for the children to wait if the small tempting reward was left in front of them. Surprisingly, however, these same children seemed quite unaware that they were vulnerable to such a temptation. Mischel (1976) asked the children whether they wanted to wait with the tempting reward in front of them or with nothing in front of them. The young children virtually all chose to wait with the tempting object in front of them, thereby increasing their chances of being tempted. In other experiments, Mischel found that the young child could be trained to adopt strategies to resist temptation. These strategies usually involved getting the child to distract himself from the tempting reward by using his imagination in some way. Most important of all though, for my purposes, was the finding that older children were better able to resist temptation than younger children when the experimenter gave no advice about helpful strategies for self-control. The implication of this finding is that the older child, being more aware of his vulnerability to temptation, spontaneously develops self-control strategies of his own. Once again we see the child's psychological knowledge having an influence on his behaviour.

Let me try to bring together the various topics that I have discussed. I have argued that the child is busy acquiring psychological knowledge. We can think of this knowledge as falling into two categories: knowledge of certain basic psychological laws which apply to his own mind and that of other people and in the second place an increasing sensitivity to his own current mental state, be it a state of temporary forgetfulness, perceptual uncertainty or partial misunderstanding. Armed with this knowledge and sensitivity the child can guide his behaviour in a more planful and deliberate fashion. In addition, it is clear that adults who are responsible for young children, even children as young as five years, must acknowledge that children try to make sense of their own behaviour: providing young children with an external reason for their behaviour may sometimes undermine the child's confidence in his own intrinsic reasons.

I want to end with a couple of cautionary remarks. Although I have argued that the child increases his psychological knowledge in the course of development, in no way do I wish to imply that the child is proceeding towards a state of psychological omniscience. Even as an adult, he will find that certain psychological processes remain difficult to understand, or inaccessible to introspection. First, the Freudian tradition reminds us that it is difficult to become aware of some of the less salubrious reasons for our behaviour. Second, some psychological processes such as the recognition of a face or a word happen far too quickly for the layman to study or explain. Third, adults are prone to deny the effect of variables which strike them as implausible. One example of this last phenomenon must suffice. Latané and Darley (1970) have studied the so-called unresponsive bystander who fails to give help to a stranger in the street even though the stranger is clearly in some kind of distress. Latané and Darley found that we are much more likely to help such a stranger if there is no-one else in sight. The more people there are present, the more we seem to abandon our responsibility, perhaps on the grounds that someone else will help instead. When Latané and Darley asked their subjects: 'Was your willingness to help the stranger in any way influenced by the presence of other people?' their subjects persistently denied that this was the case, even though the experimental results demonstrated conclusively that they had been so influenced.

It is clear then that there are some mental processes which become increasingly intelligible and accessible as the child gets older. There is a second class of mental processes which remain unintelligible and inaccessible. This means that sometimes the child's developing knowledge will enter into agreement with what psychology has established. On the other hand, the child's developing knowledge will sometimes remain in constant disagreement with what psychology has established. As psychologists, we must be alert to, and indeed try to explain, both of these developmental paths.

24.

Metacognitive skills

Ann L. Brown and Judy S. DeLoache

This reading consists of two sections from a paper by Brown and DeLoache entitled 'Skills, plans and self-regulation'. In the first section, 'Self-interrogation and self-regulation', the authors discuss the metacognitive skills that may be used in a variety of different tasks. That is, they consider those metacognitive skills that are sufficiently abstract to apply to a range of different situations. They point out that young children may not be aware of these skills, and that even once they have acquired them, they may not always see the opportunities to use them. This point is illustrated more fully in the second extract, 'Selected tasks and strategies', where Brown and DeLoache describe the application of metacognitive skills to three different activities. The activities are extracting basic information from texts, visual scanning, and retrieval processes. The authors refer to these activities because they are used in a range of situations, and because they are carried out by both children and adults. The development of metacognitive skills, and their influence on performance over a wide age range, can therefore be considered.

SELF-INTERROGATION AND SELF-REGULATION

The main premise we discuss is that when faced with a new type of problem, anyone is a novice to a certain extent. Novices often fail to perform efficiently, not only because they may lack certain skills but because they are deficient in terms of self-conscious participation and intelligent self-regulation of their actions. The novice tends not to know much about either his capabilities on a new task or the techniques necessary to perform efficiently; he may even have difficulty determining what goals are desirable, let alone what steps are required to get there. Note that this innocence is not necessarily related to age (Chi, 1978) but is more a function of inexperience in a new problem situation. Adults and children display similar confusion when confronted with a new problem: A novice chess player (Chi, 1977) has many of the same problems of metacognition that the very young card player experiences (Markman, 1977). For both, the situation is relatively new and difficult. Barring significant transfer from prior experience, the beginner in any problem-solving situation has not developed the necessary knowledge about how and what to think under the new circumstances.

The point we wish to emphasize is that children find themselves in this situation more often than do adults, and very young children may be neophytes in almost all problem situations. Thus, an explanation of why young children have such generalized metacognitive deficits (Brown, 1978b; Flavell and Wellman, 1977) is that most of our experimental tasks are both new and difficult for them. It is this lack of familiarity with the game at hand that leads to a concomitant lack of self-interrogation about the current state of knowledge and to inadequate selection and monitoring of necessary steps between starting levels and desired goals. The child's initial 'passivity' in many memory and problem-solving tasks, his failure to check and monitor his ongoing activities, and his failure to make his own task analysis could be the direct result of gross inexperience on such tasks. This does not mean that young children are incapable of self-regulation, only that they tend not to bring such procedures to bear immediately on new problems. Children are universal novices; it takes experience before they build up the knowledge and confidence that would enable them to adopt routinely the self-interrogation mode of the expert (Bransford, Nitsch and Franks, 1977).

Although absolute novices tend not to incorporate effective metacognitive activities into their initial attempts to solve problems, it is not simply the case that experts do and novices do not engage in effective self-regulation. As Simon and Simon (1978) have pointed out in their study of physics problem solvers, the expert engaged in less observable self-questioning than did the relative novice, for the processes of problem solving in this domain had become relatively automatic for the expert. The relative novice, on the other hand, showed many instances of overt self-questioning and checking. Notice that Simon and Simon's novice had received sufficient background instruction so that the basic rules for solution were known to her. We would characterize her state of knowing as being typical of the learner: acquainted with the rules of the game and beginning to acquire expertise.

We would not be surprised to find that the following pattern is typical. First, the absolute novices show little or no intelligent self-regulation. Then, as the problem solver becomes familiar with the necessary rules and sub-processes, he enters into an increasingly active period of deliberate self-regulation. Finally, the performance of the expert would run smoothly as the necessary sub-processes and their coordination have all been overlearned to the point where they are relatively automatic.

We have as yet little developmental data to suggest that such a pattern is a characteristic feature of growth during problem solving, but we predict that such a progression may be a common feature of learning in many domains. Furthermore, although age and experience are obviously intimately related, we do not believe that the growth pattern is necessarily related to age. Young children may show the same progression of naïveté to competence within simpler task domains. Evidence such as that provided by Chi's (1978) young chess experts is exactly the kind needed to support this conjecture. If we wish to understand how much of the young child's ineptitude is due to lack of expertise, rather than age *per se*, we must look at behaviour in areas in which the child is competent as well as those in which he is inefficient.

There is one other factor that might contribute to the young child's general metacognitive problem. In addition to being hampered by the novelty of most experimental situations, young children may simply not realize that certain metacognitive operations are useful in practically any situation. These general metacognitive skills are discussed at length in another paper (Brown, 1978b), and we only briefly summarize them here. The basic skills of metacognition include *predicting* the consequences of an action or event, *checking* the results of one's own actions (did it work?), *monitoring* one's ongoing activity (how am I doing?), *reality testing* (does this make sense?), and a variety of other behaviours for *coordinating* and *controlling* deliberate attempts to learn and solve problems. These skills are the basic characteristics of efficient thought, and one of their most important properties is that they are trans-situational. They apply to the whole range of problem-solving activities, from artificially structured experimental settings to what we psychologists defensively refer to as 'real world, everyday life' situations. It is important to check the results of an operation against some criterion of acceptability, whether one is memorizing a prose passage, reading a textbook, or following instructions in a laboratory experiment, a classroom, or on the street. A child has to learn these various skills, but perhaps of equal importance, he has to learn that they are almost universally applicable, that whenever he is faced with a new task, it will be to his advantage to apply his general knowledge about how to learn and solve problems.

SELECTED TASKS AND STRATEGIES

(1) Extracting the main idea

Getting the gist of a message, whether it is oral or written, is an essential communicative as well as information-gathering activity. Without this ability, children would never learn a language and would certainly never come to use that language to communicate. The ability to extract the main idea to the exclusion of nonessential detail may be a naturally occurring proclivity given, of course, a reasonable match between the complexity of the message and the receiver's current cognitive status (Brown, 1975).

In a recent series of studies (Brown and Smiley, 1977a, 1977b), we have been considering the situation in which children must extract the main theme of a prose passage, a story. Our subject population has ranged from pre-schoolers as young as three years of age to college students, and the stories are adapted to suit the different age groups. We find the same pattern across age: with or without conscious intent to do so, subjects extract the main theme of a story and ignore trivia. Older children have more highly developed scripts (Nelson, 1977; Nelson and Brown, 1978) for storytelling, but even very young children apprehend the essential gist of a story plot (Brown, 1976).

Children are misled in their comprehension of stories by the same snares that trap adults (Brown, Smiley, Day, Townsend and Lawton, 1977). Led to believe certain 'facts' concerning a main character or the location of an action, facts that never appear in the original story, children disambiguate and elaborate in the same way as adults. They falsely recognize theme-congruent distractors in recognition tests and include their pre-existing knowledge when recalling. In addition, they had difficulty distinguishing between their own elaborations and the actual story content.

If there is such essential similarity across ages in the way children construct a message from prose passages, what then is the interesting developmental trend? Not surprisingly, given the theme of this chapter, we believe that what develops is an increasingly conscious control of the naturally occurring tendency, a control that allows more efficient gathering of information.

As children mature they begin to predict the essential organizing features and crucial elements of texts (Brown and Smiley, 1977a, 1977b). Thanks to this fore-knowledge, they make better use of extended study time. If given an extra period for study (equal to three times their reading rate), children from the seventh grade up improve considerably their recall for important elements of text; recall of less important details does not improve. Children below the seventh grade do not usually show such effective use of additional study time; their recall improves, if at all, evenly across all levels of importance. As a result, older students' recall protocols following study include all the essential elements and little trivia. Younger children's recall, though still favouring important elements, has many important elements missing.

To substantiate our belief that metacognitive control governs this developmental trend, we have observed the study actions of our subjects. In particular, we have examined their physical records that can be scored objectively – notes and underlining of texts. A certain proportion of children from the fifth grade and up spontaneously underline or take notes during study. At all ages, the physical records of spontaneous subjects favoured the important elements, that is, the notes or underlined sections concentrated on elements previously rated as crucial to the theme. Students induced to adopt one of these strategies did not show a similar sensitivity to importance; they took notes or underlined more randomly. Some of the very young children underlined all the text when told to underline. Although the efficiency of physical record keeping in induced subjects did improve with age, it never reached the standard set by spontaneous users of the strategy. Furthermore, the recall scores of spontaneous producers were much superior. Even fifth graders who spontaneously underlined showed an adult-like pattern and used extra study to improve differentially their recall of important elements. When we combined all fifth graders, the efficient pattern of the spontaneous children was masked.

It should be pointed out that we do not believe there is a magical age at which children become able to detect the important elements of a text. This is obviously a case of headfitting (Brown, 1975, 1978b) – that is, the intimate relation of the child's current knowledge to the complexity of the stimulus materials. We have found that children can pick out the main ideas of much simpler texts at much earlier ages. We are currently examining whether, given this foresight, they show a concomitant decrease in the age of onset of simple strategies.

In short, knowledge about texts (or any message source for that matter) must consist of general knowledge about consistent features of all texts and specific knowledge about the particular example at hand, a specific knowledge that must be influenced by idiosyncratic characteristics such as complexity. Similarly, we would expect that strategies for learning from a text would depend on general strategic knowledge about suitable activities, but these would have to be triggered by certain specific features of the text being studied. Quite simply, if the text is so complicated that the reader cannot identify the main points, he can scarcely be expected to select them for extra study, even if he possesses the prerequisite strategic knowledge that this would be a good study ploy. Thus, we would predict that even the sophisticated college student may behave immaturely when studying a difficult text.

This brief summary of some of our ongoing research (for details see Brown and Smiley, 1977b) illustrates what we believe to be a repetitive pattern in cognitive development. What develops is often an increasingly conscious control over an early emerging process. Even young children extract the essential gist of messages if they are not misled by red herrings, such as artificially increased salience of nonessential detail (Brown, 1980). All our subjects have shown this ability to a lesser or greater extent – even preschool children (Brown, 1976), poor readers (Smiley, Oakley, Worthen, Campione and Brown, 1977), and slow learners (Brown and Campione, 1978). What develops with age are strategies and control over these strategies. Using knowledge about elements of texts, knowledge about how to study, and the interface of these two factors, the older student can become much more efficient at processing information presented in texts.

(2) Visual scanning

Our next selection of a naturally occurring ability that shows interesting refinement and increasingly conscious control with age and experience is visual scanning, the process by which one, as Day (1975) says, 'actively, selectively, and sequentially acquires information from the visual environment' (p. 154). Effective and efficient visual scanning requires a high degree of executive control, directing fixations and sequencing eye movements from one point of the visual array to another.

Visual scanning begins in the first hours of life. Even newborn infants scan visual stimuli (Salapatek, 1975) but in a very restricted fashion; the young infant is likely to limit his fixations to only one corner of a simple geometric figure (Salapatek, 1968) or to just one feature of a face (Maurer and Salapatek, 1976). The young infant's attention is drawn, almost compelled, to small areas of high contrast. He seems to have very limited voluntary control over his looking and has been characterized as being 'captured' by visual stimuli (Ames and Silfen, 1966; Stechler and Latz, 1966).

This involuntary looking gradually gives way during the first few months to much more voluntary control. By three or four months a baby scans the entire pattern, not just a single feature (Gibson, 1969), and thus becomes capable of extracting more and higher-level information. In addition, active stimulus comparison is performed (Ruff, 1975). When presented with two visual patterns, a baby looked back and forth between the two. The degree of shifting increases with age. The more similar the stimuli, the more looking back and forth the infant does, suggesting that even for infants, deployment of a strategy depends on the difficulty of the task. Thus, in the first few months of life we can see important refinements in visual scanning. The behaviour comes more and more under voluntary control and produces an ever-increasing amount of information.

The later development of visual scanning parallels the changes that occur during infancy. Many aspects of development can be attributed to the expanding role of internal, planful, self-regulation of scanning and the concomitant decreasing importance of external variables. Although the young infant gradually stops being 'captured' by simple stimuli, we see repeated examples of this same problem in older children attempting to cope with more complex tasks. The exact manifestation varies according to the situation. For example, when studying an unfamiliar irregular shape, three-year-old subjects made fewer eye movements than did six-year-olds (Zinchenko, Chzhtitsin and Tarakanov, 1963). Furthermore, the younger children fixated primarily in the centre of the figure, whereas the older children's fixations covered its more informative contours.

Although six-year-olds in the Zinchenko *et al.* study showed relatively mature scanning, if a more complex stimulus had been presented, they might have displayed immature scanning. Mackworth and Bruner (1970) showed to adults and six-year-old children sharply focused photographs containing much detailed information. The six-year-olds often became 'so hooked by the details' that they failed to scan broadly over the rest of the stimulus: 'Having arrived at a "good place" on which to rest their gaze, they seem to feel "disinclined" to leap into the unknown areas of the sharp pictures' (p. 165). Mackworth and Bruner concluded that adults possess an effective visual search programme that enables them to *coordinate* central and peripheral vision together but that children do not. Children can extract detail information centrally, and they can detect peripheral stimuli. However, they cannot execute the two operations *simultaneously*. Thus, the main problem is one of coordination and control, not the presence or absence of specific skills.

Increased cognitive control is also reflected in other important developmental changes in visual scanning. For example, children's scanning gradually becomes more systematic, indicating the presence of higher-order organization. Vurpillot (1968) filmed the eye movements of four- to nine-year-old children as they were deciding if two houses were identical. Unlike the older subjects, the youngest children rarely made the systematic paired comparisons of comparably located windows that are necessary for successful performance. Furthermore, the young children's scanning was less exhaustive. When two identical houses were shown, they often failed to look at all the windows before pronouncing the houses the same.

Another important developmental change is in focusing on the more informative areas of a visual stimulus. The older the child, the more likely he is to fixate those distinctive features that give him the greatest amount of relevant information for the task at hand (Mackworth and Bruner, 1970; Olson, 1970; Zinchenko *et al.*, 1963). Conversely, young children find it more difficult to ignore irrelevant information. Just as in incidental memory studies and in prose-studying experiments, the younger the child, the more attention he is likely to devote to stimuli that are irrelevant to the task he is performing (Pushkina, 1971).

Although by adulthood scanning has usually developed into quite an efficient, individualized process (Noton and Stark, 1971), adults are by no means immune to the metacognitive problems children experience so frequently. If required to perform a difficult scanning task, such as inspecting chest x-rays for signs of pathology (Thomas, 1968), adults (relative novices) often suffer some of the same deficiencies seen in children, e.g. failing to scan as exhaustively as necessary or failing to focus on the most informative areas.

Scanning tasks thus reveal the same general pattern illustrated by the gist-recall procedure. Scanning a visual array, like extracting the main idea, is a naturally occurring response necessary for a wide variety of tasks and for survival. As the child matures, he develops the ability to control and coordinate scanning, to make scanning a strategic action tailored to changing task demands.

(3) Retrieval processes

For our third example we have selected retrieval, considered broadly to encompass finding objects hidden in the external environment as well as retrieving information temporarily lost in memory. In both cases the subject often must use some other information to help him track down the desired object or thought. Although children use external cues to search the environment before they use internal cues to search their own memories, many of the same strategies are relevant to both activities. Furthermore, in both activities the child is increasingly able to direct and control his search procedures, that is, he achieves increasing metacognitive control, including planning ahead to facilitate later retrieval and executing a search according to a logical plan. Our discussion here will draw heavily on the work of John Flavell and his colleagues, for they have been by far the most active and creative investigators in this area.

Retrieval activities occur naturally at an early age and continue to develop over a long period of time. Even infants are capable of organizing a sequence of behaviours into a search, but their initial efforts are very limited. The earliest information we have about the development of retrieval comes from object-permanence tasks. When six- or seven-month-old infants first start searching for hidden objects, they often do something very interesting from the point of view of self-regulation. A child may initiate what appears to be an attempt to remove the cloth concealing a desired object, only to become distracted by the cloth itself. We can characterize this as a failure to maintain executive control. In the midst of conducting a search, the child appears to forget the goal and subsequently ceases those behaviours originally directed towards achieving it. A minimal requirement for the coordination and control of retrieval efforts is the ability to keep the goal in mind for a sufficient period of time and in the face of distractions.

Another interesting aspect of early retrieval activities is that even toddlers employ rudimentary search strategies, as revealed by the regular errors they make in object-permanence tasks (the Stage IV error).* Beginning at about eight months, an infant who has previously found an object hidden at one place (A) is likely to search for it again at A, even though he has just witnessed the object being hidden at a second location (B). We would say with Harris (1973) that the infant seems to employ a strategy of looking for an object in the place where he found it before. Although this strategy has obvious limitations and often causes the infant to fail in object-permanence tasks, it seems reasonable that looking for an object where he found it before would serve the child relatively well in his everyday environment. Interestingly, children as old as two years have been found to rely on this same strategy (Loughlin and Daehler, 1973; Webb, Masur and Nadolny, 1972).

We have characterized the toddler's search as strategic because it suggests the systematic execution of a plan. The degree of self-conscious participation

* Piaget (1955) distinguishes six stages in the development of the object concept. At Stage IV, children make the error of looking for an object where they previously found it even when they have seen it being moved elsewhere.

involved, however, is probably minimal. As with the other areas we have reviewed, children's retrieval processes become increasingly sophisticated as conscious, voluntary control over them intensifies. In the case of retrieval, this sophistication is clearly reflected in at least two characteristics of performance: Children become more likely to do something deliberate *at the time of storage* to facilitate later retrieval, and their attempts at retrieval become more *systematic* and efficient.

Even very young children engage in relatively simple behaviours whose sole function is to help them remember. Children as young as three years, informed that they will later have to recall the location of an object (Wellman, Ritter and Flavell, 1975) or an event (Acredolo, Pick and Olsen, 1975), show better memory than children not so informed. Thus, the children must do something to help them remember during the delay. Wellman *et al.* (1975) observed their subjects and reported that while they waited, the children in the instructed memory condition looked at and touched the location they were supposed to remember. Preschool children are also able to use a specific cue provided for them. When an external cue marking the location of an object is made available, they can use it to help retrieve the object (Ritter, Kaprove, Fitch and Flavell, 1973). In addition, they are sometimes capable of arranging a cue themselves to aid their later retrieval (Ryan, Hegion and Flavell, 1970).

Not surprisingly, the tendency to use such cues improves with age. However, even when they think to use a retrieval cue, younger children may fail to use it as effectively as older children. In a study by Kobasigawa (1974), first graders who spontaneously used an available category cue still recalled fewer items per category than did third graders. In other words, even when they thought to use the retrieval cues, the younger children failed to conduct an exhaustive search for the items associated with each cue. Istomina (1975) also noted the tendency of younger children not to execute an exhaustive search of their memories. Although some of her four- and five-year-old subjects actively attempted to recall a list of items, they did not try to retrieve items not immediately recalled. Older children, however, often showed signs of conducting an active internal search (Istomina, 1975): 'In some cases the child recalled what he had forgotten only with long pauses, during which he would try not to look at those around him, i.e. he would direct his gaze downward, to the side or screw up his eyes' (p. 31). The non-exhaustive search could result from several possible factors. The child may not check his output against a criterion of acceptability, or, alternatively, he may have a different criterion from that of the experimenter's (Kobasigawa, 1974). Or his monitoring of his own memory may be inadequate to inform him that there are items yet to be recalled. In any case, these all represent metacognition problems of one sort or another. The essential similarity of non-exhaustiveness in both visual scanning and retrieval is obvious.

We have argued that there are some essential similarities between the retrieval of objects from the environment and the retrieval of information from memory and that many of the same strategies are relevant in both cases – for example, conducting an exhaustive search. However, it is clear that external retrieval is an easier task than memory scanning. Object retrieval studies show evidence of intentional efforts to remember and the use of strategies in children as young as three years, a much younger age than that at which Istomina's (1975) children could deliberately adopt the goal of remembering and re-calling a list of words. In object-retrieval situations the cues available to aid memory are external and physically present; all the child must do is think to use them or orient to them. Thus, the problem is much simpler than one in which the child must initiate and maintain a purely internal, cognitive orienta-tion to information in memory. The latter requires a greater degree of meta-cognitive control. The child must use internal processes, cognitions, to control other internal processes.

25.

Language awareness in children

Robert Grieve, William E. Tunmer and Chris Pratt

The previous readings in this section have had a considerable amount to say about the child's developing awareness of how the mind works. The present reading is more specifically concerned with children's awareness of language. Here Grieve, Tunmer and Pratt review the evidence, and discuss when language awareness in children appears. The role that language awareness plays in children's cognitive development, and in their performance in school, is also considered. In reading this article, it should be noted that while the question of what role language awareness plays in learning to read is an obvious one, language awareness may also play an important role in other aspects of learning and development. These include the increased efficiency of communication between individuals, and more generally, the increased cognitive control that may be gained from the ability to reflect on language as a system for exchanging information.

INTRODUCTION

The phenomenon of language awareness in children has recently become a source of considerable interest to developmental psychologists and educationalists. In this paper we will try to explain why this is so, and introduce some of the problems associated with studying the phenomenon. Our procedure will be to consider why the study of language awareness is important; when language awareness typically appears; and what implications the study of it might have for developmental theory and educational practice. At a general level, language awareness may be characterized as the ability to reflect upon the structure and functions of language, as opposed to simply using it to comprehend and produce sentences. However, as we will see in a later section, the concept of language awareness is not as straightforward as it would appear.

WHY STUDY LANGUAGE AWARENESS?

To appreciate the interest of developmental psychologists and educationalists in language awareness in children, it is necessary to consider some recent thinking on the development and early education of children.

The concept of 'childhood', it has been argued (Aries, 1962), is a comparatively recent invention, for before the seventeenth century the leisure and work activities of adults and children were considered to be highly similar. While the accuracy of this thesis will not be considered here (for a critical assessment, see Tucker, 1977), it is nevertheless true that the way in which we think about children, and what we think childhood consists of, has elementary implications for both theory in developmental psychology, and practice in early education. In the present century, our view of children has been radically affected by the work of Piaget. His conclusion, that the *mentality* of the child is in important respects qualitatively different from that of the adult, has revolutionized our view of children and the study of their development. However, while Piaget's immense contribution has been generally recognized, in the past few years certain aspects of his views, especially those related to the intellectual skills and abilities of the preschool child, have attracted considerable criticism. For example, summaries of recent research suggest that rather than various cognitive skills being absent in the 'preoperational' preschool child – skills such as the ability to conserve number, the ability to classify and class include, the ability to reason, the ability to think in a non-egocentric manner – such skills are in fact evident in young children, *on entry to school* (Donaldson, 1978; Gelman 1978). Thus the intellectual limitations of the school entrant do not consist in the *absence* of such skills, but rather in their *deployment* – that is, young children are not yet able to exercise the skills they have in all contexts, but only in *some contexts*. To put the matter another way, while the preschool child does possess certain intellectual abilities, the exercise of these intellectual skills by young children is *context-dependent*, rather than *context-free*. (For further details, see Pratt and Grieve, 1980).

What motivates the transition from context-dependent to context-free (or 'abstract') thought? Donaldson (1978) has suggested that an important influence is the *types* of activities the child experiences in early school, where he is continually exposed to *different kinds* of presentations of phenomena with which he is already familiar. With respect to language and number, for example, when he arrives at school the young child has been using language for several years; and he has certain abilities to differentiate parameters that affect changes in number. So on entry to school, the child possesses certain linguistic and numerical abilities. But at school, he is required to *deploy* these linguistic and numerical abilities in new, abstract, ways. The exercise of linguistic and numerical skills therefore needs to become context-free, rather than remain context-dependent. And it is at this point that we encounter an important notion: namely, that *awareness of the nature and functions of language* is closely implicated in the child's negotiation of the transition from the limited, context-dependent thought of the preschool, to the abstract, context-free thought required in subsequent educational settings. The potential importance of the topic of language awareness in children can therefore be appreciated, and the interests of developmentalists and educationalists in the topic understood.

Saying that language awareness is closely implicated in the shift from context-dependent to abstract thought is too broad as it stands, and, to progress, attempts will need to be made to specify the nature of its implication. For example, the direction of the relationship between language awareness and intellectual functioning needs to be articulated. Likewise, the relationship between language awareness and the sorts of skills introduced in early school (e.g., learning to read) needs to be determined, as does the effect of social variables (e.g., learning to communicate with a wider range of individuals, often in a 'formal' manner) on the child's awareness of his linguistic and communicative system. However, before such questions can be tackled, we first need to know when language awareness typically appears in children.

WHEN DOES LANGUAGE AWARENESS TYPICALLY APPEAR?

A recent review of empirical studies on language awareness in children starts by stating that: 'Children begin to reflect on certain properties of language at an early age' (Clark, 1978, p. 18). What evidence is there to support this claim? Clark reviews the available evidence under six main headings. We have amended these slightly and we have used some evidence from other sources also, but the following account owes much to Clark's paper.

Making judgements about language

Children can make various types of judgements about utterances in the language, including judgements about linguistic appropriateness, form, and complexity. For example, Bates (1976) has found that four-and-a-half-year-old Italian children know that in directing requests to an elderly woman (puppet game), a less direct request (e.g. (in English) 'I would like a sweet') is more polite, and more likely to encounter success, than a more direct request (e.g. 'I want a sweet'). Several investigators have found that children from age four years can appropriately adjust their speech, either by adopting the appropriate voices for different roles in a father-mother-baby family game (Andersen, 1977, cited in Clark, 1978), or by adjusting the complexity of their speech in a game, depending on whether they are talking to a two-year-old, four-year-old peer, or an adult (Shatz and Gelman, 1973). Thus children seem to appreciate, from a comparatively early age, that certain ways of using language are more appropriate than others, depending on the age, role, status or capacities of the interlocutor.

Children can also make judgements about the complexity of utterances, and accurately attribute utterances of different complexity to interlocutors of different ages. For example, children aged five years attribute complex sentences to adults, and more primitive versions of the same sentence to children (Scholl and Ryan, 1975).

Children's appreciation of linguistic form is also evident from an early age. A four-year-old, when asked what he wanted to be when he grew up, said he wanted to be 'a dowboy' (cowboy). 'So, you want to be a dowboy, eh?' the adult replied. 'No! (irritated), not a 'dowboy, a *dowboy*.' (R. N. Campbell, personal communication, c. 1967.) While the child's use of the inappropriate form is acceptable (for he cannot pronounce the word correctly), the child appreciates that the adult's usage of that form is a tease, for the adult *can* pronounce the word correctly. Bever (1975, cited in Marshall and Morton, 1978, p. 237) has a similar example, where the child is more explicit:

Child: Mommy goed to the store.
Father: Mommy goed to the store?
Child: No, Daddy. I say it that way, not *you*!

But an even more interesting example, for a child aged two and a half years, is reported in Smith (1973):

Father: Say, *jump*.
Child: Dup.
Father: No, *jump*.
Child: Dup.
Father: No. Jummmp.
Child: Only Daddy can say *dup*!

Thus from an early age, children can make judgements about the form, complexity, and appropriateness of utterances in the language, and in doing so, they must be aware of certain social, functional and structural properties of language.

Applying rules of language

As we know from work by Berko (1958), Brown (1973), Cazden (1968) and others, children apply rules in using language. For examples, shown a nonsense figure and told it is 'a wug', then shown two of them, children can tell us that there are 'two wugs', indicating their knowledge of the rule that counts nouns in English are pluralized by the addition of final /-s/ (Berko, 1958). Or, once children have the rule that in English the past tense of verbs is formed by the addition of the suffix /-ed/, as in *jumped, walked, shouted*, etc., we may observe them applying this rule to irregular verbs, producing terms such as *digged, singed, breaked, goed*, etc. However, here we may be dealing with *implicit* knowledge about language, of which the child is not consciously aware. Is there any evidence that children are aware of such linguistic rules? As Clark points out, when children begin to make explicit comments on the matter, we can have some confidence that they do reflect on rules, as for example in the case of Leopold's daughter, who at the age of four years observed how singular and plural forms in German are distinguished: 'If there is one, you have to say *Schuh*; if there are two you have to say *Schuhe*' (Leopold, 1949). But how do we determine whether or not the child is aware of such rules at an earlier age, before he is able to make his knowledge apparent in explicit and communicable ways? In the literature, this sort of methodological issue has not received the attention it deserves.

Making corrections to language

Two common types of corrections that can be observed during the course of language development are *spontaneous repairs*, and *prompted repairs*. The former type of correction can be difficult to observe, for the minor corrections a speaker makes to the speech he is producing are often 'edited out' by the listener. This may occur not only in the case of adults listening to children (Clark, 1978; Clark and Andersen, 1979), but also in the case of children listening to adults – children may treat deliberately inappropriate adult utterances as 'unintended' slips, 'correcting' the inappropriate adult utterances into forms that make more sense (see Grieve, Hoogenraad and Murray, 1977; Hughes and Grieve, 1980). However, when 'editing out' is avoided, very young children may be observed spontaneously correcting, or repairing, their utterances. Convenient examples to illustrate the point come from Snyder (1914, cited in Clark, 1978):

> Addition of a modifier: 'Dat water – dat dirty water';
> Change of a word: 'Might take paddle out boat – might take paddle out canoe';
> Change of word order: 'Down sand beach I been – I been down sand beach'.

A different type of correction consists of prompted repairs. In this example, from Marshall and Morton (1978), the child is aged four years.

> *Child*: I brang it home from school.
> *Adult*: What?
> *Child*: I bringed it home.
> *Adult*: Eh?
> *Child*: I brung it home.

> *Adult*: Oy vay!
> *Child*: Brought!
> *Adult*: What d'you know – we finally made it!

Notice that in this example the adult does not convey to the child precisely what is wrong but only responds with a general 'What?' It is the child who identifies the problem herself and attempts to correct it. Besides correcting his own speech, spontaneously or *via* 'prompts', the child also begins to correct the speech of others, as illustrated in an example from Weir (1966):

> *David*: I don't have a raser, Anthony. I don't have dis.
> *Anthony*: David, you need an *e*raser.

Supplying interpretations of language

Trying to gauge the extent of children's language awareness by getting the child to supply interpretations of words or utterances in the language can prove problematic, especially if the attempt to do so is direct, *via* elicited definition, or paraphrase. Asking a child what so-and-so means, or whether so-and-so means the same as such-and-such, is unlikely to encounter success, and perhaps does not deserve to, for such questions are metalinguistic in character – they use language to inquire about the nature of language. Young children are said to define terms by providing indications as to the objects' functions, rather than their nature. Thus a brush is for sweeping with; a cup is for drinking out of; a blackboard is for writing on – rather than an implement consisting of a handle with bristles (e.g. for sweeping up dust); a container, usually with a handle, for holding liquids (which are drunk); or a board, usually coloured black, on which chalk marks can be made (e.g. in writing). But put this way, the differences between child-like and adult-like definitions are perhaps not as great as is usually thought. With respect to paraphrase, successful attempts have been made to elicit judgements of synonymy, provided the investigator applies attention and imagination to the character of the task the child has to complete (e.g. Hakes, Evans and Tunmer, 1980).

Segmenting units of language

The relevance of the point just made, on the extent to which the adult makes the task *congenial to the child*, can be readily appreciated with respect to studies which attempt to get children to break language down, or segment it, into its constituent sentences, words, syllables and phonemes. Several investigators have claimed that this ability is not present in children until about age six years (e.g. Bruce, 1964; Holden and MacGinitie, 1972). But others have suggested that if a task procedure is employed which is congenial to the child, evidence of an ability to segment language into its various constituents is

apparent at a younger age. For example, Fox and Routh (1975) present a
sentence and ask children to 'say a little bit' of it, progressively obtaining
identifications of linguistic constituents. Using a methodologically preferable
procedure, Tunmer and Bowey (1980) have found that children of age four
years may encounter a fair measure of success in identifying words of various
classes in word strings and sentences, provided the strings or sentences are not
so long that burdens are imposed on the child's memory.

Practising and playing with language

As we know from the observation of Weir (1962) on her two and a half-year-old
son, children may practise and play with language from an early age. Investigators of child language, and indeed any parent, have observed that young
children can be heard 'talking to themselves', often before falling asleep, or on
waking up. What Weir showed was that in such sessions, children often spend
time 'practising' phonological and grammatical aspects of language. At a later
age, language play continues. As every parent of some vintage knows, there
comes a time in children's development, usually around seven years, when a
horrible fascination with riddles sets in. 'Hey Dad, d'you know what sea
monsters eat?' 'No idea.' 'Fish and ships.' Now, the child's manipulation of
language manipulates people. Here it is interesting to notice what happens if
one fails to flinch at such riddles. 'D'you get it, Dad, d'you get it? I said: "What
do sea monsters eat", and when you said you didn't know, I said: "Fish and
ships". It's like "Fish and chips", but they're sea monsters, so it's "Fish and
ships". D'you get it now?' The child's appreciation of the joke, and associated
language awareness, are explicitly revealed. It is of course harder to be sure
about the extent to which younger children appreciate language-related
humour, although we have observed a clever language-based joke in a child
aged two years, one month (Grieve and Hoogenraad, 1976). When the child
meant to ask an adult to show him the pen-knife the adult customarily carried
in his pocket, instead of asking for the knife, he made a slip and asked for the
'fork'. 'Oh, you want the knife do you? ... Did you say "fork" just now?' At
this the child laughed, and said: 'Will you give it, spoon?'

From this brief résumé, we can see that there is considerable evidence that
children are aware of various aspects of language from an early age. In this,
other writers concur: 'The following aspects of language awareness appear,
between the ages of two and six (years): self-corrections ... in on-going
speech; comments on the speech of others; explicit questions about speech and
language; comments on (the child's) own speech and language; response to
direct questions about language' (Slobin, 1978, p. 45).

> From diary studies ... as well as recent experiments, it has become clear that
> children reflect on language well before they receive any formal teaching in

grammar: both spontaneously and in response to questions, they make remarks on pronunciation, on morphology, they correct other speakers, they
remark on meaning and form, and they may even make puns. (Berthoud-
Papandropoulou, 1978, p. 55).

But what should be noticed about such a view is the heterogeneity of the
data sources on which it is based. That is, such a conclusion, that children are
aware of various aspects of language from an early age, comes from naturalistic observation, from the child's spontaneous comments, from experimental
studies, from informal experiments. As soon as we try to sharpen the question
up: 'Precisely what aspects of language are children aware of at a specified
age?' we are in trouble, for we do not have available a methodological recipe to
help us answer this question. When children are *explicit* about aspects of the
nature and functions of language, we can have some confidence that they are
linguistically aware (Clark, 1978; Levelt *et al.*, 1978). The problem comes
when they fail to be explicit – is this because they are not aware, or because
they are unable to articulate and convey to us their awareness? Important as
this problem is, it is only beginning to be tackled in the literature. That it *is*
important is well illustrated by Read (1978), who describes some of his own
research on when children recognize relationships between certain speech
sounds (categorization of vowel pairs). While details of the particular study are
not relevant here, what *is* relevant is Read's initial observation that his task
'simply didn't work at all with five-year-olds, and it failed to elicit large
numbers of reliable, consistent judgements from six-year-olds. Only from
seven-year-olds did we receive statistically significant preferences ...' This
result was of considerable interest to Read, for: 'The appearance of the ability
to make these judgements consistently at age seven ... suggested an influence
of schooling.' That is, the result suggested that children's ability to recognize
relationships among speech sounds may have resulted from early school
experience, and that children might not recognize such relationships *before*
learning to read and write. However, as Read continued (1978, p. 75–6):
'More than a year after our first studies, a relatively small change in our
methodology considerably enhanced the success of this task with young
children .... The methodological point is that this change in the task made it
accessible to most kindergarten children, two years younger than those from
whom our earlier paradigm elicited consistent judgements.'

The moral here is fairly obvious. Unless we are careful, or fortunate, the
method we use to gauge young children's abilities may provide us with the
wrong end of the stick, and we may conclude that an ability appears as a *result*
of schooling, simply because our methodology has failed to detect the presence
of the ability in children of a younger age. Far from being the result of early
school experience, the ability in question may be present *before* the child enters
school.

IMPLICATIONS FOR DEVELOPMENTAL THEORY
AND EDUCATIONAL PRACTICE

As far as developmental theory is concerned, the implications of the study of language awareness in children have only begun to be explored. One crucial question refers to the role of language awareness in the young child's initial acquisition of language (Clark, 1978), another to the relationship between language and thought in the developing child, a topic which has exercised psychologists and philosophers for centuries. In the present context, we briefly take up this latter question, since it is particularly pertinent to implications of the study of language awareness for educational practice in the preschool and early primary school-aged child.

Consideration of the relationship between language and thought can be conveniently introduced with reference to the Whorfian hypothesis, or the Sapir-Whorf hypothesis, called after the American linguists, Sapir (1921) and Whorf (1956), who considered the matter from a cross-linguistic perspective (see Carroll, 1964). The hypothesis has at least two forms. In its *strong* form, the hypothesis states that the language we speak *determines* the way in which we think, while in its *weak* form, the hypothesis states that the language we speak *influences* the way we think. The relationship between language and thought in the developing child, and the extent to which the one might be determined or influenced by the other, has been considered by developmental psychologists. The differing views of the Genevan (e.g. Piaget, 1926; Sinclair, 1969) and Russian (e.g. Vygotsky, 1962; Luria, 1961) schools on this topic are well known (for reviews, see Bruner, 1966; Cromer, 1974). For Piaget, language is a form of symbolic representation, and cognition underlies language, rather than language cognition. For the Russian school, the young child's actions are largely determined by social influence, but as the child develops, his language and thought progressively come under the child's own control.

Recent work on language awareness in the four- to eight-year-old child shows affinity with aspects of both these approaches (which may not be as dissimilar as they first appear – see Piaget, 1962). On the one hand, several investigators have been largely concerned with the child's awareness of spoken language – one representational system – in the acquisition of another representational system: learning to read. On the other hand, other investigators have emphasized the extent to which increased language awareness affects the control the child has over his environment, especially his linguistic, cognitive and social environment.

Thus various writers concerned with the relationship between language awareness and reading have devoted attention to issues concerned with what can be termed the *analysis* and *synthesis* of language. Under the former heading, questions asked include: when can the child segment speech into its constituent sequences? When can the child segment a sentence into its constituent words? When can the child segment a word into its constituent phonemes? Here there is some literature available, reviewed by Bowey and Tunmer (1980), Tunmer and Bowey (1980), and by Lundberg (1978). With respect to synthesis, the literature is more sparse (but again, see Lundberg, 1978). Here, there has been concern with questions about the child's ability to blend sounds into words, to relate aspects of the written to the spoken language – grapheme-phoneme correspondences and so on.

Investigators of the relationship between the child's language awareness and growing control over his cognitive, linguistic and social environment tend to stress aspects of the *functions*, rather than the *structure*, of language. Thus, here we find questions about the child's ability to adjust his language (to make it simpler, or present it more slowly, or make it more polite, or whatever), depending on the capacities and status of his interlocutors. We also observe concern with the child's transition from the 'embedded thought' typical of the preschool to the 'disembedded thought' (or abstract thought) that begins to be introduced in the primary school (e.g. Donaldson, 1978). And we also find concern not only with the way the child begins to manipulate his own communications and the character of his cognitive structures, but with the way he begins to manipulate others through cognitive and linguistic means – as in the example of telling riddles, where seven-year-olds know that information is power. It can also be noticed that a recent fashion, to refer to 'metacognition' – meaning the ability to reflect on and direct one's mode of problem-solving, memory, etc. – appears essentially Vygotskian.

It should of course be noticed that those two traditions are not wholly distinct. For example, in learning to read, the child must acquire a technical vocabulary which is closely involved with both metalinguistic and metacognitive functions. 'Sound out the letters', 'What does this word say?' – such instructions/questions are pretty meaningless to a child unless he knows the meaning of terms such as 'letter', 'word', and so on. Such terms are 'metalinguistic' in character, for they are words in the language used to talk about language. As the work of Reid (1966), Downing (1969, 1979), Berthoud-Papandropoulou (1978) and others makes clear, children are frequently confused about the meanings of this technical or metalinguistic vocabulary when they start to learn to read. Indeed, Ayers and Downing (1979) have found that mastery of this vocabulary correlates highly with early reading success. But what should also be noticed is that *such a metalinguistic vocabulary possesses a metacognitive function*, for it inevitably directs the child's attention to aspects of the nature of language, not only with respect to details of its structure – e.g. that it is composed of 'letters', 'words', etc. – but also that there is a relationship between written symbols on a page, and speech – 'sounds', 'say', etc.

Indeed, a recent book on children's thinking and early education (Donaldson, 1978) lays great stress on learning to read, not only as an end in itself, but as a means whereby the child's thought becomes less restricted to particular contexts. In learning to read, Donaldson suggests, the child's awareness of language increases, and an increase in language awareness makes it easier for the child to exercise his cognitive abilities in a wide range of contexts – his thinking becomes context-free, rather than remaining context-dependent. The transition from preschool to primary school is thereby facilitated. However, as many children find it difficult to make this transition from within their own resources, they require assistance. The questions for developmentalists, and especially for educationalists, are of course: 'What kind of assistance? And when?'

Our present review suggests that all aspects of language awareness do not appear in children *only* when they get to school and begin to learn to read and write. There is a considerable amount of evidence that children may be aware of various aspects of language long before they arrive at school. We must of course be cautious here, for much of the evidence that has been reported comes from observations of the children of academic investigators. Such children tend to be verbally precocious; they are able, even encouraged, to develop cognitive and linguistic control over their environment; and they are not usually the children who find it difficult to successfully negotiate the transition to formal education. The awareness of children who *do* find the transition into formal schooling difficult may lie in a different direction – for example, exercising one's verbal abilities, or 'talking too much', might lead to trouble. For example, in some of Labov's studies on black school children in Harlem (Labov, 1972), children on interview could prove almost monosyllabic in speech, becoming verbally fluent only when the interviewer adjusted the social setting to make clear that what the child said would not be 'held against him', and where the setting involved verbal competition between children, reminiscent of the verbal games that black children play on the street (Kochman, 1970). More generally, the importance of social context, and the changes that there may be in social context between school and home environments, need to be borne in mind. An influential component in the social context of the school is the teaching profession, whose elaborated communicative code (Bernstein, 1972) may not be uniformly familiar to all students.

We therefore need to determine whether the awareness of language apparent in some children at the preschool level is generally enjoyed, or whether many children on arriving at school, and during the early school years, fail to acquire the explicit control over their cognitive and linguistic environment that 'successful' children do acquire, 'successful' in the sense of being able to negotiate the transition into formal schooling without too much difficulty.

If language awareness is important in learning to read, in being able to think in a context-free manner, in being able to adjust to formal schooling, then the need to study it is apparent. Means of identifying the extent to which children are aware of language, and at what age, need to be found. Should it prove to be the case that children who have difficulty with reading, with acquiring abstract thought, with adjusting to school, encounter these difficulties through a lack of awareness of language and the nature of the communicative process (see Robinson and Robinson, 1981), then means of enhancing their awareness could be sought.

But at this point, futurology is to be curbed. Before we try to run, we have to learn to walk, and as we hope the present paper shows, the field is still at the stage of trying to find its legs. As we have to learn to walk before we try to run, so we have to learn to stand before we try to walk. That, we suggest, is where the study of language awareness in children is at present.

26.

Play with language and metalinguistic awareness: one dimension of language experience

Courtney B. Cazden

In this final reading, we consider children's play behaviour, particularly with respect to play with language. As Cazden points out, when we use language to communicate it tends to be transparent. We rarely focus our attention on the language itself, but instead concentrate on extracting the meaning that is being conveyed. There are however times when language becomes opaque, when the system itself becomes the focus of attention. A number of these occasions were indicated in the previous reading, and include instances when corrections are made to inappropriate utterances, when children practise and play with language or when the child encounters language in the written form and is required to segment words into sounds. In the present reading, Cazden considers one of these in some detail – the one in which children spontaneously direct their attention to language as it becomes an object of their play. Unfortunately, this language play may disappear fairly early on in childhood, and consequently, some of the early creative aspects of language may be lost. Cazden suggests that those involved in the education of children should try to encourage language play, 'not at the expense of stimulation of language for communication, but in addition to it'.

Although the title speaks of play and then metalinguistic awareness, I am going to talk about them in the reverse order – first, explain what I mean by 'metalinguistic awareness' as a special dimension of language experience and its seeming importance in education; then describe one, and only one, conception of the function of 'play' in general and play with language in particular; and finally ask how we might encourage play with language in school.

METALINGUISTIC AWARENESS

It is intuitively obvious to us as language users that when either speaking or listening, our focal attention is not on speech sounds, nor even on larger units such as words and syntactic patterns. Our focal attention is on the meaning, the intention, of what we or someone else is trying to say. The language forms are themselves transparent; we hear through them to the meaning intended. As the Duchess rightly says in *Alice in Wonderland*, 'and the moral of *that* is – take care of the sense and the sounds will take care of themselves'.

However, it is an important aspect of our unique capacities as human beings that we can not only act, but reflect back on our own actions; not only learn and use language, but treat it as an object of analysis and evaluation in its own right. Metalinguistic awareness, the ability to make language forms opaque and attend to them in and for themselves, is a special kind of language performance, one which makes special cognitive demands, and seems to be less easily and less universally acquired than the language performances of speaking and listening. Our concern as educators with this particular kind of language performance comes from increasing arguments that it is at least very helpful – and maybe critically important – not so much in the primary processes of speaking and hearing as in what may be considered the derived or secondary processes of reading and writing.

The idea that such awareness is related to literacy is not new. For more than ten years we have been reading in Vygotsky (1962) that literacy depends on, and in turn contributes to, making previously non-conscious or tacit knowledge more conscious. More recently, a conference resulting in the book *Language by Ear and by Eye* (Kavanaugh and Mattingly, 1972) focused directly on the differences that must exist between learning to speak and learning to read. Mattingly, in his chapter on 'Reading, the Linguistic Process and Linguistic Awareness', says:

> Speaking and listening are primary linguistic activities; reading is a secondary and rather special sort of activity that relies critically upon the reader's awareness of those primary activities (p. 133) . . . Linguistic awareness is very far from evenly distributed over all phases of linguistic activity (p. 139). [E.g. awareness is greater for words than syllables; for syllables than sounds; and in general for units than for rules that govern their structural arrangements.] . . .

Mattingly then suggests the relationship that is the focus of this paper – the relationship to verbal play.

> There appears to be considerable individual variation in linguistic awareness. Some speaker-hearers are not only very conscious of linguistic patterns, but exploit their consciousness with obvious pleasure in verbal play, e.g. punning [and versifying, solving crossword puzzles, and talking Pig Latin] or verbal work (e.g. linguistic analysis). Others never seem to be aware of more than words . . . this variation contrasts markedly with the relative consistency from person to person with which primary linguistic activity is performed (p. 140) . . . Our view is that reading is a language-based activity like Pig Latin or versification and not a form of primary linguistic activity analogous to listening (p. 141).

If linguistic awareness is so important, what do we know about its development?

The Soviet psychologist, Elkonin (1971) argues against the 'glass theory', which is exactly what I have been calling the transparency of language. Elkonin agrees that 'the development of awareness of the language's phonological aspect . . . represents one of the most essential pre-conditions for . . . learning literacy'. But he asserts that children's playful manipulation of the sounds of words, apart from their meanings, is a natural, normal part of language development itself:

> Just as the mastery of objective reality is not possible without formation of activity with objects, exactly in the same manner is language mastery not possible without formation of activity with language as the material object with its concrete form (p. 141).

In other words, according to Elkonin, children, as part of their species-specific ability to learn language, will use elements of that language as the objects of one aspect of development not specific to humans – namely, play. Children may shift more easily than adults between using language forms transparently in inter-personal communication, and treating them as opaque objects in play. In other words, when the child's intention is to communicate, he – like the adult – can 'hear through' his language to that end; but it is hypothesized that the child can also intend to play with the elements of language for the very delight of self-expression and mastery, and does so more easily than the adult unless the latter is a poet. This brings us to consider more generally one function of play in development.

PLAY

Play, according to Peter Reynolds (1972) is the performance of segments of behaviour separated from their usual instrumental context, with the functional effect of elaborating and integrating that behaviour, and the affective effect of joy. If play is an essential part of the developmental process, then its presence or absence should make a difference. Reynolds suggests that 'What is required is an assessment of the relative survival of rehearsed versus unrehearsed performances measured in terms of the particular selective system to which the action is coupled.' In our terms, the hypothesis to be treated is that a child's play with language makes one human adaptation, literacy, easier to achieve because the child's attention has been focused on the means, the forms of language, whereas in normal communicative contexts, his attention is focused only on the end.

This hypothesis remains to be tested. Some suggestive evidence exists. Negatively, Ilse Mattick (1967), in her description of the language and cognitive development of 'children of disorganized lower-class families', specifically mentions that 'there was a lack of exploration of language and an absence of the usual play with words which facilitates increasing communicative skills and serves to extend knowledge'.

More positively, we know that many young children do play with language, and that sensitive parents and teachers value that play. Examples come from a linguist-mother, Ruth Weir (1962), a Russian listener-writer of children's stories, Kornei Chukovsky (1963), and a teacher-observer of preschool children, Harriet Johnson (1972).

In her introduction to the reissue of Harriet Johnson's book, *Children in The Nursery School*, Barbara Biber emphasizes that Miss Johnson thought that 'learning was soundest when the environment encouraged the child in his impulse to 'experiment' with the exercise of his growing powers in the widening world of experience' and she specifically included words as important objects for that experimentation. For example, Geordie, who at 24 months had a fair vocabulary, accompanied motoric activities with varied syllabication:

> As he ran: Bee, bee, bee; Lee, lee, lee; Dub, dub, dub.
> At top of slide: Ma-wee, ma-wee, ma-wee, ma-wee, A-a.

Or Mathew, as he was being undressed:

> Nolly lolly, nolly, lolly, nilly lolly, sillie Billie,
> nolly lolly.

And Donald as he ran around the roof:

> Up a lup a dup, Up a dup I go.

Because Miss Johnson's children had companions in their play, as Anthony Weir did not, two children sometimes created joint chants. For example, three-year-old Philip and Caroline in the sandbox, where meaningful communication sometimes is inserted into nonsense chant play:

> *Philip*: 'Ees not.'
> *Caroline*: 'Ees not.'
> *Philip*: 'Eh.'
> *Caroline*: 'Eh.'
> *Philip*: 'Go 'way.'
> *Caroline*: 'Go 'way.'
> *Philip*: 'Go 'way ko.'
> *Caroline*: 'Go 'way ko.'
> *Philip*: 'Go 'way ki.'
> *Caroline*: 'Go 'way ki.'

Philip: 'Aw dee, de wa, di geh.'
Caroline: 'Aw dee, de wa, di geh.'
Philip: 'My o ketty.'
Caroline: 'My o ketty.'
Philip: 'Ga de.'
Caroline: Ga de.'
Philip: 'Oh, see wain go in.'
Caroline: 'Oh, see rain go in!'
Philip: 'Ees no more holes.'
Caroline: 'Ees no more holes.'

Later, beyond the years described by Weir, Johnson and Chukovsky, comes children's delight in puns and riddles, not just turning word meanings upside down, but playing with the effects of two meanings considered simultaneously, or the transformations of parts of words for new effects. A young friend of mine, John Rosenthal of Washington, D.C., knowing of my interest in word games, has been sending me examples of the current seven-year-old culture:

Q: What word has more letters than any other in the world?
A: Mailman.

Police: You can't park here.
Driver: Why not?
Police: Read that sign.
Driver: I did. It says, 'Fine for parking'.

Q: What did Tenne-see?
A: The same thing Arkan-saw.

Q: What time did the man go to the dentist?
A: Too-th irty.

And at about the same time, from about the age of seven on, children play verbal games – to be distinguised from verbal play by the existence of rules which can be described and transmitted from one player to another, such as the classification game 'categories', sequencing-memory games like 'I pack my trunk' and games of word formation and transformation like *Ghost* and *Pig Latin*. Just as children can learn about their language from word games, so can we – linguists, anthropologists, or educators – learn about children and their language-learning processes by studying their verbal play and games.

IMPLICATIONS FOR EDUCATION

And so what can we suggest for education? We started out with the importance which the authors in *Language by Ear and by Eye* credited to awareness of language as critical for achieving literacy, and their hope that we could learn how to cultivate it. Elkonin suggested that language was in fact more opaque to children than to adults. Presumably our overly instrumental attitude towards language for communication has dulled our ability and interest in attending to non-instrumental language elements for the joy of it (outside of the few poets and creative punsters, and the many more who enjoy crossword puzzles or games like Scrabble). Elkonin also urged that this opaqueness be kept alive at all ages by valuing and encouraging verbal play at home and school. Finally, Reynolds gave evolutionary support to the value of play and, by implication, of play with language for human children.

I think we can encourage verbal play and I think we should – not at the expense of stimulation of language for communication, but in addition to it. The danger is that, when adults intervene in play, it may lose its critical characteristics and therefore its special value. We must maintain an atmosphere of familiarity and emotional reassurance, not inhibit play by directing it, or prevent its intrinsically joyful quality through external reinforcement.

In closing, I can do no better than quote Lucy Sprague Mitchell, from the section on Form in the Introduction to her *Here and Now Story Book:*

> There is no better play material in the world than words. They surround us, go with us through our work-a-day tasks, their sound is always in our ears, their rhythms on our tongue. Why do we leave it to special occasions and to special people to use these common things as precious play material? Because we are grown-ups and have closed our ears and our eyes that we may not be distracted from our plodding ways! But when we turn to the children, to hearing and seeing children, to whom all the world is as play material, who think and feel through play, can we not then drop our adult utilitarian speech and listen and watch for the patterns of words and ideas? Can we not care for the *way* we say things to them and not merely *what* we say? Can we not speak in rhythm, in pleasing sounds, even in song for the mere sensuous delight it gives us and them, even though it adds nothing to the content of our remark? If we can, I feel sure children will not lose their native use of words: more, I think those of six and seven and eight who have lost it in part – and their stories show they have – will win back to their spontaneous joy in the play of words.

Appendix

General note on statistical procedures

For readers unfamiliar with statistical analysis, the following notes on statistical tests and their interpretation are provided.

Why are statistical tests used in investigations? When an investigator compares different groups or different conditions in an experiment, he is interested in the differences in performance. But he must consider whether these differences in performance are due to the manipulation involved in the experiment, or whether they might be simply due to chance. The investigator therefore has to take account of the likelihood, or the *probability*, that the results of the experiment have occurred simply by chance, and statistical tests are used to make this possible.

There are many different types of statistical tests, for instance, the chi-squared test (χ^2), the t-test (t), and analysis of variance involving F-ratios (F). The particular test or tests used to analyse the results of an experiment will depend on many factors, including the nature of the measurements made in the experiment and the nature of the experimental design.

When an investigator has conducted a study, he uses a statistical test appropriate to the nature of his experiment, and he then proceeds to consider the probability of his results having occurred by chance. When he reports his results he first of all indicates the statistic he has used, and the value of it that has been obtained from the results of the experiment – e.g. χ^2 = (obtained value), or t = (obtained value), or F = (obtained value). Given the obtained value, the investigator can calculate the probability of the results occurring by chance. This *probability level* is normally quoted after the obtained value: e.g. 'p < .05'. What this means is that the probability of the experimental result arising simply from chance is less than 5 in 100. This .05 probability level is frequently regarded as acceptable in psychology, and the result is said to be 'significant at the .05 level'. Other probability levels are yet more acceptable – e.g. 'p < .01' means that the probability of the experimental result arising simply from chance is less than 1 in 100, while 'p < .001' means that the probability is less than 1 in 1000.

By contrast, if the probability level of the obtained result is greater than the .05 level: i.e. '$p > .05$', then this means that there is thought to be too great a probability of the result having arisen simply through chance, rather than through the manipulation involved in the experiment. In such cases, the result of the statistical test is said to be 'Not Significant' – often abbreviated to 'N.S.'. (Occasionally, some investigators will reject at the .01 level, but this is not all that common. It depends on the nature of the experiment, and the consequences of accepting or rejecting a particular experimental result.)

Further information on experimental design and the use of statistical tests is available in a range of basic texts. These include Miller (1975), Robson (1973), and Siegel (1956), all of which are suitable for the reader with no previous knowledge of statistics.

References

Acredolo, L. P., Pick, H. L. and Olsen, M. G. (1975) 'Environmental differentiation and familiarity as determinants of children's memory for spatial location', *Developmental Psychology*, **11**, 495–501.

Aebli, H. (1967) 'Egocentrism (Piaget) not a phase of mental development but a substitute solution for an insoluble task', *Pedagogica Europaea*, **3**, 97–103.

Ahr, P. R. and Youniss, J. (1970) 'Reasons for failure on the class inclusion problem', *Child Development*, **41**, 131–43.

Alleen, K., Hart, B., Bueli, J. S., Harris, F. R. and Wolf, M. M. (1964) 'Effects of social reinforcement on isolate behaviour of a nursery school Child', *Child Development*, **35**, 511–18.

Alvy, K. T. (1968) 'Relation of age to children's egocentric and cooperative communication', *Journal of Genetic Psychology*, **112**, 275–86.

Ames, E. W. and Silfen, C. K. (1966) 'Methodological issues in the study of age differences in infants' attention to stimuli varying in movement and complexity'. Paper presented at the meeting of the Society for Research in Child Development, Minneapolis, March.

Andersen, E. S. (1977) 'Learning to speak with style: A study of the sociolinguistic skills of children'. Unpublished doctoral dissertation, Stanford University.

Andersen, I. H. and Dearborn, W. F. (1952) *The Psychology of Teaching Reading*, New York: Ronald Press.

Aries, P. (1962) *Centuries of Childhood*, London: Cape.

Aronfreed, J. (1968) *Conduct and Conscience: The Socialization of Internalized Control over Behaviour*, New York: Academic Press.

Asher, S. R. and Hymel, S. (1981) 'Assessment with socially isolated and rejected children'. In J. Wine and M. Syme (eds), *Social Competence*, New York: Guilford Press.

Asher, S. R., Oden, S. L. and Gottman, J. M. (1977) 'Childrens friendships in school settings'. In L. G. Katz (ed.) *Current Topics in Early Childhood Education*, Vol. 1, Norwood, N. J.: Ablex.

Ayers, D. and Downing, J. (1979) 'The development of linguistic concepts and reading achievement'. Paper presented at the International Reading Research Seminar on Linguistic Awareness and Learning to Read, Victoria, Canada.

Barnes, D. (1971) *Language, the Learner and the School*, Harmondsworth: Penguin.

Barnes, D. (1976) *From Communication to Curriculum*, Harmondsworth: Penguin.

Bartlett, F. C. (1932) *Remembering*, Cambridge: Cambridge University Press.

Bates, E. (1976) *Language and Context: The Acquisition of Pragmatics*, New York: Academic Press.

Bateson, G. (1956) 'The message "This is play"'. In B. Schaffner (ed.), *Group Processes*, New York: Macy Foundation.

Beaver, A. (1932) 'The initiation of social contracts by preschool children', *Child Development Monographs*, 7, 1–56.

Beckmann, H. (1924) 'Die Entwicklung der Zahlleistung bei 2–6 jährigen Kindern', *Zeitschrift für Angewandte Psychologie*, 22, 1–72.

Behan, B. (1963) *Hold Your Hour and Have Another*, London: Hutchinson.

Benson, C. S. and Gottman, J. M. (1975) 'Children's popularity and peer social interaction'. Unpublished manuscript, Indiana University.

Bereiter, C. (1924) *Arithmetic and Mathematics*. San Rafael, Calif.: Dimensions.

Bereiter, C. *et al.* (1966) 'An academically oriented pre-school for culturally deprived children'. In F. M. Hechinger (ed.) *Pre-School Education Today*, New York: Doubleday.

Berko, J. (1958) 'The child's learning of English morphology', *Word*, 14, 150–77.

Berko Gleason, J. (1973). 'Code switching in children's language'. In T. E. Moore (ed.), *Cognitive Development and the Acquisition of Language*, New York: Academic Press.

Bernstein, B. (1971) *Class, Codes and Control*, Vol. I, London: Routledge & Kegan Paul.

Bernstein, B. (1972) 'Social class, language and socialization'. In P. P. Giglioli (ed.), *Language and Social Context*. Harmondsworth: Penguin, 157–78.

Bernstein, B. (1973) *Class, Codes and Control*, Vol. II, London: Routledge & Kegan Paul.

Berthoud-Papandropoulou, I. (1978) 'An experimental study of children's ideas about language'. In A. Sinclair, R. J. Jarvella and W. J. M. Levelt (eds), *The Child's Conception of Language*. Berlin: Springer, 55–64.

Bever, T. G. (1975) 'Psychologically real grammar emerges because of its role in language acquisition'. In D. P. Dato (ed.), *Georgetown University Monograph Series on Language and Linguistics*, Washington, D.C.: Georgetown University Press, 63–75.

Beyer, E. (1956) 'Observing children in nursery school situations'. In L. B. Murphy (ed.), *Personality in Young Children*, New York: Basic Books.

Biemiller, A. (1970) 'The development of the use of graphic and contextual information as children learn to read', *Reading Research Quarterly*, 6, 76–96.

Bock, R. D. (1974) 'Multivariate analysis of qualitative data'. In *Mutivariate Statistical Methods in Behavioural Research*, New York: McGraw-Hill.

Borke, H. (1971) 'Interpersonal perception of young children: Egocentrism or empathy?', *Developmental Psychology*, 5, 263–9.

Borke, H. (1972) 'Chandler and Greenspan's "ersatz egocentrism": A rejoinder', *Developmental Psychology*, 7, 107–9.

Borke, H. (1973) 'The development of empathy in Chinese and American children between three and six years of age: a cross cultural study', *Developmental Psychology*, 9, 102–8.

Borke, H. (1975) 'Piaget's mountains revisited: changes in the egocentric landscape', *Developmental Psychology*, 11, 240–3.

Bower, T. G. R. (1977) *The Perceptual World of the Child*, London: Open Books Fontana.

Bowerman, M. (1979) 'The acquisition of complex sentences'. In P. Fletcher and M. Garman (eds), *Language Acquisition*, Cambridge: Cambridge University Press.

Bowey, J. A. and Tunmer, W. E. (1980). 'The development of word awareness in children', *Education Research and Perspectives*, 7, 32–46.

Braine, M. D. S. and Shanks, B. L. (1965a) 'The conservation of a shape property and a proposal about the origin of the conservations', *Canadian Journal of Psychology*, 19, 197–207.

Braine, M. D. S. and Shanks, B. L. (1965b) 'The development of conservation of size', *Journal of Verbal Learning and Verbal Behaviour*, **4**, 227–42.

Brainerd, C. J. (1974) 'Training and transfer of transitivity, conservation and class inclusion of length', *Child Development*, **45**, 324–34.

Bransford, J. D., Nitsch, K. W. and Franks, J. J. (1977) 'Schooling and the facilitation of knowing', In R. C. Anderson, R. J. Spiro and W. E. Montague (eds), *Schooling and the Acquisition of Knowledge*, Hillsdale, N. J.: Lawrence Erlbaum Associates.

Brown, A. L. (1975) 'The development of memory: knowing, knowing about knowing, and knowing how to know'. In H. W. Reese (ed.), *Advances in Child Development and Behaviour*, Vol. 10, New York: Academic Press.

Brown, A. L. (1976) 'The construction of temporal succession by preoperational children'. In A. D. Pick (ed.), *Minnesota Symposia on Child Psychology*, Vol. 10, Minneapolis: University of Minnesota.

Brown, A. L. (1978a) 'Theories of memory and the problem of development: growth, activity, and knowledge'. In F. I. M. Craik and L. Cermak (eds), *Levels of Analysis Approaches to Cognition*, Hillsdale, N.J.: Lawrence Erlbaum Associates.

Brown, A. L. (1978b) 'Knowing when, where, and how to remember: a problem of metacognition'. In R. Glaser (ed.), *Advances in Instructional Psychology*, Hillsdale, N.J.: Lawrence Erlbaum Associates.

Brown, A. L. (1980) 'Metacognitive development and reading'. In R. J. Spiro, B. Bruce and W. F. Brewer (eds), *Theoretical Issues in Reading Comprehension*, Hillsdale, N.J.: Lawrence Erlbaum Associates.

Brown, A. L. and Campione, J. C. (1978) 'Memory strategies in learning: training children to study strategically'. In H. Pick, H. Leibowitz, J. Singer, A. Steinschneider and H. Stevenson (eds), *Application of Basic Research in Psychology*, New York: Plenum Press.

Brown, A. L. and Smiley, S. S. (1977a) 'Rating the importance of structural units of prose passages: a problem of metacognitive development', *Child Development*, **48**, 1–8.

Brown, A. L. and Smiley, S. S. (1977b) 'The development of strategies for studying prose passages'. Unpublished manuscript, University of Illinois.

Brown, A. L., Smiley, S. S., Day, J. D., Townsend, M. A. R. and Lawton, S. C. (1977) 'Intrusion of a thematic idea in children's comprehension and retention of stories', *Child Development*, **48**, 1454–66.

Brown, R. (1973) *A First Language: The Early Stages*, Cambridge, Mass.: Harvard University Press.

Bruce, D. J. (1964) 'The analysis of word sounds by young children', *British Journal of Educational Psychology*, **34**, 158–70.

Bruner, J. S. (1966) *Studies in Cognitive Growth*, New York: Wiley.

Bruner, J. S. (1971) 'The growth and structure of skill'. In K. J. Connolly (ed.), *Motor Skills in Infancy*, London: Academic Press.

Bruner, J. S. (1974) 'From communication to language. A psychological perspective', *Cognition*, **3**, 225–87.

Bryant, P. E. and Kopytynska, H. (1976) 'Spontaneous measurement by young children,' *Nature*, **260**, 772.

Bryant, P. E. and Trabasso, T. (1971) 'Transitive inferences and memory in young children', *Nature*, **232**, 456–8.

Cambourne, B. L. (1971) 'A naturalistic study of language performance in grade one rural and urban school children.' Unpublished doctoral dissertation, James Cook University.

Campbell, R. N. and Bowe, T. (1977) 'Functional asymmetry in early language understanding'. In G. Drachman (ed.) *Salzburger Beitrage für Linguistik*, Vol. 3, Tubingen: Gunter Narr.

Campbell, R. N. and Smith, P. T. (1978) *Recent Advances in the Psychology of Language*, Vol. 1, London: Plenum Press.

Carey, S. (1978) 'Less never means more'. In R. N. Campbell and P. T. Smith (eds), *Recent Advances in the Psychology of Language*, Vol. 1, *Language Development and Mother Child Interaction*, London: Plenum Press.

Carroll, J. B. (1964) *Language and Thought*, Englewood Cliffs, N.J.: Prentice Hall.

Cazden, C. B. (1968) 'The acquisition of noun and verb inflections', *Child Development*, **39**, 433–48.

Cazden, C. (1974) 'Play with language and metalinguistic awareness: one dimension of language experience', *The Urban Review*, **7**, 28–39.

Cheyne, J. 'Some parameters of punishment affecting resistance to deviation and generalization of a prohibition', *Child Development*, **42**, 1249–61.

Chi, M. T. H. (1977) 'Metamemory and chess skill'. Unpublished manuscript, University of Pittsburgh.

Chi, M. T. H. (1978) 'Knowledge, structures and memory development'. In R. S. Siegler (ed.), *Children's Thinking: What Develops?* Hillsdale, N.J.: Lawrence Erlbaum Associates.

Chomsky, A. N. (1965) *Aspects of the Theory of Syntax*, Cambridge, Mass.: MIT Press.

Chomsky, C. S. (1969) *The Acquisition of Syntax in Children from 5 to 10*, Cambridge, Mass.: MIT Press.

Chukovsky, K. (1963) *From Two to Five*, University of California Press.

Clark, E. V. (1973) 'Non-linguistic strategies and the acquisition of word meanings', *Cognition*, **2**, 161–82.

Clark, E. V. (1978) 'Awareness of language: Some evidence from what children say and do'. In A. Sinclair, R. J. Jarvella and W. J. M. Levelt (eds), *The Child's Conception of Language*, Berlin: Springer, 18–43.

Clark, E. V., and Andersen, E. S. (1979) 'Spontaneous repairs: awareness in the process of acquiring language'. Paper presented at Symposium on Reflections on Metacognition, Society for Research in Child Development, San Francisco.

Clark, M. M. (1976) *Young Fluent Readers*, London: Heinemann.

Clay, M. M. (1969) 'Reading errors and self-correction behaviour', *British Journal of Educational Psychology*, **39**, 47–56.

Clay, M. M. (1972a) *The Early Detection of Reading Difficulties: A Diagnostic Survey*, Auckland, N.Z.: Heinemann.

Clay, M. M. (1972b) *Reading: The Patterning of Complex Behaviour*, London: Heinemann.

Clough, J. R. (1971) 'An experimental investigation of the effects of a cognitive training programme on educationally disadvantaged children of pre-school age'. Unpublished doctoral dissertation, Monash University.

Cole, M., Gay, J., Glick, J. A. and Sharp, D. W. (1971) *The Cultural Context of Learning and Thinking*. London: Methuen.

Cole, M. and Scribner, S. (1975) 'Theorizing about the socialization of cognition', *Ethos*, **3**, 249–68.

Combs, M. L. and Slaby, D. A. (1977) 'Social-skills training with children'. In B. B. Lahey and A. E. Kazdin (eds), *Advances in Clinical Child Psychology*, Vol. I, New York: Plenum.

Condry, J. (1977) 'Enemies of exploration: Self-initiated versus other-initiated learning', *Journal of Personality and Social Psychology*, **35**, 459–77.

Corran, G. and Walkerdine, V. (1981) 'The Practice of Reason, Vol. 1, Reading the Signs of Mathematics'. Unpublished mimeograph.

Corsaro, W. A. (1979) '"We're friends, right?" Children's use of access rituals in a nursery school', *Language in Society*, **8**, 315–36.

Cosgrove, J. M. and Patterson, C. J. (1977) 'Plans and the development of listener skills', *Developmental Psychology*, **13**, 557–64.

Cosgrove, J. M. and Patterson, C. J. (1978) 'Generalization of training for children's listener skills', *Child Development*, **49**, 513–6.

Cromer, R. F. (1974) 'The development of language and cognition: the cognition hypothesis'. In B. Foss (ed.), *New Perspectives in Child Development*, Harmondsworth: Penguin, 184–252.

Damon, W. (1977) *The Social World of the Child*, San Francisco: Josey-Bass.

Day, M. C. (1975) 'Developmental trends in visual scanning'. In H. W. Reese (ed.), *Advances in Child Development and Behaviour*, Vol. 10, New York: Academic Press.

de Boysson-Bardies, B. and O'Regan, K. (1973) 'What children do in spite of adults' hypotheses', *Nature*, **246**, 531–4.

Descoeudres, A. (1921) *Le Developpement de l'enfant de deux à sept ans*, Paris: Delachaux & Niestle.

Diack, J. H. (1965) *In Spite of the Alphabet*, London: Chatto & Windus.

Dickson, W. P. (1974) 'An instructional device for teaching verbal skills through structured interactions between children in a communication game'. Unpublished doctoral dissertation, Stanford University.

Dion, K. K. and Berscheid, E. (1974) 'Physical attractiveness and peer perception among children', *Sociometry*, **37**, 1–12.

Dockrell, J., Campbell, R. and Neilson, I. (1980) 'Conservation accidents revisited', *International Journal of Behavioural Development*, **3**, 423–39.

Dodwell, P. C. (1963) 'Children's understanding of spatial concepts', *Canadian Journal of Psychology*, **17**, 141–61.

Donaldson, M. (1978) *Children's Minds*, London: Fontana.

Donaldson, M. (1982) 'Conservation: what is the question?', *British Journal of Psychology*, **73**, 199–207.

Donaldson, M. and Balfour, G. (1981) 'Less is more: a study of language comprehension in children', *British Journal of Psychology*, **59**, 461–71.

Donaldson, M. and Lloyd, P. (1974) 'Sentences and situations: children's judgements of match and mismatch'. In F. Bresson (ed.), *Current Problems in Psycholinguistics*, Paris: Centre National de la Recherche Scientifique.

Donaldson, M. and McGarrigle, J. (1974) 'Some clues to the nature of semantic development', *Journal of Child Language*, **1**, 185–94.

Donaldson, M. and Reid, J. F. (1982) 'Language skills and reading: a developmental perspective'. In A. Hendry (ed.) *Teaching Reading: the Key Issues*, London: Heinemann Educational Books.

Downing, J. (1969) 'How children think about reading', *The Reading Teacher*, **23**, 217–30.

Downing, J. (1970) 'Children's concepts of language in learning to read', *Educational Research*, **12**, 106–12.

Downing, J. (1979) 'Cognitive clarity and linguistic awareness'. Paper presented at the International Reading Research Seminar on Linguistic Awareness and Learning to Read, Victoria, Canada, June.

Downing, J. (1979) *Reading and Reasoning*, Edinburgh: Chambers.

Downing, J, and Thackray, D. (1971) *Reading Readiness*, London: University of London Press.

Dweck, C. S. and Goetz, T. E. (1979) 'Attributions and learned helplessness'. In J. H. Harvey, W. Ickes and R. F. Kidd (eds), *New Directions in Attribution Research*, Vol. 2, Hillsdale, N.J.: Lawrence Erlbaum Associates.

Ehri, L. C. (1978) 'Beginning reading from a psycholinguistic perspective: amalgamation of word identities'. In F. B. Murray (ed.), *The Recognition of Words*, Newark, Del.: International Reading Association.

Elkonin, D. B. (1971) 'Development of speech'. In A. V. Zaporozhets and D. B. Elkonin (eds), *The Psychology of Preschool Children* (first published, 1964), Cambridge, Mass.: MIT Press.

Ferguson, G. A. (1965) *Nonparametric Trend Analysis*, Montreal: McGill University Press.

Fienberg, S. W. (1978) *Analysis of Cross-classified Categorical Data*, Cambridge, Mass.: MIT Press.

Fishbein, H. D., Lewis, S. and Keiffer, K. (1972) 'Children's understanding of spatial relations: co-ordination of perspectives', *Developmental Psychology*, 7, 21–33.

Flavell, J. H. (1974) 'The developmental of inferences about others'. In T. Mischel (ed.), *Understanding Other Persons*, Oxford, Basil Blackwell.

Flavell, J. H. (1977) *Cognitive Development*, Englewood Cliffs, N.J.: Prentice-Hall.

Flavell, J. H., Botkin, P. T., Fry, C. L., Wright, J. W. and Jarvis, P. E. (1968) *The Development of Role-taking and Communication Skills in Children*, New York: Wiley.

Flavell, J. H., Shipstead, S. G. and Croft, K. (1978) 'Young children's knowledge about visual perception: hiding objects from others'. Unpublished manuscript.

Flavell, J. H. and Wellman, H. M. (1977) 'Metamemory'. In R. V. Kail, Jr. and J. W. Hagen (eds), *Perspectives on the Development of Memory and Cognition*. Hillsdale, N.J.: Lawrence Erlbaum Associates.

Fox, B. and Routh, D. K. (1976) 'Phonemic analysis and synthesis as word-attack skills', *Journal of Educational Psychology*, 68, 70–74.

Fromkin, V. A. (1973) *Speech Errors at Linguistic Evidence*, The Hague: Mouton.

Furman, W., Rahe, D. F. and Hartup, W. W. (1979) 'Rehabilitation of socially-withdrawn preschool children through mixed-age and same-age socialization', *Child Development*, 50, 915–22.

Garner, J. and Plant, E. (1972) 'On the measurement of egocentrism: a replication and extension of Aebli's findings', *British Journal of Educational Psychology*, 42, 79–83.

Garvey, C. (1974) 'Some properties of social play', *Merrill-Palmer Quarterly*, 20, 163–71.

Gates, A. L. (1947) *The Improvement of Reading*, 3rd edn, New York: Macmillan.

Gelman, R. (1972) 'Logical capacity of very young children: number invariance rules', *Child Development*, 43, 75–90.

Gelman, R. (1977) 'How young children reason about small numbers'. In N. J. Castellan, D. B. Pisoni and G. R. Potts (eds), *Cognitive Theory*, Vol. 2, Hillsdale, N.J.: Lawrence Erlbaum Associates, 219–38.

Gelman, R. (1978) 'Cognitive development', *Annual Review of Psychology*, 29, 297–332.

Gelman, R. and Gallistel, C. R. (1978) *The Child's Understanding of Number*, Cambridge, Mass.: Harvard University Press.

Gelman, R. and Shatz, M. (1977) 'Appropriate speech adjustments: the operation of conversational constraints on talk to two-year-olds'. In M. Lewis and L. A. Rosenblum (eds), *Interaction, Conversation, and the Development of Language*. New York: Wiley, 27–61.

Gelman, R. and Tucker, M. F. (1975) 'Further investigations of the young child's conception of number', *Child Development*, 46, 167–75.

Gibson, E. J. (1969) *Principles of Perceptual Learning and Development*, New York: Appleton-Century-Crofts.

Gibson, E. J. and Levin, H. (1975) *The Psychology of Reading*, Cambridge, Mass.: MIT Press.

Glucksberg, S., Krauss, R. M. & Higgins, E. (1975) 'The development of referential communication skills'. In F. D. Horowitz (ed.), *Review of Child Development Research*, Vol. 4, Chicago: University of Chicago Press.

Goodluck, H. and Roeper, T. (1978) 'The acquisition of perception verb complements'. In H. Goodluck and L. Solon (eds), *Papers in the Structure and Development of Child Language*, University of Massachusetts Occasional Papers in Linguistics, Vol. 4.

Goodman, K. S. (1967) 'Reading, a psycholinguistic guessing game'. In H. Singer and R. Ruddell (eds), *Theoretical Models and Processes of Reading*, Newark, Del.: International Reading Association.

Goodman, K. S. (ed.) (1968) *The Psycholinguistic Nature of the Reading Process*, Detroit: Wayne State University Press.

Goodman, K. S. (1969) 'Analysis of oral reading miscues: applied psycholinguistics', *Reading Research Quarterly*, **5**, 9–30.

Goodman, K. S. (1981) Letter to the editor, *Reading Research Quarterly*, **16**, 477–8.

Gottman, J. (1979) 'Detecting cyclicity in social interaction', *Psychological Bulletin*, **86**, 338–48.

Gottman, J., Gonso, J. and Rasmussen, B. (1975) 'Social interation, social competence and friendship in children', *Child Development*, **46**, 709–18.

Gottman, J. M. and Parkhurst, J. T. (1980) 'A developmental theory of friendship and acquaintanceship processes.' In A. Collins (ed.), *Minnesota Symposia on Child Psychology*, Vol. 13, Hillsdale, N.J.: Lawrence Erlbaum Associates.

Grice, H. P. (1975) 'Logic and conversation'. In P. Cole and J. Morgan (eds), *Syntax and Semantics*, Vol. III, *Speech Acts*, New York: Academic Press.

Grieve, R. (1971) 'Some studies of language use and class inclusion.' Unpublished doctoral dissertation, University of Edinburgh.

Grieve, R. and Hoogenraad, R. (1976) 'Using language if you don't have much'. In R. J. Wales and E. C. T. Walker (eds), *New Approaches to Language Mechanisms*, Amsterdam: North Holland, 1–28.

Grieve, R., Hoogenraad, R. and Murray, D. (1977) 'On the young child's use of lexis and syntax in understanding locative instructions', *Cognition*, **5**, 235–50.

Gronlund, N. E. (1959) *Sociometry in the Classroom*, New York: Harper & Row.

Guillaume, P. (1971) *Imitation in Children*, Chicago: University of Chicago Press.

Hakes, D. T., Evans, J. S. and Tunmer, W. E. (1980) *The Development of Metalinguistic Abilities in Children*. Berlin: Springer.

Halliday, M. A. K. (1968) 'Language and experience', *Educational Review*, **20**, 2, 95–106.

Halliday, M. A. K. (1975) *Learning How to Mean*, London: Arnold.

Harris, P. L. (1973) 'Perseverative errors in search by young infants', *Child Development*, **44**, 28–33.

Harris, P. L. (1978) 'Tekstbegrip bij jonge kinderen'. In J. de Wit, H. Bolle, and J. M. van Meel (eds), *Psychologen over het kind*, Vols. 5/6, Groningen, Wolters-Noordhoff.

Harris, P. L. and Singleton, W. M. (1978) 'The child's understanding of measurement'. In R. Glaser and S. Fokkema (eds), *Cognition and Instruction: Proceedings of the N.A.T.O. Conference*.

Hartup, W. W., Glazer, J. A. and Charlesworth, R. (1967) 'Peer reinforcement and sociometric states', *Child Development*, **38**, 1017–24.

Hayes, J. R. (1972) 'The child's conception of the experimenter'. In S. Farnham-Diggory (ed.), *Information Processing in Children*, New York: Academic Press.

Heathers, G. (1955) 'Emotional dependence and independence in nursery school play', *Journal of Gen. Psychology*, **87**, 37–57.

Hewson, S. (1978) 'Inferential problem solving in young children', *Developmental Psychology*, **14**, 93–8.

Hetherington, E. M., Cox, M. and Cox, R. (1979) 'Play and social interaction in children following divorce'. Paper presented to the Society for Research on Child Development, San Francisco, March.

Hocker, M. E. (1963) 'Reading materials for children based on their language patterns of syntax, vocabulary and interests'. Unpublished master's thesis, University of Arizona.

Hocking, M. (1977) 'Verbal interpretation in the infant classroom and its place in the learning process'. Unpublished doctoral thesis, University of Bristol.

Hogan, R. (1973) 'Moral conduct and moral character: a psychological perspective', *Psychological Bulletin*, **79**, 217–32.

Hogan, R. and Mills, C. (1976) 'Legal socialization', *Human Development*, **19**,261–76.

Holden, M. H. and MacGinitie, W. H. (1972) 'Children's conceptions of word boundaries in speech and print', *Journal of Educational Psychology*, **63**, 551–7.

Hollenbeck, A. R. (1978) 'Problems of reliability in observational research'. In G. P. Sackett (ed.), *Observing Behaviour*, Vol. 2, Baltimore: University Park Press.

Hoogenraad, R., Grieve, R., Baldwin, P. and Campbell, R. N. (1978) 'Comprehension as an interactive process'. In R. N. Campbell and P. T. Smith (eds), *Recent Advances in the Psychology of Language*, Vol. 1, *Language Development and Mother-Child Interaction*, London: Plenum Press.

Hoy, F. A. (1974) 'Predicting another's visual perspective: a unitary skill?' *Developmental Psychology*, **10**, 462.

Huey, E. B. (1908) *The Psychology and Pedagogy of Reading*, New York: Macmillan.

Hughes, M. (1978) 'Selecting pictures of another person's view', *British Journal of Educational Psychology*, **48**, 210–19.

Hughes, M. (1981) 'Can preschool children add and subtract?' *Educational Psychology*, **1**, 207–19.

Hughes, M. and Grieve, R. (1980) 'On asking children bizarre questions', *First Language*, **1**, 149–60.

Huttenlocher, J. and Presson, C. (1973) 'Mental Rotation and the perspective problem', *Cognitive Psychology*, **4**, 277–99.

Hymel, S. and Asher, S. R. (1977) 'Assessment and training of isolated children's social skills'. Paper presented at the biennial meeting of the Society for Research in Child Development, New Orleans.

Inhelder, B. and Piaget, J. (1964) *The Early Growth of Logic in the Child*, London: Routledge & Kegan Paul.

Ironsmith, M. and Whitehurst, G. J. (1978) 'The development of listener abilities in communication: how children deal with ambiguous information', *Child Development*, **49**, 348–52.

Isen, A. M., Riley, C. A., Tucker, T. and Trabasso, T. (1975) 'How does a child understand part-whole relations?' Paper read at Society for Research in Child Development, Colorado, April.

Istomina, Z. M. (1975) 'The development of voluntary memory in preschool-age children', *Soviet Psychology*, **13**, 5–64.

318   *References*

Jagger, J. H. (1929) *The Sentence Method of Teaching Reading*, London: Grant.

Jefferson, G. (1974) 'Error Correction as an Interactional Resource'. *Lang. Soc.*, **2**, 181–99.

Jennings, J. R. (1970) 'The effect of verbal and pictorial presentation on class-inclusion competence and performance', *Psychonomic Science*, **20**, 357–8.

Johnson, H. M. (1972) *Children in The Nursery School* (first published, 1928), New York: Agathon Press.

Johnson, S. M. and Bolstad, O. D. (1973) 'Methodological issues in naturalistic observation: some problems and solutions for field research'. In L. A. Hammerlynck, L. C. Handy and E. J. Mark (eds), *Behaviour Change*, Champaign, Illinois.

Josephson, J. (1977) 'The child's use of situational and personal information in predicting the behaviour of another.' Doctoral dissertation, Stanford University. (Dissertation Abstracts International. 1977. 38. 1967B-2443B. (University Micro-films No. 77-25. 688).)

Kagen, J., Kearsley, R. and Zelazo, P. (1975) 'The emergence of initial apprehension to unfamiliar peers'. In M. Lewis and L. Rosenblum (eds), *Friendship and Peer Relations*, New York: Wiley.

Kalil, K., Youssef, Z. and Lerner, R. M. (1974) 'Class-inclusion failure: cognitive deficit or misleading reference?' *Child Development*, **45**, 1122–5.

Karmiloff-Smith, A. (1979) 'Language development after five'. In P. Fletcher and M. Garman (eds), *Language Acquisition*, Cambridge: Cambridge University Press.

Kavanaugh, J. F. and Mattingly, I. G. (eds) (1972) *Language by Ear and by Eye: the Relationship between Speech and Reading*, Cambridge, Mass.: MIT Press.

Kendler, T. S. and Kendler, H. H. (1967) 'Experimental analysis of inferential behaviour in children'. In L. P. Lipsitt and C. C. Spiker (eds), *Advances in Child Development and Behaviour*, Vol. 3.

Klahr, D. and Wallace, J. G. (1972) 'Class inclusion processes'. In S. Farnham-Diggory (ed.), *Information Processing in Children*, New York: Academic Press.

Kobasigawa, A. (1974) 'Utilization of retrieval cues by children in recall', *Child Development*, **45**, 127–34.

Kochman, T. (1970) 'Towards an ethnography of black American speech behaviour'. In N. E. Whitten and J. Szwed (eds), *Afro-American Anthropology*, New York: Free Press, 145–62.

Kohlberg, L. (1968) 'The child as a moral philosopher', *Psychology Today*, **2**, 25–30.

Kohn, M. (1966) 'The child as a determinant of his peers' approaches to him', *Journal of Gen. Psychology*, **109**, 91–100.

Kohnstamm, G. A. (1963) 'An evaluation of part of Piaget's theory', *Acta Psychologica*, **21**, 313–56.

Krauss, R. M. and Flucksber, S. (1969) 'The development of communication: competence as a function of age', *Child Development*, **40**, 255–66.

Labov, W. (1972) 'The logic of nonstandard English'. In P. P. Giglioli (ed.), *Language and Social Context*. Harmondsworth: Penguin, 179–215.

Latané, B. and Darley, J. M. (1970) *The Unresponsive Bystander: Why Doesn't He Help?* New York: Appleton-Century-Crofts.

Lee, L. C. (1973) 'Social encounters of infants: the beginnings of popularity'. Paper presented to the International Society for the Study of Behavioural Development, Ann Arbor, Michigan, August.

Leopold, W. F. (1949) *Speech Development of a Bilingual Child*, Evanston, Illinois: North-western University Press.

Lepper, M. R., Greene, D. and Nisbett, R. E. (1973) 'Undermining children's intrinsic interest with extrinsic rewards: a test of the overjustification hypothesis', *Journal of Personality and Social Psychology*, **28** 129–37.

Levelt, W. J. M., Sinclair, A. and Jarvella, R. J. (1978) 'Causes and functions of linguistic awareness in language acquisition: some introductory remarks.' In A. Sinclair, R. J. Jarvella and W. J. M. Levelt (eds), *The Child's Conception of Language*. Berlin: Springer, 1–14.

Light, P. (1974) 'The role-taking skills of four-year-old children'. Unpublished doctoral dissertation, University of Cambridge.

Light, P. H., Buckingham, N. and Robbins, A. H. (1979) 'The conservation task as an interactional setting', *British Journal of Educational Psychology*, **49**, 304–10.

Lockhart, K. L., Abrahams, B. and Osherson, D. N. (1977) 'Children's understanding of uniformity in the environment', *Child Development*, **48**, 1521–31.

Loughlin, K. A. and Daehler, M. A. (1973) 'The effects of distraction and added perceptual cues on the delayed reaction of very young children', *Child Development*, **44**, 384–8.

Lundberg, I. (1978) 'Aspects of linguistic awareness related to reading'. In A. Sinclair, R. J. Jarvella and W. J. M. Levelt (eds), *The Child's Conception of Language*, Berlin: Springer, 83–96.

Luria, A. R. (1961) *The Role of Speech in the Regulation of Normal and Abnormal Behaviour*, Oxford: Pergamon.

McCraw, L. W. and Tolbert, J. W. (1953) 'Sociometric status and athletic ability of junior high school boys', *The Research Quarterly*, **24**, 72–80.

McGarrigle, J. and Donaldson, M. (1974) 'Conservation accidents', *Cognition*, **3**, 341–50.

McGarrigle, J., Grieve, R. and Hughes, M. (1978) 'Interpreting inclusion: a contribution to the study of the child's cognitive and linguistic development', *Journal of Experimental Child Psychology*, **26**, 528, 50.

McGrew, P. L. and McGrew, W. L. (1972) 'Changes in children's spacing behaviour with nursery school experience', *Human Development*, **15**, 359–72.

McGrew, W. C. (1972) *An Ethological Study of Children's Behaviour*, New York: Academic Press.

Mackay, D., Thompson, B. and Schaub, P. (1970) *Breakthrough to Literacy: Teacher's Manual*, London: Longman.

McKenzie, M. (1977) 'The beginnings of literacy', *Theory into Practice*, **16**, 315–24.

Mackworth, N. H. and Bruner, J. S. (1970) 'How adults and children search and recognize pictures', *Human Development*, **13**, 149–77.

Macnamara, J. (1972) 'Cognitive basis of language learning in infants', *Psychological Review*, **79**, 1–13.

McNeill, D. (1970) *The Acquisition of Language*, New York: Harper & Row.

Maratsos, M. P. (1973) 'Nonegocentric communication abilities in preschool children'. *Child Development*, **44**, 697–700.

Markman, E. (1973) 'The facilitation of part-whole comparisons by use of the collective noun "family"', *Child Development*, **44**, 837–40.

Markman, E. M. (1977) 'Realizing that you don't understand: a preliminary investigation', *Child Development*, **48**, 986–92.

Markman, E. M. and Seibert, J. (1976) 'Classes and collections: internal organization and resulting holistic properties', *Cognitive Psychology*, **8**, 561–77.

Marshall, H. R. and McCandless, B. R. (1957) 'Relationships between dependence on adults and social acceptance by peers', *Child Development*, **28**, 413–19.

Marshall, J. C. and Morton, J. (1978) 'On the mechanics of EMMA'. In A. Sinclair, R. J. Jarvella and W. J. M. Levelt (eds), *The Childs Conception of Language*, Berlin: Springer, 225–39.

Mattick, I. (1967) 'Description of the children'. In *The Drifters: Children of Disorganized Lower-class Families*, Boston, Mass.: Little Brown.

Maurer, D. and Salapatek, P. (1976) 'Developmental changes in the scanning of faces by young infants', *Child Development*, **47**, 523–7.

Meacham, J. A. (1977) 'Soviet investigations of memory development'. In R. V. Kail and J. W. Hagen (eds), *Perspectives on the Development of Memory and Cognition*, Hillsdale, N.J.: Lawrence Erlbaum Associates.

Meadows, S. (1977) 'An experimental investigation of Piaget's analysis of class inclusion,' *British Journal of Psychology*, **68**, 229–35.

Meek, M. (1982) *Learning to Read*, London: Bodley Head.

Menninger, K. (1969) *Number Words and Number Symbols*, Cambridge, Mass.: MIT Press.

Menyuk, P. (1969) *Sentences Children Use*, Research Monograph No. 52, Cambridge, Mass.: MIT Press.

Millar, S. (1968) *The Psychology of Play*, Harmondsworth: Penguin.

Miller, G. A. (1974) 'Toward a third metaphor for psycholinguistics'. In W. B. Weimer and D. S. Palermo (eds), *Cognition and the Symbolic Processes*. Hillsdale, N.J.: Lawrence Erlbaum Associates.

Miller, S. (1975) *Experimental Design and Statistics*, London: Methuen.

Mischel, W. (1974) 'Processes in delay of gratification'. In L. Berkowitz (ed.), *Advances in Experimental Social Psychology*, Vol. 7, New York: Academic Press.

Mischel, W. (1976) 'Cognition and the delay of gratification'. Pressented at University of Michigan Psychology Department Colloquium.

Mitchell, L. S. (1948) *Here and Now Story Book*, New York: Dutton.

Moore, S. (1967) 'Correlates of peer acceptance in nursery school children', *Young Children*, **22**, 281–97.

Much, N. and Shweder, R. A. (1978) 'Speaking of rules: the analysis of culture in breach'. In W. Damaon (ed.), *New Directions for Child Development*, Vol. 2, *Moral Development*, San Francisco: Jossey-Bass.

Mueller, E., Bleir, M., Krakow, J., Hagedus, K. and Cournoyer, P. (1977) 'The development of peer verbal interaction among two-year-old boys', *Child Development*, **48**, 284–7.

Murphy, M. D. and Brown, A. L. (1975) 'Incidental learning in preschool children as a function of level of cognitive analysis', *Journal of Experimental Child Psychology*, **19**, 509–23.

Neilson, I. and Dockrell, J. (1982) 'Conservation tasks as interactional settings'. In G. Butterworth and P. Light (eds), *Social Cognition*, Brighton: Harvester Press.

Nelson, K. (1977) 'Cognitive development and the acquisition of concepts'. In R. C. Anderson, R. J. Spiro and W. E. Montague (eds), *Schooling and the Acquisition of Knowledge*, Hillsdale, N. J.: Lawrence Erlbaum Associates.

Nelson, K. and Brown, A. L. (1978) 'The semantic-episodic distinction in memory development'. In P. Ornstein (ed.), *Memory Development*, Hillsdale, N.J.: Lawrence Erlbaum Associates.

Noton, D. and Stark, L. (1971) 'Eye movements and visual perception', *Scientific American*, **224**, 34–43.

Nucci, L. P. (in press) 'The development of conceptions of personal issues: a domain distinct from moral or societal concepts', *Child Development*,

Nucci, L. P. and Turiel, E. (1978) 'Social interactions and the development of social concepts in preschool children', *Child Development*, **49**, 400–407.

O'Connor, R. D. (1969) 'Modification of social withdrawal through symbolic modeling', *Journal of Applied Behavior Analysis*, **2**, 15–22.

Oden, S. and Asher, S. R. (1977) 'Coaching children in social skills for friendship making', *Child Development*, **48**, 495–506.

Olson, D. R. (1970) *Cognitive Development: the Child's Acquisition of Diagonality*, New York: Acadmic Press.

Olson, D. R. (1977) 'From utterance to text: the bias of language in speech and writing', *Harvard Educational Review*, **47**, 257–81.

Palermo, D. S. and Molfese, D. L. (1972) 'Language acquisition from age five onward', *Psychological Bulletin*, **78**, 409–28.

Parke, R. and Walters, R. (1967) 'Some factors influencing the efficacy of punishment training for inducing response inhibition', *Monographs of the Society for Research in Child Development*, **32**, (1. Serial No. 109.)

Parten, M. (1932–3) 'Social participation among preschool children', *Journal of Abnormal Social Psychology*, **27**, 243–69.

Peel, E. A. (1967) 'A method for investigating children's understanding of certain logical connectives used in binary propositional thinking', *British Journal of Mathematical and Statistical Psychology*, **20**, 81–92.

Peterson, C. L. (1974) 'Communicative and narrative behaviour of preschool-aged children'. Unpublished doctoral dissertation, University of Minnesota.

Peterson, C. L., Danner, F. W. and Flavell, J. M. (1972) 'Developmental changes in children's response to three indications of communicative failure', *Child Development*, **43**, 1436–8.

Phillips, E. L., Shenker, S. and Revitz, P. (1951) 'The assimilation of the new child into the group', *Psychiatry*, **14**, 319–25.

Piaget, J. (1926) *The Language and Thought of the Child*, London: Routledge & Kegan Paul.

Piaget, J. (1929) *The Child's Conception of the World*, New York: Harcourt Brace.

Piaget, J. (1932) *The Moral Judgement of the Child*, London: Routledge & Kegan Paul.

Piaget, J. (1951) *Play, Dreams, and Imitation in Childhood*, London: Routledge & Kegan Paul.

Piaget, J. (1952) *The Child's Conception of Number*, London: Routledge & Kegan Paul.

Piaget, J. (1953) 'How children form mathematical concepts', *Scientific American*, **189**, 74–9.

Piaget, J. (1955) *The Child's Construction of Reality*, London: Routledge & Kegan Paul.

Piaget, J. (1962) 'Comment on Vygotsky's critical remarks concerning the language and thought of the child'. In L. S. Vygotsky, *Thought and Language*, Cambridge, Mass.: MIT Press.

Piaget, J. (1970) *Genetic Epistemology*, New York: Columbia University Press.

Piaget, J. (1977) *The Grasp of Consciousness*, London: Routledge & Kegan Paul.

Piaget, J. and Inhelder, B. (1956) *The Child's Conception of Space*, London: Routledge & Kegan Paul.

Piaget, J. and Inhelder, B. (1969) *The Psychology of the Child*, London: Routledge & Kegan Paul.

Piaget, J., Inhelder, B. and Szeminska, A. (1960) *The Child's Conception of Geometry*, London: Routledge & Kegan Paul.

Pratt, C. and Grieve, R. (1980) 'The role of language awareness in cognitive development', *Education Research and Perspectives*, **7**, 69–79.

Pushkina, A. G. (1971) 'Mechanisms of transposition of relations in preschool-age children'. *Soviet Psychology*, **9**, 213–34.

Putallaz, M. and Gottman, J. (1981) 'Social skills and group acceptance'. In S. R. Asher and J. M. Gottman (eds), *The Development of Children's Friendships*, Cambridge: Cambridge University Press.

Read, C. (1978) 'Children's awareness of language, with emphasis on sound systems'. In A. Sinclair, R. J. Jarvella and W. J. M. Levelt (eds), *The Child's Conception of Language*, Berlin: Springer, 65–81.

Reid, J. F. (1958) 'A study of thirteen beginners in reading', *Acta Psychologica*, **14**, 294–313.

Reid, J. F. (1966) 'Learning to think about reading', *Educational Research*, **9**, 56–62.

Reid, J. F. (1970) 'Sentence structure in reading primers', *Research in Education*, **3**, 23–37.

Reid, J. F. (1972) 'Children's comprehension of syntactic structures found in some extension readers'. In J. F. Reid (ed.) *Reading Problems and Practices*, London: Ward Lock Educational.

Reid, J. F. (1975) *Breakthrough in Action: An Evaluation of Breakthrough to Literacy*, London: Longman.

Reid, J. F. and Donaldson, M. (1978) *Letter Links*, Edinburgh: Holmes McDougall.

Reid, J. F. and Low, J. (1972) *Link-Up*, Edinburgh: Holmes McDougall.

Reynolds, P. (1972) 'Play and human evolution'. Stanford University Medical Center. Paper presented at the annual meeting of the American Association for the Advancement of Science.

Riskin, J. and Faunce, E. E. (1970) 'Family interaction scales, III: Discussion of methodology and substantive findings', *Archives of General Psychiatry*, **22**, 527–37.

Ritter, K., Kaprove, B. H., Fitch, J. P. and Flavell, J. H. (1973) 'The development of retrieval strategies in young children', *Cognitive Psychology*, **5**, 310–21.

Robinson, E. J. (1981) 'The child's understanding of inadequate messages in communication failure: a problem of ignorance or egocentrism?' In W. P. Dickson (ed.), *Children's Oral Communication Skills*, New York: Academic Press.

Robinson, E. J. and Robinson, W. P. (1976a) 'Developmental changes in the child's explanation of communication failure', *Australian Journal of Psychology*, **28**, 155–65.

Robinson, E. J. and Robinson, W. P. (1976b) 'The yound child's understanding of communication', *Development Psychology*, **12**, 328–33.

Robinson, E. J. and Robinson, W. P. (1977a) 'The child's understanding of like-like communication failures', *Australian Journal of Psychology*, **29**, 137–42.

Robinson, E. J. and Robinson, W. P. (1977b) 'Development in the understanding of causes of success and failure in verbal communication', *Cognition*, **5**, 363–78.

Robinson, E. J. and Robinson, W. P. (1978a) 'Explanations of communication failure and ability to give bad messages', *British Journal of Social and Clinical Psychology*, **17**, 219–25.

Robinson, E. J. and Robinson, W. P. (1978b) 'Development of understanding about communication: message inadequacy and its role in causing communication failure', *Genetic Psychological Monographs*, **98**, 233–79.

Robinson, E. J. and Robinson, W. P. (1978c) 'The roles of egocentrism and of weakness in comparing children's explanations of communication failure', *Journal Experimental Child Psychology*, **26**, 147–60.

Robinson, E. J. and Robinson, W. P. (1981) 'Ways of reacting to communication failure in relation to the development of the child's understanding about verbal communication', *European Journal of Social Psychology*, **11**, 189–208.

Robson, C. (1973) *Experiment, Design and Statistics in Psychology*, Harmondsworth: Penguin.

Rogers, S. (in press) 'The effects of external variables on the language of children aged 5–7 years', *Communication and Cognition*.

Rose, S., Blank, M. and Spalter, I. (1975) Situational specificity of behaviour in young children', *Child Development*, **46**, 464–9,

Ruff, H. A. (1975) 'The function of shifting fixations in the visual perception of infants', *Child Development*, **46**, 857–65.

Ryan, S. M., Hegion, A. G. and Flavell, J. H. (1970) 'Nonverbal mnemonic mediation in preschool children, *Child Development*, **41**, 539–50.

Sachs, J. and Devin, J. (1976) 'Young children's use of age-appropriate speech styles in social interaction and role-playing', *Journal of Child Language*, **3**, 81–98.

Sackett, G. P. (1977) 'The lag sequential analysis of contingency and cyclicity in behavioural interaction research'. In J. Osofsky (ed.), *Handbook of Infant Development*, New York: Wiley.

Sacks, H. (1967) Unpublished lecture notes, University of California at Irvine.

Salapatek, P. (1968) 'Visual scanning of geometric figures by the human newborn', *Journal of Comparative and Physiological Psychology*, **66**, 247–58.

Salapatek, P. (1975) 'Pattern perception in early infancy'. In L. B. Cohen and P. Salapatek (eds), *Infant perception*, Vol. 1, New York: Academic Press.

Sapir, E. (1921) *Language*, New York: Harcourt Brace.

Scholl, D. M. and Ryan, E. B. (1975) 'Child judgements of sentences varying in grammatical complexity', *Journal of Experimental Child Psychology*, **20**, 274–85.

Shapiro, B. and Ogilvie, D. (1974) 'Manual for assessing social abilities of one-to-six-year-old children (Harvard Preschool Project). Unpublished manuscript, Harvard School of Education.

Shatz, M. and Gelman, R. (1973) 'The development of communication skills: modifications in the speech of young children as a function of listeners', *Monographs of the Society for Research in Child Development*, **38**, (5, Serial No. 152), 1–38.

Sheppard, J. L.(1973) 'Conservation of part and whole in the acquisition of class inclusion,' *Child Development*, **44**, 380–83.

Shipley, E. F. (1974) 'The Piagetian class-inclusion task: an alternative explanation. Technical report XIX: The acquisition of linguistic structure'. University of Pennsylvania.

Schultz, T. R. and Butkowsky, T. R. (1977) 'Young children's use of the scheme for multiple, sufficient causes in the attribution of real and hypothetical behaviour', *Child Development*, **48**, 464–69.

Siegel, S. (1956) *Nonparametric Statistics for the Behavioural Sciences*, New York: McGraw-Hill.

Silverman, I. W., Rose, A. P. and Phillis, D. E. (1979) 'The "magic" paradigm revisited', *Journal of Experimental Child Psychology*, **28**, 30–42.

Simon, D. P. and Simon, H. A. (1978) 'Individual differences in solving physics problems'. In R. S. Siegler (ed.), *Children's Thinking: What Develops?* Hillsdale, N.J.: Lawrence Erlbaum Associates.

Sinclair, H. (1969) 'Developmental psycholinguistics'. In D. Elkind and J. H. Flavell (eds), *Studies in Cognitive Development: Essays in Honour of Jean Piaget*. Oxford: Oxford University Press, 315–36.

Sinclair, J. Mc. R. and Coulthard, R. N. (1975) *Towards an Analysis of Discourse: The English Used by Teachers and Pupils*, Oxford: Oxford University Press.

Singleton, L. C. and Asher, S. R. (1977) 'Peer preferences and social interaction among third-grade children in an integrated school district', *Journal of Educational Psychology*, **69**, 330–36.

Slobin, D. I. (1978) 'A case study of early language awareness'. In A. Sinclair, R. J. Jarvella and W. J. M. Levelt (eds), *The Child's Conception of Language*, Berlin: Springer, 45–54.

Smiley, S. S., Oakley, D. D., Worthen, D., Campione, J. C. and Brown, A. L. (1977) 'Recall of thematically relevant material by adolescent good and poor readers as a function of written versus oral presentation,' *Educational Psychology*, **69**, 381–7.

Smith, F. (1978) *Reading*, Cambridge: Cambridge University Press.

Smith, N. V. (1973) *The Acquisition of Phonology: A Case Study*, Cambridge: Cambridge University Press.

Snyder, A. D. (1914) 'Notes on the talk of a two-and-a-half year old boy', *Pedagogical Seminary*, **21**, 412–24.

Spitzer, L. K. (1967) 'Selected materials on the language experience approach to reading instruction'. IRA Annotated Bibliography No. 13, Newark, Del.: International Reading Association.

Stechler, G. and Latz, E. (1966) 'Some observations on attention and arousal in the human infant', *Journal of the American Academy of Child Psychiatry*, **5**, 517–25.

Stevenson, R. L. (1879) *Essays of Travel*, Republished by Chatto & Windus, London (1920).

Stocking, S. and Arezzo, D. (1979) *Helping Friendless Children: A Guide for Teachers and Parents*, Boys Town, Nebraska: The Boys Town Center for the Study of Youth Development.

Strickland, R. (1962) 'The language of elementary schoolchildren: its relation to the language of reading textbooks and the quality of reading of selected children', *Bulletin of the School of Education, University of Indiana*, **38**, 2.

Tapp, J. and Kohlberg, L. (1971) 'Developing senses of law and legal justice', *Journal of Social Issues*, **27** (2), 65–91.

Tatarsky, J. H. (1974) 'The influence of dimensional manipulations on class-inclusion performance', *Child Development*, **45**, 1173–5.

Thomas, E. L. (1968) 'Movements of the eye', *Scientific American*, **219**, 88–95.

Tisak, M. (1977) 'Preschool children's ability to make moral and prosocial judgements'. Unpublished honors thesis, University of California at Berkeley.

Tough, J. (1977) *The Development of Meaning*, London: Unwin Education Books.

Trabasso, T., Isen, A. M., Dolecki, P., McLanahan, A. G., Riley, C. A. and Tucker, T. (1978) 'How do children solve class-inclusion problems?', In R. S. Siegler (ed.), *Children's Thinking: What Develops?* Hillsdale, N.J.:Lawrence Erlbaum Associates.

Trevarthen, C. (1974) 'Conversations with a two-month old', *New Scientist*, **62**, 230–35.

Troike, R. C. (1970) 'Receptive competence, productive competence, and performance'. In J. A. Alatis (ed.), *Georgetown University Round Table on Languages and Linguistics, 1970*, Washington D.C.: Georgetown University Press.

Tucker, N. (1977) *What is a Child?* London: Open Books/Fontana.

Tunmer, W. E. and Bowey, J. A. (1981) 'The development of word segmentation skills in children'. In A. Nesdale, C. Pratt, R. Grieve, J. Field, D. Illingworth and J. Hogben (eds), *Advances in Child Development: Theory and Research*, Perth, W. Australia: NCCD, 122–30.

Turiel, E. (1974) 'Conflict and transition in adolescent moral development', *Child Development*, **45**, 14–29.

Turiel, E. (1978a) 'The development of concepts of social structure: social convention'. In J. Glick and A. Clarke-Stewart (eds), *The Development of Social Understanding*, New York: Gardner Press.

Turiel, E. (1978b) 'Social regulations and domains of social concepts'. In W. Damon (ed.), *New Directions in Developmental Psychology*, Vol. 1, *Social Cognition*, San Francisco: Jossey-Bass.

Turiel, E. (in press) 'Domains and categories in social cognitive development'. In W. Overton (ed.), *The Relationship Between Social and Cognitive Development*, Hillsdale, N.J.: Lawrence Erlbaum Associates.

Udelson, T. A. M. (1975) 'The syntactic patterns of a group of Chicago school children: hesitations and spontaneous speech'. Unpublished Ph D thesis, Northwestern University.

Vurpillot, E. (1968) 'The development of scanning strategies and their relation to visual differentiation', *Journal of Experimental Child Psychology*, 6, 632–50.

Vygotsky, L. S. (1962) *Thought and Language*, Cambridge, Mass.: MIT Press.

Wales, R. J. (1974) 'Children's sentences make sense of the world'. In F. Bresson (ed.), *Les Problemes actuels en psycholinguistique*, Paris: P.U.F.

Wallington, B. A. (1974) 'Some aspects of the development of reasoning in preschool children'. Unpublished doctoral dissertation, University of Edinburgh.

Warner, S. A. (1966) *Teacher*, Harmondsworth: Penguin.

Webb, R. A., Masur, B. and Nadolny, T. (1972) 'Information and strategy in the young child's search for hidden objects', *Child Development*, 43, 91–104.

Weber, R. M. (1970) 'A linguistic analysis of first-grade reading errors', *Reading Research Quarterly*, 5, 427–51.

Weir, R. H. (1962) *Language in the Crib*, The Hague: Mouton.

Weir, R. H. (1966) 'Some questions on the child's learning of phonology'. In F. Smith and G. A. Miller (eds), *The Genesis of Language*, Cambridge, Mass.: MIT Press, 153–68.

Wells, C. G. (1974) 'Learning to code experience through language', *Journal of Child Language*, 1, 213–69.

Wells, C. G. (1977) 'Language use and education success: an empirical response to Joan Tough's *The Development of Meaning* (1977)', *Research in Education*, 18, 9–34.

Wells, C. G. (ed.) (in press) *The Interactive Context of Language Development*, Cambridge: Cambridge University Press.

Wells, G. and Raban, B. (1978) *Children Learning to Read*. SSRC Final Report No. HR 3797/1. School of Education, University of Bristol.

Wellman, H. M. (1977) 'Tip of the tongue and feeling of knowing experiences: a development study of memory monitoring' *Child Development*, 48, 13–21.

Wellman, H. M., Ritter, K. and Flavell, J. H. (1975) 'Deliberate memory behaviour in the delayed reactions of very young children', *Developmental Psychology*, 11, 780–87.

Weston, D. R. (1978) 'Act rule relations and the meaning of rules: children's reasoning about social conventional issues and moral issues'. Unpublished master's thesis, University of California, Berkeley.

Whitehurst, G. J. and Sonnenschein, S. (1978) 'The development of informative messages in referential communication: knowing when versus knowing how'. In W. P. Dickson (ed.), *Children's Oral Communication Skills*, New York: Academic Press.

Whorf, B. L. (1956) *Language, Thought, and Reality*, New York: Wiley.

Wiggins, J. S. (1973) *Personality and Prediction*, Reading, Mass: Addison-Wesley.

Wilkinson, A. (1976) 'Counting strategies and semantic analysis as applied to class inclusion', *Cognitive Psychology*, 7, 64–85.

Winch, P. (1958) *The Idea of a Social Science*, London: Routledge & Kegan Paul.

Winer, G. A. (1974) 'An analysis of verbal facilitation of class-inclusion reasoning', *Child Development*, **45**, 224–7.

Winer, G. A. and Kronberg, D. D. (1974) 'Children's responses to verbally and pictorially presented class-inclusion items and to a task of number conservation', *Journal of Genetic Psychology*, **125**, 141–52.

Wohlwill, J. F. (1968) 'Responses to class-inclusion questions for verbally and pictorially presented items', *Child Development*, **39**, 449–65.

Youniss, O. and Furth, H. G. (1973) 'Reasoning and Piaget', *Nature*, **224**, 314–15.

Ziff, P. (1972) *Understanding Understanding*, Ithaca, N.Y.: Cornell University Press.

Zimbardo, G. (1977) *Shyness*, Reading Mass.: Addison-Wesley.

Zinchenko, V. F., Chzhi-tsin, B. and Tarakanov, V. V. (1963) 'The formation and development of perceptual activity', *Soviet Psychology and Psychiatry*, **2**, 3–12.

Name index

Subject index